An Introduction to Christianity

An Introduction to Christianity examines the key figures, events and ideas of two thousand years of Christian history and places them in context. It considers the material as well as the spiritual dimensions of this multi-faceted faith, and explores its interactions with culture and society. The volume pays particular attention to the ways in which Christianity has understood, embodied and related to power. It shows how the churches' long-standing commitment to 'higher power', both human and divine, has been repeatedly challenged by alternative allegiances to 'power from below', both sacred and secular. By tracing the history of Christianity to the beginning of the third millennium, this book explores the ways in which churches of north and south have reacted to the rise of modem democracy and the cultural turn to subjective life.

LINDA WOODHEAD is a Senior Lecturer in Christian Studies at Lancaster University. She has written extensively on Christianity, culture and society. Recent books include *The Spiritual Revolution: Why Religion is Giving Way to Spirituality* (2004) (with Paul Heelas); *Predicting Religion* (2003) (with Grace Davie and Paul Heelas); *Religions in the Modern World* (2002); and *Peter Berger and the Study of Religion* (2001).

An Introduction to Christianity

Linda Woodhead

CAMBRIDGE
UNIVERSITY PRESS

CAMBRIDGE
UNIVERSITY PRESS

University Printing House, Cambridge CB2 8BS, United Kingdom

Cambridge University Press is part of the University of Cambridge.

It furthers the University's mission by disseminating knowledge in the pursuit of education, learning and research at the highest international levels of excellence.

www.cambridge.org
Information on this title: www.cambridge.org/9780521786553

© Linda Woodhead 2004

First published 2004
Fifth printing 2009

A catalogue record for this publication is available from the British Library

ISBN 978-0-521-45445-2 Hardback
ISBN 978-0-521-78655-3 Paperback

Contents

Illustrations

List of illustrations

Maps

Introduction

This book is about success: about Christianity's rise to power and its growth over two millennia to become the largest religion in the world today. It is also about failure: about Christianity's loss of influence in modern times and the precipitous decline in churchgoing that has taken place in many parts of the west since the 1960s.

In order to understand these mixed fortunes this volume considers the development of Christianity over two thousand years. It focuses on the changing relations between Christianity and society and looks, in particular, at the ways in which Christianity has related to power. It considers how Christian institutions and individuals have understood, articulated and embodied power, and how they have related themselves to political, economic, cultural and military power. Above all, the book considers Christian history in terms of two competing models of power – power from on high and power from below – and the consequences of the churches' tendency to favour the former over the latter.

The volume is divided into two parts, with a hinge in the sixteenth century. The first traces the way in which Christianity in the pre-modern period established itself as a major power first in the near east and then, increasingly, in the west. It shows that its success was due in large part to the way in which the Catholic version of Christianity was able to adopt and embody power from on high and form alliances with secular powers operating according to the same model. For both, power was monarchial. It comes from above and is exemplified in the control exercised by the strong, who are few, over the weak, who are many. The church laid claim to such power early on by representing it as the possession of a sovereign God who delegates it to his authorised representatives on earth: to bishops and clergy, emperors and kings. Rather than giving explicit legitimation to the exercise of arbitrary, tyrannical or despotic power, however, the church developed an ideology of rule that spoke of the godly exercise of dominating power in terms of the paternalistic care of the 'father' for his 'children'. It taught that a just, harmonious and ordered hierarchical society would be brought into being by general obedience to a loving heavenly Father and to his (male) deputies on earth – in government, church and home.

Yet the model of paternal-monarchial power was not the only one in the Christian repertoire. Right from the start it competed with an alternative model in which power was exemplified in the life of a 'Lord', Jesus Christ, who had lived and died in a way that overturned expectations of sovereign, dominating power. Rather than garner power for himself or exercise it over others, Jesus had tried to establish a 'kingdom' in which the mighty were cast down and the poor were exalted. The power of which he spoke was not a power of control over the many by the few, but the power of love between equals. After Christ's death and resurrection, this power was given to all who followed him through the gift of the Holy Spirit. As such, sacred power was understood not as the institutionalised and regulated power of the church, its clergy and the secular leaders they supported, but as the possession of all those who lived by the Spirit of Christ – however humble. Over the centuries different groups of 'radicals', whether lay or monastic, would repeatedly emerge in Christian history to support this model of power from below, and to disrupt existing religious and secular forms of power from on high in the process.

Though the two halves of this book consider the pre-modern and modern periods respectively, we see that the fault line between the two runs jaggedly and erratically through both time and place. It opens up whenever and wherever the model of power from on high starts to be overthrown by that of power from below. Thus the modern world comes into being when power, rather than being seen as the possession of sovereigns and monarchs (earthly and heavenly) to whom individuals must submit their lives, comes to be seen as the possession of each individual subject. Since each one is sovereign in his or her own right, power is now thought to come from below, and to be bestowed by 'the people' on their rulers, rather than the other way round. From this point on, life is seen as something to be lived freely by each individual in his or her own way, rather than according to the rules and laws of others (unless individuals choose to endorse such rules). In the very broadest sense this process may be referred to as one of 'subjectivisation' – since each individual becomes a sovereign subject, rather than the subject of a sovereign.

The second part of the volume traces the way in which Christianity both supports this transition to modernity and fights against it, becoming internally fractured in the process. Thus some movements, such as the Protestant Reformation, support some aspects of power from below (such as the redistribution of power to an emerging middle class) while resisting others (such as the emancipation of women). Others, such as the Roman Catholic church, fiercely resist the redistribution of power from on high *tout court*, and in doing so ensure that movements of nationalism, revolution, democracy and feminism will take on a broadly secular rather than religious profile. In Europe, ecclesiastical resistance to the processes of modernisation and subjectivisation tends to be strong. In the USA, by contrast, the churches become important allies and supporters of the transition to capitalist democracy.

Despite protracted struggles, it is only in the late twentieth century that the model of power from below truly comes into its own with the extension of democratic arrangements to more countries and constituents, with growing affluence in many parts of the globe, and with the widespread breakdown of established structures of authority. At exactly the same time that power from below comes into the ascendant as subjectivisation intensifies, Christianity enters a period of severe decline in much of the west, particularly Europe – but strong growth in large parts of the southern hemisphere. The final part of the volume explores this situation, and shows how it relates to wider issues of social and individual power and empowerment.

I have tried to write this book in a way that will appeal to a wide audience. My aim throughout has been to strike a balance between offering a fresh interpretation of Christianity and providing the basic information that a reader or student new to the area will require. The bias falls slightly towards the former aim, not least because there are already a number of excellent and informative textbooks on church history. But although the book offers a thematisation of history rather than a compendium of facts, it supplies what is needed in terms of key dates, figures, events and so on. In order to prevent this information from clogging the text, some of it has been pulled into the suggestions for further reading at the end of each chapter, and summarised in the 'Chronology' at the end of the book.

For the same reason it has been impossible to acknowledge all my sources, despite the fact that a book of this scope draws on the work of an army of other scholars. I have tried to take account of the latest scholarship without neglecting earlier illuminations of the relation between Christianity and society. Sometimes my interpretation runs closely along the lines of a long-established scholarly consensus; sometimes – when the evidence prompts it – it strikes off in a different direction. (So much new and exciting work bearing on the history of Christianity has appeared in the last two decades that the time seemed ripe for some new departures.) I have indicated some of my most outstanding debts in the suggestions for further reading. I should also like to acknowledge the invaluable influence and assistance of a number of colleagues and friends including John Davies, Paul Heelas, Henry Kirk, Gillian Taylor, and Jan Jans. Both Ellen Clark-King and David Martin read and commented on an early version of the manuscript and gave me advice and encouragement at a critical stage, as did the readers and referees of the book proposal. John Clayton and Alex Wright commissioned the book, and Kevin Taylor and Kate Brett at Cambridge University Press were helpful and supportive editors.

Even though this *Introduction* draws on the work and assistance of many others, it inevitably conveys a personal vision of Christianity. It arises out of a life-long engagement with Christian life and thought at both a personal and a professional level. At different times in my life I have attended Anglican and Roman Catholic schools, worshipped in a variety of churches and been employed by the Church of England. For the last twelve years I have studied and written about Christianity from within a faculty of social sciences in a university with a secular constitution, and I have been engaged in empirical research within congregations in the UK and abroad. My area of research expertise in contemporary Christianity explains the book's particular interest in the modern period, and my location in a faculty of social sciences explains my general approach. Though my reactions to Christianity have been as mixed as what I have encountered, my fascination with this rich and complex religion has been constant. Writing this book has given me the opportunity to stand back, to consider Christian history in the broadest perspective, and to try to present as truthful an interpretation as I can. My intention has been to stimulate, to engage and to provoke – but certainly not to have the last word.

The last word, in any case, belongs to the actors and not the interpreters of history. A simple scheme of interpretation, such as the one concerning different modes of power that is offered in this book, is effective only as a frame within which the twists, turns and ironies of events that burst its bounds can stand out in sharper relief. Its value lies not in its universal applicability, but in its ability to cast light on Christianity's past as well as on the present direction of things.

In this regard, my hope is that one thing the framework offered here highlights most clearly is the difficulty that Christianity – so long self-identified with power from on high – has had in supporting manifestations of power from below. One consequence has been a reflex within the churches to return to more conservative and 'authoritative' forms of the faith – a tendency very evident today. Yet the ability of Christianity to survive in the highly subjectivised cultures of late modernity may in fact lie not in the churches' ability to forge an authoritative social vision, but in their ability to give spiritual support and inspiration to individuals in the living of their unique lives. If there is a single 'big question' that this book raises it is whether Christianity can subjectivise without losing its soul.

Part I

The Christian revolution: ascent to power

I

How Christianity came to power

The Word of God [Jesus Christ] . . . is the Lord of All the
Universe; from whom and through whom the king, the beloved
of God, receives and bears the image of His Supreme Kingship,
and so steers and directs, in imitation of his Superior, the helm
of all the affairs of this world.[1]

So wrote Eusebius (c. 260–c. 339), bishop of Caesarea, in celebration
of thirty years of imperial rule by the Roman emperor Constantine.
Three centuries had passed since the death of Jesus. Eusebius had reason to rejoice. Under Constantine Christianity had changed its status
from being a cult within the mighty Roman empire to being an officially
tolerated religion. Encouraged by Christians such as Eusebius, Constantine had readily accepted the status of deputy of Christ. With the blessing
of the 'Supreme King' in the heavens, his ambition to become supreme
king on earth was gaining new impetus and legitimacy.

One of the most skilful, powerful and ruthless of the Roman emperors,
Constantine had harboured ambitions to unify and expand the Roman
empire even before his 'conversion' to Christianity in 312. During the
course of his long reign – from 306 to 337 – his commitment to Christianity increased until it became the favoured religion of the empire. The
reasons appear to have been political as well as personal. Christianity
offered something unique in the ancient world: an exclusivist, universalist, monopolistic monotheism focused on a single all-powerful God.
Roman religion was generally pluriform and tolerant. It accepted the
existence of many gods and welcomed new ones without any difficulty.
The Jews were different, for like the Christians they worshipped a universal, exclusive God and accepted converts, but their religion remained
largely ethnic nevertheless. Rooted as they were in the Jewish tradition,
Christians worshipped the same universal, 'jealous' God as the Jews –
the God of the Hebrew scriptures that the Christians turned into their

'Old Testament'. But they presented him not just as the God of Israel, but as the mighty Lord of the entire universe, beside whom all other gods were not just imposters but 'demons'. They believed that this mighty God had sent his Son Jesus Christ to earth to proclaim his rule and to throw open the gates of heaven to all who would repent, turn from their old gods and old ways, and give total loyalty to him.

It was this exclusivism that many Romans found troubling and that may have been a major cause of the sporadic persecution, both popular and official, unleashed against Christians between 64 CE and 313 CE. It was not that the Romans could not tolerate this new religious group; what they could not tolerate was its intolerance. The most damaging charge against the Christians was that of 'atheism', for instead of respecting other gods they ridiculed and condemned them and claimed that they were evil spirits leading people astray. This was not only insulting; it was a threat to individuals, families, communities and the empire – whose welfare, it was widely believed, depended upon cultivating the continuing favour of a multitude of gods. Christians astonished Romans with their zealous loyalty to a single God and their willingness to die rather than offer sacrifice to other gods.

But as well as leading to persecution, it was this exclusivism that helped bring Christian monotheism to power in the empire. It lent Christianity many advantages: single-mindedness and strength of purpose; a drive to achieve unity in its own ranks and among its own followers; followers who were loyal and devoted; a commitment not just to spread the new religion but to destroy its rivals. Above all, however, Christian monotheism succeeded because it proved such a useful tool for emperors and rulers. 'As there was one God, so there was one King,' wrote Eusebius in the oration quoted above.[2] An all-powerful God who demanded total loyalty from his followers, even unto death, had a natural appeal for Constantine and many of his successors. Not only was the task of securing and maintaining unity within the existing bounds of the empire made easier by the adoption throughout its territories of a single faith in the one God, but the ambition to destroy rival political powers and establish a world empire could be legitimated and furthered by alliance with a jealous God of supreme power.

The realisation of this vision was not easy, and it would be many years before a unified church, built around belief in a God of almighty, exclusivistic power from on high, would win the support even of most

Christians, let alone of a sizeable proportion of the empire. For not all Christians gave their allegiance to this version of Christianity, and not all 'pagans' (as the Christians called Romans who did not convert to their cause) were won over to it – indeed, paganism would survive right through to the medieval period, perhaps beyond.

The version of Christianity that eventually triumphed in the Roman empire after Constantine may be called 'Catholic' ('universal') Christianity. Those who were its champions, such as Eusebius, described it simply as 'orthodoxy'. Every other form of Christianity they labelled 'heresy', and the heretics even more than the pagans were their sworn enemies. According to Eusebius' version of church history, it is orthodoxy that comes first, and heresy that springs up later as a deviation or, as he calls it, an 'innovation'.[3]

In fact, as this chapter will show, things were not as simple as Eusebius would have us believe. The 'early church' was no such thing. Rather, it was an unregulated mix of all sorts of different religious and spiritual groups, all of whom looked back to the inspiration of Jesus Christ, but who interpreted his legacy in different ways and constructed very different sorts of 'church' in the process. Among them was the embryonic Catholic church, which would ultimately win out and destroy its rivals so comprehensively that in most cases our knowledge of them is patchy and comes by way of Catholic denunciations. Even our knowledge of Jesus and of the earliest days of Christianity is mediated to us through this tradition. For in the face of alternative collections of Christian scripture, Catholic Christianity ruled on what should be included in the official canon of the 'New Testament' and what should be left out. Likewise, it attempted to destroy and outlaw rival Christian scriptures, and to leave only its own accounts of the first centuries of Christian history – such as Eusebius' influential *Ecclesiastical History*.

It is for these reasons that this chapter opens not with the birth of Jesus, but with the coming to power of the Catholic church under the patronage of Constantine. Having set this framework, it proceeds by way of a more straightforwardly chronological framework. It begins by discussing the spiritual ferment of the first few centuries of Christian history and the rise of several competing versions of Christianity, all inspired in one way or another by Jesus Christ and the events surrounding him. It goes on to consider in more detail the emergence of Catholic Christianity and its eventual triumph over its rivals, both Christian and pagan. It then takes the story forward by showing how church and empire entered into ongoing alliance (a subject that is continued in the next chapter). It ends with a brief consideration of the way in which Catholic and imperial Christianity was eventually strengthened through the incorporation of potentially rivalrous forms of ascetic and monastic Christianity.

Spiritual ferment

The Roman empire provided the formative context for the birth and early development of Christianity. So significant – and ultimately beneficial – did this context prove that some Christians, including Eusebius, believed that God had deliberately shaped history in this way. Their belief was strengthened by the fact that Jesus was born at exactly the time that Rome reached a peak of power and stability under Augustus.

The empire was built and sustained by force. A militaristic people led by a deeply competitive aristocracy, the Romans conquered the western Mediterranean world by the end of the third century BCE and the eastern Mediterranean in the second and first centuries BCE. In 31 BCE a single autocratic ruler, Octavian Caesar, emerged victorious from a long civil war and was named Augustus by senate and people four years later. Under this new leader the Roman empire became a single administrative unit with clear frontiers, stretching from the English Channel in the north to Sudan in the south and from Spain in the west to Syria in the east. The principal task of subsequent emperors was to defend this huge territory and maintain stability within it, and the creation of a stable and well-ordered hierarchy of control and authority became a priority. To that end new alliances were gradually forged between emperor and the ancient elites of Roman society (the senatorial and equestrian classes) and below them the local municipal elites; self-government by indigenous rulers in the regions was increasingly replaced by direct Roman rule (with a civil service developing in the process); and the army became a defensive force permanently stationed in strategically important parts of the empire and bound by loyalty to its emperor.

Though ultimately undergirded by military might, the empire tended to mask its crude power under a rhetoric of *civilitas* or civility. Emperors promoted themselves not only as mighty conquerors but as benevolent and paternal rulers and protectors of their people. Likewise the ruling elites were marked off not only by wealth and power, but by their cultural achievements. Increasingly they shared a common literate culture

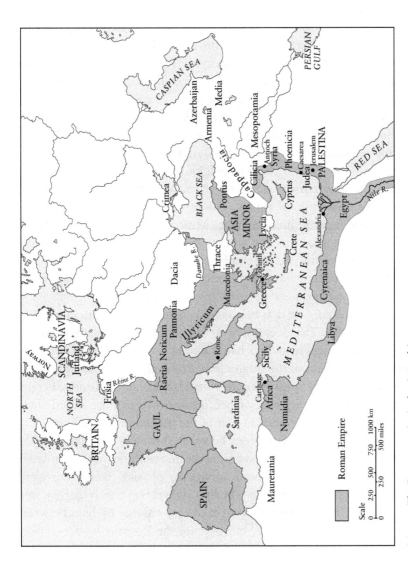

Map 1   The Roman empire in the time of Augustus

(*paideia*) across the empire, a culture that drew on Hellenistic as well as Latin sources and gave rise to significant work in such areas as philosophy, history and literature during the first to third centuries CE. In the eastern half of the empire Greek was the universal language of culture, while Latin occupied the same place in the west. Though some individuals outside the cultural elite might have a working knowledge of Latin and Greek, the masses would be betrayed by their use of vernaculars, as well as by their more general exclusion from the culture of *paideia*.

Social and political order in the empire was further reinforced by religion. While a few of the elite may have pursued a personal religio-philosophical quest, and the majority may have been largely indifferent to religious matters in their day-to-day lives, all would make public obeisance to the gods of Roman religion. Like the earlier Greek gods from whom they borrowed certain characteristics, these were anthropomorphic, supernatural beings. The principal Roman gods were the supreme god Jupiter, Juno his wife, Minerva the goddess of the arts, and Mars the god of war and vitality. Temples of increasing splendour were dedicated to the gods by emperor and elites, and designated priests would perform ritual worship on behalf of the wider society. Far from being a religion of personal or small-group empowerment, then, this was civic religion, a religion that helped legitimate the status quo in locality, town and empire. This does not mean that it was insincere; the Romans believed that things would go badly wrong if the gods were not honoured, and the peace of the empire (*pax Romana*) was indistinguishable from peace with the gods (*pax deorum*). It was only in times of crisis that the demands of such religion became intrusive; in more settled times it could be taken for granted as part of the natural order of things.

Behind the appearance of order, however, there was also considerable movement and even dislocation during the first centuries of the Christian era. Such movement was social as well as physical, and there were important connections between the two. Travel was relatively easy, not only because the Mediterranean offered easy passage by boat between so many parts of the empire, but because the Romans built excellent roads wherever they ruled. Increasing numbers of merchants, traders and businessmen moved freely across the empire, as well as to more distant lands, and they began to form a new section of the population – mobile, cosmopolitan, questing and relatively affluent. Just as mobile in social terms were the increasing numbers of men from families of modest means who could now aspire to a job in the expanding bureaucracies of the empire. Such 'new men' (*viri novi*) sought employment as orators, lecturers, teachers and officials in an expanding imperial civil service. Their means of admission was a literary education, which had formerly been reserved for the elite. Very occasionally one of these new men might rise to the highest level in Roman society. The most famous example is the emperor Pertinax, who ruled for three months in 193 CE. The son of a freedman who had become a schoolteacher, he became a teacher himself, and was singled out by a senator – a friend of his father's former master – who secured him a post as an army officer. From thence he was admitted to the equestrian order, and ultimately became a senator. But for every Pertinax there were thousands of other highly cultured, cosmopolitan and ambitious men who might share or even exceed the cultural and intellectual attainments of those with social power, but would never be able to join their ranks.

Such individuals found themselves cut loose from the existing structures of the social world. No longer part of the stable, labouring rural classes or of the rich and powerful upper classes, their status has been described by some scholars as 'liminal' or 'dislocated'. Such descriptions might also apply to some of the high-born women of the Roman empire who belonged mainly to the affluent families of the empire, but whose sex barred them from full access to social power. As the daughters of powerful men (in whose *potestas* or power they continued until the death of their fathers) and as the wives of influential men, they were accorded considerable respect. A good wife was considered an important asset to a well-born man, and might have considerable power as head of his household, not to mention considerable wealth as a widow (if she had inherited from her father). In order to fit them for these roles, Roman women were often educated to a reasonable level, though they were unable to receive the higher education in rhetoric that equipped men for public life. Roman satirical writers mock their desire to discuss everything and occupy themselves non-stop with poetry, dancing, music, business, social life, sports events, concerts, parties, travelling. But though they might move freely within towns and cities, women could not hold public office, and had little say in legal and administrative matters. They were liminal because they could glimpse the sources of social power – political, economic, ideological – to which they could never really lay claim.

Below the mobile and liminal sections of the population was a mixture of occupations, roles and statuses, most of which were tied closely to agriculture. The overwhelming majority of the population of the empire worked the land, and lived in villages or towns from which they rarely moved. They made up 80–90 per cent of an empire that probably had a total population of around 70 million. Yet they were far from a homogeneous mass. Some owned their own land and may have accumulated reasonable wealth. Increasing numbers were 'citizens' of the empire, as emperors became more willing to enfranchise entire cities or regions. Some were freemen who sold their labour, while others were slaves. At the bottom of the pile were those who had neither land, job nor possessions. These dispossessed, some of whom could not even afford a decent burial, were a serious problem for the empire. Inevitably, some of the poorest were women, especially those who had been widowed and left without an inheritance.

While the evidence remains limited, it is reasonable to suppose that the mobile minds of the first three centuries of the Christian era were key actors in the spiritual ferment that occurred at this time. Thrown back on their own personal skills and resources, they might embark upon a quest for a meaning, truth, power and belonging that would lead them to sample different religions. There they might find not only new truths, but new social spaces from which they could act on the world and their own lives in ways that might otherwise have been impossible. These spiritual seekers of the early centuries found themselves at the centre of a religious ferment that was partly of their own making. Traditional forms of religion were being reinterpreted and new forms invented. Greek philosophy, Jewish religions and new options with a Christian inspiration were the resources that were mined and reconfigured in the drive to build new spiritual homes. During the first and second centuries CE the boundaries between them proved highly permeable.

HELLENISTIC PHILOSOPHIES

Philosophy occupied an important place within the culture of *paideia* (which is not to say that many of the aristocracy actually read works of philosophy). Most prestigious of all was the tradition of ancient Athenian philosophy, in which the key figures were Socrates, Plato, Aristotle, Epicurus and Pythagoras. Though all had died by the third century BCE, schools had formed around them that maintained living traditions of thought and exploration. These had continued into the second century CE, which witnessed a revival of interest in philosophy and a reinvigoration of several of the ancient schools. What was novel about this revival was that for the first time philosophy travelled from the confines of elite society into the world of the newly mobile and cosmopolitan social groups of the empire. This philosophical revival was part and parcel of the spiritual ferment of the time, since no hard and fast distinction was drawn between philosophy and religion. Both were concerned with the nature of reality (metaphysics) and the proper human response to this reality (morality), and both gave rise to communities or schools (Latin, *scholae*; Greek, *didaskaleia*) of dedicated and often ascetic followers.

Different schools propounded different teachings, though there was room for disagreement and debate within each. Views of the cosmos ranged from those of the Stoics on the one hand (who argued that it was a living, ensouled body) to those of the Platonists on the other (who regarded it as matter shaped by a demiurge, a lower god responsible for creation). The Platonic understanding was particularly influential within the religious ferment of the day. Though there was a range of Platonic schools and teachings, all drew a clear distinction between spirit and matter, and regarded the former as the higher and more real principle. Some viewed matter as merely inert, others as positively evil. They distinguished it from spirit not only by the fact that it was the object of sense-perception, but because it was changeable. (Change was regarded as a sign of imperfection and finitude – only what was static could be infinite and perfect.) Thus the highest reality was immutable and, as such, represented the eternal principle not only in human beings, but in the universe as a whole. Contemplation was therefore the highest goal in life – for in contemplation the spiritual, ideational, aspect of a human being unites with the perfect, formless 'Idea' that lies beyond the material world and leaves behind the body. For some forms of Platonism, this 'Idea' was an impersonal principle, for others a divinity. In either form, Platonism fed the increasingly widespread belief that this material world is fleeting and insubstantial, and that a higher realm lies beyond.

The philosophical revival of the second century also helped give expression to a truly universalist morality. Centuries before, Socrates and Plato had ridiculed the class-based and locality-based customs of the ancient city-dwelling Greeks and contrasted them with a system of universal values based on a philosophical understanding of human nature. Second-century and third-century philosophers of almost every persuasion did the same; by its very nature Hellenistic philosophy tended to be concerned with the universal rather than with the particular. Not surprisingly, such a morality appealed to the interests and concerns of the homeless minds in the empire, cut loose as they were from the ancient and particular claims of family and locality, and newly aware of how little separated them in achievement (if not attainment) from their 'betters'. While they may have been interested in philosophy, however, few would have joined the rarefied ranks of a philosophical school. The influence of philosophy came about not directly, but indirectly, as philosophical ideas fed into the new forms of religion which were appearing across the empire.

JEWISH RELIGIONS

Jewish religion was another possible port of call on the map of the spiritual seeker. While Palestine was the homeland of the Jewish people, there had long been substantial communities of Jews in many cities of the Roman empire and Babylonia (the Jews of the 'diaspora'). Many such Jews were highly Hellenistic; that is to say, they had absorbed much from Greek culture. (In many parts of the empire, Hellenistic empires had preceded the Roman empire.) Despite the hostility that arose in the wake of Jewish revolts against Roman rule, Judaism had long been tolerated in the Roman empire, not only because Jews outside of Palestine were not normally disruptive, but because the Romans had respect for any ancient religion – and that of the Jews presented itself as one of the most ancient. In addition, some Romans appear to have been attracted to Judaism because of its profoundly ethical monotheism. Its discipline and respect for the Law seems to have exercised a natural appeal within a society with high respect for the family, law and order.

A significant obstacle for non-Jews who wished to join the Jewish community was that it remained a largely ethnic religion. That is to say, it was the religion and the culture of a particular people. The Jews believed themselves to be a chosen people, set apart by God. Most were simply born Jewish, and, while it was possible to join their ranks by choice as well as by birth, to do so was to leave one's own culture and people to join another. For those who became Jews, their difference would henceforward be inscribed by very deep markers: ritual circumcision in the case of a man, as well as obedience to laws, such as those of dietary purity, that set one apart from gentile society. While a number of Romans took the option of becoming 'God-fearers', loosely affiliated members of a Jewish community, it is understandable that few took the more radical step of becoming full members of the Jewish race.

Yet Jewish religion was itself in a state of flux at this time, and there were many mobile minds within it. The inter-testamental Palestinian Judaism of Jesus' and Paul's day was characterised by a variety of interpretations of Jewish religion and its Law on the part of competing individuals and parties (who nevertheless seemed to work within a framework of mutual toleration and even of interchange). All had to respond to the challenge of Roman occupation of Israel's 'promised land', and all were subject to the inevitable tensions that generated for a people who claimed to be subject to no rule but God's. The most influential parties of Jesus' day included the hereditary priests, who controlled the temple in Jerusalem (the ritual centre of Judaism); the conservative party of Sadducees; and the more popular Pharisees, who sought to spread an intense piety among ordinary men and women. Eschatological expectation was high. In the desert by the Dead Sea an apocalyptic group at Qumran had withdrawn from society in order to form a self-contained community of perfect obedience and purity, ready for the imminent coming of God. There were also parties such as the Zealots, who wished to overthrow the Romans and restore God's kingdom by direct political intervention and violent rebellion.

Jewish anger at Roman occupation led to two major rebellions in Palestine in 66–70 CE and 132–5 CE, both centred on Jerusalem. In putting down these uprisings the Romans destroyed the Jewish temple and turned Jerusalem into a Roman city. Communities such as that at Qumran were destroyed, and parties and groups associated with the temple died out. But the Pharisaic party survived, and some of its rabbis (teachers) set about creating a form of Judaism (later referred to as 'rabbinic Judaism') suitable for the new conditions in which the Jewish people found themselves. They were particularly concerned with Jewish Law, and their debates concerning the Law were eventually written down as the *Mishnah*.

Rabbinic Judaism appears to have had little impact outside Palestine until later centuries. Even before the Jewish revolts, most Jews lived outside Palestine in the diaspora, and after the revolts Judaism's centre of gravity moved more decisively towards them. Such Judaism was often deeply Hellenised, and centred around daily or weekly worship in synagogues. The synagogues were lay-led, may have allowed women positions of leadership, and at this time seem to have had little connection with rabbinic Judaism. In the towns and cities of the diaspora, a few Jews developed new, highly Hellenised, interpretations of Judaism. The most notable was the philosopher Philo (c. 20 BCE–c. 50 CE), who lived in the intellectual centre of Alexandria in Egypt. Philo dealt with the biblical passages that were most objectionable to a Hellenistic frame of reference by allegorising them – by claiming that their 'material' or 'fleshly' meaning concealed a deeper 'spiritual' sense. Where the Bible spoke about God as if he had a body, for example, this should be read not literally but allegorically. Philo championed an ascetic-philosophical mode of life, and articulated the ideal of a godly monarchy. It is a measure of the spiritual interchange of the time that Philo would in the long run prove more influential for Christian intellectuals than for Jewish.

JESUS AND PAUL

In the first century CE a new ingredient was added to the spiritual melting pot of the time by a variety of individuals and groups who looked to the legacy of a Palestinian preacher and wonder-worker called Jesus for authority. Some were Jews, as Jesus himself had been, and others were 'gentiles' (non-Jews). Though their numbers were tiny, by mid-century they might be found not only in Palestine but in a number of Roman cities around the Mediterranean.

The man who inspired these groups is known to us only by way of the documents his followers produced – particularly those that were later authorised by the Catholic form of Christianity. Apart from a brief and much disputed reference in the work of the Jewish historian Josephus, we have no other sources of knowledge about Jesus of Nazareth. None of the documents produced by the early Christians were historical in the modern sense of the word. They were written 'for effect' – to cultivate faith in existing believers, to stimulate conviction in others, to reassure Romans that they need have no fear of this new religion, to persuade Jews that this was indeed the messiah foretold in their scriptures, and so on.

In the first decades after Jesus' death in or around 33 CE nothing at all was written down about him. His memory was preserved by word of mouth. Papias, a Christian leader from early in the second century, is reported by the early church historian Eusebius to have said, 'I supposed that things out of books did not profit me so much as the utterances of a voice which lives and abides'[4] – for it was much easier to check the credentials and reliability of a speaker whom one could meet, and who may have known Jesus or known someone else who did, than those of an unknown author. By the mid-first century, however, things did begin to be written down. Some of the earliest documents that survive are letters (epistles) such as those of Paul, written by Christian leaders to Christian groups. It also seems that some of Jesus' sayings began to be written down and to circulate in the form of collections (though those that have survived intact are 'apocryphal'; that is, they were not included in the canon of authorised scripture).

But by the end of the first century the most popular genre relating to Jesus had become that of a gospel (literally, 'good news'). A gospel usually presents key events and teachings from the life of Jesus within a unified narrative framework. A very large number of gospels were pro-duced – far more than the four (Matthew, Mark, Luke and John) that are included in the New Testament canon. A number of these 'apoc-ryphal' gospels are still extant. To complicate matters further, even the four canonical gospels exist in many different versions. It seems that early Christians used the genre of gospel as a way of presenting their own particular interpretation of Jesus – as a mode of theological con-struction rather than of strict historical record. The name ascribed to each gospel – Matthew, Mark, etc. – may be that of the leader to whom a gospel writer and his or her community owed primary allegiance.

Given the complexity of the source material, the quest for the histor-ical Jesus is therefore one that is unlikely ever to reach its destination. Nevertheless, some measure of scholarly agreement has built up about at least the key events in the life and death of Jesus. Few doubt that he was indeed raised in Nazareth in Galilee, the northern territory of Palestine, and that he was a Jew of relatively humble background. His ministry, which was confined to his fellow Jews, seems to have taken place chiefly in Galilee and among its largely rural population, but was sometimes extended to the southern territory of Judea and to its chief city of Jerusalem. Jesus was a charismatic teacher who offered his own, occasionally controversial, interpretations of the Jewish scriptures, and who performed miracles. As such he was probably not an unusual figure;

there are records of other itinerant preachers and wonder-workers active in the same areas at the same time.

As for his death, the narrative of Jesus' being handed over to the Romans by the Jewish authorities in Jerusalem during a Passover festival and executed by crucifixion is considered broadly reliable by most scholars. Though the reasons for this brutal but not unusual execution are less clear, there is plenty of evidence to suggest that the Jewish and Roman authorities would have been quick to take decisive action to quell any sort of disturbance. The Jewish leaders in particular, whose power was tied up with that of the temple in Jerusalem, may have been particularly keen to show their control over their own people – for on such control their standing with their Roman overlords depended. And while there is no clear evidence that Jesus directly criticised Roman rule, there is much more evidence that he – perhaps like many of his countrymen – criticised the authority, wealth and power of the Jewish leaders in Jerusalem.

About the central themes of Jesus' teaching there is less consensus, not only because there are so many different versions of this teaching (if one takes into account non-canonical documents), but because even the teachings recorded in the New Testament show considerable variation not only between gospels but between gospel manuscripts. (Only about half the verses in the gospels are variant-free, and there is considerably more variation in verses that record Jesus' words than in passages of narrative.) If we rely on those areas where there is some agreement, however, it seems likely that Jesus preached a simple message that called for total commitment to a God of love. Since this Father God loves his children without limit, they too are to love him and one another with equal recklessness and disregard for the consequences. Even the most pressing of earthly commitments and loyalties must be subordinated to this imperative of infinite love. Those who give themselves completely to God and to one another in this way enter into his kingdom (or 'rule') – and the meek, poor and humble are more likely to win a place than the powerful and proud. Thus the radicalism of Jesus' message was addressed first and foremost to the individual. It did not demand the overthrow of existing social arrangements, or the organisation of a new community, or the reorganisation of Israel. Though all these things may follow, Jesus called only for the total surrender of the individual human heart.

The simplicity and openness of this basic message – and the fact that there is room for dispute about even this most minimal interpretation – indicates the huge scope that existed for those who followed Jesus to fill in the gaps: the nature of God; the nature of the love he demanded; the ethical imperatives that would spell out what was required; the status and authority of Jesus himself. This process of interpretation and clarification is evident already in the New Testament documents themselves, and accounts for the variation between them. Different Christians and different communities could, and did, fill in the gaps somewhat differently. This is not to say that there was an unlimited freedom in what could be said and done; but it is certainly true that Christianity offered its followers a wide range of options and opportunities for spiritual experimentation (and for quarrying of existing traditions).

Where the key question of Jesus' own status and significance was concerned, there was wide scope for variation. Some of Jesus' Jewish followers appeared to believe that he was an inspired teacher, perhaps a prophet, even the messiah – but that he was human rather than divine. (Jewish religion tended to draw a clear line between the creator and creatures.) But from very early on, many other Christians (including some Jews), believed that he was something more, and that in him the human and the divine came into uniquely close relationship. Belief in the resurrection – that Jesus was not a normal mortal but had been raised from the dead and now dwelt in the heavens – was a key element in such conviction. But his uniqueness could be spelt out in a huge variety of ways, as so much of the history of Christian thought indicates.

Yet there were, and are, two poles of interpretation within which the many options for those who believe that Jesus was not just a man but a God-man can fall. On the one hand Jesus can be presented as the human incarnation of an almighty God of infinite power. As such, he may be represented as the Son of God, who 'humbled himself for a season' (without compromising his true divine nature) before returning to his rightful place at the right hand of a God of power from on high. On the other hand, Jesus may be interpreted as revealing what is truly divine and eternal by way of a fully human life of love, self-sacrifice, empowerment of others, and a refusal to exercise dominating power. In the former interpretation, his divinity is revealed in the exercise of power from on high; in the latter it is revealed in the exercise of power from below. In the former he is a king and judge who is to be obeyed and worshipped (by self-sacrifice); in the latter he reveals the divine possibilities of the human condition, and inspires others to follow him in the path of deification (by self-realisation). As we shall see in later chapters, both views can take fully trinitarian forms.

In the mid-first century we see the earliest interpreter of Jesus' status whose writings survive, St Paul, tending towards the former pole of interpretation, as would the Catholic strand of Christianity, which began to develop later in the century and drew (selective) inspiration from Paul's writings. As Paul's letters indicate, however, his was not the only possible interpretation of Jesus, for it is clear that he was often contending with alternative views within the early Christian groups to which he was writing.

Paul had little or no interest in Jesus' teachings or in his deeds on earth. For his attention, hopes, authority and sense of purpose were focused upon the risen Christ, whom Paul claimed to have met in an experience in which he was caught up into heaven (II Cor. 12.2–4; I Cor. 9.1). The only earthly event that really mattered for Paul was the resurrection of Christ and his subsequent ascension into heaven. It was the resurrection that proved Christ's divine status and confirmed that he was truly 'the Lord' (as Paul liked to call him). Moreover, it was the resurrection that indicated to Paul that Christ was part of God's plan for the world, which had begun with the creation of Adam and was ending with the sending of a 'second Adam'. Paul, drawing on the Jewish tradition in which he was trained, interpreted the resurrection as a sign of God's intervention to draw all things to a close and to bring history to a glorious consummation.

For Paul, then, Jesus is not a mortal man but a living spiritual being, whose power is available to all who have faith in him. His power flows directly from God, and is offered to those who have faith in him by the gift of the Spirit. Possession of the Spirit will not only transform believers' lives in the here and now; it will make them ready for the imminent irruption of God into history, and guarantee them a place in the kingdom of God that is to come. But in order to receive the Spirit they must 'die' to their old lives and be reborn into Christ. Sin, the flesh and the powers and principalities of this world must be renounced in order that the faithful may become 'incorporate' in the body of Christ.

As the image of membership in the body suggests, such 'new life' is social rather than individual; it is life lived for God and for one another. Those who have been born again through the Spirit become members of *ekklesia* (the church), a new society, called out of the world and into the fellowship of Christ.

Bearing this extraordinary message, Paul became the spokesman for a new form of religion that drew on Jewish as well as Hellenistic sources, but that distinguished itself from both by its transfiguration of existing forms of religion into a new cult focused on the Spirit-Christ. With its focus on the universal God revealed in Christ, it sought to draw *all* people, both Jew and gentile, into its ambit. Just as Constantine would much later dream of a universal world empire, so Paul envisaged a universal religion in which the whole of humanity would live in harmony as children of the one God. In *ekklesia*, Paul said, there is 'neither Jew nor Greek, slave nor free, male and female, for you are all one in Christ Jesus' (Gal. 3.28). The price of such universalism was renunciation of all that had previously made one Jewish or Greek, male or female – if that in any way conflicted with one's own or another's faith in Jesus Christ. The reward was new life in this world, and everlasting life in the world to come. Existing identities must be abandoned in order to become a 'son of God' by being possessed by the Spirit of Christ. Those who rejected Jesus would remain in thrall to sin and death.

The social force of Paul's version of Christianity lay in the rituals, cult and community in which he gave it material form. This was no ethereal, individual mysticism but a powerful social movement. To become a Christian was to abandon loyalty to competing institutions and to join one of the Christian communities over which Paul now tried to assert his authority. The passage from the old life to the new would be marked by the powerful rite of baptism, now interpreted as a passage from death to life. And for those who received baptism, their incorporation into Christ would be marked on a weekly basis by participation in the eucharist, in which the elements of bread and wine would be consumed as symbols of his flesh and blood. Paul's letters are full of practical instruction about how these rituals are to be conducted and understood, how worship should be performed, and how Christians are to live – as well as what they must believe. And through them all runs the concern for unity: not just that members of Christian communities must be united in love for one another (under the leadership of Jesus and his apostle Paul), but that the separate communities must unite with one another – through such practical means as financial support.

Thus Paul's letters provide us not only with an invaluable snapshot of the early development of Christian thought and ritual, but with some tantalising glimpses into the life of some the earliest Christian communities. Together with the other glimpses offered by the Acts of the Apostles (in the New Testament), this is our only source for knowledge of these groups. What we see is considerable diversity in organisation, belief, loyalties and practices – a diversity that Paul is always keen to resolve into unity, and that Acts is careful to downplay. The communities appear to have been made up of quite a wide cross-section of society, though perhaps with a concentration of the mobile middle classes. Women were prominent, though restrictions on their activity were already being laid down. Most of the communities to which Paul writes appear to be predominantly gentile, though there were also Jewish-Christian groups, particularly in Palestine (the most important of which was located in Jerusalem and led by James the brother of Jesus). The communities appear to have been supported financially by their wealthier members (who therefore had considerable power), with some experimenting briefly with a communion of goods. While their members appear to have carried on their everyday occupations, they subordinated every previous loyalty to the new, overriding authority of God and his *ekklesia*. They looked forward eagerly to the time when God would bring history to an end and, when that hope did not quickly materialise, to the risen life that they hoped to enjoy. Yet in several instances Paul had to rein in spiritual enthusiasm, rebuking people for going too far in their renunciation of the existing order of things – for family loyalties and social hierarchies must still be respected and political authorities obeyed.

Highly radical in its spiritual teaching, Paul's version of Christianity thus retains a social conservatism. It was rooted in his theology as much as in any pragmatic motive, for Paul's God is ultimately a male Father God of power from on high. Just as Christ obeys the Father, so Christians must obey Christ 'their head' and his authorised representatives such as Paul. Equally, wives must obey their husbands, children their parents, and slaves their masters. Yet such conservatism had to be reinforced by those of Paul's successors who wrote the so-called deutero-Pauline letters, for Paul's teaching also had a more radical and potentially subversive edge. For if the Spirit is offered to all, then all may claim the mind of Christ, and all may reject external authorities in favour of the voice of the Spirit within. Some groups, as we shall see in a moment, did indeed follow this subversive path of power from below. And the fact that some claimed Paul's authority in doing so would, as we shall see below, render his teaching somewhat suspect to the emerging Catholic tradition for some time to come.

GNOSTICISM

Paul's letters were probably written between about 40 and 60 CE. This was the time of the earliest Christian groups and writings, and of considerable fluidity. Some order began to be imposed on the early Christian documents by the integrative work of gospel writers, first by Mark, in around 60–80 CE, then in Matthew, Luke and John some time between 80 and 120 CE. 'Apocryphal' gospels were produced over the same period. The turn of the first century also saw other competing attempts to give order and coherence to Christian thought and life and to shape the 'true' church of God. It is during this time that the Catholic tradition takes shape (see below), and that alternative communities and scriptures compete with it for followers.

During the course of the second century an important source of competition consolidated into what its Catholic rivals called 'gnosticism'. Since it embraced widely different groups and views, not all of which were Christian, and since it drew on Jewish, Hellenistic and far-eastern as well as Christian sources, its unity was clearer in the minds of its opponents than in historical reality. Gnosticism appears to have been divided into many different schools, some under the leadership of a charismatic teacher (such as the mid-second-century Basilides in Alexandria, and Valentinus in Alexandria and then Rome – both Christian gnostics), and some of a looser and more egalitarian structure. Women and men may have participated on equal terms.

Developed second-century and third-century gnosticism had roots in older communities and writings, such as the surviving proto-gnostic *Gospel of Thomas* (60–80 CE). Even some of the Pauline communities display gnostic tendencies in their preference for a more 'spiritualised' version of Christianity than he was prepared to support. For these proto-gnostics, death to their old lives meant that they were free to leave behind the obligations and restrictions of the existing socio-material world in order to embrace the radical possibilities of their new birth as creatures of the spirit (whether that meant imagining new forms of socio-economic arrangement, new gender roles or new sexual freedoms). As we see in the *Gospel of Thomas*, the gnostic tendency also favoured a subjectivisation of Christianity, which understood divine power not as standing over and above the believer and demanding subordination, but as an inner potential activated by the Spirit – even a divine spark within. Some distinguished between an enlightened inner group of 'pneumatics' (from *pneuma*, spirit) and a wider group of 'psychics' (from *psyche*, mind). Paul and later Catholic theologians, by contrast, tended to favour a more materialist interpretation of Christianity that insisted upon the good and God-given status of the created order and the overriding power of God above.

Some later gnostics articulated their views by way of sophisticated metaphysical and cosmological schemes, and offered their followers access to a secret and hidden *gnosis* (knowledge). Such schemes drew heavily on existing scriptures, including those of the Jewish people. Yet gnostics tended to be decidedly hostile to the 'Old Testament' God and the world he created. Drawing on Platonic ideas, some spoke of him as a 'demiurge', an inferior god responsible for shaping the lower world. They argued that the world he had made, and in which human beings are condemned to live, is plainly evil and imperfect. Yet human beings are not wholly of this world. Reinterpreting the story of creation in Genesis, some gnostics maintained that human beings had within them a divine spark, identical with the unchanging Spirit that is the goal of true spiritual striving. This spark had become trapped in a body of flesh within this lower world. Thus the goal of spiritual striving is escape from the existing order of things in order to reunite with the higher divine source of all reality.

Far above the God of the Old Testament, some gnostics believed, there was a higher being who transcends human categories and who is 'One', the source and ground of all things. This oneness consists of a creative female as well as a static male principle. It is from this duality, and particularly from the generative principle of the female (Wisdom), that the cosmos comes into being, with different 'aeons' (spheres of cosmic reality) being generated by the female principle. Instead of being subject to God's control, however, rebellious Wisdom seeks to create autonomously, and in doing so gives birth to the 'abortion' that is the material world. It is in the course of this catastrophic expulsion of matter that sparks of divine spirit find themselves cut off from their source and trapped far from home. Many gnostics believed that the ascent through the heavenly spheres back to the divine source would take place fully only after death and release from the material body, and that their secret teaching supplied the knowledge (including the passwords) that would enable souls to ascend sphere by sphere back to the origin of all things.

Christian versions of gnosticism were distinguished by the significance they ascribed to Christ. Many saw him as the heavenly redeemer, who had been sent from the 'place of fullness' (*pleroma*), where God dwells, to reverse the process of creation by recalling human beings to their divine source. While he assumed a body, it was not part of his essential reality, for he was pure spirit. As such, he did not really die on the cross. Nor was he the saviour of sinners. Rather, he came to show human beings what they truly are and must become for themselves. As the *Gospel of Thomas* puts it: Jesus said, 'If you bring forth what is within you, what you bring forth will save you. If you do not bring forth what is within you, what you do not bring forth will destroy you' (45: 29–33). Or the gnostic teacher Monoimus (quoted by the anti-gnostic Christian writer Hippolytus):

> Abandon the search for God and the creation and other matters of a similar sort. Look for him by taking yourself as the starting point. Learn who it is within you who makes everything his own and says, 'My God, my mind, my thought, my soul, my body.' Learn the sources of sorrow, joy, love, hate . . . If you carefully investigate these matters you will find them in yourself.[5]

Given such beliefs it is not surprising that in sociological terms gnosticism seems often to have been characterised by tightly knit communities that kept themselves separate from wider society. While adherents may still have had to function in, for example, the economic sphere, they would presumably have done so with a detachment born from their knowledge that their true home was elsewhere. An egalitarianism in internal organisation was related to belief in the equal divinity of each individual. If all, or even some, are Christ-like, then it would be inappropriate to have a hierarchy of power like that which was developing in Catholic Christianity. Not surprisingly, then, we find representatives of the latter attacking it for precisely this lack. Thus Tertullian attacks 'the behaviour of the heretics' in the following terms:

> How frivolous, how worldly, how merely human it is, without seriousness, without authority, without discipline, as fits their faith! . . . They enter on equal terms, they listen on equal terms, they pray on equal terms . . . All are proud, all promise knowledge . . . Their ordinations are improper, superficial, changeable . . . And so, today one man is a bishop, tomorrow another . . . Even members of the laity are charged with the duties of a priest.[6]

This egalitarian spirit seems to have extended even to women in some gnostic circles, and was another cause of criticism on the part of anti-gnostic Christian writers such as Tertullian and Hippolytus. In the same passage quoted above, Tertullian notes 'how brazen' the gnostic women are, for 'they dare to teach, to dispute, to exorcise, to promise cures, even perhaps to baptise'. This relative openness to women on the part of the gnostics is reflected in the higher status accorded them in some of the gnostic gospels. One group of gnostic sources claims to have received its secret tradition of gnosis via Mary Magdalene. In the *Gospel of Philip*, for example, we read that

> the companion of the [Saviour is] Mary Magdalene. [But Christ loved] her more than [all] the disciples, and used to kiss her [often] on her [mouth]. The rest of [the disciples were offended] . . . They said to him, 'Why do you love her more than all of us?' The Saviour answered and said to them, 'Why do I not love you as (I love) her?' (63: 32–64: 5)

Similarly, both the *Gospel of Mary* and the *Pistis Sophia* ('Faith Wisdom') record disputes in which Mary teaches with authority on the basis of her intimate knowledge of the living and resurrected Christ, but is rebuked for her presumption by Peter. In both cases Peter is overruled, and Mary's authority vindicated.

Equally striking is the attribution of female characteristics to the God-head, already noted above. God is sometimes spoken of as a dyad who embraces both masculine and feminine elements; some groups prayed to God as 'Father and Mother'; and the divine Mother is thought of as the first universal creator who brings forth all creatures, as well as the Wisdom that enlightens them. Yet Wisdom cannot act alone, and is perfected only through subjection to the masculine principle. Likewise, while women could occupy the highest ranks of gnosticism, their destiny was fulfilled in uniting with the male principle. In the *Gospel of Thomas*, Simon Peter says to the disciples:

'Let Mary leave us, for women are not worthy of Life.' Jesus said,
'I myself shall lead her, in order to make her male, so that she too may
become a living spirit, resembling you males. For every woman who will
make herself male will enter the Kingdom of Heaven.' (51: 19–26)

While much gnosticism appears to have been ascetic, calling for complete renunciation of sexual activity to the point of castration, there were
also gnostics who regarded the embodied life on earth as a preparation
for eventual spiritual union with God, and who may have treated sexual
intercourse as an anticipation of that state.

OTHER RADICAL CHRISTIAN GROUPS

At the same time that some of the most successful gnostic groups were
coming into their own in the mid-second century, other radical Christian
groups were also attracting large numbers of followers. The Catholics
we shall consider in a moment. Before that, we need to consider some
equally important and influential variants of early Christianity with
which they would have to compete. While they share something of the
spiritualising tendency of gnosticism, these groups tended to anticipate
a church form of organisation and more universalist, exclusivist forms
of monotheism.

As with gnosticism, the tendency of later Catholicism to destroy or
selectively reproduce the writings of its enemies means that evidence and
information about such groups are sketchy. They appear to have flourished away from the great urban administrative centres of the empire
in regions such as Syria, where the landscape was one of villages and
smaller, less cohesive towns. Here, as in the Palestine of the original Jesus
movement, it proved possible to sustain more radical visions of Christianity than that of the respectable Christian householders who began
to form the core of the emerging Catholic tradition.

As in the teaching of Paul, whom some of these groups revered, the
message of these alternative Christian groups was that the coming of
Christ into the world had 'made all things new'. But what their members envisaged was not a mild tinkering with the world, but a wholesale overthrow of the existing order in anticipation of the kingdom of
peace that Christ had initiated. Like the gnostics, they therefore sought
to live lives not 'in the world', but 'in the Spirit'. To a greater extent
than Paul had allowed, they experimented with new personal and social

possibilities. One of the most obvious ways in which they did so was by renouncing sexual relations. At a stroke this set them free not only from the powerful force of sexual desire, but from the entire existing structure of male–female relationships, children, households, and family responsibilities and entanglements. The liberation was perhaps greatest for women. In many radical groups ascetic men and women could now live and work side by side as spiritual equals, anticipating the state of total liberation that had been bought by the death and resurrection of Christ. They believed that they had become angels on earth, and/or that they had regained the status of Adam and Eve before the fall.

Such groups included the Montanists, a pneumatic group founded by Montanus and two female prophets, Priscilla and Maximilla, in the mid-second century, and the 'Encratites', probably a collective term imposed by later opponents on many different radical spiritual groups, including those in Syria inspired by the influential teacher Tatian. The latter produced an influential harmony of the gospels, the *Diatessaron*, in the mid-second century, which was probably more widely read than the canonical gospels, but which was gradually expunged by Catholic Christianity (so effectively that there is no extant version).

But the most successful of these groups seems to have been that version of Christianity developed by Marcion, an affluent ship-owner and merchant who moved to Rome from Asia Minor in the first part of the second century. In 144 Marcion abandoned the emergent Catholic church in order to found an alternative 'true' church. Unlike the teaching of gnostics such as Valentinus, who was beginning his career in Rome at the same time, Marcion's version of Christianity had a good deal in common with Catholic Christianity. He mirrored the emerging hierarchical form of the Catholic church by establishing a three-fold order of bishops, priests and deacons (but diverged by offering ordination to women). He also devised a lively set liturgy, formulated clear and precise doctrines, and established a canon of scripture made up of the works of Paul and Luke, which pre-dated the Catholic canon, and to which the Catholic church would be forced to react by establishing the alternative 'New Testament' that we have today.

But Marcionism offered a more radical teaching than its Catholic rival. Marcion's most significant move was to abandon the entire Jewish heritage of Christianity. For him, as for the gnostics, the creator God of the Old Testament was an inferior and vengeful demiurge. Jesus had come to preach the true God, a God of spirit and of love. Instead of trapping us in the structures of a lower world, the God of Jesus Christ loves us, forgives us and sets us free. By dismissing the Jewish God and his scriptures, Marcion liberated Christians from what he regarded as the restrictive prohibitions of the Law, and allowed them to wander into a new world of gracious social possibility. No longer bound by the old ties of family and kinship, Christians were to follow Christ in showing love and mercy to all. As he put it, 'This is the basic and most absolute goodness of Christ, that such goodness should be poured out to total strangers, to those to whom we owe no debt of kinship, as a free act of will.'[7]

Marcionism was no minority sect. In many parts of the empire, Marcionism *was* Christianity. The sense of threat to the Catholic version of Christianity is evident in the church father Tertullian's lament that Marcion's church 'filled the entire world'.[8] According to the polemical writings of the Syrian father Ephraem, Marcionism was still flourishing in the fourth and fifth centuries, not just in Italy but as far afield as Egypt, Mesopotamia and Armenia. It would require a formidable rival to displace it.

The emergence of Catholic Christianity

Catholic Christianity differed from its rivals in many ways. And as it vied with them for control of a growing (but still tiny) Christian population, these differences tended to sharpen.

Early in the second century a Christian leader from Antioch, Ignatius, was arrested and taken in captivity to Rome to be executed. As he travelled he wrote to Christian communities who recognised his authority, and laid down for them – as Paul had done more than a generation earlier – a clear picture of the organisational form to which they should conform. Since some of these letters survive, and since they give access to one of the earliest and clearest statements of the Catholic Christian point of view, they supply important information.

Just as Paul's theology implies a practical set of social arrangements, so does that of Ignatius. He writes not for the joy of discussing the nature of God for its own sake, or to inspire individuals to pursue their own spiritual paths, but to show how belief in the God of Jesus Christ implies membership of a uniform and hierarchically constituted social body, the church. The loose arrangement of offices in the Pauline communities is now tightened up into a defined clerical order of bishops (*episkopoi*), priests or elders (*presbyteroi*) and deacons (*diakonoi*). For Ignatius this is no merely human, optional arrangement, for it reflects the heavenly hierarchy. Thus the bishop's authority reflects that of God himself, and the bishop is the focus of unity for Christians on earth just as God is in the heavens. To be a Christian is not merely to obey God; it is also to obey the bishop. For the bishop, in Ignatius' view, is the very image or 'type' of God (*typos theou*). As Ignatius puts it in his *Epistle to the Smyrneans* (*Epistle to the Smyrneans* (8)):

> Avoid divisions as the beginning of evils. All of you follow the bishop as Jesus Christ followed the Father, and follow the elders as the apostles; and respect the deacons as the commandment of God. Let no man perform anything pertaining to the church without the bishop . . . Wherever the bishop appears, there let the people be, just as, wherever Christ Jesus is, there is the Catholic church. It is not lawful apart from the bishop either to baptise, or to hold a love-feast [eucharist]. But whatsoever he approves, that also is well-pleasing to God, that everything which you do may be secure and valid.

Thus heavenly power from on high is channelled into a hierarchy of sacerdotal power on earth, and ordinary lay Christians are turned into obedient servants rather than precocious sons and daughters of God. What is more, far from blowing where it will, the Spirit of God is channelled into the sacraments of baptism and eucharist, which, according to Ignatius, only a clergyman has the power to administer. Direct access to divine power becomes the privilege of the clerical orders.

The Ignatian vision is inherently patriarchal. God is a male God and Father, and his supreme headship of the church is not unlike the male headship of the household that was enshrined in Roman law as *patria potestas* (the power of the father). The patriarchal image is likewise applied to bishops and priests ('fathers in God'). It is no coincidence, then, that women appear to have been excluded from the clerical orders from the very start. This was one thing that differentiated Catholic Christianity from some more spiritualised forms of Christianity and gnosticism. Another was the Catholic church's more positive evaluation of marriage and the household. Indeed, it seems likely that early Catholicism had a particular appeal to respectable householders within the most influential cities of the Roman empire. Rather than undermining the domestic realm and the system of male domination it helped support, Catholicism sought to perfect it by insisting on the indissolubility of the marriage bond and the importance of dignified and orderly hierarchical relations between husband and wife, parents and children, owners and slaves – a development already evident in the deutero-Pauline letters.

For the first few centuries of Christian history, this church type of Catholic Christianity would compete with more alternative forms for the title of orthodoxy. Many of the latter were closer to the shape of a 'school', being smaller in scale, looser in organisation and more egalitarian in their internal relations. The evidence suggests that Christianity developed sporadically and at different rates in different areas of the empire, with different versions becoming dominant in different cities and regions. There were probably large swathes of the empire, most notably in Syria and Egypt, where Catholicism failed to make any headway at all in the first and second centuries. In Edessa, for example, the evidence suggests that Marcionism was the dominant form of Christianity at this time, while in Egypt the gnosticism of Basilides held the equivalent place. Meanwhile, in much of 'the Orient', including Arabia, Samaria, Transjordania and Babylonia, no form of Christianity was able to make headway because of the strength of existing religions. This explains why Catholic Christianity was therefore forced north and west, towards Rome and Europe and through Asia Minor. The apostle Paul had played a pioneering mission role in Asia Minor, though by no means all his churches became Catholic. (Galatia, for example, seems to have become Montanist and Philippi gnostic.)

In the event it appears to have been the church in Rome that became the most important stronghold of the Catholic tradition, and it was here that the Catholic church was nurtured even when it was making little headway elsewhere. A church of power from on high developed in a city of power. Though Paul had written to the church in Rome, his authority proved ambivalent, since heretical groups such as the Marcionites and many of the gnostics also claimed him as an inspiration. For that reason, perhaps, the Catholic church in Rome preferred to base its claim to orthodoxy on its links with the apostle Peter. Its bid for power was given extra weight by Rome's status as the capital of the Roman empire, as well as by the fact that Christianity had been established there soon after Jesus' death. Nevertheless, Catholic Christianity in Rome in the second century faced a life-and-death struggle in its own stronghold against both Valentinian gnosticism and Marcionite Christianity.

This struggle helped Catholicism define itself and consolidate its identity. It had been slow to develop a sophisticated theological position, having been outpaced by the achievements of gnostic thinkers. When its theology did begin to take shape, it would be moulded by reaction to competing 'heretical' groups, and adopt a critical-defensive as well as a creative-constructive stance in the process. This is evident in the pioneering work of the 'orthodox' theologian Irenaeus (c. 135–c. 200), the bishop of a relatively new Catholic community in Gaul. The title of his most important work is telling: *An Indictment and Overthrow of the 'Knowledge' Falsely So-Called,* known to later generations simply as *Against Heresies* (probably completed around 185 CE). Irenaeus' concern is with authority and its location. His argument, against gnostics and Marcionites alike, is not simply that it lies in the scriptures (for the heretics too appealed to the scriptures), but that it lies in 'that tradition which is derived from the apostles, and which is safeguarded in the churches through the successions of clergy'.[9] Like Ignatius, in other words, he argues that the truth is handed down from Christ to the apostles to the clergy in a direct line of succession. It is summed up in a 'rule of faith' authorised by the (Catholic) church, and is identical with the plain truth (rather than with some esoteric interpretation) of the scriptures. In conscious defiance of his opponents, Irenaeus spells out this plain truth in strongly materialist terms: the one true God created this material world; both it and its inhabitants were created good; such goodness is restored in Christ; salvation is available by way of the material sacraments distributed by the ordained priesthood of the one true – Catholic – church. And with this church, Irenaeus insists, 'because of its position of leadership and authority, must needs agree every church, that is, the faithful everywhere'.[10]

The progress of Catholic Christianity throughout the second and third centuries was aided by a number of factors, both internal and external. Of the former, five seem particularly important.

First, legitimacy. It seems very likely that Rome was one of the first places to which Christianity spread from Palestine in the decades after Jesus' death, and that it did indeed have direct links with the apostle Peter, whose recollections may well have formed the basis of Mark's gospel (also said to have been written in Rome). We know from Paul's letter to the Romans that there was already an established Christian community there by 50 CE, and that the community was well acquainted with the Hebrew scriptures. In many ways, however, the actual histori-cal facts are less decisive than the presentation of history by the church in Rome, which carefully established its legitimacy by insisting on its unique status as the church founded by Peter, the foremost of the apos-tles, whom Christ had singled out as 'the rock' on which the church would be built.[11]

Second, organisational strength. Unlike alternative forms of Christian-ity, the Catholic tradition developed a tightly knit ecclesiastical structure that was both sacramental and sacerdotal. Ignatius' vision prevailed, with the bishop becoming the leader of the local group and the focus of unity for the wider church. His authority was conferred by historic apostolic succession from Jesus Christ. To him and to his priests was reserved the exclusive right to administer the sacraments, which became the focus of ritualised forms of worship. Organisational unity was fur-ther enhanced by the organisation of local groups (led by a priest) into 'dioceses' or 'sees' under the control of a bishop, which were in turn part of the wider area of jurisdiction of a 'patriarchate'. The earliest patriarchates were those of Jerusalem, Rome, Antioch and Alexandria, with Constantinople being added in the fourth century.

Third, unity. Catholic Christianity's organisational strength helped secure its unity. Its hierarchical system of leadership turned what might otherwise have been a loose federation of independent congregations into a universal church. The episcopal system allowed bishops to become a focus of unity since they could meet together in councils to settle disputes and make new rulings, impose a uniform discipline upon 'the faithful', and promulgate and police a unified system of ritual and belief. Unity in belief was furthered by two means: by a gradual formation of an authorised canon of scripture (which would become the New Testament) and by an equally gradual formulation of what Irenaeus had called the 'rule of faith', that is, an agreed system of Catholic belief. Ultimately, of course, unity was secured by belief in a single, jealous God, who demanded exclusive adherence to his truth.

Fourth, material resources. While the evidence is patchy, it appears that the Catholic strand of Christianity was able to mobilise consider-able material resources, and that the promise of financial support often encouraged other churches to join the Catholic fold. Early Christian documents from Antioch and Corinth (where the Catholics seem to have been fighting for survival) thank Rome for its donations of money. Such money would have had many uses, ranging from buying the freedom of Christian slaves to paying for salaried clergy. Its source appears to have been substantial donations from wealthy Roman Christians.

Fifth, constituency. It was noted above that the appeal of Jewish religion, even of a Hellenised type, was limited by virtue of its ethnic character. The appeal of radical and gnostic forms of Christianity was limited by the opposite tendency. Since their gaze was on the spiritual rather than on the material world, they rejected the significance of all the elements so central to Judaism – the land, biological community, food and purity laws, circumcision in the flesh. They were universal communities of the spirit rather than particular communities of the flesh, with an ascetic tendency. Yet this meant that they were exclusive in another way, for they were intense, elective communities that rejected the material and everyday world in favour of a higher world of pure spirit. Much was demanded of their followers, not only in terms of education, but of lifestyle and commitment. Those who joined were asked to leave behind the existing social order and its ties of kinship and affection. While the rewards of this world-rejection may have been high, so too was its price. It is perhaps not surprising that some gnostic groups distinguished between the 'elect' and a larger group of less committed followers who may not have been ready to sever their ties with the world in quite so dramatic a fashion, just as Judaism distinguished God-fearers from ethnic Jews.

Given their demanding teachings and strenuous demands, it seems quite likely that the primary appeal of these non-Catholic Christian groups was to the new educated and literate classes of the empire rather than to the masses and the ordinary householder. But these new men and women represented only a fraction of the population of the empire. Inevitably, then, a religion that could appeal more widely – and disrupt the order of the household less – would have a better chance of success. In this respect, the Catholic version of Christianity seems to have scored highly. Its very name signalled its openness to all comers and its dislike of the esoteric and elitist. Its teachings were relatively simple. It demanded high moral standards, but not necessarily asceticism and a rejection of the world. It was possible to become a faithful member of the Catholic church without renouncing one's normal occupation or family ties. Salvation was promised to all, not merely to an elect. And there were benefits – not least material help – for all sections of society, including the very poor.

It was a difficult balancing act to maintain. On the one hand, in order to be truly 'catholic' and open to all, Catholic Christianity could not demand as much from its followers as many more esoteric groups could. Nor could it risk alienating Romans by appearing too counter-cultural and socially disruptive. On the other hand, it could not appear too worldly or compromised – particularly in the face of competing groups of strenuous other-worldliness. The solution seems to have been found in the idea of self-sacrifice. Where Catholicism was potentially limitless in its demands was in its requirement that its members sacrifice body, mind and spirit to God, neighbour and church. Far from disrupting social and ecclesiastical order, such sacrifice served to strengthen it – as wives gave themselves in obedience to their husbands, slaves to masters, citizens to rulers, laity to clergy and so on. The most potent symbol of such self-sacrifice became that of the martyr. Catholicism quickly developed a huge martyrological literature in which the tales of the heroic deeds of male and female martyrs were told in vivid and gory detail. No-one could accuse the Catholic church of being lukewarm if it had such men and women as its heroes. And yet it was not that the sacrifice of power was itself seen as God-like, for God was all-powerful. Rather, it was the fitting posture for those who served this sacred power from on high, and it would bring its rewards in terms of empowerment in the life to come.

All these factors aided the growth of Catholic Christianity. Alone they might not have been enough to guarantee its success, or its eventual triumph over what it labelled 'heresy'. But in combination with external factors they bestowed a unique advantage. The first such factor was the diversity and disunity of the 'heretical' groups, which were unable to unite even in a loose association reflecting a common purpose. This inability counteracted the probable numerical superiority of these groups aggregated together, and gave Catholic Christianity an enormous advantage in the long run. The second external factor, almost certainly the most important of all, was the developing alliance between the Catholic form of Christianity and the Roman empire, an alliance made official by Constantine.

Christianity and empire
EARLY CHRISTIANITY AND THE EMPIRE

From the first, many Catholic Christians seem to have been at pains to reassure their Greco-Roman neighbours that their religion constituted no threat to the empire. A whole genre of 'apology' (*apologia*, speech for the defence) developed in the course of the second century in the work of Catholic writers such as Quadratus, Aristides, Justin Martyr and Theophilus of Antioch. Their reassurances were reasonable. Pre-Constantinian Christians could not have challenged the political or economic power of the empire even if they had wanted to do so, for their numbers were tiny. But in any case they did not want to. Catholic Christians may have wished to change men and women's intimate and domestic lives and create new communities, but they had no interest in changing the structures of the empire. Nor, unlike some more radical forms of Christianity, did they wish to withdraw from the world to create alternative modes of existence. In so far as Christianity had an impact on the empire, apologists were keen to stress, its effects were wholly beneficial, for Christians would prove better citizens, more loyal slaves, more trustworthy partners in business.

Thus the early versions of Christianity failed to establish any form of social ethic. Far from challenging even the most apparently unchristian arrangements in the wider social world, such as the institution of slavery, Christianity may even have had the long-term of effect of prolonging slavery. (Like women, slaves were excluded from the Catholic priesthood.) The most that Christian teachers commended was a change of heart whereby slave-owners would became more merciful, the rich more charitable, and rulers more just. Even where Christianity could and did formulate strong ethical teachings – in relation to the intimate life of its own communities and the household – it tended, as we have seen, to endorse the existing orders of social and gender domination.

Yet the reassurances of Christian apologetic were not enough to allay the suspicions of many Romans or to prevent some acts of violence against Christianity. While the number of Christian martyrs and the intensity of persecution tended to be exaggerated by Christian writers, for whom martyrdom was a most powerful witness to the truth of their religion, Christianity *was* attacked, both with the pen and with the sword. There were a number of reasons. One was simply the secrecy of Christian gatherings and rituals, which gave rise to unsubstantiated

Plate 1 Christ Helios, from the pre-Constantinian necropolis below St Peter's (Rome)
  Early Catholic Christianity drew much from the hierarchies of the Roman empire, both earthly and heavenly. In this mosaic, probably from the late third century, the figures of Christ, Apollo and the sun god merge. Constantine also seems to have combined worship of the sun god (*sol invictus*) with that of the Christian God. Both could be understood in the same terms: as powerful, universal lords of the heavens.

41

rumours: that they met at dead of night, sacrificed babies and practised cannibalism, incest and other perversions. While the more educated Greco-Roman critics might ignore these rumours, they had their own reasons to dislike Christianity (though not to persecute it). From the perspective of many literate and cultured 'pagans', Christianity lacked almost everything that would have won natural respect: antiquity, respect for tradition and for ancestors and for reason. It was newfangled, open to all comers, more interested in faith than in reason and philosophy, and based on absurd miracles such as the rising of a dead man. But, far more important from the point of view of the Roman authorities and some popular uprisings, Christianity was dangerous because it refused to respect the civic order by sacrificing to the Roman gods. As we have already noted, such exclusivism might be viewed as disloyal or uncivil, or it might be regarded as downright subversive.

Until the third century, persecution of Christians tended to be localised and sporadic. This reflected the situation in the empire, where rule was mainly through the *ordo* of legally constituted town councils and the local dignitaries. The emperor was a distant, benevolent figurehead. After about 230, however, intense pressure on the borders of the empire led to political and economic disruption and unsettlement of the *pax Romana*. The response was to centralise power in the person of the emperor, and to impose a more direct form of rule across the empire, with less scope for local autonomy. One result, which aided the growth of Christianity, was to increase the number of educated men required to staff a growing bureaucracy – many of whom would be attracted to Christianity and take up many of the positions of leadership within it. The other, much more dangerous result was that, as the importance of an imperial cult increased, dissent was less likely to be tolerated, and persecution could be organised more systematically and on an empire-wide scale. Different emperors pursued different policies in relation to the churches. Some let Christianity alone; some tolerated Christians as long as they participated in public ceremonies; some outlawed Christian gatherings and demoted any in the civil service who professed Christianity; and some executed those who refused to sacrifice. Inevitably, many Christians apostatised (renounced their faith in the face of persecution). The question of whether they could be readmitted to the church in more settled times was one that would split many Christian communities in the century that followed.

CONSTANTINE AND THE CATHOLIC CHURCH

The fact that the greatest of the persecutions occurred under the emperor Diocletian (284–305) made the total reversal of his policy under his immediate successor Constantine seem more miraculous to Christians, such as Eusebius, who were disposed to see history as the outworking of God's purposes. In the version of the story popularised by Eusebius, Constantine was converted to the Catholic form of Christianity before the Battle of the Milvian Bridge in 312, when he saw a cross in the sky and the words, 'In this sign conquer.'[12] The following year the emperor issued the Edict of Milan, granting toleration to all religions and restitution to Christianity. Thereafter he extended increasing favours to the Catholic church, donating an imperial palace and lands (the Lateran), freeing the clergy and the church from certain burdens of taxation, embarking on ambitious programmes of church-building and the production of Christian Bibles, and lending his support to Christian initiatives to destroy paganism and pagan temples (even when, as was common, seizure and destruction by Christian mobs involved lethal force). A religion once persecuted became a religion not only tolerated but actively supported.

The reasons for Constantine's conversion to Christianity were briefly discussed at the start of the chapter, and the advantages of combining an expansive imperial project with missionary monotheism were noted. (A significant fact that Eusebius fails to mention is that Constantine appears to have been embarking on a campaign to conquer the Persian empire at the time of his death.) So far as domestic policies were concerned, Constantine's conversion also gave him a means of consolidating unified control, and of breaking with the continuing power of Rome and the old (pagan) ruling classes. The break was marked by the establishment of a new capital at Constantinople on the Black Sea in 330. A Christian rather than a pagan city, the rise of this new Rome would mark the beginning of a late antiquity in which Christianity and empire would develop hand in hand.

It is hardly surprising that Constantine favoured the Catholic version of Christianity over its rivals, and in so doing guaranteed its triumph. Not only was this form of Christianity ascendant in Rome, and therefore accessible to Constantine; it had also won some converts in high Roman society – including the wives of important officials in the city. It was the form of Christianity least threatening to the established hierarchical social order. By the early fourth century it had also developed a robust form of management and control over its own life and that of its members, and was demonstrating an ability to extend itself and mobilise its supporters right across the empire. It was also rapidly becoming a centralised system of power from on high. The effect of Constantine's co-option was to reinforce these tendencies. In sociological terms, imperial sanction accelerated a shift away from tightly knit local gatherings of 'the saints' to a universal church whose doors were open to all comers, and that wished to save the whole world rather than turn away from it. In theological terms, God became an ever more distant and powerful monarch and ruler over all. Just as the emperor might model himself on the Christian God, so the Catholic Christian God was likely to be modelled on the emperor. As Eusebius said of him: 'The Father and Maker gives commands like a supreme ruler by imperial fiat; the divine Word, who holds the second place to him . . . subserves his Father's behests.'[13]

The embrace of dominating, almighty power was expressed in architecture and ritual. Before Constantine Christians met chiefly in private houses. Not only was this arrangement practical, given the danger that designated Christian places of worship would be confiscated or destroyed in periods of persecution; it was also fitting for a religion whose sphere of operation was the intimate and private life of individuals and families. As Christianity became an increasingly public and civic religion, however, it was appropriate that one of the emperor's first acts should be to commission a number of grand churches. Their form was not that of a temple, but of a meeting hall or basilica. Rather than catering for intimate, face-to-face gatherings, such buildings favoured worship of a more imposing and awe-inspiring nature. The liturgy became more formalised and dramatic, and regional variations were dropped in favour of more standardised forms. Clergy were robed in vestments modelled on the costume of the ruling Roman elites, which signalled their status and difference from the laity, and an all-high God was worshipped with appropriate splendour. Disciplines such as penance, which had previously been administered on an informal and one-to-one basis, inevitably had to change in order to fit the requirements of what was becoming a mass religion. Likewise, teaching became more formal and authoritative. Clergy and bishops gave regular expositions of scripture from the pulpit, which catechumens (those being prepared for baptism) as well as interested laity were expected to attend. Unlike more radical forms of non-Catholic Christianity, such teaching did not take the form of dialogue or conversation, but was presented as the authorised interpretation of God's revealed and unquestionable Word as contained in the canonical scriptures. (The first undisputed list containing the twenty-seven books of the New Testament is found in the *Festal Letter* of Athanasius, written in 376.)

The dominion of the Catholic church was furthered by the conquest of space and time. Besides the building of basilicas and baptisteries throughout the empire, monuments and shrines were erected for martyrs and saints. Relics of martyrs were also brought into churches and placed under their altars, turning them into even more potent seats of holy power. Very often the shrines of the martyrs became the focus of a new nexus of social relationships, providing cohesion for the region in which they were found, and consolidating the power of the bishop. Further afield, Constantine's mother, Helena, played a major role in Christianising the 'Holy Land' by erecting monuments and churches over the main sites associated with Christ's life, death and resurrection. At the same time, the church's calendar was formalised, standardised and extended. Christians had long established Sunday as their day of rest in distinction from the Jewish sabbath, but this division of time was made official by Constantine. Gradually the year also came to be also punctuated with a rhythm of Christian feasts and fasts, of which the most important were Easter (the commemoration of Jesus' resurrection), the 'Holy Week' that led up to it, and the forty days of Lent (a time of fasting and preparation for Easter and for baptism, which took place at Easter). Spaces in between began to be filled with festivals celebrating the great saints and martyrs. The sacred space and time of the pagan past was slowly being overlaid and suppressed.

ESTABLISHING ORTHODOXY

Unity by way of centralisation, discipline, control and the imposition of uniformity became ever more important for Christianity under imperial aegis. If the Catholic church was to be an agent of unity in the empire, it had better be unified itself. What is more, it had better win the entire population of the empire – and beyond – to its cause. After 313 such matters became the concern not just of church but of emperor. And the means at the church's disposal altered accordingly: not just spiritual, intellectual and moral persuasion, but financial inducement, legal measures and, if necessary, brute force.

There were very significant forces of disunity to be overcome. Paganism remained entrenched. Gnosticism, Marcionism and other early forms of heresy still posed a considerable threat. And new forms of heresy were gaining ground. The latter took two main forms. On the one hand there were rigorist churches that split from the parent Catholic body early in the fourth century because of what they regarded as the laxness of the latter in readmitting to the communion of the faithful those who had apostatised. The most important were the Melitians in Coptic Egypt and the Donatists in Africa and Numidia. On the other hand there were the Arians, followers of the Alexandrian cleric Arius (c. 250–336). While both might be lumped together as heresy, Arianism raised questions of doctrinal definition, while the rigorist groups raised questions about ethics, ecclesiology, authority and the Christian life. The struggle with both forms of opposition had the effect of forcing rapid and rigorous development of Catholic self-definition, as well as encouraging exclusivist and persecuting tendencies.

Both the Melitians and the Donatists claimed to represent the true Catholic church, establishing themselves around bishops who remained free from any taint of apostasy or undue lenience towards those who had weakened in times of persecution. In both cases the central religious issue may also have had the effect of mobilising ethnic and regional loyalties. More ready to compromise than the Donatists, the Melitians eventually collapsed before the greater might of Athanasius' alliance of the Catholic church with desert asceticism (see below). But the Donatist schism proved far more enduring, and it severely tested Constantine's ability to control Christian faction within his empire. His first move was to restrict financial privileges to the 'official' Catholic party. His second was to refer the issue to two successive councils of bishops. When the Donatists rejected the councils' decisions, he resorted to force. But martyrdom and persecution failed to eradicate this self-styled church of the martyrs that 'suffers persecution but does not persecute', as its leaders put it. It was during a brief period of toleration under the short reign of the pagan emperor Julian (361–3) that Donatus formulated his famous question, 'What has the emperor to do with the church?'[14] Even under renewed persecution in the later fourth and fifth centuries, and even under the theological onslaught of Augustine (see next chapter), the

Donatists' remained the dominant church in north Africa. It survived until the seventh century, when Christianity of all kinds was eroded under the influence of the invading Moors.

The battle with Arianism took a different course. It was complicated by intense and prolonged theological debates and by internal church politics. Of the latter, the most important had to do with rivalries between different patriarchates, particularly between the ancient and intellectually venerable see of Alexandria, the increasingly powerful upstart see of Constantinople, and the established Catholic stronghold in Rome. Not only doctrine and immortal salvation but the worldly fortunes of individuals, churches and regions were at stake.

The controversy was focused on the long-standing debate about the status of Jesus. It concerned the proper understanding of the relation between Father and Son. Arius' concern appears to have been to protect the transcendence, immutability and unknowability of God. These characteristics had long been ascribed to divinity by the Greek philosophical tradition, particularly Platonism, and by the Alexandrian school of theology, which owed much to this tradition. In Arius' view, Christ was a unique divine being, the 'only begotten' son of the Father, but must be sharply distinguished from God himself. Christ was willed by God, and was the principle of creation through which everything else was made. He was not a creature like a human being, but neither was he the creator. He was the Word, the one who reveals God, the knowable one who points to the Unknowable.

Though he had supporters in high places, Arius' views divided the church in several regions and led to his condemnation by his archbishop, Alexander. Following precedent, councils were called to discuss the issues, but even the intervention in writing by Constantine did not lead to a resolution. In 325 the emperor therefore personally convened a major council at Nicea attended by about 230 bishops from both east and west. Nicea settled on a creed that anathematised the views it took to be Arian ('that "there was [a time] when he was not" and "he came to be from nothing"'), and affirmed instead that Jesus Christ was 'only-begotten from the substance (*ousia*) of the Father; God from God, Light from Light, true God from true God, begotten not made, consubstantial (*homoousios*) with the Father'. Although the formula was almost unanimously agreed at the council of Nicea, it did not settle the arguments. Its very breadth and ambiguity were part of the problem, since many Arians and 'semi-Arians' also accepted it. Arianism continued to win support, not least among barbarian tribes in the north, such as the Goths – no doubt as a marker of both their similarity to and their difference from 'Roman' Catholic Christianity.

It was not until a Nicene party began to form under the informal leadership of Athanasius (c. 300–73), Alexander's successor as bishop of Alexandria, that the battle lines between Arianism and Catholicism really hardened. Athanasius insisted on the unique authority of the Nicene statement and the authoritative status of Nicea as an 'ecumenical council' (a council of the whole church). He and his supporters rejected any Arian-type formulations that seemed to diminish the Son and deprive him of divine being and saving power. Athanasius understood that a great deal depended on this issue, for if Jesus were not divine then the hope of salvation through him would be weakened. And with it the power of Catholic Christianity, which rested on the unique authority of the saviour it proclaimed and the sacraments it distributed, would be diminished. Christian uniqueness and its exclusive ability to save would be undermined if it could proclaim only a demigod.

In the event it was not only Athanasisus but also the remarkable trio of Gregory of Nyssa, Basil of Caesarea and Gregory of Nazianzus (the 'Cappadocian fathers', since all came from the region of Cappadocia in modern-day Turkey) who shaped the course of orthodox theology in the later fourth century by developing formulations that eventually led to an agreed Catholic 'trinitarian' theology. This theology insisted on the same substance (*homoousios*) not only of Father and Son (as at Nicea), but of Father, Son *and* Holy Spirit. At the same time, the Cappadocians protected the difference between the three by insisting that they were three different instantiations (*hypostases*) of the one divine substance (just as in Platonic thought three different human beings are three different instantiations of a single 'humanity'). The Cappadocians explained these differences in terms of the origins of each of the persons of the Trinity: the Father is the cause, the Son the only-begotten, and the Spirit proceeds from the Father.

Yet unresolved issues concerning Jesus Christ and his relation to God still remained and continued to be provoked by the stubborn persistence of Arianism. One of the main concerns of the Arian parties was that, if the Son was really of a nature or substance identical to the Father, then that seemed to imply that the Father suffered and died and was subject to human weakness. This was wholly unacceptable to Christian minds shaped not only by the Platonic conviction that God could not suffer or change, but by the need to insist upon God's almighty power. The Arian solution was to make Christ different from God, thus preserving monotheism and safeguarding God's impassibility. The Nicene party shared the assumption that God could not suffer, but also wanted to affirm the full divinity of Christ. The danger was that they would turn Christ into a divine being who merely *appeared* to be human. This must be avoided because, as Gregory of Nazianzus realised, 'that which is not assumed is not healed' – if Jesus does not share our full humanity, then he cannot save us. Again, the power of Catholic Christianity as a uniquely powerful religion of salvation would be diminished.

Two solutions were proposed. One, associated with Nestorius and the see of Antioch (the Antiochene position), maintained that Jesus is fully God and fully human, but that the human and the divine are distinct in him. Therefore, when the Bible speaks of Jesus learning, weeping, suffering and dying it refers to his humanity, and when it speaks of his power, his miracles and his resurrection it refers to his divinity. The other proposal, associated with Cyril and the see of Alexandria (the Alexandrian position) maintained that the two natures are united in the one Christ, and that the Word is the subject of all Christ's actions – all that Christ is and does has God the Word as its subject. In order to explain his finitude and suffering, some Alexandrians maintained that the Word self-consciously adapted his behaviour at certain moments to what befitted a man, saying that he felt distress or did not know only for the benefit of his hearers. Both solutions ensured that God's almighty power from on high was not compromised by Christology: the thought that Christ's suffering and finitude might convey something real about the nature of God was not entertained. Suffering was understood as an indication of God's grace and condescension, but not as a sign that his power could be understood as anything other than almighty.

The dispute between the Antiochene and Alexandrian schools was eventually settled by the intervention of Leo, bishop of Rome (who thereby struck a vital blow for the supremacy of Rome), and by the Council of Chalcedon of 451 (discussed in more detail in the following chapter). Chalcedon represented something of a compromise between the two positions, but was not enough to prevent the schism of churches that favoured the Nestorian position, most notably those in Persia. By the

49

sixth century other 'non-Chalcedonian' churches of a monophysite persuasion would also separate from the Catholic, Chalcedonian tradition.

The fourth to sixth centuries were therefore decisive for the settling of the dogmatic boundaries of the Catholic tradition – of trinitarian orthodoxy. Though it was not abolished, 'heresy' was now clearly labelled as such, and was quite literally pushed to the fringes of empire. Imperial legislation went hand in hand with credal formulation. As one of the edicts of the great Christian emperor and legislator Theodosius (ruled 379–95) put it:

> We command that those persons who follow this rule [of trinitarian faith] shall embrace the name of Catholic Christians. The rest, however, whom we adjudge demented and insane, shall sustain the infamy of heretical dogmas, their meeting places shall not receive the name of churches, and they shall be smitten first by divine vengeance and secondly by the retribution of our own initiative, which we shall assume in accordance with the divine judgement.[15]

Theodosius compelled the nominal assent of all to a comprehensive formula of 'Catholic truth', produced laws against Arians and other heretical movements, proscribed the celebration of pagan sacrifices, and closed remaining temples – or had them turned into churches. From Rome in 407 issued the decree to the west that 'if any images stand now in the temples and shrines, they shall be thrown from their foundations . . . Altars shall be destroyed in all places.'[16] Only Judaism was now officially tolerated.

Christian separation from both Judaism and paganism in the fourth and fifth centuries was equally decisive. Though Catholic Christianity owed far more to Judaism than did many more gnostic variants of Christianity, this did nothing to diminish its virulent polemic against the Jews and their stigmatisation as murderers of Christ. Many shared Eusebius' view that the destruction of Jerusalem by the Romans was punishment of the Jews by God for killing his only Son. One of Constantine's first acts after conversion had been to enact legislation against the Jews, renewing a prohibition on proselytism and making it punishable by death.

In relation to paganism, the official adoption of Christianity by the emperor gave Christians a chance to give paganism a taste of its own persecuting medicine, and violent destruction of pagan temples by Christians became commonplace. Yet paganism did not die so easily, as the brief reign of the pagan emperor Julian 'the apostate' (361–3) demonstrated. Many high-born Romans continued to despise the Christian upstarts and the destruction of an older way of life, and many ordinary people continued to sacrifice to their ancestral gods. Yet the tide of imperial power was against them, and the coffers of the empire were now financing churches and clergy rather than pagan temples and their priests. It has been estimated that, during the course of the fourth century, Christian numbers increased from five million to thirty million – getting on for half the empire.[17]

Within the Catholic church, too, boundaries had hardened and organisation sharpened. The brightest and most able men of the increasingly large literate middle class could now find a comfortable home as bishops and priests. As such they found themselves in positions of considerable power and influence, and were often the most influential figures in the local community. Their responsibilities grew as they became functionaries of empire and church with jurisdiction in the area of law as well as of morals. What is more, with the gradual suppression of 'pagan' support systems, including cult groups, retirement and obsequies insurance societies, civic banquets, and distribution of surplus offerings at temples, the Christian clergy stepped forward to take over many welfare and charitable functions. Increasingly, Christianity offered all that an ambitious man might desire: not only authority, respect, security, a salary and a career structure, but a framework in which to discipline the body, exercise the mind and direct the longings of the heart.

The incorporation of asceticism

As the previous section shows, the battle against heresy was also a battle on the part of the Catholic tradition against alternative forms of Christianity, and on the part of the empire against disunity. Originally, Christianity had attracted many of the homeless minds of the empire. After Constantine, many were happy to be assimilated to the world and find a home – and real power – therein. But others remained convinced that the Christian calling was still to be homeless in this world, for their true home lay elsewhere. Christians were called to be nothing less than 'angels', witnesses to the breathtaking possibilities of human life that had been revealed by the re-creation of the earthly Jesus as the transfigured and resurrected Christ.

While church and empire might fight against those who held such views in gnostic and radical Christian groups or in Donatism and Meletianism, there were many within Catholic ranks who nevertheless felt the force of the rigorist ideal. The Catholic tradition had always been able to point to the martyrs in its ranks as evidence that Catholics were no less dedicated than their rivals. But, as martyrdom ceased with the ending of persecution, non-Catholic groups seemed in danger of capturing the moral and spiritual high ground. The answer lay in the incorporation of asceticism in an organised monastic form into the heart of ecclesiastical life. 'Monasticism', the seventh-century romance *Barlaam and Joasaph* explained, 'arose from men's desire to become martyrs in will, that they might not miss the glory of them who were made perfect by blood'. One of the great achievements of Constantinian Christianity was to co-opt asceticism to its cause, thus turning what might have been a revolutionary influence into a reforming one.

The task was accomplished not only with the aid of Constantine, but through the skill of several of those church leaders who also played a decisive role in the battle against heresy, including Athanasius, Jerome (c. 340–420), Ambrose (c. 340–97), Augustine (354–430) and the Cappadocian fathers. Like their opponents, their campaign would focus on the body – both social and physical – and its control. For the meaning of asceticism came to be identified not only with the control of the mind and the will (and ultimately the Spirit) over the body, but with Christian integrity and self-determination in a world that constantly threatened to overwhelm it. Each fought the demons in its own way and each grew more powerful in the process.

The roots of this distinctive attitude to the body go back as far as Paul, who had combined an emphasis on the significance of the body in the religious life with a preference for celibacy. Within high culture, Platonism – and the Jewish, Christian and gnostic groups that drew from it – had long championed a philosophical-ascetic ideal (prominent, for example, in Philo and Origen). At the popular level martyrdom helped to reinforce the Christian ideal of total control over the body. By emphasising the appalling nature of the fatal wounds inflicted upon their bodies by sword, fire, wild beasts and so on, the immensely influential Christian *Lives* and *Acts* of the martyrs highlighted a heroic ability to overcome the flesh. (So much was this so that some of the women martyrs are declared to have become male: they have overcome their fleshly and sexual selves to such an extent that their true spiritual self has been revealed – the assumption being that the form of true humanity must be male, since the God in whose image man is made is male.) As the martyrological literature also emphasises, what the martyrs do is to imitate and recapitulate the sufferings of Christ on the cross and the sacrifice of the body.

Although the cessation of Roman persecution meant that the martyrs' total victory of spirit over flesh could no longer be won in the arenas and public spaces of imperial Rome, it began to be enacted in the antisocial world of the desert. Ascetic Christianity of the desert developed in the fourth century in Egypt, Palestine and Syria. Interestingly, both the former and the latter had long been areas where 'orthodox' Christianity had found it hardest to win the battle against 'heresy', and the various forms of desert Christianity may have been an extension of this heretical tradition. By venturing out into this no-man's-land where the demons made their habitations, Christians left behind them not only the structures of empire, but also those of the consolidating Catholic church. Here the obligations and burdens of political, economic, religious and domestic life fell away – not only were there no taxes to pay, there were no tithes either. (Roman complaints about the greed, violence and irresponsibility of monks 'who eat more than elephants'[18] are common.) Men and women could pursue the ideal Christ had set before them in total freedom. They could either live on their own in the isolation of a cave or some other sheltered place, or form themselves into loose communities of ascetics. In the early literature, the latter form of monasticism is classified as 'coenobitic' (*koinos*, common; *bios*, life) and distinguished from the more individualistic 'eremetical' monasticism (*eremos*, desert). The former is associated with the monk Pachomius, the latter with Antony.

On the ground, however, this distinction may have been blurred. What seems to have happened is that certain ascetic individuals achieved influence due to their wisdom, ascetic feats or miraculous powers. In some cases, informal communities would form around their leadership; in others, a formal community with buildings, rules and loose organisation would develop; in still others these leaders would become central points in a network of teachers who would be visited by seekers after wisdom. All, however, owed more to a 'school' model of Christianity than to the 'church' of Catholicism. When we read the *Sayings of*

Plate 2   Monastery of St Catherine, Sinai (Egypt)

One of the oldest surviving Christian monasteries, St Catherine's was constructed by order of the Emperor Justinian between 548 and 565, and survives to this day. A fortress, shrine and small town, it illustrates the way in which the ascetic ideal was co-opted by the Catholic church and empire.

the Desert Fathers, we find that the authorities of the Catholic tradition – scripture, sacraments and priesthood – have little place. Instead, we find something closer to a wisdom tradition. In the desert men stand before God as equals, and those who have authority earn it by the rigour of their lives and the wisdom of their words. The attainment of control over bodily appetites – for food, sex and money – is admired and celebrated. So too is the ability to seek and discern God, and to direct others towards him. But all this must be accompanied by humility. Even the most perfect monks must not lord it over others, and must never judge any man:

> Once a brother in Scete was found guilty, and the older brethren came in assembly and sent to the abbot Moses, asking him to come: but he would not. Then the priest sent to him, saying: 'Come: for the assembly of brethren awaits thee.' And he rose up and came. But taking with him a very old basket, he filled it with sand and carried it behind him. And they went out to meet him, asking, 'Father, what is this?' And the old man said to them, 'My sins are running behind me and I do not see them, and am I come today to judge the sins of another man.' And they heard him, and said naught to the brother, but forgave him.[19]

In many ways, then, Christianity in the desert seems to have developed an alternative model of power to that of the Catholic tradition. As such, it might have posed as serious a threat to Catholicism and empire as the other, more organised forms of 'rigorism' mentioned above. In the event, however, the threat was not only contained but turned to Catholicism's advantage, for desert Christianity was not only co-opted to the Catholic cause but presented as a vital piece of evidence for the latter's authentic ascetic credentials. Two strategies combined to effect this coup. The first was political: Catholic bishops won over ascetic leaders by extending to them the protection and benefits that their church could offer – and by ordaining them. Before long, nearly all monks and ascetics were brought within the oversight of a local bishop. The second strategy was a literary one. The same church fathers who had penned sophisticated doctrinal arguments in the defence of doctrinal orthodoxy now turned their talents to the production of much more influential *Lives* of the desert fathers. The latter were extremely effective, not only in winning converts to Christianity (the young Augustine, for instance, was inspired by reading Athanasius' *Life of Antony*), but in furthering the Catholic cause. In

Athanasius' hands, for instance, Antony became a model of obedience rather than of independence, and of humble imitation of Christ rather than of heroic striving after human perfection. It was not his wisdom that was highlighted, but his subjection to 'the Word'. His ethical conduct is presented as being of far greater significance than his teaching; his reverence for scripture, sacraments and bishops is woven into the narrative, and his opposition to heresy – particularly Arianism – and unfailing loyalty to the Catholic church are made crystal clear.

Instead of being left outside the church, then, the monastic ideal was brought inside. The major effects were to harness the dangerously free-floating power of the ascetics, and to bolster the rigorist credentials of Catholicism. Asceticism itself was changed in the process. In the west, in particular, it began to be interpreted in terms of the conquest of sin rather than the refinement of humanity into the likeness of God, and its social and political radicalism tended to be diminished in the process. The effects on the internal life and organisation of the Catholic church were profound as well. Above all, the incorporation of asceticism served to reinforce the hierarchical nature of the church and its understanding of power as control of the weak by the strong. God's control over his church and a bishop's control over his flock were now echoed and reflected in the imperative of the soul's control over the body. Not only must a believer's external and public life be lived in obedience to higher power, but even the most private and intimate stirrings of the body and its desire must be constantly controlled. Increasingly, this idealised hierarchy of control came to be symbolised in patriarchal terms: power and control were understood as male, and subjection as female. Thus divine order was a system in which a Father God and a male saviour ruled over 'his bride', the church. Within the church, this was replicated in a system of exclusively male clerical control over weaker brethren, with images of 'children', 'sheep' and so on becoming common. And in relation to the individual person, such ordering meant that the body must be subject to the control of the higher, more manly soul.

This hierarchical system of patriarchal power is vividly illustrated by the increasing importance given to virgins in the Catholic church. Groups of celibate women, both widows and younger unmarried women, appear to have been important within Christianity from the very start. By refusing to marry and have children, Christian virgins were not only refusing the one publicly acceptable role open to women; they were undermining the entire social order, which depended upon women for its renewal in the most literal sense. As we have seen, many such women seem to have carved out powerful roles for themselves within the more sectarian and 'school' forms of Christianity. The virulence of much early Catholic polemic against women's speaking, preaching and teaching in public seems to be clear evidence of the fact that it was a relatively common occurrence. The co-option of asceticism by the Catholic church, however, included the co-option of women virgins. And, in a profound reversal, they ceased to be revolutionary symbols and became, instead, one of the most potent symbols in the Catholic repertoire of total submission to divinely authorised male authority.

Instead of being seen as autonomous equals to men in the new life of freedom that had been opened up by Jesus Christ, these women were henceforward to be understood in terms of the guiding metaphor of a 'bride of Christ'. As Athanasius instructed them:

> When you have found him, hold on to him, and do not leave him until he brings you into his bedroom. He is your bridegroom. He is the one who will crown you . . . Wait for him; gaze on him with your mind; speak to him; rejoice with him; take everything from him. For when you are fed by the Lord, you will lack nothing.[20]

Unlike the male ascetics, whose voices we can still hear, we know of these women only through the male clerical voices that extol and instruct them. This is fitting, for the command that is given them again and again is that of silence. Church leaders such as Athanasius battled hard against existing arrangements, including the financial independence of many women ascetics, the practice of male and female ascetics living together, and the practice of women teaching other women. Instead, he strove to gather all virgins into the church, under the oversight of the bishop. There they would listen to the Word in humble and grateful silence, a powerful image of the perfect Christian life to be held before other Christian men and women. As 'brides of Christ' they did not threaten and undermine the institution of marriage in the way that autonomous women ascetics had done. Rather, they modelled the perfect obedience that all wives must show to their husbands, and upheld the institution of marriage – albeit to a heavenly rather than to an earthly bridegroom.

For Athanasius and some other church leaders, the virgin was the perfect symbol of the Christian life because she had renounced all power; not only the economic and political power that was closed to women in any case, and power in the religious sphere, which the Catholic church had put out of bounds, but even power in the sphere of sexual and domestic life, which was the one remaining arena where women might assert themselves. There could be no better model of total subjection to power from on high – the power both of the clergy and of God.

As we shall see in the chapters that follow, however, the containment of ascetic power was only partially successful – as, for related reasons, was the containment of women. Through the incorporation of monasticism, the church developed into a two-tiered society, with ascetics, both male and female, being regarded as higher than the rest. The church's division between ascetic and non-ascetic Christians overlaid its earlier one between clergy and laity. The results were often complex. In relation to women, it meant that the highest form of Christian life in spiritual terms, asceticism, was opened up, while the most powerful in this-worldly terms, ordination, remained closed.

Thus, while the Catholic church treated all men and women as potentially equal before God, in the organisation of its institutional life it tended to favour a pyramidal hierarchy of power. Divine power from on high descended through Christ to bishops and thence to the people, becoming more and more diffuse as it did so. This structure echoed that of the Roman empire, and made the two natural partners. What God was to the church, the emperor was to the empire, and the superimposition of the two systems of rule upon each other only increased the power of each and reinforced masculine domination in both church and society. At the same time, however, tensions were created between religious and political sources of power. Which had ultimate authority, and how did the power of the church relate to that of empire? The model favoured by Eusebius positioned the emperor as deputy of Christ with authority over the church. Others – not least Augustine, and a succession of bishops of Rome – disagreed and developed more complex models of state–church relations that sought to safeguard the authority of the church and the autonomy of the sacred. The next chapter considers how the supremacy of the emperor was upheld in eastern Christianity, while an ideal of papal supremacy shaped the increasingly separate development of Christianity in the west.

Further reading
THE CONTEXT OF EARLY CHRISTIANITY

Until recently, early Christianity tended to be the preserve of church historians, and late antiquity of classical historians. By bringing the two into relation with each other, Peter Brown revolutionised scholarship in this area. His *The Making of Late Antiquity* (Cambridge, MA: Harvard University Press, 1978) offers an engaging introduction to a classical world that both resists and incorporates Christianity. Gillian Clark's *Women in Late Antiquity* (Oxford: Clarendon, 1994) offers an accessible treatment of its subject. In *Religions of Late Antiquity in Practice* (Princeton, NJ: Princeton University Press, 2000), Richard Valantasis has gathered together a useful collection of primary religious texts, including Christian ones.

EARLIEST CHRISTIANITY

The New Testament scholar E. P. Sanders has helped further understanding of the historical Jesus by placing him in the context of Palestinian Judaism. See, for example, *The Historical Figure of Jesus* (London: Allan Lane, 1993). Dominic Crossan's somewhat controversial *The Historical Jesus: The Life of a Mediterranean Jewish Peasant* (Edinburgh: T. & T. Clark, 1991) is another influential attempt to sift what can be known about the historical Jesus, and offers a useful three-fold chronological scheme for categorising earliest Christian writings. Paula Friedrikson's *From Jesus to Christ: The Origins of the New Testament Images of Jesus* (New Haven, CT: Yale University Press, 1988) offers a balanced survey of the different ways in which the earliest Christian communities interpreted Jesus. Wayne Meeks's *The First Urban Christians* (New Haven, CT: Yale University Press, 1983) sets Paul and the Pauline communities in sociological context and offers a vivid and concrete portrait of these early Christian groups. Richard Valantasis's introduction to, translation of and commentary on *The Gospel of Thomas* (London and New York: Routledge, 1997) serves as a useful starting point for engagement with early Christian apocryphal literature.

'HERETICAL' GROUPS

Walter Bauer helped change the way we view early Christianity by arguing that it was 'heresy' that came first and 'orthodoxy' that followed. See his pioneering study *Orthodoxy and Heresy in Earliest Christianity* (Philadelphia, PA: Fortress, 1971), which, though not an easy read, repays the effort. Giovanni Filoramo's *A History of Gnosticism* (Cambridge, MA: Blackwell, 1990) offers a comprehensive and detailed overview of the phenomenon. A more popular treatment can be found in Elaine Pagel's *The Gnostic Gospels* (London: Weidenfeld and Nicolson, 1980). Henry A. Green's *The Economic and Social Origins of Gnosticism* (Atlanta, GA: Scholars, 1985) offers a thoroughgoing sociological treatment of gnosticism. Rowan Williams contextualises the Arian crisis in *Arius: Heresy and Tradition* (London: Darton, Longman and Todd, 1987).

THE DEVELOPMENT OF CATHOLIC CHRISTIANITY

Eusebius' *History of the Church* (or *Church History*) is available in a number of translations and editions, including Penguin Classics (1965). It is an easy and enjoyable read. There are many accessible accounts of the early church; Stuart G. Hall's *Doctrine and Practice in the Early Church* (London: SPCK, 1991) is one of the best. Ramsey MacMullen's *Christianizing the Roman Empire (AD 100–400)* (New Haven, CT: Yale University Press, 1984) and W. H. C. Frend's *Martyrdom and Persecution in the Early Church* (Oxford: Blackwell, 1965) consider the often hostile relations between Christianity and paganism. For wide-ranging anthologies of early Christian documents see J. Stevenson (ed.), *A New Eusebius: Documents Illustrating the History of the Church to AD 337* (new edition, London: SPCK, 1987), and J. Stevenson (ed.), *Creeds, Councils and Controversies: Documents Illustrating the History of the Church AD 337–461* (new edition, London: SPCK, 1989). William R. Schoedel's *Ignatius of Antioch: A Commentary on the Letters of Ignatius of Antioch* (Philadelphia, PA: Fortress, 1985) illuminates the emergence of the Catholic form of Christianity.

THE GROWTH OF ASCETICISM AND MONASTICISM

Peter Brown's *The Body and Society* (London: Faber, 1990) considers the development of asceticism and monasticism in the early church from Paul to Augustine, and is the classic work in the field. David Brakke's *Athanasius and the Politics of Asceticism* (Oxford: Clarendon, 1995) influenced the final section of this chapter. The *Sayings of the Desert Fathers* is available in a number of translations, and is still compelling as living spiritual literature as well as a historical document. E. A. Clark's *Ascetic Piety and Women's Faith* (Lewiston, NY: Edwin Mellen, 1986) was a pioneering work on women and asceticism, and Susannah Elm's *'Virgins of God': The Making of Asceticism in Late Antiquity* (Oxford and New York: Oxford University Press, 1994) builds on such work.

Churches of east and west in the early Middle Ages

> He who has founded his church in the west, his church has
> not reached the east; the choice of him who has founded his
> church in the east has not come to the west . . . My church is
> superior . . . to previous churches, for these previous churches
> were chosen in particular countries and in particular cities. My
> church shall spread in all cities, and its gospel shall reach every
> country.[1]

The previous chapter explored the way in which dreams of universal dominion helped shape the fortunes of early Christianity and support the rise to power of the Catholic church. Such dreams lost nothing of their allure as antiquity gave way to the Middle Ages. Men of power still imagined themselves at the helm of great empires, and they were men of religion as well as of politics – for as yet there were no secular empires, only religious ones.

Yet the Christian empire was threatened by competing powers, both religious and political. The words above are those not of a Christian but of Mani (216–76), the founder of a new universal religion that, he believed, would supplant those that had come before, including Christianity. Mani's dream faltered because his religion failed to form an adequate alliance with political power. The next great world empire, the Islamic, did not make the same mistake. Its dramatic rise to power from the seventh century, and its rapid seizure of territories belonging to the Roman empire, would have serious consequences for the development of Christianity. So too would the collapse of the western empire under the pressure of incursion by 'barbarian' tribes from the north.

In spite of all this, the Romano-Christian dream of universal dominion refused to die. This chapter and the next explore the way in which it continued to shape and animate Christianity from late antiquity through the Middle Ages, but took new forms in the process. This chapter begins the story by charting the ways in which eastern and western Christianity developed separate identities as they attempted to maintain their allegiance to power from on high in increasingly divergent ways.

In the east, where Roman-Byzantine imperial power was threatened but not defeated by rival empires, the church continued in its role as privileged partner of the state until the defeat of the empire by the Ottoman Turks in 1453. In the west, where Roman power retreated after the fifth century, the church would stake a claim to earthly as well as to spiritual power from on high in its own right. The difference was due to theological as well as political factors for, as we saw in the previous chapter, the church in the west had long been more suspicious of the empire than the church in the east, and more prone to ask, 'What has the emperor to do with the church?' Yet the question would now be raised by the western church, not in repudiation of worldly power from on high, but out of a growing desire to share and even to control it. It was this, together with a combination of propitious circumstances, that inspired the vision and pursuit of 'Christendom': of a united territory in the west under the control of the Catholic church based in Rome.

What we witness, as the chapter unfolds, is an extension of the churches' power that begins to render the distinction between 'sacred' and 'secular' redundant. In the east, church and state work together in the defence of a fully Christian empire. In the west, the rich and pluriform culture that was explored in the previous chapter gives way to a simpler and more monolithic culture based on the Bible and institutionalised in the monasteries and courts of great rulers. The latter becomes an integral part of an aristocratic culture that owes as much to the Germanic tribes as to the classical world, and in which power is based on blood and the sword. Power is also concentrated at the local level, and takes personal rather than impersonal (bureaucratic or judicial) forms. It is exercised, above all, by kings and bishops, normally working in harmonious relationships of mutual support.

But for at least half the period under consideration, the centre of gravity of the Christian world remained in the east rather than in the west. The Latin world remained peripheral to the political and cultural centres that dominated the early medieval world: Constantinople, Damascus, Baghdad. By any measure of power – cultural, economic, political or military – the eastern empire and church would for many centuries be superior to anything to be found in the west. At the same time that the western church was struggling to maintain Christian culture and learning, the theology of the eastern church was growing to maturity. As it did so, it nurtured a tradition of sacred power from below, in which God's power is made manifest not through the subjection of the human being but through its divinisation.

Given that the leading edge of Christianity remained in the east rather than in the west for much of this period, our narrative begins there, before shifting to the west and considering the consequences of the gradual separation of a previously unified religion and empire into two halves.

The church in the east

In December 537 the emperor Justinian entered the completed church of St Sophia (in Greek, 'Hagia Sophia', which means Holy Wisdom) in his capital city, Constantinople. He had commissioned this 'Great Church' five years earlier; it was to be the largest Christian building in the world. Legend has it that as he looked about him he murmured, 'Solomon, I have surpassed thee' – even the ancient temple of Israel in Jerusalem could not compare with Justinian's achievement. St Sophia stands in Constantinople to this day, though Constantinople is now Istanbul, in Turkey rather than in the Roman empire, and the Great Church has served as mosque and tourist attraction.

The architecture of St Sophia marked a departure from the earlier style of Christian building that had developed under the patronage of Constantine. The first Christian 'basilicas' were longitudinal (longer than wide) with a central 'nave', an aisle on each side, and a semicircular 'apse' containing the altar and situated opposite the entrance door. Their style was derived directly from the large public buildings that could be found in most Roman cities and that were used for a variety of purposes, including public gatherings, law courts, audience halls and throne rooms. Given its ready associations with power, grandeur and holiness (the emperor's statue or throne was often situated where later Christians would place an altar), it is not surprising that Constantine selected the same architectural form for the churches he commissioned across the empire. Though every bit as grand, St Sophia was different. It was square rather than rectangular, and reached its climax not in an apsed sanctuary but in a massive central dome, a shallow saucer 33 m (107 ft) across and pierced around its rim with forty windows. Internally, it was decorated with mosaic in gold and decorative patterns, which were illuminated by the flickering yellow light of carefully positioned gold lamps and candles. The impression – quite intentionally – was of heaven brought down to earth, or earth caught up to heaven.

While St Sophia was not without classical precedents – the most obvious being Hadrian's domed Pantheon in Rome – it speaks of the way in which classical architecture was beginning to be influenced by Christianity. The overall effect of the Great Church is quite different from the clearly defined circular space of the Pantheon, for its boundaries advance and recede in an array of semi-domes, apses, and columned galleries, with its great dome appearing to float above them all. St Sophia may well have been influenced by the circular baptisteries and mausoleums being built to house the bodies of Christian saints, particularly in the east. It was also shaped by the needs of an increasingly dramatic 'divine liturgy' that was punctuated by hymn-singing and ritual processions through the congregation. This liturgy began with the 'mass of catechumens': a solemn procession of deacons and priests carrying scriptures and icons, followed by readings from the scriptures, a sermon and prayer. This led on to the 'mass of the faithful', which was opened by another procession in which the elements of bread and wine, representing the body of Christ, were carried to the altar. Previously celebrated in the sight of the whole congregation, the eucharist now became a secret and solemn rite performed by the clergy in the 'holy of holies' behind the 'iconostasis', a screen placed between the congregation and the altar. After the consecration, the clergy would appear from behind the iconostasis with the sacraments; they themselves received in 'two kinds' (bread and wine), while the laity would receive by intinction (bread dipped into the wine). While St Sophia stood at the heart of the eastern empire, the imposition of uniformity within that empire meant that parallel eucharistic celebrations in similar, though much smaller, churches would take place simultaneously, effectively binding a whole people into an ethnic and political unity through shared ritual.

St Sophia symbolises the transition from the classical western empire to the Christian eastern empire, later called the Byzantine empire. The immediate causes of this transition were external. The most obvious was the loss of large swathes of western territory to barbarian tribes after the fifth century. But even before that, as his relocation of the Roman capital in the east demonstrates, Constantine had realised that the empire's heart had shifted. This was true in both cultural and geopolitical terms. The Roman empire could survive the loss of its western portion. Most of its

Plate 3   Interior of St Sophia, Constantinople (Istanbul)

food and raw materials came from the east, and almost all the culture that needed to be taken seriously had arisen in the eastern Mediterranean, Syria-Mesopotamia and Iran. Though the emperor Justinian (527–65) tried with limited success to restore some of the western territories, including parts of north Africa and Italy, he would be the last emperor to do so.

It was also in the east rather than in the west that the Roman empire's real political rival was to be found: the revived Persian empire. Under the Sasanian dynasty, which ruled the territories of Iran and Mesopotamia from the third century until the seventh, Persia engaged in a number of both aggressive and defensive military engagements with the eastern Roman empire. Both empires aspired to control the same territory: the 'fertile crescent' that stretched down from the Black Sea in the north, through the eastern Mediterranean and Transjordania, down the Nile to Ethiopia in Africa (the latter being the ancient empire of 'Axum'). Raw materials and manpower abounded in these regions, and the territory was far more important to an empire aspiring to superpower status than were north Africa and the west. Thus the swift and unexpected Arab conquest of much of this region in the seventh century, together with its overthrow of the Persian empire itself, broke the stalemate between Rome and Persia and established a new world power greater than either: the Islamic empire. Though it survived the Muslim onslaught, the Byzantine empire was much diminished by it, losing control of Syria, Palestine, Egypt and north Africa, and retaining only its heartlands around Constantinople in Asia Minor. From this point on its only opportunity for expansion lay northwards into Romania and the Slavic lands (see ch. 6).

There were also important internal forces at work in the reshaping of the Roman empire. Since the time of Constantine, one of the most significant had been the growing alliance between church and state, and again Justinian's construction of St Sophia serves as a powerful symbol. There was no contradiction in an emperor building a church, for, as deputy of Christ, the emperor was head of both church and state. Just as St Sophia was seen as a model of heaven on earth, so the Byzantine state was viewed by its rulers and subjects as an earthly image of the heavens above. This justified a hierarchical social order with one absolute ruler, an emperor supreme over all his subjects, both clerical and lay. The carefully scripted imperial procession to St Sophia in Constantinople enacted this understanding on a regular basis. It was led by standard-bearers, clearing the way. Behind them, in ascending rank order, came the civil and the military hierarchies. Finally, the emperor himself processed, robed in splendid garments and surrounded by the imperial guard and the eunuchs of the bedchamber. The procession passed before the capital's population, organised according to their various occupations. When it reached St Sophia the emperor would be received by the patriarch and the bishops, before disappearing with them behind the iconostasis while the elaborate rituals surrounding the holy mysteries were enacted. On leaving the church, he would distribute gold to the poor.

Since the Byzantine emperor was the representative of God on earth, he naturally had a special relationship to the church. The very conception of a Christian empire meant that the church was part of the polity, a department of state under the direction of the emperor. It meant that there was no clear distinction between religion and politics, the spiritual and the temporal, what was Caesar's and what was God's. The emperor was responsible for upholding God's order in the empire and among his subjects, both clerical and lay. It was also the emperor who elected and appointed the patriarch, and had ultimate responsibility for maintaining and codifying correct doctrine and church order as well as more obviously 'secular' law. In the latter task he was assisted by a growing 'civil service' of cultured laymen and clergy. Yet this was not a form of 'Caesaro-papism', in which the emperor is also a chief priest, for, although the Byzantine emperor was able to participate in some of the privileges reserved for clergy – such as entering the sanctuary behind the iconostasis and receiving communion in both kinds – he was not a member of the clergy. This opened up a limited space for the clergy to exercise independent power, even to exercise outright opposition to the emperor if he was deemed 'heretical'. Of course, given the increasing power of the church and the monastic orders within the empire from the time of Justinian onwards, it was important for the emperor to maintain the clergy's goodwill; but this was generally achieved through close involvement in church affairs rather than by a policy of non-interference.

The relation between church and state in the Byzantine empire was thus one of interdependence, in which earthly and heavenly power were not clearly distinguished, but in which the state had overall control of the church. The advantages to both parties were considerable. On the one

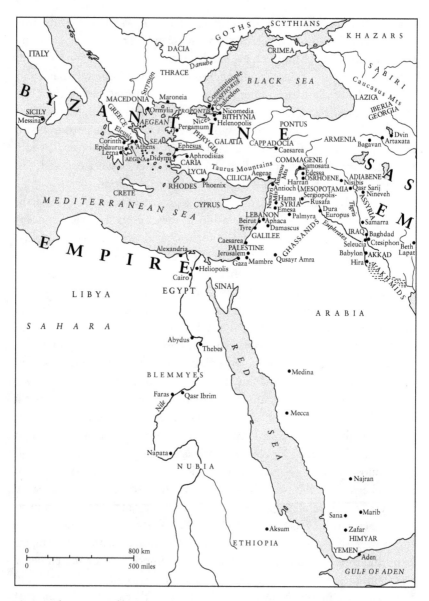

Map 2 The empires of late antiquity

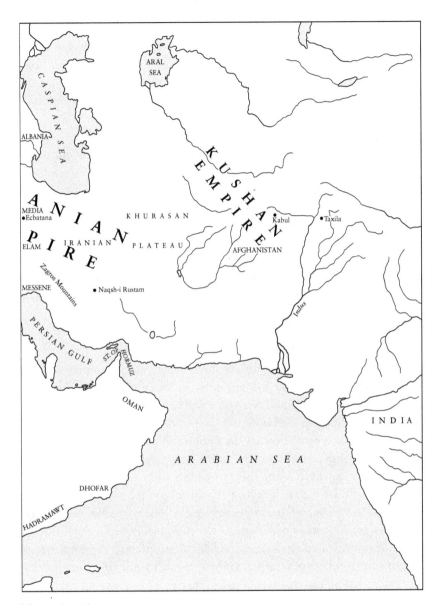

Map 2 (*cont.*)

hand, the church served to legitimate the political and social hierarchy, making them seem part of a natural and God-given order. On the other, the church benefited from imperial protection and patronage. In both cases, the relationship led to a powerful concern with unity and order. Christianity helped unify the empire, while the empire helped unify the church, a church that was already beginning to separate itself from the western church and to think of itself as the one true 'Orthodox' church. Well aware of this dynamic, Justinian and his successors took considerable care to uphold and impose unity in Christian doctrine in the face of the theological disputes that Nicea had been unable to lay to rest. They also closed down 'pagan' academies, including the famous academy in Athens, so bringing to an end the dominance of the classical curriculum. From then on, the church would have sole responsibility for education, and classical learning would take place in a Christian framework rather than vice versa. In the long run, however, this drive to impose imperial and ecclesiastical unity seems to have given impetus to the very forces of disunity it was seeking to destroy.

The separation of the non-Chalcedonian churches

Despite the loss of its western territories, the eastern empire continued to consider itself *the* Roman empire. Its emperor was the Holy Roman emperor, and its subjects still referred to themselves as *Romanes* or *Romaioi* ('Romans' in Latin and Greek respectively). Until the Arab conquests of the seventh century the Byzantines retained control of Syria, Palestine and Egypt (despite temporary Persian seizure of near-eastern territories in 614). While the subjects of this still extensive empire were proud to consider themselves Roman, this did not, however, mean that they were always happy to accept the rule of Constantinople, its emperor or its patriarch. Instead of serving as the straightforward force for unity that Constantine had envisaged, the Christianisation of the empire was also having the effect of reinforcing the separate identity of its great cities and exacerbating the rivalries between them.

The problem was that, while Christianity could indeed legitimate the central power, it could also empower opposition from the margins. Thus the churches in Rome and Constantinople became engaged in a battle to assert primacy over each other and over other patriarchates, while the churches of Antioch (in Syria) and Alexandria (in Egypt) tried to exercise independent power and forge temporary alliances with Rome and the pope or with Constantinople and its emperor as and when this might best serve their purposes. From the fifth century onwards, when it declared itself an independent church with its own patriarch, the church in Persia also began to consolidate its power and identity. Not only did Christianity hasten such fragmentation by dividing the empire into patriarchates with their own leaders; the translation of the Bible and Christian literature into regional languages (for example, Coptic in Egypt; Syriac in much of the near east), together with the development of distinctive Christian liturgical and theological traditions in different areas, reinforced the creation of separate identities.

Since the Catholic church had tried to establish the unity of Christianity on the basis of common belief (Irenaeus' 'rule of faith'), internal disagreements and disaffiliations now tended to be played out by way of doctrinal disputes. Just as the establishment of 'centres' of Christianity (Rome, Constantinople) was inseparable from the creation of 'peripheries' (Egypt, the near east, etc.), so the attempt to establish uniform belief throughout the empire often led to disagreement and schism. In both cases that which was designed to ensure unity also had the effect of unleashing disunity. Under the culturally tolerant regime of the earlier polytheistic Roman empire, matters of belief had rarely been able to become a focus for division. In any case, as we saw in the last chapter, 'philosophy' had been a pursuit that attracted only a few earnest souls. The intellectual and moral seriousness of Catholic Christianity, however, combined with its wide appeal to the expanding middle classes, made it a new and powerful force. Intellectual debate and instruction could now take place not only in academies for the elite, but in monasteries and churches as well as in the homes of the urban middle classes. Given the exclusivist tendencies of Catholic thought, this huge expansion of intellectual activity meant that theological dispute could now have serious political consequences.

While the Council of Nicea in 325 was the most successful of all the ecumenical councils in uniting churches throughout the Roman empire (albeit fairly gradually, the Persian church, for example, accepting Nicea's authority only in 410), even Nicea could have the effect of crystallising schism. Thus several of the 'barbarian' tribes who conquered the western territories of the empire adopted Arianism as their official religion, thereby establishing a safe distance between themselves and Rome while at the same time drawing on the same source of ideological power and prestige as Rome. (Only when greater advantage could be gained by allying with the Roman empire did they finally convert to Nicean 'orthodoxy'.) But whereas Nicea gradually became a focus of unity, the Council of Chalcedon of 451 proved far more enduringly divisive.

As the previous chapter has documented, Chalcedon was one of a number of councils that were called to settle the dispute between Alexandria and Antioch, and it attempted to maintain the unity of the empire by offering a formulation acceptable to both parties. The Alexandrians maintained a 'monophysite' position, arguing that there was only 'one nature' in Christ, while the Antiochenes, following the teaching of Nestorius, the patriarch of Constantinople (c. 386–c. 451), took a 'dyophysite' position, arguing that there were 'two natures' in Christ, the human and the divine. By affirming that Christ's nature was 'without division, without separation', and that Mary his mother was *theotokos* or 'God-bearer', the resulting 'Definition of Chalcedon' seemed to endorse the monophysite position; but in saying that Christ was recognised 'in two natures, without confusion' it could also be seen to affirm the dyophysite position associated with Nestorius and his followers.

While it was intended to close down the controversy between monophysites and Nestorians, Chalcedon also had the effect of energising both positions. The former grew dominant in north Africa and Syria, while the latter dominated Antioch and spread into Persia (and from there into India and China through the trade routes). Each position, in other words, came to define a periphery over against the 'Chalcedonian' Christian centres of Rome and Constantinople. In a desperate attempt to maintain unity, successive emperors attempted reconciliation with either one or the other position – and whichever they chose inevitably alienated the other. In the end, the monophysite territories proved more important to the survival of the empire than did the Nestorian, and the price Justinian had to pay to try to win their loyalty was the condemnation of Nestorianism (a condemnation that, by cutting the ties between Nestorian Christianity and the empire, greatly aided the survival and growth of Nestorian Christianity in the territories of Rome's enemy, Persia). Both the sixth and seventh centuries saw further Roman imperial attempts to reconcile Chalcedonian Christianity with moderate monophysitism. The doctrine of 'monoenergism', for example, taught that, while Christ has two natures, one divine and one human, he possesses a single activity (or 'energy' in Greek usage); and this won some acceptance from monophysites in Egypt and Armenia, as well as from both Rome and Constantinople. Faced by mounting Chalcedonian theological opposition, however, the formula of a single 'energy' was transformed into that of a single will ('monothelitism'). Despite growing opposition from Rome, as well as from 'orthodox' Chalcedonian theologians in the east, such as Maximus the Confessor (c. 580–662), monothelitism survived as an imperially backed church doctrine until the Council of Constantinople of 680–1. In the context of the rising threat from Islam, and the obvious and increasingly irreconcilable divisions within Christianity, the attempt at reconciliation with monophysite churches was never again attempted. Yet again, an attempt to achieve unity had served only to open a new division, and 'Catholic' concern to impose doctrinal unity had given rise to a split between Chalcedonian and non-Chalcedonian churches.

The fate of Nestorian and monophysite Christianity – as well as of contemporaneous faiths such as Manicheism – indicates the vital importance for religion of political support in the ancient and medieval worlds. Though Manicheism had been designed by its founder as a universal faith, without political backing it was unable to become either a 'world religion' or a national faith, despite winning pockets of followers in north Africa, Asia, the Balkans, Italy, central Asia and even China. Likewise, without political backing, non-Chalcedonian Christianity suffered a serious setback in many areas conquered by Islam – including Arabia, Iran and Mesopotamia, Syria and Palestine.

Monophysite Christianity tended to survive best where it had become the indispensable marker of national and ethnic identity. Thus monophysite churches still exist today in Syria, Egypt (as 'Coptic' Christianity), Ethiopia and Armenia. To take the latter as an example, Christianity became integral to the maintenance of ethnic identity in a country whose location made it subject to repeated conquest and occupation – by Persians, Arabs, Turks and Russians. Armenia was the first nation officially to embrace Christianity (in the fourth century), and the Armenian script was actually invented in order to make possible the translation of the Bible and other Christian writings into the national language. Similarly, Ethiopia (more accurately, the kingdom of Axum in north Ethiopia) adopted Christianity as a national faith in the sixth century, translating the Bible and other Christian writings into Ethiopic or 'Ge'ez', which remains the liturgical language to this day even though it died out as a spoken language in the early Middle Ages. Revealingly, Ethiopia's national epic, the *Kebra Nagast* or *Glory of Kings*, which may contain material dating back to the sixth century, tells the story of the righteous Christian king Kaleb, who travels to Jerusalem to meet the Roman emperor and agrees to partition the known world between Ethiopia and Byzantium; but a prophecy put into the mouth of St Gregory the Illuminator, the apostle of Armenia, declares that Byzantium will be destroyed by Persia, while Ethiopia will last for ever. The story indicates not only the sense of common purpose that united the monophysite world from as far apart as Armenia and Ethiopia, but the ability of monophysitism to enable peripheries to lay claim to the sources of power that the centre believed to be its own. Thus in the *Kebra Nagast* it is Ethiopia that has the duty of keeping alive the pure legacy of both Rome and Christianity, in place of an empire gone astray.

Again demonstrating the interdependence of religion and politics, Nestorian Christianity's period of greatest flourishing was under the Persian empire. Though the ancient dualistic religion of Zoroastrianism was the official state religion of the Sasanians, the Persians tended to adopt a policy of cultural pluralism rather than of religious exclusivism. When under threat, however, the state and its religion could adopt an exclusivistic and persecuting stance; Christianity suffered as a result, particularly because of its close associations with Byzantium. The rejection of Chalcedonian Christianity in favour of Nestorianism therefore made Christianity politically acceptable within Persia in a way that would not otherwise have been possible. Fully aware of the advantage of allying itself with Persia and marking itself off from Rome, the church in Persia increasingly became a national church with a 'catholicos' (the equivalent of 'patriarch' in the west) whose election was ratified by the shah (ruler of Persia, 'king of kings').

Blocked off by rival forms of Christianity in the west (and suffering from increasing competition first from monophysitism and then from Islam in Iran), Nestorianism expanded eastwards. Its Asiatic missions began in the fifth century, and followed the trade routes as far as Afghanistan and India. The *Christian Topography* of Kosmas Indikopleustes (c. 535) records the presence of Syrian Nestorian bishops and Christians along the coasts of India and Sri Lanka. Most numerous in Malabar, the members of these Christian communities became, for the most part, an aristocratic elite whose social ranking as merchant traders became embedded in the caste system. Further east, Nestorians are first attested at the Chinese court in 635, and they built up a significant presence in China that lasted until the ninth century, and revived again under Mongol patronage in the thirteenth and fourteenth centuries. In both places, however, Christianity was generally seen as a religion of foreigners. Because it failed to find a patron to replace Rome or Persia, because it competed with religions such as Buddhism, Confucianism and Hinduism, which were already ethnically and politically entrenched, and because it did not become the distinctive marker of a particular nation or people, Nestorian Christianity never managed to gain more than a foothold in the territories to which it spread. Even in its Persian heartland, it failed to survive the onslaught of Islam.

Byzantine Christianity
By sweeping away the Persian empire and conquering most of the former territories of Byzantium, Islam managed in less than a century to attain the superpower status that had long eluded its predecessors. (The Islamic state was ten times larger than that of Byzantium, with a budget fifteen times greater.) To some extent the early Islamic empire achieved this remarkable feat by building on what had gone before. Its founder, the prophet Mohammed, was well acquainted with the religions of the Roman and Persian empires. Just as Christianity saw itself fulfilling and superseding Judaism, so Islam was presented as the fulfilment of both these faiths, with Mohammed as the last and greatest of the prophets in the long line from Abraham to Jesus. As such, Islam was a more intensive and inclusive monotheism than those that had preceded it.

It was an intensive monotheism because – unlike Christianity – it acknowledged only one God, not a Trinity. Those who joined the community of the Prophet, the *umma*, left behind existing tribal loyalties and hierarchies and were answerable to none but God. At the ethical and doctrinal level the unity of Islam was also more securely safeguarded by the Koran than it was in Christianity by the Bible. The former was believed to be directly dictated by God to the prophet Mohammed, and had neither the loose boundaries nor the internal diversity of the Christian Bible. Even its language, Arabic, was regarded as sacred and unalterable.

It was an inclusive monotheism not only because it welcomed any who wished to convert, but because, instead of attempting to destroy competing faiths, it was happy to tolerate religious pluralism in its territories – so long as non-Islamic faiths accepted their subject position. Unlike the Byzantine empire, then, the early Islamic empire and its successors did not embark upon costly attempts to impose doctrinal unity. Not only were other monotheisms tolerated, but the ruling dynasties of the Islamic empire – first the Umayyads, then the Abbasids – actually depended upon the existence of non-Muslims for revenue through taxation.

Islam was also internally inclusive in the sense that it made no sharp distinction between clergy and laity or between church and state. All were subject to God; all were called to do his will; all were capable of heeding the call. Though a religious leadership developed, the idea of a hierarchy in which some stood in a closer relationship to God due to their clerical office did not develop. Nor, consequently, did a struggle for power between religious and political leaders. Islam empowered all who would submit to the one God and Mohammed his prophet. Such radical egalitarianism was undoubtedly a part of Islam's appeal to the previously despised nomads at the fringes of 'civilised' society who became its devastatingly efficient early shock troops.

In the long run, Islam's toleration, together with its rapid spread and the mass conversion within its territories, led to the fragmentation of the Islamic empire after the tenth century. Its very success meant that an increasing diversity of people further and further from the original Arab heartlands of Islam came to feel that they had an independent stake in what was effectively becoming a worldwide Islamic commonwealth linked by cultural rather than political bonds. Yet this politico-cultural unit was no less significant on that account; it had more believers and greater territory than Christianity could claim, freedom of trade and travel between its constituent parts, a rich cultural life, and the power of absorbing and converting whole peoples (such as the Turks) and turning their energy to its account.

Despite the loss of its territories, and despite its relegation to the political periphery, the eastern Roman empire survived and developed in the context of Muslim expansion. Indeed, it was from the seventh century onwards that many of the most characteristic features of an empire that can now be truly labelled Christian and Byzantine, rather than Roman, came into being. Equally, it was at this time that the separate identity of that variety of Christianity that is now identified as Byzantine,

Orthodox or Eastern Orthodox was consolidated. In many respects Orthodoxy developed in self-conscious isolation. Its relationship with the western church became increasingly strained, while Islam and various Slavic peoples were encountered for two long centuries (until around 840) as the enemy that repeatedly attempted to seize territory and sack Constantinople itself.

Under these pressures the reduced Byzantine empire became a compact political entity with a more coherent, largely Greek, culture and population. By contrast with the later western Roman empire, where outside attack by barbarian tribes led many of the rich and powerful to migrate from the cities to their country estates, the rural areas of the Byzantine empire were now abandoned to villagers and the troops who defended them, while those who could fled to Constantinople. The empire had long been run from Constantinople by the emperor and a metropolitan elite of civil servants and clergy. Now this centralisation became even more pronounced. With no local urban elites to stand between the villagers and the central administration, the emperor's power over his people increased. So too did the power of the church, with Orthodoxy playing a crucial role in the maintenance and intensification of a Byzantine sense of identity and divine destiny.

In these circumstances, the liturgical heart of Orthodoxy was strengthened. Whereas the western church would continue to channel its intellectual energy into the formulation of precise doctrinal statements (especially after the sixteenth century, as we shall see in the second half of this volume), the eastern church would find the focus of its unity and identity in its liturgy. Not that Orthodoxy set little store by credal formulations. On the contrary, the first seven 'ecumenical councils' (i.e. councils of the whole church, such as Nicea and Chalcedon), together with the writings of the church fathers, were considered infallibly authoritative. So too was scripture, though it was believed that scripture could not be correctly interpreted without the guidance of the patristic material. So perfect and so entire was the truth laid down in all these writings that all that remained after the last council (the second Council of Nicea, 787) was to safeguard and repeat this truth. (Thus, in the fifteenth century, Simon of Thessalonica insisted in the very title of his *Against Heresies* that he has inserted nothing of his own, but has collected everything from the holy scriptures and from the fathers.)

Plate 4   Interior of St Sophia: mosaic of the Virgin and Child, Constantine and Justinian
   In this tenth-century mosaic Constantine offers the city of Constantinople to the Virgin
Mary and Christ-child, and Justinian offers St Sophia. In return the Virgin and Child were
expected to protect the empire dedicated to them.

Yet it was in liturgy that Orthodox truth was made real, witnessed to, embodied and brought to life. The great imperial liturgy at St Sophia in Constantinople continued to be performed regularly, with each local town and village echoing it in its own church and celebration. In this way, daily, weekly and annual ritual celebrations united the baptised in 'the body of Christ' into a compact and united body of people. Following the model of St Sophia, all Orthodox churches were designed to bring heaven down to earth. Generally built on a small scale, their interiors were richly decorated with coloured glass mosaic and, in some cases, with painted icons. The central dome represented heaven, from which Christ Pantocrator (ruler of all) looked down; the twelve apostles supported the dome; the apse was the cave of Bethlehem, and in its dome was the Mother of God and her child; round the walls were the images of the saints, betokening the church on earth. The altar was the table of the Last Supper, and the ciborium above it the Holy Sepulchre. In the liturgy all these supernatural beings were really present, the eucharist

Plate 5   Interior of St Sophia: mosaic of the Deesis: Christ with Mary and John the Baptist (detail)

This thirteenth-century mosaic was probably commissioned by the emperor to express gratitude for Byzantine victory over the Latins, and may be compared with the image on the previous page (plate 4). Here Mary has been supplanted by Christ (holding a gospel book) as the focus of veneration, and she (out of shot on the left) and John the Baptist pay homage to him. Christ is depicted in terms appropriate to a model Christian emperor: powerful but gentle, sovereign but compassionate.

itself being the regular representation of Christ's passion on earth, an enactment of God become man.

The practical effect of this concentration on the liturgy was to strengthen the power not only of the heavenly beings who were the object of the cult, but of the clergy who maintained it, and of the emperor who stood in the place of Christ on earth. Terrestrial and celestial orders were shaped in imitation of each other. To give just one example, the non-payment of taxes became classified as a sin. As such, it was believed that it would be recorded in the detailed registers of sins kept by the demons who dwelt between earth and heaven, and would have to be confessed and expiated. In exactly the same way, the failure to pay taxes, annotated in registers by the emperor's collectors, could be expiated only by payment or torture.

Just as the liturgy became increasingly codified and regulated by 'tradition', so too did the life of the emperor and the empire itself. (The daily rituals by which the life of the Byzantine emperors were regulated are recorded in detail in the tenth-century *Book of Ceremonies*.) The aim was that everyone in society should conform to his or her correct role. Imitation (*mimesis*) was the aim, not change or innovation. God did not change. His truth, laid down in the early centuries of Christianity, did not change. His church and his society should not change.

Yet Byzantine church and society were never as monolithic or as unchanging as the Byzantines themselves might have liked to present them. Nor did creativity dry up in theology. Even as the Islamic threat developed in the seventh century, Orthodoxy produced some of its most important thinkers, most notably Maximus the Confessor and John of Damascus (c. 655–c. 750). Both brought to the fore a theme that had long been central in early Christian life, particularly in asceticism and monasticism: deification (*theosis*). This, they argued, was the purpose of prayer, of the liturgy, of the incarnation itself: God became human so that man could become divine. Whereas the Latin tradition, under the influence of Augustine, tended to set an unbridgeable gulf between man and God by way of their doctrine of the fall and original sinfulness (see below), Orthodox theology interpreted the incarnation as proof of the affinity between God and humanity. Eastern theologians did not teach that the fall had completely corrupted humanity or destroyed human freedom to turn to God and receive the Holy Spirit. Through the gift of the Spirit, human beings were still called to become 'gods' (Ps. 82.6; John 10.34), 'partakers of the divine nature' (II Pet. 1.4).

These ideas were tested and refined during the controversy that came to a focus in the eighth century over the use of icons. What lay behind the crisis is still not entirely clear, but at some level it certainly appears to represent a clash between different understandings of sacred power and the ways in which it could be appropriated. The icons were stylised portraits of Christ and the saints, often painted on board, which had become the cherished possessions of many eastern churches, monasteries and private individuals. For many Byzantines, monastic and lay, icons had the same concentrated spiritual power as relics of saints in the west. In popular culture legends abounded of the miraculous powers of icons: how an icon had cured a sick man, made a barren woman fertile or caused an empty well to fill. (Equally, icons, like relics, could have political uses at the highest level; when the Arabs besieged Constantinople in 717, for example, an icon of Mary was carried around the walls to ensure protection.) Yet a succession of emperors and their advisors outlawed the use of icons. Influenced by the ban on images in the Ten Commandments, and perhaps by the strictness of Islamic observance of this ban, they feared that icons were in fact displeasing to God. They may also have realised that the power of icons had become threatening because it was too diffuse, and could no longer be brought under centralised imperial power. Thus the icons could empower individuals and groups in a way that was potentially dangerous to power from on high.

Monks and monasteries were among the most powerful supporters of the 'iconodule' (pro-icon) cause, and the growing power of monasticism in the empire was an important factor in the eventual official defeat of iconoclasm in 843. So too were the ideas of theological defenders of icons, including John of Damascus and Theodore of Stoudion (752–826). Their arguments helped reinforce four increasingly characteristic emphases of eastern theology. First, since God had truly become man (Chalcedonian orthodoxy), man could truly become God (and since God had truly become man – and become circumscribed – he could be depicted). Second, God is Trinity – not merely a Father God, but a God who is God in Father, Son and Holy Spirit. Third, God is nevertheless ultimately unknowable – not just because of human finitude, but in his very essence. (Thus the icon represents the *hypostasis* but not the *ousia* of God, and is worthy of veneration but not worship.) And fourth, the liturgy is the heart of Orthodox life, and the ground of authority for Orthodox belief (for it was by appeal to liturgical practice and the sacraments that the iconodule case was made).

Even though they eventually triumphed, the danger of such views, so far as the preservation of imperial and ecclesiastical power and unity was concerned, was that they could lead to an unregulated diffusion of divine power, spiritual individualism and 'pride', and the proliferation of cults of 'holy men'. Thus the concentrated power of the church, channelled into the divine liturgy and sacraments and guarded by the clergy, might be dissipated into the branching channels of individual human ambition and aspiration. Yet the theology of John and Maximus contained an inbuilt safeguard, for they both made it clear that divinisation is possible only through regular participation in the liturgy and the sacraments and through obedience to the church's teaching. Holy men are not created outside the church, and holiness is not primarily an individual pursuit. Rather, it must be understood as part of the much larger purpose of God, begun and revealed in Christ, in which the whole creation – brought to a focus in the church – is gradually transformed into its heavenly prototype by the power of God.

The balance between openness to the mystery of God and the power of the Spirit on the one hand and adherence to fixed tradition on the other proved hard to maintain. The listing of heresies and the compilation of anthologies of patristic teachings, often arranged into manuals of *Questions and Answers*, became a central theological activity in the later empire. Yet a mystical tradition continued, most importantly in the monasteries. Its most important manifestation came in the Hesychast movement (from *hesychos*, quiet) and an accompanying tradition of theological reflection. The latter began in the eleventh century, with the work of Simeon (949–1022), 'the New Theologian', and continued into the fourteenth. Despite his reverence for tradition, Simeon's theology gave a new authority to the place of experience in the religious life. Theology, he believed, meant above all the knowledge that monks attain when they are transformed and divinised through contact with God. The goal of all thought and all striving was not knowledge, or even contemplation, but the vision of God in which the individual is transfigured, just as Jesus had had been. 'Christ', Simeon wrote, 'has a union with the Father similar to the one we have with Christ.'[2] Not only did believers become incorporate in Christ; he became incorporate in them: 'Christ is my hand and Christ is my foot . . . and I am the hand of Christ and the foot of Christ'[3] – not only in the life to come, but in the present life.

In following the doctrine of divinisation to this point, Simeon articulated one of the most important theological accounts of sacred power as power from below – God's power working in and through believers so that they might realise their own divine nature. As God says to him in a vision: 'Yes, I am God, the one who became man for your sake. And behold, I have created you, as you see, and I shall make you God.'[4] Yet Simeon's theology was also profoundly 'apophatic'. For, in an intensification of the 'negative' tradition of theology that stemmed from the Cappadocian fathers and the ascetic tradition, Simeon insisted upon the necessity of negating all affirmations about God as falling short of his true mystery. What the mystic is caught up in, he argued, was not the divine essence but the 'light' of God, the self-communication that flows from God's being. In divinisation human beings are transformed by this light, transformed by the energies of uncreated divine power. This tradition of mystical theology was developed by followers of Simon, perhaps most notably by Gregory of Palamas in the fourteenth century. Ultimately, such apophatic theology, growing out of mystical experience and basing itself on direct experience of the energies of God, would stand as the distinguishing mark of an eastern as opposed to a Latin and western theology.

But the growing division between the churches of east and west had political as well as theological dimensions. The traditional date for the so-called 'schism' between churches of east and west is 1054, when patriarch and papal legates excommunicated each other in the course of a dispute concerning liturgical customs followed by Greek churches in Italy. This event was merely a symptom of rivalry between papal and patriarchal power that had been developing for centuries, and that had earlier come to a head in 836, when the pope disputed the election of the patriarch Photius. The antagonism between pope and patriarch was intensified by rivalry over mission territories such as Bulgaria. But it was the Crusades that sharpened antagonism into hatred. This hostility became irreversible when western crusaders – who had always claimed to be acting in co-operation with the east – attacked Constantinople itself, proceeded to occupy the city and other lands, and retained power in Byzantium from 1204 to 1261. Even though the emperor eventually regained control of Constantinople, the episode resulted in permanent fragmentation of rule within Byzantine territory.

When the time came, Byzantium no longer had the resources to resist the new Islamic threat posed by the Ottoman Turks. It made desperate attempts to forge a union with Rome in order to secure western protection against this formidable enemy. A Greek delegation of more than seven hundred travelled to Italy for discussions, which ended in the Council of Florence of 1439. Points of liturgical and theological dispute were covered, including the Latin addition of a sentence to the creed, stating that the Holy Spirit proceeded not 'from the Father' but 'from the Father and the Son' (the *filioque*). An agreement was made, very much on Latin terms. (The *filioque*, for example, was accepted.) Yet, in the event, the pope failed to send military assistance. The rapprochement was, in any case, resisted by the majority of Byzantines, for whom the price of submission to papal authority was simply too high to pay. Constantinople fell to the Turks in 1453, and the Byzantine empire was at an end.

Yet Eastern Orthodoxy survived even this final conquest. It survived under Islamic rule, and it survived in less restricted circumstances in the lands of Serbia, Bulgaria, Romania and Russia, to which it had been carried by Byzantine missionaries from the ninth century onwards. Conversion to Christianity not only provided these emerging nations with a sense of identity and unity, but encouraged them to adopt imperialist aspirations. Though Constantinople struggled to maintain ecclesiastical jurisdiction over the churches in these areas for as long as possible, they eventually sought and won national 'autocephalous' (self-governing) status. Both Bulgaria and Serbia also came to pose a considerable political threat to Byzantium due to their growing sense of imperial purpose. In the end, however, it was Russia that took up the imperial crown from a defeated Byzantium and proclaimed itself the 'New Rome' under a 'tsar' (a Caesar). Christianity was first embraced in 'Kievan Russia', the polity centred on Kiev, which lasted from 988 to the early thirteenth century, when it was invaded by the Mongols. As Mongol power waned in the fourteenth and fifteenth centuries and the principality of Moscow emerged as the new centre of power in Russia, Orthodoxy grew in influence here as the official religion. In 1448 the Russian church centred on Moscow finally obtained autonomy from the patriarchate of Constantinople. Heavily influenced by Byzantine traditions, it nevertheless developed its own autonomous interpretations of Orthodox belief and practice, and grew to become the largest and most powerful Orthodox church in the world (see ch. 6).

Augustine and the Latin tradition

The gradual separation of the churches of east and west was reinforced by the divisions of language. Greek had long been the language of philosophy and culture within the Roman empire, though Latin was the native tongue of the Romans. More cosmopolitan and cultured citizens of the Roman empire would often have facility in both languages. As the two halves of the empire grew apart, however, Greek became increasingly exclusive to the eastern empire, and Latin to the west. Greek remained the more prestigious language. It was, moreover, the preferred language of Christianity in the sense that the New Testament was written in Greek, the councils and controversies of the early church had been conducted in Greek, and a majority of the church fathers had written in Greek.

Increasingly cut off from the continuing theological disputes of the eastern churches, the developing tradition of Greek-speaking theology and the world of Greek philosophy and learning, western Christian thought began to develop its own distinctive themes and approaches. It was resourced by Latin translations of the Bible, most notably Jerome's 'Vulgate' (completed 405), by the works of the early Latin fathers, by Latin liturgies, by tales, biographies and narrative traditions in Latin and vernacular languages, and by the development of western monastic traditions. The increasing centralisation of the western church upon Rome served only to reinforce the tendency to make Latin the official language of an increasingly distinctive western Christian tradition.

To a much greater extent than in the east, the work of a single theologian – a Latin who struggled to read Greek – had a uniquely formative and continuing influence upon the western church. Augustine of Hippo ('St Augustine') was born in 354 in north Africa at a time when there was still space in the Roman empire for a plurality of religio-philosophical traditions to exist side by side, even though the die had officially been cast in favour of Christianity. Influenced by a Christian mother and a classical training in rhetoric in Rome, Augustine's intense personal and spiritual quest led him first to Manicheism and then, by way of the works of the Platonists and the preaching of Bishop Ambrose of Milan, to Christianity. After his baptism in 387 and his consecration as bishop of Hippo in north Africa (where he served from 395 until his death in 430), Augustine not only took up the practical duties of a church leader with zeal and determination – as in his fight against the Donatists – but pursued an extraordinarily fruitful theological career. As we shall see throughout this volume, the enormous body of writings that he produced would influence the western tradition from then on.

A central theme that had guided Augustine's personal religio-philosophical quest, and that would unify much of his theology, was that of sin and evil. For Augustine, the appeal of the Manichees had lain in their powerful explanation of the pervasiveness of evil in terms of a cosmic war between good and evil, and the attraction of Platonism had been in its more sophisticated account of evil as the privation of good. His conversion to Christianity came when he became convinced that it alone offered a practical and effective remedy for sin – through the grace offered by God in Jesus Christ.

For Augustine, sin represented not merely a failure of the will, but a power that overwhelms the human person and takes control of both body and soul. As he explains in his *Confessions*, it is the force that led him to steal pears as a child even though he was not hungry, to indulge in sexual pleasure with his concubine even though he wanted neither marriage nor children, and to resist conversion to the God of Jesus Christ even though he knew he must finally submit. Sin affects the body just as much as the mind and the soul: it is sin that makes the eyelids grow weary when reading, the concentration wander when studying, and the penis become erect independent of any conscious intention.

Augustine moved these reflections from the personal to the political by tracing the effects of sin in relation not only to the human body but to the body politic. In the *City of God* he told the story of humankind from the beginning (the creation of Adam and Eve) to the present (the sacking of Rome by Alaric the Goth in 410). Augustine's explanation for the fall of Rome was not that Christians had neglected to worship the Roman gods, as their critics charged, but that Rome had succumbed to the cosmic power of sin unleashed by the transgression of Adam and Eve at the beginning of time and evident in the course of human history ever since. Rome had became a 'city of man', which worships self to the neglect of God, in contrast to the part-earthly, part-celestial 'city of God', which worships God to the neglect of self.

Pessimistic though it was in its estimation of human nature and its abilities, of human social and political endeavour in general, and of the Roman empire in particular, Augustine's negativity was balanced by a positive vision focused not only on a God of love but on the original goodness of the created order, including human beings. For, once he had repudiated the influence of Manicheism, Augustine never again spoke of sin as a force equal in power to God and his goodness. Instead he characterised it as willed and wilful disorder – the deliberate perversion of the order that God had intended by sinful human beings. This vision was given historical and even cosmological form in a series of commentaries on Genesis. According to Augustine's reading, Adam and Eve disrupt the perfection of the created order – including their own human perfection – by disobeying God and eating from the forbidden tree. They do so in abuse of the free will that God had given them as part of their human glory. God is in no way responsible for the evil that they have brought into the world, an evil manifest in a disobedience that spreads outwards from their relation to God to affect their relationship with one another and with their own bodies. Augustine believed that all human beings, with the exception of Christ, inherit this 'original sin' from their first parents.

And yet there is a solution. It arises not from the travails of an all-sinful and impotent humanity but from the initiative of an all-loving and omnipotent God. It lies in submission, in humans' becoming obedient to God as well as to the order of things he has ordained. The answer is for human beings to resume the status of grateful children that Adam and Eve had assumed before the fall. Since they are powerless to effect this themselves, they can do so only by surrendering to God and allowing him to overpower them. 'Grant what you command, and command what you will', was his plea.[5] Even then there is no guarantee of salvation. Human beings deserve death on account of their inherited sin. Yet out of his unfathomable love and mercy an inscrutable God may save a handful to eternal life.

The social, ecclesiastical and political implications of Augustine's theology were clear and unmistakable: those who are outside the Catholic church will be damned, and it is entirely within the church's right and responsibility to call on the state to take whatever measures may be necessary to prevent this terrible outcome. Those Christians who denied the authority of the Catholic church, such as the Donatists, should be 'compelled to come in' – through violence if necessary – for the sake of their own souls.[6] Likewise, paganism must be destroyed by force as well as by persuasion. 'For', as Augustine exhorted his congregation, 'that all superstition of pagans and heathens should be annihilated is what God wants, God commands, God proclaims!'[7] It was also the church's duty, he believed, to help the state enforce order in a world of sin. 'It is you', he wrote of the Catholic church, 'who make wives subject to their husbands . . . you set husbands over their wives; you join sons to their parents by a freely granted slavery, and set parents above their sons in pious domination . . . You teach slaves to be loyal to their masters . . . You teach kings to rule for the benefit of their people; and you warn the peoples to be subservient to their kings.'[8]

Yet Augustine's exclusivism was also tempered not only by his own love of classical learning, but by a tolerance and even compassion that stem from his realism about the pervasiveness of sin and resist all attempts to turn the church (or monasteries) into enclaves of the 'saints' (the morally perfect). It was this that provoked his long-standing battle with the British monk Pelagius over the issue of grace and free will. Augustine declared that sin was all around, within the church as well as outside it, and that only God was in a position to judge who would be saved and who damned, and to determine who would suffer which fate (the doctrine of predestination). The church must therefore be a universal church that welcomes all comers, and never pretends to be identical with the ranks of the saints, whose identity will not be revealed until the last judgement. Given the strength of his belief in a good and loving God and an originally good creation, Augustine was also an opponent of the ultra-ascetics who would deny the body altogether; against them he defended the institution of marriage and sexual relations within it. Yet sex, in his view, was still tainted by sin, must be indulged in only for the good of procreation, and was inferior to the monastic and celibate life that he favoured.

The influence of Augustine's thought in the west derived not merely from its astonishing power and breadth, but from its 'fit' with the shape of the Christianity that gradually emerged in the context of a shattered Roman empire. Despite internal controversies and external threats, the church in the east retained the support of empire and consolidated its position as the inseparable ideological counterpart of this power. In the east, heaven and earth continued to touch at a number of points, not only in the emperor himself and in the divine liturgy, but in the lives of those men (and occasionally women) who had become living sacraments, active embodiments of a God made human. In the west, by contrast, where the collapse of empire had left the church exposed, the golden age in which God came down to earth seemed always a thing of the past. Augustine's theology spoke not of divinisation but of fall. The very course of human history came to be read through this lens: not as Eusebius' glorious tale of co-operation between church and state in inexorable fulfilment of God's purposes, but as the story of the endless disruption of God's good purposes by human sinfulness. The saints, though important, were from thenceforward in the west to be found among the dead rather than among the living.

Augustine's theological scheme – one might call it an 'economy of submission' – meshed well with a society that was becoming increasingly feudal as powerful rulers and dynasties began to seize power and literally 'lord it over' subjected men and women. It also supported a universal (catholic), hierarchical, sacramental and sacerdotal model of the church, whose roots stretched back to Ignatius, but that was to be further consolidated in the centuries after Augustine. Equally, Augustine's views supported the growth of monasteries and monastic orders in the Middle Ages, for it was in these oases of sanctity that the corruptions of the world could be exchanged for a life of perfect love and obedience: here the uncontrollable stirrings of the body and sexuality could be mastered; here obedience could be nurtured; and here the ideal of perfect holiness could shine like a beacon in an otherwise darkened world. Though apparently pessimistic, in a world of poverty, scarcity and political instability, Augustine's message carried considerable hope. The hope was of escape – escape from the pains and cares of this fragile, limited and chaotic world into the eternal order of the City of God, both in this life and in the next.

The making of Christendom

Augustine lived at a time of transition. The mighty power of the Roman empire in the west was disintegrating. Its collapse was a gradual and patchy affair. It came not by way of confrontation with a mighty rival empire, but through a series of skirmishes, treaties, sieges and battles with the different barbarian tribes that were pushing westwards looking for land. Some of these tribes had formerly serviced and supplied the empire from behind its frontiers, and had adopted aspects of its culture, not least its religion – albeit in Arian guise. Though Rome was sacked by Attila the Hun in 452 and the last western emperor was deposed in 476, and although these events had powerful symbolic resonance, Roman culture and institutions continued to function in the west, often under barbarian control, until well into the sixth century. The old Roman way of life was kept alive in small pockets of culture, most notably in the villas and estates of Italy and Gaul to which a few wealthy landowners had retreated (and more widely, we may assume, among the rural population). The post-Constantinian Christian-Roman way of life survived better, as can be appreciated from the fact that two of the most important western Christian writers of the time, Cassiodorus (died 583) and Boethius (c. 480–524), reached high office in the civil service of Theodoric, king of the (Arian) Ostrogoths. Other Romans migrated east, where imperial life continued relatively undisturbed, and the west suffered serious depopulation. After Justinian's attempt to win back western territories in the sixth century (which resulted chiefly in the establishment of a lavish new western imperial capital in Ravenna), the enterprise was never repeated.

To speak of 'the west' in late antiquity and the early Middle Ages as if it were a unified territory is to anticipate a situation that had not yet come into being. The Roman empire had never controlled all of the region we now call 'Europe', and even the extensive territories over which it had exercised dominion were now under the control of a variety of constantly changing regimes. Nor was it not only the east that was threatened by the new power of Islam. As well as seizing the western empire's former territories in Africa, Islam had conquered parts of southern Italy and Spain by the early eighth century, and would continue to lap the boundaries of the west for much of the medieval period. Despite its survival under new rulers, the church was not in a position to impose unity on this patchwork of rule and misrule. Not only did it have no mechanism of widespread political or military control, but even its cultural reach was limited. Most of the barbarian tribes were Arian; others – most notably the Franks – worshipped their own gods. (The Frankish king, Clovis, accepted Catholic baptism in about 496, and a close collaboration between the Franks and the Catholic church would be an important feature of western history from then on, as we shall see below.) Territories in the north – some of which had never been under Roman control – also continued in their ancestral traditions. Even within its own ranks, Catholicism continued to be troubled by internal dispute and defection, and its leadership's ability to impose unity was severely curtailed by the lack of state support.

In this situation the idea of a unified western church with the power to bring order and unity to the west might have seemed far-fetched. And yet it was this ideal – the ideal of Christendom – that would eventually emerge out of the ruins of the Eusebian-Constantinian project in the west. It marked an entirely new phase in Christian history, for neither in theory nor in practice had the ideal of a civilisation controlled by a centralised church emerged before. Inspired by it and carried along by a combination of chance, luck and good judgement, by the high Middle Ages the western church would manage to establish a dominance over state and society that had never before been achieved and would never again be repeated (see next chapter). Though this dominance was always fragile and would be severely challenged and curtailed after the medieval period (the theme of the second half of this volume), its legacy lives on, not least in the existence of a region with sufficient unity to be labelled 'Europe'. The creation of 'the west' in this enlarged sense was thus the achievement of a church built on the ruins of the western Roman empire, and was testament to the way in which it was able to reactivate the universalising potential of sacred power from on high in dramatically changed circumstances.

The western church's achievement can be attributed to a combination of powerful cultural and institutional resources and a set of adventitious and unplanned social, economic and political circumstances that the church was able to turn to its advantage. It was not so much that western Christianity evolved a grand sociopolitical programme that it then put into action, as that such a programme gradually emerged out of interaction with developing events in a way that no-one could or did foresee. Even with the advantage of hindsight, the process is so complex that scholars still struggle to explain it adequately; but it is clear that a combination of factors was involved, some of which had to do with the internal development of western Christianity, others with developments external to the church.

POLITICAL AND ECONOMIC OPPORTUNITIES

The Roman empire was gradually succeeded by a world in which regional aristocracies strove to maintain local power, often with the assistance of the local bishop and/or monastery, and often under the fragile overlordship of a warrior king or emperor. In the west as a whole there was no single head or centre, but shifting and crosscutting networks of power and influence. Territory was seized or retained by any who had sufficient military power to do so, and the 'states' that emerged had little of the infrastructure that we normally associate with this word. Normally they had a single ruler, who might be called lord, emperor, prince, bishop, prince-bishop or king – titles that themselves testify to the dissolving boundary between sacred and secular, church and state. Since the size of these early 'states' was dictated by what their ruler could realistically control and defend, they tended to be relatively small.

Yet it was the very weakness of these shifting centres of rule that lent strength to Christianity. Being so underdeveloped in almost every respect – politically, culturally, economically – they needed Christianity in a way that more powerful states and societies would not have done. As the only credible inheritor of the mantle of the Roman empire in the west, the emerging papacy was quick to take advantage and to claim something of the prestige and authority once attaching to empire. Its credibility was enhanced not only by the fact that its seat was in the ancient capital of Rome, but because it was the only institution that could now claim a unifying presence across the former territories of the western empire. Yet the power of the papacy was severely limited, not least by the breakdown of efficient means of communication across the empire, and in practice it tended to be the local bishop who wielded greater power in the territory over which he presided.

The church's position was also aided by economic factors. In what had become a rural subsistence economy, it managed to accrue considerable economic power. The fact that many churches and monasteries were well endowed with land had huge significance in a world in which the collapse of a money economy made this the most valuable resource. In order to strengthen their power, in the eyes of both God and man, rulers and aristocrats began to endow the church with even more wealth by establishing churches and monasteries. Since the latter were increasingly widely spread throughout the west, they gave Christianity a ubiquitous presence that would in time enhance its role as a pan-European communications network and focus of unity. As yet, however, Rome could not take full advantage of these factors, since local rulers still regarded the church's property as their own property, and Rome had as yet established the right neither to appoint clergy nor to claim ecclesiastical property as its own.

IDEOLOGY OF RULE AND SUBMISSION

In these circumstances, it was the church's growing cultural or ideological capital that was perhaps its greatest asset. Even before the collapse of the Roman empire the Catholic church had been swift to take charge of culture in both east and west. Now its control of literacy, of education and, increasingly, of ideas, gave it the monopoly of a scarce and valuable resource. The church was the only institution in the west that could train and supply the administrators of whom rulers increasingly had need. It was the only one that could offer even a minimal education to the people of a territory and so help shape, and reshape, their ideas and behaviour by offering a worldview within which to live. And it alone had a legal expertise based around a body of written law – not only its own law ('canon law'), but Roman law as well.

All these advantages would be fully exploited only after the eleventh century. In the early medieval period they were still less important than the single fact that Christianity offered secular rulers an ideology of rule. It told kings, princes, lords, magnates and knights who they were and what duties they had, it legitimated their power and placed it under the seal of divine approval, and it sanctioned the increasingly rigid hierarchical social structure that had emerged across Europe as part and parcel of a feudal society. What Christianity offered, in other words, was not merely an ideology of rule, but an ideology of rule *and* submission. As such, it was able to serve as the indispensable ideological component of the emerging feudal states of Europe.

It was a remarkable pope, Gregory I ('Gregory the Great', pope from 590 to 604), who did much to capitalise on this ideological opportunity. He did so by pulling together some of the church's ideological resources in order to formulate a highly influential ideal of Christian rule and submission. Several Germanic rulers had already started to draw on biblical models of kingship for their self-understanding, comparing their lands to Israel and their rule to Moses who had established Israel as the chosen nation by promulgating the law. Gregory continued this tradition, taking King David as his model of a just ruler, divinely exalted from humble origin, wise and respectful of God's law, and responsible to his people. Yet he was also quick to point out that the dire fate of Israel under her less worthy rulers served as a warning of what could happen if a ruler tried to overreach himself and stray from God's law – and from obedience to the church.

But Gregory went further. In a short work entitled the *Regula Pastoralis* ('Pastoral Rule'), written in 593, he outlined a sophisticated understanding of the proper Christian use of power that owed as much to his later training as a monk as to his earlier employment in the public administration of the Byzantine empire. Far from shunning power, Gregory believed that it was the task of leaders in both church and society to embrace it wholeheartedly and bring it under the banner of Christ. What this meant in practice was not only that all power derived from the Christian God, but that this power must be exercised with humility, benevolence and condescension rather than in a tyrannical fashion. As he puts it:

> Care should be taken that a ruler show himself to his subjects as a mother in loving-kindness, and as a father in discipline. And all the time it should be seen to with anxious circumspection that neither discipline be rigid nor loving-kindness lax . . . there ought to be in rulers both compassion justly considerate, and discipline affectionately severe.[9]

Influenced by Benedict's model of the ideal abbot, which is discussed below, Gregory produced an inspiring ideal for every Christian rector ('ruler', from the Latin, *regere*), Gregory's generic term for all authority. Power was to be concentrated in the hands of the few for the sake of the many. It was power from on high, but it was no longer the unconstrained power of an emperor or a warrior-king, but a more responsible and paternalistic power that humbled itself as God had done in Christ, and in so doing won divine sanction. In keeping with this understanding of power from on high exercised in a mode of humble condescension, Gregory famously described his own role as pope as that of 'a servant of the servants of God'.

Gregory's ideal of fatherly benevolence could be appropriated not only by temporal rulers, but by clerical ones as well. It spoke directly not only to kings, but also to bishops and popes. It was entirely appropriate to the personal relationships of mutual dependence around which feudal society was established. For, rather than being free to exercise their power without limitation, medieval rulers were bound to powerful 'vassals', who might be lords in their own right, who swore homage to their king, and who gave military and courtly service in return for protection and/or land. Even the larger, more centralised states such as the growing Frankish kingdom did not have the ability to levy taxes, and had to pay their large numbers of armed, personal retainers by land grants, which created the vassal solider as a potentially autonomous power base. Vassal soldiers in turn would have their own clients, including the peasants, who worked the land. Social relationships therefore tended to be small-scale, localised and face to face, even when they took a hierarchical form. And such relationships were likely to work best in a society in which hierarchy was seen as ordained by God, and was oiled by a paternalism that was benevolent rather than tyrannical.

In addition to strengthening and shaping the power of ruler, bishop and abbot, Gregory also helped strengthen the hand of the papacy. There were external factors at work here too. Islamic conquest of competing patriarchates had left Rome in a natural position of leadership in the west, and Gregory was quick to contest the patriarch of Constantinople's right to use the title 'ecumenical patriarch' (patriarch of the whole Christian world). What is more, the collapse of the western empire had undermined the status of Rome – whose population was reduced from around a million to fewer than 50,000 – and left a power vacuum into which the ecclesiastical establishment could move. The gradual accumulation of territory in Italy – the so-called 'Papal States' – began to make the bishops of Rome rich and powerful territorial rulers in their own right.

Even before Gregory, Pope Gelasisus I (died 496) had capitalised on this situation by articulating an early and influential account of church and state as a dualism of powers in which the priestly and imperial jurisdictions should function in a reciprocal fashion, but in which the spiritual power of the church in Rome seemed to take precedence. But it was Gregory I who took the most decisive step in formulating a coherent and systematic theology of church–state relations in which the former became sovereign, and who in so doing helped place the papacy at the centre of things.

MISSION FROM ON HIGH

Gregory's vision of the papacy as the focus of a new western, Christian civilisation took practical shape in his diplomatic and missionary programme. In 596 he commissioned a monk from his own monastery in Rome, Augustine of Canterbury (died c. 609), to travel to south-eastern England to win converts. Augustine managed to convert the king of Kent and his subjects and establish an Anglo-Saxon church. An ensuing complex of conquests, alliances and marriages in turn led to yet more monasteries and missionaries. Most prominent among the latter were Willibrord (died 739), who became evangelist of Frisia with the protection of its ruler, Pippin II, and Boniface (c. 680–754), the 'Apostle of Germany', who reformed the church in France in association with Pippin III. The Anglo-Saxon mission to Europe was carried out in close and continuous reference to Rome, with both Willibrord and Boniface being consecrated by the papacy as bishops in the lands to which they brought the gospel.

Missionary activity – or 'preaching' as it was then called – proved an important internal factor in the establishment of Christendom. While some missions were commissioned by the pope himself, others were initiated by independent missionaries whose energies and achievements were then harnessed by Rome. One of the earliest examples was Patrick (c. 390–460), who carried Christianity from Britain to Ireland, where a strongly ascetic form of Christianity developed in relative isolation. In turn, Ireland produced and exported its own missionary monks such as Columba (c. 521–96) and Aidan (died 651), who took the gospel to Scotland and northern Britain, and Columbanus (c. 543–615), who led a mission to Gaul.

Whether under direct or indirect papal control, much of this early medieval missionary effort can be described as mission 'from on high' in a number of senses. For one thing, its agents tended to be educated and cultured Christian monks and clergy who often worked with the authorisation or commission of Rome, and who directed their energies to converting kings and rulers who would then use their secular power to enforce the Christianisation of their territories. Such 'conversion' usually took the form of mass baptism, perhaps combined with the destruction or Christian rededication of pagan sites.

Thus mission often took place in close collaboration with political power, and in some cases under the direct control of political rulers and in the deliberate pursuit of territorial interests. In a number of instances, perhaps most notably in the conquest of Saxony by Charlemagne in the eighth century, Christianity was imposed by force. In that example it was used as an instrument of cultural domination and imposed on a society that was violently and deliberately dislocated in order to be remade in a Frankish-Christian image. In other, more celebrated cases, however, missionaries worked from a position not of strength but of weakness. They often faced considerable danger in venturing to the edges of Christian civilisation to spread the gospel, and their letters and biographies record the hardships they had to endure.

Christian mission was also from on high in the sense that a key factor in its success appears to have been the power of the culture and regime by which it was imposed or with which it was associated. In 723–4 Boniface received a letter from his mentor, Bishop Daniel of Westminster, giving him advice on how to win pagans to the gospel. Daniel was firmly of the opinion that faith should be won by reasoned argument, and the arguments he proposed for persuading the pagans are revealing:

> This also is to be inferred . . . while . . . the Christians possess fertile lands, and provinces fruitful in wine and oil and abounding in other riches they [the pagan gods] have left to them – the pagans, that is, with their gods – lands that are always frozen with cold, in which these [gods], now driven from the whole globe, are falsely thought to reign.[10]

Non-Christians, in other words, were to be convinced of the truth of the Christian religion by the greater power and effectiveness of the Christian God in achieving material success for his followers. The evidence was all around them. 'There must also often be brought before them the might of the Christian world,' Daniel advised Boniface.[11] For people struggling for material survival, such arguments would have made a good deal of sense. They could be strengthened by an appeal to fear, as Daniel shows when he strengthens Boniface's hand with a further argument: the pagans might think that they are propitiating their gods by offering them sacrifices, but they have no idea who the most powerful god is; in fact they may therefore be offending rather than propitiating the most high God.

That is not to suggest that people turned to Christianity solely out of a concern with worldly power. Worldly power was of little significance unless backed by the higher power that was believed to control the course of events. It was the higher power of the Christian God – not of his subjects – that really mattered. For this was a power that controlled not only the slender and fragile span of this life, but what lay beyond. In our main source of knowledge of the early development of Anglo-Saxon Christianity, Bede's *Ecclesiastical History of the English People*, we hear of a public debate in which Christianity is commended to an unconverted Anglo-Saxon king in the following terms:

> This is how the present life of man on earth, King, appears to me in comparison with the time that is unknown to us. You are sitting feasting with your earls and thegns in winter time; the fire is burning on the hearth . . . and all inside is warm; while outside the wintry storms of rain and snow are raging and a sparrow flies swiftly through the hall . . . it flits from your sight, out of the winter storm and back into it again. So

> this life of man appears but for a moment: what follows, or, indeed, what
> went before we know not at all. If this new doctrine [Christianity] brings
> us more certain information, it seems right that we should accept it.[12]

In a world where the presence of death was as real as that of life, a
religion that spoke with the confidence born of following a Lord who
had returned from the grave could have a profound appeal.

Thus Christianity has often been commended to potential converts
chiefly on the grounds that its God was greater and more powerful
than all other gods. We have seen the same strategy at work in the
spread of early Christianity in the Roman empire. But there the message
was that this God would tolerate no other gods. In 'the conversion of
Europe', as it would subsequently be called, the missionary strategy
appears to have begun on a more pragmatic note. The early missionaries
did not so much deny other religions as trump them. Many pagan shrines
were rededicated to Christian saints, and gradually these saints began to
attract the awe and reverence that had previously been attached to their
predecessors. Similarly, Christian festivals began to displace pagan ones
as both time and space were gradually won for the Christian cause.

Through its cult of the saints and its sacramental system, Christianity
offered immediate contact with an all-powerful God. The relics of holy
men and the sacraments of water, bread and wine were tangible and
reassuring tokens of God's presence in an insecure world. They could be
mobilised to terrify as well as to comfort. Thus the scary statue-reliquary
of St Foy (plate 6) from Conques in France, for example, would be
carried out to manors that, monks claimed, belonged to them, and used
to pacify their owners. To have such power on one's side was the main
thing, and submission to the Christian God – even if one continued to
pay respect to other gods – must have seemed like a wise strategy.

MONASTICISM

In the absence of any developed structure of parishes or dioceses, the
spread of monasticism in the early Middle Ages also played a vital role in
the gradual consolidation of Christianity on the ground. In many parts of
the early medieval world the average person's contact with Christianity
would more likely be by way of a local monastery or nunnery than
through a local church, since a developed parochial system dates from
later in the medieval period.

Plate 6   Reliquary statue of St Foy, late tenth century (detail of the head)
   Designed to contain the remains (relics) of a saint, a reliquary was an object of dangerous potency. The power resided in the relics themselves, which were believed to retain something of the supernatural of the saint. Like power of an earthly ruler, it could be turned against those who failed to respect it.

As noted above, western monasticism had developed in a way that made individual asceticism and world-rejection the exception rather than the norm. The *Rule* was provided by one of Gregory the Great's heroes, St Benedict of Nursia (c. 480–c. 550), who composed it for the guidance of a small monastic community he had established at Monte Cassino, between Rome and Naples. He was well acquainted with the history of Christian monasticism, and his *Rule* was influenced by the desert fathers, and by Augustine, Caesarius of Arles, Basil of Caesarea, John Cassian, and the roughly contemporary *Regula Magistri* ('Rule of the Master'). A relatively short and highly practical document, this *Rule* had an unparalleled influence upon western monasticism, gradually lending it a unity unknown in the east, where monastic establishments continued to be autonomous units independent of any wider rule or 'order', and stamping it with an activist and practical, rather than a contemplative, orientation.

Benedict's *Rule* pivots around the central image of a powerful but loving 'father' and 'master' to whom total obedience is owed. Such a one is God, and such a one is the abbot, the leader of the monastery, who has received his authority from God. Just as the abbot must surrender his will to the Father, so the monks must surrender their wills to the Father in the person of the abbot. In the words with which the *Rule* opens: 'Hearken, my son, to the precepts of the master and incline the ear of thy heart; freely accept and faithfully fulfil the instructions of a loving father, that by the labour of thy obedience thou mayest return to him from whom thou hast strayed by the sloth of disobedience'.

Though it inculcates total destruction of the individual will, the tone of Benedict's *Rule* is generally moderate and gentle. The power it envisages is not that of an absolute ruler, but that of a loving father who seeks the best for his 'flock' and admonishes them only for their own good. Though the chief focus is on the life of the monastery and its members, there is no sharp rejection of 'the world'. Instead of advocating other-worldly ascetic contemplation, Benedict proposes an ordered life of daily communal worship, scripture reading and manual labour. Monks are exhorted to 'relieve the poor, clothe the naked, visit the sick, bury the dead, and help the afflicted',[13] and, though their lives are to be lived chiefly within the monastery, it is clear that they were also allowed to work outside it with the abbot's permission.

This Benedictine spirit of benevolent paternalism seems to have won sympathy and converts for Christianity within a world where there was often no alternative system of welfare or education, or a more compelling vision of social order and individual discipline. Their inhabitants, both male and female, were chiefly drawn from aristocratic families, and as such the monasteries melded seamlessly into the fabric of early medieval society. There were monasteries for both men and women, together with some 'double monasteries' in which a powerful and high-born abbess might control both the monks and the nuns. Though they might serve the interests of Roman Christianity through loyalty to the pope, most monasteries were established and financed not by the church but by wealthy lay rulers and landowners. In this way mission and monasticism went hand in hand, with newly converted rulers establishing monasteries in their territories, and monasteries establishing and strengthening Christian regimes.

Monasteries helped preserve and extend Christian learning, particularly through their reverence for the Bible. Such reverence was expressed through the careful preservation, copying and ornamentation of scripture. One of the world's greatest works of art, the Lindisfarne Gospels, for example, was produced by monks on Holy Island, off the coast of north-east England, in the early years of the eighth century. The 'illuminations' of its Latin script fuse a dazzling range of influences: pre-Roman Celtish metalwork, Roman mosaic pavements and brooches, Italian and Byzantine sacred portraits and icons, even patterns from carpets produced in Coptic Egypt. Such books would be carried by the Irish and Anglo-Saxon monks across the heartlands of Europe in their missionary expansion, where the art of illumination and the work of manuscript production would be continued in the new monasteries they helped to found. The act of producing such a book represented a new form of asceticism, influenced by that of the Egyptian desert, yet adapted to a new context. It required the same spiritual and physical endurance, but it issued in something that would help spread the gospel to pagan lands and would enhance the power and prestige of any to whom it belonged. Here the Word became flesh not in the bodies and souls of men living in the desert like angels, but in sacred books.

Sacred power was also brought down to earth in the west – as in the east – in the magnificent buildings, churches and ornamentations of the monasteries and, above all, in their liturgy and music. Though Benedict had emphasised the importance of communal worship and laid down rules for its conduct, it was the liturgical side of his *Rule* that would be most elaborated in the west in the centuries that followed. Such development was supported by the patrons of monasticism, not least by the great Frankish dynasty the Carolingians. Pippin III, for example, influenced the musico-liturgical development of the west by introducing Roman chant at Metz cathedral. As in the Byzantine empire, rulers were quick to grasp that the splendour of worship enhanced the power not only of

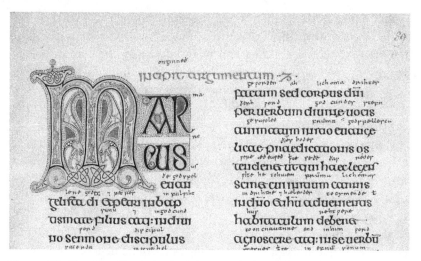

Plate 7   The illuminated letter 'M' from the Gospel of St Mark, Lindisfarne Gospels

Probably written between 715 and 720, the Lindisfarne Gospels were dedicated to St Cuthbert (bishop of Lindisfarne, 634–87) by the monastic community who took his name and established a 'cult' around him. A major cult of a saint had come to require a beautiful gospel book.

God but of the ruler. Awe generated in worship could be most directly transferred to the ruler by the borrowing of ecclesiastical rituals, such as anointing, for ceremonies in which his kingly status was confirmed. And by the tenth century, on a page of a gospel book made for his imperial church in Aachen, Otto III would be depicted in the form of Christ seated in majesty. But such symbolism would have had no power had the worship of monasteries and cathedrals not been able to generate genuine awe, reverence and devotion to Christ on the part of Otto's subjects. During the early medieval period monasteries became yardsticks of Christian living, centres of Christian learning, bases of missionary activity, nodal points of local administration and economic organisation, sources of liturgical development, and powerhouses of sacred power.

Although the above factors enhanced the power of the church in the west, they did not lead directly to the creation of Christendom. Instead of supporting a universal Christian civilisation under papal control, they favoured the rise of territorial churches – the churches of the Franks, of the Anglo-Saxons and so on. Rulers and aristocrats might be enthusiastic supporters and patrons of churches and monasteries, but they regarded them chiefly as their own assets. In most places the church was completely in the hands of feudal lords and bishops and their king. As we shall see in the next chapter, the realisation of the more universal ideal of Christendom and a new 'Holy Roman' empire seems to have come about largely as an unforeseen result of the gradual expansion of the kingdom of the Franks into the largest power in the west. For as this kingdom expanded into an empire by way of its conquest of much of central Europe, so its state church gradually became a quasi-imperial church – with the pope quickly staking a claim to spiritual leadership. He alone, it seemed, had a power ancient and wide-ranging enough to legitimate the expansive claims of the emerging Christian empire.

Further reading

LATE ANTIQUITY

The encyclopedic volume on *Late Antiquity: A Guide to the Postclassical World* (Cambridge, MA: Belknap Press of Harvard University Press, 1999), edited by G. W. Bowersock, Peter Brown and Oleg Grabar, is an excellent resource for information on Roman, Byzantine, Persian and Islamic cultures from the mid-third century to the eighth. So is Garth Fowden's monograph *From Empire to Commonwealth: Consequences of Monotheism in Late Antiquity* (Princeton, NJ: Princeton University Press, 1995), whose synoptic view and argument about the significance of universal faiths influenced this chapter and the previous one.

Judith Herrin's *The Formation of Christendom* (Princeton, NJ: Princeton University Press, 1989) and Peter Brown's *The Rise of Western Christendom: Triumph and Diversity AD 200–1000* (Malden, MA: Blackwell, 1996) offer elegant, wide-ranging accounts of the fate of the Roman Empire from late antiquity to 800 and 1000 respectively. See also Peter Brown's *Society and the Holy in Late Antiquity* (London: Faber, 1982).

BYZANTINE CHRISTIANITY

J. M. Hussey's *The Orthodox Church in the Byzantine Empire* (Oxford: Clarendon, 1990) is an important source. There are in addition a number of histories of the Byzantine empire that give attention to the role of the church. See, for example, Steven Runciman's *The Byzantine Theocracy* (new edition, Cambridge: Cambridge University Press, 2003), Dimitri Obolensky's *The Byzantine Commonwealth: Eastern Europe, 500–1453* (London: Weidenfeld and Nicolson, 1971) and Cyril Mango's *Byzantium: The Empire of New Rome* (London: Weidenfeld and Nicolson, 1980).

Jaroslav Pelikan's *The Spirit of Eastern Christendom (600–1700)* offers an account of the development of Orthodox thought (Chicago, IL: University of Chicago Press, 1974). Tia Kolbaba's *The Byzantine Lists: Errors of the Latins* (Urbana, IL: University of Illinois Press, 2000) offers a scholarly introduction to this neglected genre. Andrew Louth has written a number of useful studies of the eastern mystical tradition. See, for example, his studies of *Maximus the Confessor* (London and New York: Routledge, 1996), *St John Damascene* (Oxford: Oxford University Press, 2002) and *Denys the Areopagite* (London: Geoffrey Chapman; Wilton, CT: Morehouse-Barlow, 2002).

THE MAKING OF THE WESTERN TRADITION

R. W. Southern's *The Making of the Middle Ages* (London and New York: Hutchinson's University Library, 1953) provides an extremely helpful introduction to the subject, as do R. A. Markus's *From Augustine to Gregory the Great* (London: Variorum Reprints, 1983) and *The End of Ancient Christianity* (Cambridge: Cambridge University Press, 1990). Augustine's achievement is analysed by Peter Brown in *Augustine of Hippo: A Biography* (London: Faber, 1967), and Augustine's works are readily available in translation. His *Confessions* is a good place to start.

On the rise of the papacy see Geoffrey Barraclough, *The Medieval Papacy* (London: Thames and Hudson, 1968). On religion and kingship see Walter Ullman, *The Carolingian Renaissance and the Idea of Kingship* (London: Methuen, 1969) and E. H. Kantorowicz, *The King's Two Bodies* (Princeton, NJ: Princeton University Press, 1957). On relations between church and state, see Janet L. Nelson, *Politics and Ritual in Early Medieval Europe* (London and Ronceverte, WV: Hambledon, 1986).

Benedict's *Rule* is short, accessible and available in a number of translations. On the development of western monasticism see David Knowles's *Christian Monasticism* (London: Weidenfeld and Nicolson, 1969). On the evangelisation of the west see Richard Fletcher, *The Conversion of Europe: From Paganism to Christianity, 371–1386* (London: HarperCollins, 1997).

3

Christendom: the western church in power

> The Emperor Constantine in Christ Jesus . . . to the most holy
> and blessed father of fathers, Silvester, bishop of the Roman city
> and Pope . . . .
>
> Inasmuch as our power is earthly, we have decreed that it shall
> venerate and honour [the Pope's] most holy Roman Church and
> that the see of blessed Peter shall be gloriously exalted above
> our empire and earthly throne. We attribute to him the power
> and glorious dignity and strength and honour of the empire, and
> we ordain and decree that he shall have rule as well over the
> four principal sees, Antioch, Alexandria, Constantinople, and
> Jerusalem, as also over all the churches of God in all the world.[1]

It is generally accepted that Pope Stephen II (752–7) set the western
church on a novel course when he appealed to King Pippin III of the
Franks to restore conquered papal lands, and bestowed on him the title
Patricius Romanorum. In so doing, Stephen was turning his back on
the eastern empire in favour of what he hoped would become a new
empire with its centre in Rome. This move was justified, to later generations at least, by *The Donation of Constantine*, quoted above, a forgery
from the eighth century, whose authenticity was queried only in the
fifteenth. Purportedly written by the emperor Constantine on the eve of
his move to Constantinople, it bestowed power in the west to the pope
of the time and to his successors. Not only did it present the pope as
head of the church in the whole world, including the east; it even had
the emperor himself bow down before the plenitude of papal power.

The Frankish church reached its highest point under Charlemagne
(c. 742–814) and the Carolingian dynasty to which he belonged. Charlemagne united northern parts of the Roman empire with the more newly
won mission territories of northern Europe to create a territory extensive
enough to be thought of as an empire. Certainly Charlemagne himself
seems to have been influenced by an imperial ideal, one that was fed
not only by the legacy of Rome but by the universal-imperial dynamics of Christianity itself, absorbed in part through a Latin translation
of Eusebius. The idea of a revival of the Roman empire in the west,
with Charlemagne as its head, led to Pope Leo III's crowning of Charlemagne in St Peter's in Rome in 800 to the acclamation, 'Emperor of the

Romans'. Heavily laden with symbolic meaning, this act was at one and the same time a subversive assertion of Roman Christian independence from the east (which of course still considered itself to be the true Roman empire) and a claim to supreme power on the part of both Charlemagne and the papacy. For Charlemagne, the coronation established him as the most powerful Christian ruler in the west, a theocratic king-priest who was responsible for the temporal and spiritual welfare of his people. For Leo and his successors, however, the coronation indicated the supremacy of the papacy, since it was the pope who had the power to anoint the emperor, not vice versa.

Implicit in the coronation of Charlemagne, in other words, was a struggle between sacred and secular power that would be played out throughout the Middle Ages and beyond. More immediately, it forms a central theme in the reign of Charlemagne and in the formation of Carolingian political theology. On the one hand, Charlemagne tried to claim all power for himself by taking over not only political but also spiritual control of his territories. He actively masterminded the Christianisation of the Carolingian empire, nominating bishops, convening church councils, appointing Christian scholars, theologians and artists, promulgating church law, and promoting better Christian education for both clergy and laity. On the other hand, the powerful and active Carolingian bishops constantly checked Charlemagne's power not only by promoting their collective role, but by placing kingship on a Gregorian rather than a Eusebian footing. They spoke of the complementarity of royal and episcopal governments and emphasised the paternal authority of spiritual over temporal rulers. In their view the authority of the secular ruler was not absolute, but depended upon his respectful obedience to divine, human and ecclesiastical law. The king was king only so long as he used his God-given powers justly and wisely.

Though Charlemagne may not have been in wholehearted agreement with the Frankish bishops, his power was probably not secure or absolute enough for him to disagree too forcefully in practice or in theory. For Charlemagne was still bound by typically feudal ties of reciprocity, being heavily dependent on the election, consent and support of the clergy and his powerful lords. In addition, as his coronation makes clear, neither he nor his bishops were able to ignore the competing claims of papal authority. While they might act as the powers in their land, their power was checked by their ties to the church in Rome and by the fact that the

Frankish church could not claim to be the universal church. It was in order to claim the latter title that Charlemagne had to ally himself with Rome and the papacy. This would continue to be true for later Romano-Germanic emperors, most notably Otto I and his successors, who also made alliances with Rome in their bid to inherit control of what was now coming to be called 'the Holy Roman empire'. Otto II (973–83) replaced the title of *Imperator Augustus,* which had been habitually borne by his father, with that of *Imperator Romanorum.* His son, Otto III, installed himself in Rome and proclaimed the restoration of the Roman empire.

The fact that no one secular power ever became powerful and extensive enough to rule over the whole of Europe turned out to be to Rome's advantage. Had a pan-European empire emerged, it might have taken control of the church. But, when the Holy Roman empire lost power to rival states, a papacy that had become skilled in diplomatic negotiation with the various powers in Europe simply made alliances elsewhere. The fact that no single political power was able to unite the west meant that the church could now step up and claim that role. Unlike the church in the east, in other words, the western church was gradually being set free from dependence upon secular power. With that freedom came new opportunities, ideas, institutions and the social programme necessary to exploit them.

By the eleventh century it was thus the church in the west rather than in the east that had managed to expand its power. This power took the form of the European-wide Christian civilisation we call Christendom. Its universal impetus was visible not only in its conquest of a territory more extensive than that of the western Roman empire at the height of its power (and a population that was bigger still), but in its continuing efforts to win back the lost territories of the eastern empire by pushing back the Muslims. As soon as the means became available, it would also be visible in the expansion of the Catholic church into new territories such as 'Latin' America (see ch. 7).

Never before or since has Christianity achieved such intensive and extensive centralised power, both religious and political. It was a power from on high, flowing downwards through a series of mediations from an almighty Father God through the pope to the clergy and finally to the laity. This spiritual pyramid reinforced a social one as medieval society grew increasingly stratified. In the theology of later medieval scholastic

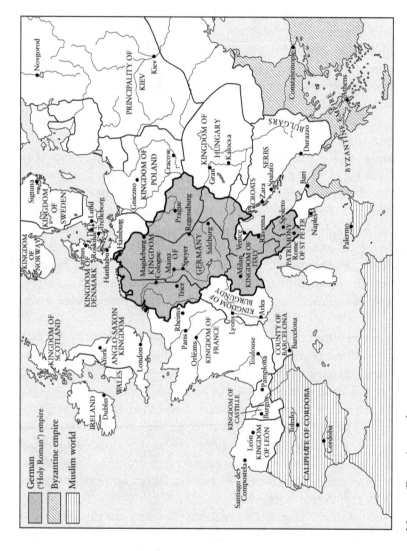

Map 3 'Europe' around AD 1000

Legend:
- German ('Holy Roman') empire
- Byzantine empire
- Muslim world

KINGDOM OF NORWAY

KINGDOM OF SWEDEN

Sigtuna

KINGDOM OF DENMARK
Aarhus
Roskilde · Lund
Haithabu · Trelleborg
Hamburg

IRELAND
Dublin

KINGDOM OF SCOTLAND

WALES
ANGLO-SAXON KINGDOM
York
London

PRINCIPALITY OF KIEV
Novgorod
Kiev

KINGDOM OF POLAND
Gniezno
Cracow

KINGDOM OF HUNGARY
Gran · Kalocsa

KINGDOM OF GERMANY
Magdeburg
Cologne
Mainz
Trier
Speyer
Prague
Regensburg
Salzburg

CROATS
Zara
Spalato

SERBS

BYZANTINE EMPIRE
Constantinople
Athens

BULGARS
Durazzo
Bari

KINGDOM OF ITALY
Milan · Venice
Ravenna
Spoleto

PATRIMONY OF ST PETER
Rome
Naples
Palermo

KINGDOM OF BURGUNDY
Arles
Lyons

KINGDOM OF FRANCE
Rheims
Paris
Orléans
Toulouse

COUNTY OF BARCELONA
Pamplona
Barcelona

KINGDOM OF CASTILE
Burgos
Toledo

KINGDOM OF LEÓN
León
Santiago de Compostela

CALIPHATE OF CÓRDOBA
Córdoba

theologians such as Thomas Aquinas, this order would be dignified as natural and God-given. Yet the order and uniformity of Christian society were more fragile than its defenders might admit. Profound intellectual and spiritual as well as socio-economic changes were in train throughout the high Middle Ages. The church's attempt to maintain unity was constantly challenged by various forms of dissent. Such dissent came from within as well as from without. As we shall see, the growing power of the church was challenged not only by rival claims to power on the part of secular rulers but by alternative Christian visions of poverty and power from below.

Papal power

Just as Pope Gregory I had helped lay the foundations of Christendom in the sixth century, so in the eleventh Pope Gregory VII (pope from 1073 to 1085) played a major role in completing the construction. 'Cometh the hour, cometh the man', and the hour was propitious. As we have seen, the position of the church in the west had been greatly strengthened. It was now the single most extensive power network within Europe, its power being ideological, political and economic. What is more, Europe had achieved a certain stability. By 1000 the last invaders – Viking, Muslim, Hun – had been pushed back. Where states had been established, stability was tending to enhance their powers and aid their growth, though no single power had been able to establish a lasting dominance. Gregory was the right man to seize the hour. Since taking monastic vows as a young man, Hildebrand (as he was then called) had served a succession of popes and become a trusted advisor. He had thought long and hard about the role of papacy and church in the west, and had already set in train a number of reforms designed to strengthen the position of both. When he became pope in 1073 he was entering into his own.

What Gregory saw with such clarity was that if the church were to take control in the west it would be necessary for it to shake off the secular ('lay') control that had so far made that impossible. Instead of being in captivity to individual emperors and kings, the church must become free to establish its supremacy. Even before becoming pope, Gregory had worked to ensure the church's independence in relation to papal elections by framing a decree that made cardinal bishops (later simply called 'cardinals') rather than secular leaders responsible for the election of a new pope. When he himself was elected pope, Gregory took his campaign further by attempting to stop lay appointments to clerical posts, particularly episcopal ones. At one level this was a moral battle against 'simony', the practice of buying and selling divine offices. At another it was an economic battle, for many clerical posts were supported by a substantial endowment of land, the income from which was used to support the clerics who served in them. As such, these 'livings' were significant material goods worth a great deal not only to their beneficiaries but to the lay rulers in whose gift they were, who could use them to buy favour and loyalty. The same was even more true of bishoprics, since the office of bishop was by now one of the most ancient and powerful in Europe. To abolish the power of lay patronage would be to win an important economic and political as well as moral victory for the church. At the same time Gregory also launched a campaign for clerical celibacy. There were economic as well as moral motives at play here too, for, if clergy were married with children, not only did they cost more to support, but there was always the danger that the Christian priesthood would turn into a hereditary priesthood, with livings passed down from father to son. While the practice of clerical celibacy dated back to the rise of Christian asceticism in the late third century, it was by no means universal. In the east most parish priests were married, though bishops – who were drawn from the monasteries – were celibate. In the west, however, while celibacy had long been the ideal for all clergy, there were many from the highest to the lowest who kept wives or mistresses either openly or covertly.

One of the reasons that Gregory's reforms eventually succeeded was that they won a significant degree of popular as well as clerical support. The trading of the best clerical offices by rulers and aristocrats and their families had inevitably generated widespread resentment. The most important long-term effect of Gregory's reforms, however, was to raise the status of the clergy and set them much further apart from the laity than had previously been the case. For the first time 'the church' became identified with 'the clergy'. It was clergy who now acted as God's representatives on earth, and lay people who simply received their services. In Gregory's view the clergy should be both moral and spiritual exemplars, whose growing power over the laity would be justified by their moral purity and higher learning. Their literacy and their use of Latin set them apart from the masses, and their celibacy set them apart from rich and poor alike. The deliberate effect was to create a hierarchy of power in society in which the clergy stood above both the ruling classes and the labouring classes. The hierarchy would extend to the church, in which the pope would command the bishops, the bishops the clergy, and the clergy the people.

Given his desire to establish clerical difference, it is not surprising to find that asceticism was central to Gregory's reforms. As we saw in chapter 2, a connection between asceticism and the church's bid for power had been established at least as early as the time of Athanasius. There may be several reasons for this. For a start, 'purity' involves being set apart. To reject sex, marriage and family is to set oneself apart in the most obvious physical and material way. In addition, purity and asceticism involve control. The ascetic is one who has complete control over all that might otherwise control him – over his appetites, his body, women, and 'the world'. Thus asceticism should be seen not only in terms of the renunciation of inferior forms of power, but in terms of a quest for the higher power of total self-control. What is more, asceticism releases huge amounts of time and energy that would otherwise be expended on more 'mundane' tasks. As such, it produces an individual who can become a hugely valuable asset to an institution such as the church. As we have seen in relation to the Benedictine rule, surrender of the will in obedience to the abbot (or bishop) was presented as a central part of the spiritual discipline of the monastic life. Gregory's reforms aimed to secure and harness all these energies for a revitalised church capable of taking control of Europe.

What Gregory helped to establish, in other words, was Christendom: a west united under the rule of the Roman Catholic church and its clergy. Though this rule would be indirect, being mediated through secular powers, it would be no less powerful for that. Secular rulers would be under the control of the church, and would act as its instruments. The church would set the direction of law and social policy by reference to divine law, and secular rulers would help implement it, thereby bringing into being a truly Christian civilisation – for the very first time. In this scheme of things, the pope would be the most powerful sovereign of all. As Gregory put it in his letters:

> The pope can be judged by no-one;
> The Roman church has never erred . . .
> The Roman church was founded by Christ alone . . .
> All princes should kiss his feet.[2]

This grandiose vision went a step beyond what had been imagined by early Christianity, Eusebius or even Augustine. The only problem was that secular rulers were not always as enthusiastic about it as the papacy. They wanted to be in control just as much as the church did, and the effect of the attempted papal power-grab was to initiate a continuous, fluctuating power struggle between secular and religious authority. Roman church and revived Roman empire became locked in a rivalry of imperial projects, both claiming absolute power for themselves. Christendom was not to be established without a struggle.

By the time of Gregory VII's pontificate three secular powers were in the ascendant in Europe – the English, the French and the German/'Holy Roman'. Since it was the last of these that still had the most plausible claim to imperial power, it was with the Holy Roman empire that Gregory clashed most fiercely. The clash focused over Gregory's reforms in the areas of both church property and lay investiture. When the emperor Henry IV continued to make his own nominations of bishops, Gregory reproved him. The emperor responded by calling a synod of German bishops at Worms in 1076, at which he deposed the pope. In return, Gregory excommunicated Henry. Excommunication had considerable force, for it not only carried the threat of eternal damnation in the next life, but released Henry's subjects from the obligation to obey him and to honour his rule and property. Faced by insurrection, Henry was forced to seek absolution from the pope, though their continuing rivalry led later to Henry's forcible eviction of Gregory from Rome, which may have hastened the latter's death. The bitterness of the contest and the nature of the claims that Gregory made in his struggle for supremacy over Henry and other secular powers become evident in his letters dating from this period. In Gregory's view papal power rests not only on the dignity of the office but on the personal goodness and humility of individual popes. Explicitly invoking Gregory I's *Regula Pastoralis*, Gregory VII therefore calls all kings and princes to 'humbly obey' the Holy Church, lest their 'pride' invoke God's wrath and judgement:

> Let them not seek to subject themselves or to subjugate the Holy Church; but above all let them strive, by recognising the teachers and fathers, to render due honour . . . For if we are ordered to honour our fathers and mothers after the flesh – how much more our spiritual ones! And if he who has cursed his father or mother after the flesh is to be punished with death – what does he merit who curses his spiritual father or mother?[3]

Like his predecessor Gregory I, Gregory VII distinguishes between the power-seeking of secular rulers which is selfish, and that of spiritual leaders which is selfless. Like his predecessor too, he calls secular leaders to submit to the papacy not as subjects to a monarch so much as sons to a loving father.

This rhetoric of benevolent papal paternalism did not convince the most powerful leaders in Christendom, for the struggle for power between church and state continued for centuries. While some so-called 'settlements', such as the 'Concordat of Worms' drawn up in 1122, helped ease disputes by distinguishing between the church's spiritual power and the state's temporal power, such formulations tended to be too open to interpretation to settle matters for good. Affairs were further complicated by the fact that successive popes' attempts to win supreme power for themselves often threatened not only the interests of secular rulers but also those of bishops. Still powerful men in their own right, the bishops might shift allegiance from king to pope and back again, depending on who was most likely to support their interests in a particular situation. Yet in so far as allegiance to the papacy gave them independence from their territorial ruler and a court of appeal against him, the bishops gradually tended to become allies rather than opponents of papal power. This process was greatly strengthened by Rome's increasing success in winning the right to make episcopal appointments. If the papacy had a powerful episcopate supporting them across Europe, and if this episcopate could in turn influence the clergy and people in their care, then Rome's power would be secure. Not surprisingly, then, the medieval popes worked hard to establish a clear 'diocesan' and 'parochial' structure across Europe, such that every area would be under the jurisdiction of a parish priest, every parish priest under the jurisdiction of a bishop, and every bishop subject to an archbishop, who would be directly answerable to Rome.

The gradual colonisation of European space was also secured by a system of direct papal control. This worked in two ways. First, popes ruled not only through their clergy but through 'legates' directly answerable to their papal employer. Some legatine offices were permanent (sometimes awarded to a bishop), but many legates were troubleshooters who could be sent into a territory to sort out any problems arising. As the direct representative of the pope, legates had considerable power, and acted as agents of his will. Second, direct papal power across Europe was

Plate 8 *Pope Gregory VII Absolving Henry IV*, by Federico Zuccaro (c. 1540–1609)
    Commissioned for the *sala regia* in the Vatican palace, this post-Reformation painting captures the symbolic significance of King Henry's submission to Pope Gregory for the official Catholic understanding of church supremacy over the state.

greatly strengthened by Rome's growing role in the formulation and enforcement of law. The expansion and systematisation of church and church-administered law constituted a key element in the consolidation of Christendom after the eleventh century, so much so that every notable pope from 1159 to 1303 was a lawyer. As legal expertise grew up in and around Rome from the mid-eleventh century, the papacy became a centre to which anyone in Europe could appeal to have a dispute settled. Since they could appeal directly to the pope, so bypassing secular rulers and courts as well as local ecclesiastical ones, this served to strengthen direct papal control. In formulating ever more exalted claims for papal power, successive popes played up this legal role to the full. The 'keys' that Christ had handed to the papacy via Peter were now interpreted as conferring authority not only to convict and absolve sinners, but to command the world in moral, legislative and judicial matters. Canonist writers developed the use of the term 'universal ordinary', meaning that anyone could appeal to the pope, without reference to any intermediary, in virtue of his 'plenitude of power' (*plenitudo potestatis*).

While the concept of *plenitudo potestatis* was derived from a letter of Pope Leo I (440–61), its mature development in relation to papal power took place in relation to the full flowering of papalist theology in the late thirteenth and early fourteenth centuries. From the doctrine of 'two swords' formulated by Bernard of Clairvaux (1090–1153) the argument developed that the pope had control over the swords of both spiritual and temporal judgement and merely granted secular rulers the use of the latter (as well as having the right to crown and depose them). Pope Innocent III (pope from 1198) went further by claiming not only that he had the right to judge and control earthly rulers, but that his judgements had divine authority because he was the mediator between God and man. This prompted a further canonical distinction between the pope's 'ordinary power' (*potestas ordinata*) and the extraordinary or absolute power (*potestas absoluta*) that he exercised as 'Vicar of Christ', a title increasingly used after the mid-twelfth century. In the context of his quarrels with the French monarchy, theological supporters of Pope Boniface VIII (pope from 1294 to 1303) refined the theory of papal plenitude by deriving it from Christ's unlimited earthly lordship (*dominium*), and defining the pope's jurisdiction over things as well as persons. Boniface's bull *Unam sanctam* of 1302 is often regarded as the most extreme of all claims to papal power. In its claims to absolute dominion it seems to have abandoned even the restraint offered by a Gregorian invocation of humility and paternalism. Its background was the threat to church power and property posed by the emergence of strong national monarchs ruling kingdoms with increasingly centralised financial, judicial and legislative structures of their own.

It was Boniface who suffered the first serious defeat of the mature papacy at the hands of a rising national monarchy, that of Philip IV of France. The increasing hostility between the two men signalled a profound reversal of the collaboration between the pope and the kings of France that had been a steady force in European politics for two centuries. Their argument was over money and power, over whether the French clergy should continue to pay taxes to Rome rather than to their king, and over whether the clergy could remain immune from the law of the land. On both counts, Philip demonstrated that his power within his own nation was greater than that of the pope. In a final show of strength he had Boniface arrested in the papal palace at Anagni in 1303. Philip's intention had been to capture the pope and bring him to France. Though Boniface died before this could be done, Clement V (pope from 1305 to 1314) voluntarily took up residence in Avignon in 1309, exposing himself and his next six successors to the charge of becoming puppets of the French king.

Yet the return to Rome in 1377 only led to a worse situation, the so-called 'Great Schism' of 1378–1414. The schism came about when the election of an Italian pope, Urban VI (pope from 1378 to 1389) was opposed by non-Italian cardinals when he refused to return to Avignon. In retaliation they elected a second pope, Clement VII (pope from 1378 to 1394), who set up residence in Avignon. Christendom was split between two lines of popes until 1409, and among three lines from 1409 to 1414. The situation was exacerbated by the fact that different national rulers allied themselves with rival popes. As the problem dragged on, the 'conciliarist' movement took shape in an effort to bring the schism to an end. The solution proposed by the conciliarists was to call a general council to reform the church and appoint a legitimate pope. After an abortive attempt that resulted in three rival claimants for the title, the Council of Constance (1414–18) finally elected Martin V as pope and ended the Great Schism.

The overall effect of the schism was to weaken papal power, not only because it allowed opportunities for secular rulers to take further control over the finances and personnel of the churches in their lands, but because it had given rise to a conciliarist theory of church government, which aimed to subordinate the power of the pope to that of a church council.

The popes' struggles with increasingly powerful monarchs had revealed their Achilles' heel: lack of military power. The church was weak in means of coercion, and this was the most important respect in which it fell short of being a state. It was not for want of trying. Later medieval theologians had abandoned early Christianity's suspicion of violence. Even as late as the Battle of Hastings in 1066, those who took part were made to undertake heavy penance for taking part in violent confrontation. By the time of Aquinas, however, a theory of 'just war' had been developed, which legitimated the use of violence on the part of states when it had a just cause and was prosecuted in a just manner. Likewise, Christianity had civilised the warrior tradition of early Europe through the ideal of the chivalrous knight who bore arms for the protection of the weak and defenceless. The Crusades constituted the most important manifestation of this ideal, as well as the most notable attempt by the church to mobilise military power on her own behalf and under her own direct control. They revealed a growing Christian intolerance of religious difference, which will be discussed in more detail below. And they signalled that the universalising, expansive tendency so evident in Constantinian and early post-Constantinian Christianity, but checked by the circumstances of the early Middle Ages, remained potent.

Beginning in 1095 and continuing until the fifteenth century, these continuous expeditions to the eastern Mediterranean were first designed to recover the Holy Land from Islam, then to retain it in Christian hands, and later to counteract the expanding power of the Islamic Ottoman empire. Crusades were proclaimed and supported by popes, bishops and theologians, and crusaders were encouraged by a wide range of privileges including tax immunity, protection of property, indulgences, and the award of the status of martyr in the event of death. As in Constantine's day, the cross once more became the symbol of power, conquest and military might rather than of suffering and death.

The motivations for crusade were multiple, but so far as the papacy was concerned two stand out. The first was the attempt to reunite the two halves of the empire and their two churches, eastern and western – on terms favourable to the west, of course, and with Rome as the centre of power. The second, closely connected, was to push back the power of Islam. By so doing the entire territories of the former Roman empire might be regained, and the church returned to its former glory – or better. The destruction of Islam and its followers would be a welcome bonus. Despite the relations between Christians and Muslims that had developed in some parts of Europe, most notably in Spain, and despite the fact that until relatively recently Christians had been able to travel freely in Islamic territories, the Crusades set up a total antithesis between Christian and Muslim. Pope Urban II defined it thus when he preached to the First Crusade at Clermont in 1095: 'What a dishonour it would be for us if this infidel race, so justly scorned, which has shrunk from the dignity of man and is a vile slave of the devil, should defeat the chosen people of God . . . On the one hand the enemies of the Saviour will be fighting, on the other his friends.'[4]

Despite their stated aim of aiding their eastern brethren, the Crusades also served to worsen relations with Byzantine Christianity. Both over-awed and disgusted by what they found, the crusaders eventually turned on their former allies (see ch. 2). When the eastern empire finally fell to the Turks in 1453 the pope of the day, Pius II, immediately wrote to the Turkish conqueror offering to make him emperor of the Greeks in return for his submission to papal authority.

Despite initial success in capturing Jerusalem (in 1099) and establishing four crusader states, Christian control was repeatedly threatened by Islamic power, and the last Christian stronghold in Acre was finally lost in 1291. When crusading activities in the Holy Land became less rewarding, the crusading spirit could be turned inwards on Europe itself. A crusade was launched against heresy in southern France (see below), and the *Reconquista* (reconquest) of Spain took on the tone of a religious war after the mid-eleventh century. In both cases the victors seized large tracts of land from those they defeated. By the end of the thirteenth century the Spanish Muslims were confined to the tiny kingdom of Granada. Overall, however, the attempt to vanquish Islam had been no more successful than the attempt to reunite Christendom.

The long-term failure of the Crusades to achieve their goals mirrored the failure of the papacy to achieve lasting and effective military power. Papal dreams of a militia of St Peter, secular rulers obedient to command, knights sworn to faithful service and mercenaries in the pay of Rome, an Inquisition capable of policing Europe – all did a great deal to strengthen papal power in the late Middle Ages, but none was sufficient. The result was a church that was never freed from dependence upon the consent of secular rulers in the exercise of coercion, a dependence that would eventually prove fatal to the attempt to establish permanent Christian control in Europe.

Scholasticism

It was in relation to ideological power that Christianity's control was perhaps the most secure over the longest period. Here the great explosion of energy, activity and achievement first took place in the twelfth century. Its institutional basis was provided by the new universities, which some-times grew out of earlier cathedral schools. While the latter were founded in order to train clergy for local dioceses, after the late tenth century a number – particularly in northern France – had masters who became renowned enough to attract students from much further afield. The conditions for a more sustained intellectual and educational environ-ment were eventually realised in twelfth-century Paris (for theology) and Bologna (for law). A second infusion of energy was given to the scholastic enterprise in the thirteenth century by the rise of mendicant orders or orders of friars, the Franciscans and the Dominicans. Given the centrality of preaching to their ministry, the friars came to play a key role in the later development of the universities and scholasticism.

Scholasticism provided the ideological basis of Christendom, just as Christendom provided the political and material basis of scholas-ticism. Each was as ambitious as the other in its confidence and scope. Just as Christendom aimed to be a unified Christian civilisation, so scholasticism sought to consolidate all learning in a single system. Its grand unified theory of all things would capture and secure the truth once and for all. Such total knowledge would be achieved by way of a method that essentially consisted of gathering together all avail-able texts and harmonising their truths through comparative evalua-tion and interpretation. It was this method, above all, that unified the scholastic enterprise. It would begin with a question, gather together the sentences from various texts that had a bearing upon it, and adju-dicate between them in order to arrive at the correct answer. It was an approach that relied on the assumed authority of the texts that were consulted, but, by allowing the scholar and his pupils to decide between them in coming to a conclusion, it also offered considerable scope for the exercise of individual reason and the creation of theological celebrities.

To the schoolmen who worked on them, the texts the scholastic method sought to distil and harmonise represented the whole of human knowledge from the creation to the present day. They fell into two main categories: the 'classical' works of ancient Greece and Rome, and the Christian writings that had succeeded them and that included not only the Bible but the writings of the church fathers in both Greek and Latin – though it would be in Latin that the texts would be read, debates conducted and scholastic works prepared. (The recovery and translation into Latin of a number of classical texts preserved by Islam were significant stimuli to scholasticism.) A scholastic theologian would obviously have to be a man of huge erudition to have mastered all these texts, yet there were still sufficiently few in circulation to make the achievement possible. As time went on, scholastics were also able to draw on existing compilations of 'sentences', rather than having to start from scratch. (The *Sentences* (c. 1157) of Peter Lombard became the standard text.) Their task was also simplified by the fact that not all texts were regarded as having equal authority. Since Christian texts were written in the light of God's revelation in Christ, they embodied a more perfect and complete knowledge than the classical writers could have achieved, and had a corresponding authority. But the greatest authority of all was the Bible, and it was in the light of scriptural guidance, therefore, that the mass of other texts could be sifted and systematised.

Underlying this whole procedure was the belief that the present generation was closer to unified and unifying knowledge than any generation since the fall. In paradise, Adam and Eve had had perfect knowledge, but their disobedience had led to its loss. Ever since, men of learning had tried to recover what had been lost, and major advances had been made by the Old Testament writers as well as the classical writers such as Plato and Aristotle. Yet it was only those who were able to see in the light of Christ who could bring this knowledge to perfection. Even now the task was incomplete, having been set back by the destructive forces of the barbarian invasions; but huge strides were at last being made. By standing on the shoulders of giants, the scholastics believed that they could see further than ever before. Their goal of laying hold of the truth in its wholeness was never merely theoretical. While theological truth had a beauty of its own, it was also the blueprint of Christendom. What the theologians discovered about reality, the lawyers would draft as law, and the church and its secular allies would enforce. By such means God's kingdom would be anticipated on earth, and men and women would be prepared to enter it in its fullness after death. The sense of purpose of medieval scholasticism was intense.

While they strove for agreement in universal truth, the scholastics did so by way of a disputation that was often public. Truth was arrived at through argument. Inevitably this involved important disagreements among different teachers, their pupils, and the works they produced. The early scholastics who laid the foundation of the whole enterprise – men such as Anselm of Laon, Hugh of St Victor, Abelard, and Peter Lombard – by no means agreed on all points. Yet the ground of hope was that the system that was coming into being through their work was unified not only by a common method but by a coherent view of God, the creation, fall and redemption of humankind, and by the church and the sacraments through which the redeeming process was extended to individuals. Soon this would be systematised for the benefit of Christendom in such a way that, while instruction would still need to be crowned by individual acts of faith and devotion, no-one need be in any doubt about the essential contours of saving truth – or that the Catholic church was its guardian.

While the basis of systematic theology and law had been fully articulated by the end of the twelfth century, it was during the thirteenth that scholastic theology achieved its greatest systematic expression in the work of the Dominican friar Thomas Aquinas (c. 1225–74). Aquinas' thought gained a new impetus from newly available translations of Aristotle's work, particularly on natural philosophy. What this provoked was a theology of astonishing breadth and scope that was capable of forming the metaphysical and ethical basis of medieval Christendom, a basis on which the Catholic church would seek to re-establish itself in later ages. In Aquinas' work, the modification of Augustine's position that had gradually been taking place under scholasticism can be seen in its clearest outlines. For Augustine, sin was the most striking feature of human beings and the world, and the Christian life was understood as an attempt to overcome this through laying hold of God's grace. What this meant in practical terms was that the church must always be set apart from the world. While secular rulers have a place ordained by God, it is the lowly one of holding back sin rather than the exalted one of establishing a Christian society on earth. For Aristotle, by contrast, human beings (particularly aristocratic men) are naturally endowed with the capacity of reason, which allows them to discern and pursue a natural human *telos* (end, purpose) – a state of flourishing; of well-being and well-doing (*eudaimonia*).

What Aquinas achieved was a synthesis of these apparently opposite positions that could provide a powerful rationale for Christendom. He did this by thinking not in terms of a dichotomy between sin and redemption, as had Paul and Augustine, but in terms of a natural and harmonious relation between the 'natural' and the 'supernatural'. Without the action of saving, supernatural grace, human beings and the world exist in a state of nature. Even so, they are made by God and, despite the imperfections caused by the fall, they retain the basis of a God-given order in their natural constitution. It is this order that reason is capable of comprehending. Even without revelation, then, men were capable of knowing something of the truth, of discerning good from bad, and of proving God's existence. All these things are possible on a natural, rational basis. Yet, without revelation, a perfection of knowledge is impossible.

For Aquinas, the natural requires the supernatural to attain its proper end – the vision of God. As he put it in his great *Summa Theologica*, 'grace does not abolish nature, but perfects it' (1–1, 1, 8). By the exercise of reason alone the classical writers had been able to discern the natural virtues such as courage and justice, but it had required scriptural revelation before the supernatural virtues of faith, hope and charity could be made known. Only then could the natural virtues fall into their proper place and the whole be perfected. On the basis of the same logic Aquinas argued that the church was called not to abandon or condemn or reject the world, but to perfect it. Secular rulers are a necessary and good part of the natural order, but the supernatural services of the church are required for the perfect society to be achieved. Yet existing social and economic realities can in the main simply be accepted as natural, with the church in a position of supremacy over them, for it is in the latter that they find their proper goal and end.

The practical implication of Aquinas' thought was that the church achieved supremacy in society not by trying to shape it in a Christian mould, but simply by ruling over it. So long as its supremacy was accepted, the natural would be perfected through submission to the supernatural. In this way the unprecedented power of the medieval church was made possible by sanctifying 'the natural' rather than by trying to transform it into something else. Institutions such as the family, private property, male domination, violence and even serfdom and slavery were generally accepted as part of the natural order of things just as they were. This was possible because the natural order was – for mainly contingent reasons – one that did not pose too many challenges to either the organic and communitarian or the hierarchical and patriarchal ideals that Catholic Christianity sought to validate. What Aquinas called the natural order of things could therefore be accepted as God-given but in need of the perfecting agency of the church, just as his theology declared.

One result of this fortuitous alliance between scholastic theology and the medieval social order was that changes in the latter inevitably unsettled the former. This, in part, accounts for the gradual disintegration of scholasticism after about 1300 (see below). Such decay was also the result of dynamics within scholasticism itself. Since it had been premised on the possibility of achieving a unified agreed knowledge, the continued existence of disagreement and disputed areas proved highly damaging to the entire enterprise, as did scholasticism's inability to incorporate new forms of knowledge, from mysticism to history and science. The overarching ambition of the scholastic project was gradually proving its undoing – but, despite increasing criticism, its force was far from spent. For one thing, some of the architects of the downfall of scholasticism in the late medieval period, from Duns Scotus to Ockham, still worked in a recognisably scholastic mode even as they overturned Thomistic principles (see below). For another, as we shall see in later chapters, the methods of scholasticism and the achievement of Aquinas would be revived after the medieval period not only by some Protestant theologians, but by the Catholic church of the nineteenth century.

Orthodoxy and heresy, power and powerlessness

The structural and ideological developments we have been tracing brought the Catholic church, and a monarchial papacy, to a position of unprecedented power in the high Middle Ages. Christianity now presented itself as a compact constellation of doctrinal, ethical and ritual commitments with a firm institutional basis and an assured place in society. Above all, it was unified. If there was a single ideal that the church now upheld above all others, it was that of unity. The church itself must be unified, a hierarchy of clergy and people acting as a single body. Its teaching must be unified; it presented the whole truth about all things (subject, of course, to natural human fallibility). And Christendom as a whole must be unified, a unified church undergirding the unity of western society.

Even though Christendom represented the outcome of a long process of development culminating in recent strenuous reform, it presented itself as timeless. Scholasticism used texts in an ahistorical and decontextualised fashion. All that mattered was how they fitted into the unified system of Christian truth, not what their original context or meaning might have been. Likewise, the sovereign, monarchial, papal church represented itself as a return to the way things had been at the beginning – as *The Donation of Constantine* proved. The golden age for Christendom was always the past. There was no sense of ongoing progress, development or change. As in the eastern church, that which was subject to change was viewed as imperfect. God did not change; why should his church? If anything, society was getting worse, not better. Since the days of Christ, men had drifted further and further from Christian truth. The only hope was an apocalyptic one: for the irruption of God into human history to bring the present sorry state of things to an end, to separate the righteous from the wicked and to inaugurate the kingdom of heaven in its fullness.

In the meantime, however, the church – together with the earthly rulers subject to its commands – was there to act as the bulwark against even greater sinfulness and to be the place where salvation could be tasted through the sacraments that it alone could distribute. What was required was no arrogant human striving towards divinisation, but faith and obedience towards one's superiors – God, the clergy, rulers and nobles. In short, the powerless must submit themselves to the powerful, women to men, and all to God.

One of the greatest achievements of the medieval church was to communicate this understanding to the entire population. Though those who were involved in developing papalist ideology and scholastic theology belonged to the very highest echelons of society, and though their work was aimed at maintaining the church at the highest level, their work also had a significant impact lower down in society. A major effect of the Gregorian reforms had been to improve the quality, status and distribution of the local clergy, so that most people's chief contact with the church would no longer be by way of the local monastery, but by the parish priest. One of his functions would be to disseminate truth from on high – from Rome and the schools – to those in his care. Through an increasingly effective line-management system that connected pope to bishop, bishop to clergy, and clergy to laity, that which was said and done in Rome might reach the ear of almost every man and woman in Christendom.

For that to happen, however, it was necessary that everyone should come to church. One step was to provide enough buildings of suitable grandeur. The high Middle Ages was an unprecedented era of church-building. Though the population was growing rapidly, there would be enough new, stone-built churches and cathedrals to cater for them. Many would be as imposing as the authority they represented. In his chronicle of the time, the Burgundian Ralph Glaber recorded that

> When the third year after the millennium dawned, churches were to be seen being rebuilt over all the earth, but especially in Italy and Gaul . . . each Christian community was driven by a true rivalry to have a finer church than that of its neighbours. It looked as though the world was shaking itself to take off its old age and to reclothe itself in all areas in a white cloak of churches.[5]

A second step was to legislate for regular church attendance. In 1215 the Fourth Lateran Council laid down that

> All the faithful of both sexes shall after they have reached the age of discretion faithfully confess all their sins at least once a year to their own priest, and perform to the best of their ability the penance imposed, receiving regularly, at least at Easter, the sacrament of the eucharist . . . otherwise they shall be cut off from the church during life, and deprived of Christian burial at death.[6]

One thing this decree indicates is the way in which penance was becoming the most important of the seven sacraments of the Catholic church (the others being baptism, confirmation, marriage, ordination, the eucharist, and extreme unction). It required individuals to confess their sins before their priest and to discharge the prescribed penance in recognition of the 'absolution' the priest would confer. It was a discipline that enabled the church to enforce its morality by way of a system which, though external to individuals, could be internalised to become part of their very self-understanding.

Penance helped encourage an approach to the religious life in which the aim of all striving was to avoid sin in order that one's soul might be saved rather than damned. This negative and somewhat forensic under-standing of the moral life went hand in hand with the development of belief in purgatory. In the Augustinian scheme of thought there were only two options after death: heaven for the few and hell for the many. Purgatory opened up a third option, since it was a supernatural state or place appropriate for those who were neither all bad nor all good but somewhere in between. Through continued merit-building and sin-avoidance after death they might eventually work their way out of pur-gatory and into heaven. Since this might seem like a purely human effort, however, scholastic theologians including Aquinas refined a theory that postulated a store of infinite merit collected by Christ and the saints, on which penitents might draw. Sinners might lay hold of such merit even before death by buying an 'indulgence'. Issued in order to help raise money for papal and episcopal causes such as crusades, indulgences released those who purchased them from the post-mortem penalty they would otherwise have to pay for sins committed.

In this and other ways Christendom became part of the warp and woof of everyday life. It played a major role not only in the management of sacred matters, but more mundane ones as well – from the adminis-tration of charity to the settlement of disputes. Above all, it offered a unified framework within which life would be lived from cradle to grave. It provided people with major life rituals, with their view of the cosmos, their ethical code, their community centre and their source of story and legend. It structured time, from the week to the year. And it served as a source of sacred power for the protection of life here and now – and preparation for the life to come.

The Catholic church appeared to have established a monopoly. No longer was it chiefly imposed from above; it also took root below – in all sections of society. It appeared to have defeated its competitors. Paganism had been largely suppressed. Arianism had died out centuries before with the gradual conversion of all the Germanic tribes to Catholi-cism. The eastern church had challenged its western counterpart in only a few disputed areas where their jurisdictions clashed (particularly in disputed mission territories). Yet the Catholic monopoly would have to be constantly defended. All monopolies require vigilance, and all monopolies tend to provoke rivalry. But, in the case of the Catholic monopoly, the situation was even more fragile. For, having identified its rule with the preservation of a godly, timeless unity, any threat to such unity at any level of church or society would pose a serious threat – not only to the Catholic monopoly, but to the ideology that sustained it. It would therefore be impossible to tolerate any form of dissent, disagreement or difference. Anything that did not fit the organic unity of Christendom would have to be ignored, assimilated or destroyed.

APOSTOLIC POVERTY

The imposition and maintenance of unity ('catholicity') would have been hard even in settled times; and the high Middle Ages was far from settled. We have already noted the papacy's constant battle to establish and maintain its sovereignty over increasingly assertive political leaders. But it was not only the political landscape that was shifting, for the socio-economic profile of the west was also undergoing significant change.

From the end of the twelfth century to the fourteenth society polarised into two main groups: the powerful (*potentes*) and the powerless (*pauperes*). A new dividing line emerged, setting the rich against the poor, the strong against the weak, the nobles against the common people. The former consisted not just of the old landowning class, but of those who had been climbing up the socio-economic ladder and now included not only wealthy merchants but 'clerks' – the literate, university educated, proto-professionals whose skills were in increasing demand. Despite significant variation within this ruling class, and enormous disparities of wealth, its members nevertheless consolidated themselves into a single, hereditary and legally privileged 'nobility' who distinguished themselves by universal adherence to the title, values and code of the knight. Their position was reinforced by new laws defending property and inheritance. And as the *potentes* consolidated their status, so the rest of the population found itself increasingly subjected to their control and treated as a single servile class. The status differences between those who worked the land in the early Middle Ages – including free men and serfs, small landowners and property-less vassals – tended to diminish as the nobles gathered more and more land and wealth to themselves.

Social change was thus bound up with economic transition. The productivity of the land had been steadily increasing with the use of more intensive methods of cultivation and new technologies such as the plough and the watermill. Those who could take advantage grew wealthy out of the surpluses that could now be produced, while those who did not were economically subjected. The population of the west more than doubled between the late tenth and mid-fourteenth centuries, growing from about 22 million to about 54 million. Towns grew rapidly. Some became powerful and self-sufficient enough to become self-governing. (In northern Italy, Flanders and the Rhineland, several cities underwent an expansion to the point where they began to attain the dimensions of a modern town.) Not only did towns become the sites of new trades producing new goods; they also created a system of markets, which exchanged the products of the countryside for those of long-distance commerce and urban manufacture. Merchants and moneylenders took advantage. Authority became more impersonal and distant, with the personal justice administered by local ruler or bishop being replaced by governing institutions of new force and effectiveness. Such institutions, whether civil or ecclesiastical, were staffed by the new cadre of permanent, educated officials, for in every sphere of life the demand for expert knowledge and a new form of rationality was becoming more urgent. Europe, in other words, was gradually being transformed from a society of gift exchange to a money economy – with profound results for its structure of values and social custom.

In many ways the church was integral to the changes. It began to develop its own bureaucracy; its authority became more centralised in Rome and more impersonal; its power grew through the development of international judicial functions; its clergy filled many of the new administrative posts, and their education and status ensured that they would be identified with the *potentes*, not the *pauperes*. By developing a system of fees, collections and ecclesiastical taxation (the tithe), the church also became the first great beneficiary of the transition to a money economy and managed to appropriate a significant proportion of the money in circulation. What is more, the church's official teaching served both to legitimate the interests of the powerful and to pacify the powerless by presenting the present order of things as the God-given order of things – thus masking the nature of the changes that were under way and so inhibiting protest against them.

So far as public perception and its own self-perception were concerned, however, the church must be seen to rise above the changes that were taking place. If it was to be the focus of social unity it could not afford to be identified too closely with any particular sector of society or any particular interest group. Its own preferred image of society was an organic unity composed of three 'orders': those who pray (*oratores*), those who fight (*bellatores*), and those who labour (*laboratores*). Though they existed in a God-given hierarchy of command, each order needed the other, and together they made up the body of Christendom. And, though it insisted that the duty of the poor was to submit to the rich and powerful, the church was also very clear about its duty to the needy. Without countenancing any form of social change or upheaval, it took very seriously the duty of charity. If the church were to be a focus of unity for the whole of society, it could not be seen to side with one segment against another.

But some Christians went further. They believed that the church was there not just to care for the poor, but to imitate them. If it was to be true to its calling – and to the Lord who had called it into being – it should be a church not just *for* the poor but *of* the poor. From the eleventh century onwards more and more women and men in Europe responded to the call of the *vita apostolica* – the apostolic life, modelled on the life of poverty and obedience of Jesus' first followers. A shift in morality occurred. *Avaritia*, the desire for money, began to rival *superbia*, pride, as the mother of all vices, while poverty-and-powerlessness came to be seen as the mark of the true Christian. (The spiritual ideal of *paupertas*, which animated the great reforms of the eleventh century, means not just poverty but powerlessness.) The shift became visible in the way in which the divine was depicted. Though God the Father remained a God of power, who was still often depicted as a king enthroned in heaven or as a hand pointing down from the heavens to the earth, there was also a shift of emphasis towards the depiction of God's gentleness, love and even powerlessness. This is most obvious in the rise of devotion to the human Christ rather than to the supernatural, and in more realistic depictions of both Christ and his mother Mary. For the first time Christ's suffering, weakness and death on the cross were depicted in moving detail. The figure of the monarch-Christ – Christ as king, Christ as judge, Christ as conqueror – remained, but alongside him a man of love, compassion and humility began to appear in the art and devotion of the west.

One of the first spheres to manifest a desire to return to an earlier, purer, simpler, more 'apostolic' way of life, and to disentangle the church from worldly concerns, was monasticism. A direct spur appears to have been a revival of the eremitical (hermit) tradition, which was still alive in the east and which influenced those who came into contact with Greek Basilian monks in Latium, Calabria and Sicily. From this contact came the first monastic reforms in Italy at the end of the tenth century and the beginning of the eleventh, which culminated in the creation of the new orders of Prémontré, Grandmont, Chartreuse and Cîteaux. The latter (the Cistercians), under the leadership of St Bernard of Clairvaux, was the most successful, particularly in northern Europe. Its aim was to foster a spirituality of simplicity, purity and poverty of life. Tellingly, the Cistercians ceased to receive children into the cloister, thus confirming a new view of the religious vocation as freely chosen by the individual. And, though they followed an austere rule, organised themselves with military precision, and used martial metaphors to describe their vocation (it was not an accident that the chief crusading orders adopted its *Rule*), Cistercians such as Bernard also introduced a deeply affective form of piety that stressed the intensity of the love that draws each believer out of love of self into selfless love of God. Like some later women mystics (see below), Bernard placed particular emphasis on the close and loving relationship between the soul (the bride) and Jesus Christ (the bridegroom).

By the twelfth century the monastic reforms had begun to stall. Even the reformed orders had grown wealthy and 'compromised'. They seemed set apart from the poor in society, part of an old order of society, not the new. A more innovative development was the rise of the Augustinian canons or canons regular. The Augustinians were a movement of clergy who gathered in small communities in towns and cities, held all things in common, followed a revised rule of St Augustine, and obeyed a superior. Yet even the Augustinians were unable to accommodate the spiritual needs of the growing numbers of lay men and women who wished to live lives of total dedication to God not in the cloister but in the world. Often on their own initiative, rather than as members of some wider movement or organisation, such people turned their back on existing social conventions and dedicated themselves wholly to a life of apostolic poverty. For a woman, this might mean rejecting marriage and pooling her resources with other like-minded women (for the cities opened up new opportunities for economic independence). For a man, it might mean embarking on a life of itinerancy. Instead of being settled

Plate 9   The Gero Crucifix, Cologne Cathedral (Germany)
   It was in the early medieval period that Christ began to be depicted as suffering and
dying on the cross; before then it was his triumph over death that was emphasised. This
innovative tenth-century crucifix from Cologne illustrates how Christian art and devotion –
to Christ's sacrifice, symbolised and repeated in the eucharist – could develop hand in
hand.

and taking a vow of 'stability' as western monasticism had required,
men now took to the road in order to spread the gospel just as Jesus'
disciples had done. Instead of securing themselves against the world in
strongholds of godly order, they remained within the world in order
to convert it, and instead of seeking riches and power they sought to

witness to the poverty and powerlessness that Christ had voluntarily embraced.

There is no doubt that the flowering of the apostolic ideal in the twelfth and thirteenth centuries was related to a number of changes both internal and external to the church. The growing disparity between the powerful and the powerless was clearly an important factor in this new 'witness' against the dangers of the world, and the movement may even be read as a protest against rapid social change – though the protestors tended to be from the higher classes rather than the lower, and to advocate charity, not social change. Disappointment at the failure of Gregorian ecclesiastical reform may have been a further factor; for those who had hoped for the emergence of a truly spiritual church cut free from the bonds of temporal power, Rome's growing wealth and power were major provocations. Above all, the rise of the apostolic ideal seems to signal a growing desire on the part of the laity for a more active, engaged, subjectivised form of spirituality – for religious experience at first hand. Liberated from feudal ties, increasingly mobile and literate, with new opportunities for independence, some of the most devout souls in the population made new demands on the church and ushered in a new style of piety. For these people it was no longer enough to have clergy and monks live out the religious life and receive the sacraments on one's behalf; the *homines novi* (new men and women) wanted to live holy lives for themselves.

The spirituality they pursued was something ancient as well as something new. Its most powerful backing came from the gospels themselves, from the teaching and example of Jesus and his first disciples: 'Be perfect as your holy Father is perfect'; 'Sell all you have and give to the poor'; 'Take no thought for the morrow'; 'Take nothing for the journey except a staff – no bread, no bag, no money in your belts'; and 'If you want to be perfect, go, sell your possessions and give to the poor, and you will have treasure in heaven. Then come, follow me.' Like reformed monasticism, the apostolic spirituality may have been inspired by the eremitical tradition of solitary, ascetic pursuit of holiness. It seems unlikely that the role of the hermit had ever died out completely in the west, and the 'holy man' or 'holy woman' had long been an important figure in local life. Activated by changed social circumstances, then, these fragments came together to inspire a new generation of spiritual enthusiasts.

Rome's attitude was cautious and ambivalent. It could hardly denounce the ascetic and apostolic ideals. But it was uncomfortable with any spiritual movement that was not under its direct control in the way that monasticism was. And the new spirituality carried at least an implicit criticism of the church. Against a centralised institution that was growing increasingly wealthy and powerful, partly through the expansion of its legal functions, the new spirituals set the example of the poverty and humility of Christ, his refusal to legislate ('Who made me a judge over you?'), and his single-minded devotion to the task of preaching. Like him, they sought to win men and women for God not by coercion but by persuasion. Like him, they went out to the poor rather than expecting the poor to come to them.

As in the fourth century, so in the thirteenth, the most successful strategy that the church adopted was to neutralise the potential threat by bringing it under its own authority. This was the policy developed by the astute Pope Innocent III (1198–1216). It was first put into practice in relation to Francis of Assisi (c. 1181–1226), an itinerant from central Italy, whose loyalty to 'holy mother church' led him to travel to Rome to seek papal approval for the new order of followers or 'friars' gathered around him (later called the Franciscans or Friars Minor). It was followed by Innocent's acceptance of another new 'order', that of the Dominicans under the leadership of Dominic (c. 1172–1221). The Dominicans, also called the Friars Preachers, were less radical than the Franciscans in their embrace of poverty, and were much more quickly clericalised. Given their twin aims of preaching the gospel and eradicating heresy, the Dominicans provided vital support in the task of defending the unity of Christendom – as the work of Aquinas shows.

The co-option of the Franciscans proved harder. Deeply committed to an ideal of radical poverty that made them critical of the growing wealth of their order, some of Francis's followers – the 'Spirituals', later the Fraticelli – became schismatics and won condemnation from the papacy for their efforts. Inspired by the apocalyptic prophecies of Joachim of Fiore (c. 1135–1202), they looked forward to a new era of the Spirit, where all men and women would be equals before God. Yet even the more moderate Franciscans could threaten the unity of Christendom. Their potential to do so was in some ways increased rather than diminished by the way in which their order developed a growing presence in

Plate 10   *St Francis Renounces All Worldly Goods*, by Giotto (c. 1266–1337), Assisi (Italy)
    Giotto conveys the scandalous nature of Francis's embrace of poverty through the reac-
tion of Francis's father (on the left), who has to be restrained from laying hands on his son.
Francis's 'true' fathers, a bishop of the church and God the Father (the hand of blessing
in the sky), protect him.

church circles and in the schools and universities of Europe, where many Franciscans became distinguished teachers. As we shall see below, the work of Franciscan scholastics such as Duns Scotus (c. 1265–1308) and William of Ockham (c. 1285–1347) would play a major role in destabilising the scholastic consensus.

ENEMIES OF CHRISTENDOM

For every itinerant preacher who became a friar, there were many more who remained independent of the church's control. And for every woman who joined a monastery in the high Middle Ages, there were more who wished to live a life of perfect holiness within the world. Such people proved hard for the church to control, and posed a serious threat to its authority. Even if their views were completely orthodox – as the majority seem to have been – their failure to submit to the existing structures of ecclesiastical life made them enemies of Christendom. Violence against the enemies of Christendom, which began in the eleventh century with the burning of heretics at Orléans but remained sporadic, became a growing feature in the life of Europe towards the middle decades of the twelfth century, and by the mid-thirteenth century it had been institutionalised in a comprehensive apparatus of persecution. Having begun chiefly at the initiative of secular rulers – with some courageous resistance from churchmen – the church, under papal leadership, had taken an increasingly active part in rooting out and punishing heresy. The crises of the fourteenth century, which included war, famine, economic depression, plague (the Black Death) and depopulation, only made the situation worse.

The church also played an active role in constructing its enemies. Heresy can arise only in the context of the assertion of (doctrinal) authority. That which did not fit into the existing model of Catholicism and could not be brought within Rome's control was represented as wholly 'other' – the mirror image of the true church and the true Christian. 'Heresy', Aquinas wrote, 'is a sin which merits not only excommunication but also death, for it is worse to corrupt the faith which is the life of the soul than to issue counterfeit coins which minister to the secular life. Since counterfeiters are justly killed by princes as enemies to the common good, so heretics also deserve the same punishment.'[7] The analogy with a forger of currency is instructive: the heretic passes off falsehood for truth. He might appear to be dealing in the same currency as the true

Christian, but the currency is counterfeit. As such, the heretic is an anti-Christian belonging to an anti-church and seduced by the Antichrist. The figures of Satan and the Antichrist, often merged into one, played a growing role in the medieval imagination. All who were against Christ must be for Christ's enemy. They were children of darkness, not of light, in league with the devil, guilty of despicable crimes (often sexual), and engaged in the attempt to set up an anti-church and undermine Christendom. Such crimes were attributed to all the enemies of Christendom: to Christian 'heretics', Jews, lepers, homosexuals.

By the thirteenth century the church was systematically hunting its enemies and subjecting them to trial, often with the help of the secular powers. The Fourth Lateran Council had made it the duty of bishops to identify and punish heretics, and had laid down a range of sanctions. But the papacy rapidly took more direct control of the process by setting up inquisitors (often Dominican friars) to act on its behalf, condoning the use of torture and authorising the secular authorities to execute those found guilty of heresy. Thus 'the Inquisition' was born, its finishing touches being supplied by Pope Innocent IV in the bull *Ad Extirpanda* (1252). Its activities spread rapidly throughout Europe. In some areas, such as Spain, the Inquisition quickly came under secular control; in others it remained an arm of the papacy. The Inquisition would descend suddenly on a town, deliver a sermon requesting information regarding any heretics in the area, and set up its court in order to try the accused. It played a major role in the construction of heresy, not least by extracting – sometimes under torture – confessions concerning trysts with the devil, nocturnal sabbaths and appalling crimes. In addition, the Inquisition made the classification of heresy into a science, drawing up great lists of heresies derived from the work of the church fathers (for heresy was seen as constant throughout history). Thus contemporary forms of Christianity that appeared to deviate from Catholic orthodoxy were assimilated to Arianism, Manicheism, gnosticism, and so on. The effect was generally to attribute to heresy far greater coherence, rigour and internal consistency than was really the case. Most medieval 'heretics' appear to have been individuals and intellectuals whose religious enthusiasm and exploration led them outside the bounds of customary tradition. Yet the task of the hunter of heresy was to show that they belonged to coherent movements with systematic theologies (anti-churches with anti-theologies). By this means disparate elements were converted into fragments of a larger picture – a monster by which their adversaries believed themselves to be threatened.

One of the largest and most unified of the heretical movements, which therefore became something of a model for the rest, was Catharism. The Cathars or Albigensians (from the town of Albi, which was a centre of the heresy) believed themselves to members of the true, pure church, as distinct from the existing church, which had betrayed the faith of the apostles. Their leaders practised ascetic austerity, and a distinction was drawn between the 'Perfect' – followers who had renounced the world and lived in strict poverty – and the ordinary 'Believers', who did not. By 1200 the heresy had spread widely in southern France and parts of Italy, particularly in the region of Languedoc, which was not yet part of France. Catharism appears to have won widespread support, winning the allegiance of merchants, nobles and peasants alike, and thus having access to military and economic power. In answer to an appeal from Pope Innocent III in 1209 the barons of the north of France marched southwards in a crusade against the Cathars, and eventually succeeded in annexing the territory of Languedoc. In the period 1231–3 an inquisition was established to root out what remained of the heresy by unrelenting persecution. Catharism was largely destroyed by the early fourteenth century.

The way in which ecclesiastical and secular rulers' construction of heresy could actually bring a coherent heretical movement into being where none had previously existed is shown clearly by Waldensianism. Peter Waldo (or Valdes), a successful merchant in Lyons, was a contemporary and northern European counterpart of St Francis. In about 1175 he gave away all his worldly goods and pursued an apostolic life of poverty and preaching. Followers rallied to him, and his ideal of lay people living in simple poverty met with approval at the Third Lateran Council (1179). The proviso, however, was that they must obtain the permission and supervision of the church authorities before preaching. When they failed to do so, they were condemned by the archbishop of Lyons and excommunicated by Pope Lucius III in 1184, who also decreed that they be punished by the Inquisition. The Waldensians fled, gradually organising themselves into an alternative 'true' church that denied the authority of the Catholic clergy and sacraments and allowed men (and probably women) to preach from the scriptures in the vernacular. They gradually spread throughout much of Europe, but were strongest in central and eastern Europe. Despite inquisition and crusade against them they survived, and small numbers still exist in the Piedmont region of Italy today.

Perhaps the least directly threatening of all the so-called heretics were the Beghards and Beguines (male and female members of the same 'movement'). Far from being a unified, large-scale movement, these were groups of men and women who gathered together in the same neighbour-hood of a city and attempted to live lives of semi-monastic purity within the world. On the whole they appear to have been loyal to the church and its sacraments, and many won significant clerical support. Despite this they were subjected to a growing level of persecution after the thirteenth century. (For more on the Beguines and their persecution see below.) By the fourteenth century the Beghards and Beguines were sometimes assim-ilated to another heretical 'movement', the Brethren of the Free Spirit. The charges made against both groups were often the same: that they believed in the possibility of human perfection (deification/autotheism), and that they were antinomian, since they held that the perfected person has no heed of moral rules. Some distinguished and highly educated writ-ers who displayed the same 'mystical' or 'gnostic' tendencies – particu-larly in the golden age of mysticism in the fourteenth century – hovered on the edge of heresy and condemnation. Propositions from the writ-ings of the Dominican mystic Meister Eckhart (1260–1328), for example, were condemned after his death. Others were not so lucky. Marguerite Porete, for example, the author of *Mirror of Simple Souls*, was burnt in 1310. From the writings that survive, it seems apparent that charges of gnosticism or even of deification, in the sense that a Greek theolo-gian such as Simeon the New Theologian might have meant it, were often unfounded. While it may be true that many 'heretics' pursued an active experience of God with ardour and enthusiasm, and while some were rewarded with an experience of mystic union with Christ, such 'subjectivism' was often highly ascetic – humans came into the pres-ence of God not by virtue of their own abilities and endowments but by renouncing their selves by way of severe austerity and discipline. Very often the reception of the church's sacrament, particularly the eucharist, was an integral part of such spirituality. For this reason it seems more appropriate to speak of a mysticism of negative subjectivism rather than of positive – God made known not *in* the self but through the destruction of self; union with God achieved by grace, not by nature.

The treatment of Jews, who by this time constituted a sizeable and widely spread population within the borders of Christendom, was both similar to and different from that of heretics. What was similar was that they too were treated as an anti-church, and they too were suspected of conspiracy and a plot to take over the world (a mirror image of the church's own universalist tendencies). Despite sporadic violence such as the massacre that took place in the Rhineland in 1096 during the First Crusade, developing ecclesiastical law suggested that the Jews were to be handled not through destruction but through containment. Like lepers, they were to be segregated and marked out rather than destroyed. The Fourth Lateran Council forced them to wear a distinctive badge. Their 'sin of unbelief' made them, in Aquinas' words, 'subject to perpetual servitude . . . their goods are at the disposal of the ruler; only he must not take from them so much that they are deprived of the means of life'.[8] But special protection easily turned into special abuse. There were sporadic persecutions and mass expulsions, first from England, then from France and eventually from Spain. Despite such persecutions, a sizeable Jewish population survived in Europe throughout the medieval period: many Italian states did not expel the Jews, they remained in parts of Germany, and the largest population became concentrated in Poland. It was not until the Reformation era that the church instituted and encouraged the ghetto.

The outbreak of persecution after the eleventh century requires an explanation, not least because persecution had not been a feature of life in the west for many centuries. The drive for unity and uniformity under centralised Catholic control was clearly one factor. The growing power of the church, and its increased control over certain means of coercion, were others. In some cases the church was able to persuade secular leaders to do its bidding in this matter, or was able to stir up popular sentiment. The ethos of the Crusades must also have played its part. But the most important factor of all may be that all those who attracted persecution posed not just an imaginary but also a genuine material threat to some particular interest group in society whose position was both powerful and fragile. In the case of the Jews, it was the clerks (the new literate class) who were threatened – for the Jews were not only better educated than most Christians, but also the most natural candidates to occupy the roles that the *literati* wanted for themselves. And in the case of the heretics, it was the power of the clergy and of Rome that was threatened – for anyone who claimed the power to preach was claiming a share of their sacred power. Worse than that, however, the embrace of poverty and the criticism of power from on high, which were such common features of medieval heresy, threatened not only the church's wealth and position, but that of the growing class of the rich and powerful in society. However irrational charges of diabolic trysts and nocturnal sabbaths might seem, persecution often had a basis in rational self-interest.

Late scholasticism: theologies of ecclesiastical power and powerlessness

Challenges to the reigning mode of Catholic power from on high, as well as reinforcements of it, also came from the ranks of intellectuals and academics, particularly after the thirteenth century. A range of intellectual influences fed late medieval theology and philosophy, including intense meditation on the work of Augustine, access to a growing range of classical texts in Latin translation (including the work of some of the Greek fathers), and the outworking of the Franciscan ideal of apostolic poverty. Most theology still took place in the scholastic mode – hence the term 'late scholasticism' – but it questioned aspects of the Thomistic synthesis. Only Renaissance thinkers departed significantly (though not entirely) from the scholastic method (see ch. 4).

The most important of the late scholastics, including Duns Scotus and William of Ockham, are often remembered for their intensified doctrine of divine power. In relation to the doctrine of God, one of their chief theological preoccupations was with an insistence upon the totally unconstrained nature of the divine will. This will, they argued, was completely free and unlimited, even by the moral law. God could do whatever God willed, and whatever God willed was good. As Duns Scotus put it, 'the will of God is the norm and the ground of justice'. Thus they took issue in general with Aquinas' belief that God's will was bound by reason and goodness, and in particular with his statement that 'given the things which actually exist, the universe cannot be better'. One of the consequences of this extreme theological voluntarism was an emphasis on the doctrine of predestination – that God has willed the salvation of some and the damnation of others. This emphasis was deepened in the work of Thomas Bradwardine (c. 1290–1349) and Gregory of Rimini (c. 1300–1358), both of whom defended a doctrine of double predestination according to which God foreordained the election of some to salvation and of others to damnation. All of these late scholastics, the latter two in particular, were strongly influenced by Augustine's thought, and keen to defend his doctrine of grace against what they regarded as the neo-Pelagian tendency of the times.

The main preoccupation of the late scholastics, however, as indeed of all fourteenth- and fifteenth-century theology, was not with the doctrine of God or even of salvation, but with the doctrine of the church (ecclesiology), a topic that had been almost completely neglected by earlier scholasticism (though not by the lawyers). This interest was stimulated by one or more of the three schisms of the time: the papal schism, the east–west schism and the Hussite schism (see below). It was also a response to the assertion of papal power that has been reviewed above, and to the challenges to this power represented in different ways by the Franciscan tradition and the conciliar movement. Far from concerning itself solely with the nature and constitution of the church, this work spilled out to consider the proper nature of state–church relations and, as such, formed a starting point for early modern political theory.

As is clear from the work of Ockham, the greatest political theologian of all the late scholastics, the defence of divine power could lead not to a defence of unconstrained papal power but, on the contrary, to a sense of the limitations of that power. Under the influence of the Franciscan movement to which he belonged, Ockham understood the chief function of the church and the papacy to be that of teaching and preaching, rather than the administration of law and justice. He also believed that the Franciscan ideal of poverty and powerlessness should extend to both the church and the world, to both the clergy and the laity. He took issue with Pope John XXII's condemnation of the Franciscan ideal of extreme poverty. But his most subversive contribution of all was to deny to the papacy or even to the clergy the prerogative of teaching and jurisdiction within the church and Christendom.

Ockham attributes the ability to discern true doctrine and oppose heresy as given to all parts of the church, lay as well as clerical, and he attributes a special though not exclusive authority to theologians as well as to general councils. At the same time, he distances himself from the more enthusiastic conciliarists, who had wrenched infallibility from the pope only to attach it to a general council. For the cautious Ockham, truth and authority cannot be located with such certainty.

Checks and balances are always needed, in church, in state, and in the relation between the two. In his political theology, Ockham therefore envisages, not church control of the state or state control of the church, but an equality between the two that will make possible mutual correction and service. Ockham therefore defends both papal and imperial or kingly rule, but qualifies both by holding them responsible not only to each other but also to those they rule (or serve) and, above all, to 'the evangelical law'.

Ockham's ecclesio-political stance was rooted not in a belief in the goodness or reasonableness of human beings but, on the contrary, in an Augustinian insistence on human sinfulness and fallibility. It was because of this fallibility that the higher divine law is more likely to be faithfully interpreted by the whole body of the church than by a small number. Yet there are also glimpses of a more positive principle at work, for Ockham also invokes the natural freedoms of humankind established by God, including a freedom from coercion, whether secular or ecclesiastical. Invoking a favourite text on the gospel law as the law of freedom (Jas. 1.25), Ockham argues that this includes not merely freedom from slavery to sin and the Mosaic law, but from every external form of servitude that lacks rational justification.

Working partly within the Augustinian tradition established by his predecessors in Oxford, including Scotus and Ockham, John Wyclif (c. 1330–84) also defended a Franciscan ideal of Christian powerlessness and dispossession against that of a plenitude of power. Working in an English context and in support of the English monarchy, Wyclif concluded that the secular monarch rather than the pope should have a monopoly of coercive power – as a remedy against sin, as Augustine had thought – and that such power should extend even over church affairs. In Wyclif's view the secular ruler should thus take over the ownership of clerical property, in order to keep the church 'pure'. Wyclif, in other words, went a long way towards envisaging a national church, and his efforts in this direction were strengthened by his support for the project of translating the Bible from Latin into the emerging national languages of Europe.

In his later writings Wyclif sought to put ecclesiastical life on an alternative footing to the papal and canonical one that had developed since the eleventh century. His alternative authority was both Christological and scriptural, as laid out in *The Truth of Holy Scripture* (1378). This argued for the Bible's inerrancy and sufficiency, as well as for its direct accessibility to all Christians. The dangerous freedom this might allow the individual in interpreting God's will was, however, tempered by an insistence on the public authority of the monarch and and of ecclesiastical councils convened by him in matters of interpretation. Despite condemnation from the English bishops and from Rome, Wyclif enjoyed the protection of his king and university, and escaped persecution. His influence lived on in the following he attracted not only in England (the Lollards), but in Bohemia, where his disciple Jan Hus (c. 1372–1415) led the 'Hussite' movement. Both Wyclif and Hus were condemned at the Council of Constance in 1415; Wyclif's condemnation was posthumous, but Hus suffered death at the stake.

Yet the most serious challenge to papal and ecclesiastical power – in terms of content if not of influence – was posed not by the late scholastics but by the early Renaissance thinker Marsilius of Padua (c. 1275– c. 1342). Marsilius' radicalism was made possible not only by his close reading of Aristotle and his political ideas, but by his location in Padua, one of the prosperous, self-sufficient and self-governed city-states of Italy. In *Defensor Pacis* ('Defender of the Peace', 1324), Marsilius proposed an earthly society that would be completely free of papal and clerical control. Indeed, it would be free of any form of monarchial rule. Marsilius' revolutionary proposal was that the city would be governed not from on high but by the people themselves, or at least 'the weightier part thereof, which represents the whole body'.[9] (As in classical republicanism, women would be excluded.) The advantage, he believed, was that better laws would be framed thereby – laws that achieved the ultimate political aim of 'living well' by serving the interest of all rather than the interest of a minority. While it might be necessary to have a single ruler for practical reasons, the ruler would be subservient to the people rather than vice versa. Above all, there would be no clerical control, since the papal claim to plenitude of power was, in Marsilius' view, the chief cause of political instability in his day.

More Aristotelian than Augustinian, Marsilius' republican vision was undergirded by a positive, though not unrealistic, view of human nature: 'Most of the citizens are neither vicious nor undiscerning most of the time; all or most of them are of sound mind and reason and have a right desire for the polity and for the things necessary for it to endure.'[10] From the different starting point flowed a different conclusion: since human beings were not mired in sin, they did not need to be passive recipients of a law from above mediated by the clergy. Instead, they could frame their own legislation in their own interests. For Marsilius this did not make the church redundant; it merely meant that it should confine its work to spiritual matters rather than to worldly. Influenced by the Franciscan programme, Marsilius insisted that when Jesus said, 'My kingdom is not of this world', he meant, 'I have not come to reign by temporal rule or dominion, in the way in which worldly kings rule.'[11] Far from seeking a plenitude of earthly power and wealth, Jesus renounced both. Likewise, he refused to be a judge over men. And in refusing 'rulership or coercive judgement in this world', Christ set an example that all the clergy should follow.[12] In Marsilius' view, the role of the clergy was to preach, not to legislate. In this world the 'evangelical law' of the church could and should shape men's actions, but it was only in the next world that they would be punished for not obeying it.

What Marsilius envisaged, in other words, was a 'spiritual church' whose programme could never be translated into a worldly society. In so doing, he undermined the entire vision of Christendom, and did so in the name of the gospel as well as in the name of Aristotle. That which Aquinas had tried to unite – the natural and the supernatural, the classical and the Christian – Marsilius separated with crystalline clarity. As if this was not enough to bring down papal condemnation on his head, he also branded Pope John XXII (1316–34) a heretic for his denial of Franciscan poverty, and insisted not only that the church should own no property, but that the only head of the church was Christ. In Marsilius' view, the church should be run by a general council, which would be assembled in times of need by an earthly ruler. Bishops, including the bishop of Rome, would be subject to the authority of the council. *Defensor Pacis* was anathematised by John in 1327 and placed on the *Index* of prohibited books in 1559. Forced to flee the University of Paris, Marsilius spent the rest of his life in exile in the Bavarian court, along with other supporters of the Franciscan programme including the minister general of the order and William of Ockham. They were later defeated by Pope John in their attempt to install a Spiritual Franciscan as anti-pope.

The feminisation of piety

The period with which this chapter deals had not started well for women. By concentrating power in the hands of the clergy and the papacy, the reforms of Gregory VII had concentrated it in the hands of men. One of the most obvious symptoms was the declining status of women's religious orders and of the women (abbesses) who led them. Such institutions had played a key role in the earlier Middle Ages, not only as centres of learning and order within an unstable world, but as social spaces in which women could escape their otherwise inescapable destiny as wives and mothers and pursue a life of sisterly piety. The many tales of the dramatic escapades of medieval girls who defy their families and evade their potential suitors – in one case by hiding, suspended by her fingertips, from the canopy of the four-poster bed in which she was to be seduced – testify to the way in which early medieval society tolerated this significant threat to its customary sexual order. After Gregory, however, the power of the convents was much curtailed, not only by banning 'double monasteries' but by bringing all convents under stricter clerical supervision. A new emphasis upon the importance of liturgy and intercessory masses within the monastic life made nuns increasingly dependent on the services of ordained clergy. Measures were also taken to ensure that women religious were more strictly enclosed within the walls of their convents ('claustrated'), with opportunities for contact with the outside world being reduced to a minimum. In the great period of monastic foundation from the early tenth century to the early twelfth, the fortunes of women in the monastic life suffered a sharp decline.

If we take the number of women who were canonised (recognised as saints) in the medieval period as an index of their changing status within the church, we see a significant decline between the early Middle Ages and the Gregorian period. The progressive centralisation and clericalisation of the church had involved taking control of the process of canonisation, which was now based not so much on popular acclaim but on a formal process administered from Rome. While the new process did not exclude the recognition of women saints, the wider reforms of which it was part seem simply to have left women with no public role within Christendom. Equally, the power of women was being diminished by the slow shift from a feudal, aristocratic society to a more mobile, urbanised, money-based one. Until this time the social power of women had rested largely upon land, which they were able to possess in their own right before they were married and after they were widowed, and which they would generally administer and control even when married, due to the frequent absence of husbands engaged in military campaigns.

Inheritance at this time was bilineal rather than patrilineal, with property passing down both female and male lines of descent, and it was not uncommon for dowries to be given with bridegrooms rather than with brides. In early medieval society, then, the figure of the powerful woman with an important public role was relatively common, within both the monasteries and the great houses of the time. Both the 'lady' and the abbess might be powerful landowners and employers in their own right, and there were often important social and economic ties between monasteries and the landowning dynasties that endowed them not only with wealth but with daughters and sons. By curbing the power of secular rulers within church affairs, the Gregorian reforms also curbed the power of women.

In the later Middle Ages, however, women began to regain a more central position within Christendom. The number of women canonised between 1151 and 1347 rose significantly. Though the evidence is patchy, there seem to have been a number of reasons for this. One of the most important was that attempts to control and limit the influence of women's monasticism had simply failed. The revival of monasticism that began at the end of the eleventh century appears to have inspired women as much as men. When the new order of the Cistercians was instituted, its founders had had no intention of including women in their austere monasteries. Indeed, given the aggressive, colonising, martial nature of Cistercian organisation, symbolism and rhetoric, this seemed like a supremely male order in both its theory and its practice. Yet almost as soon as the order began to expand, nunneries following Cistercian customs began to spring up all over Europe. The fact that they had no formal place in the structure of the order, and were largely ignored in its official legislation, merely gave them greater autonomy of development. Once the order did start to take notice, its concern was to bring the women under its discipline and curb their power. From 1213 the ruling body of the Cistercian order tried to enforce strict enclosure upon nuns, to commit them to the control of an abbot, to have them make regular confession only to authorised confessors, and to ensure that no more nunneries were attached to the order. They failed. By the end of the thirteenth century the number of Cistercian nunneries outnumbered the foundations for Cistercian monks in many parts of Europe.

In many ways the upsurge of female monasticism in the central Middle Ages represented a revival of the spiritual power of aristocratic ladies, which had waned with the demise of the double monasteries of the early Middle Ages. By and large the new nunneries were populated by women of high social standing, with the more humble sisters performing menial tasks. But it is to these nunneries of the later Middle Ages that we owe the remarkable fact that, for the first time in Christian history, we begin to hear women's voices. Previously we have heard only the voices of men. Now, for the first time, we have women's words. In some cases these words were written down by male scribes. In others, women themselves mastered the written word. Though women were unable to enter the schools or universities, a few nunneries allowed a small number of them to attain a level of literacy that enabled them to contribute directly to Christian literature and theology for the first time. In the thirteenth century the German convent of Hefta, for example, became famous for the accomplishments of its nuns, who wrote learned scientific and theological treatises in Latin. In the fourteenth and fifteenth centuries a few educated nuns, of whom Catherine of Siena (1347–80) was the most notable, even managed to win for themselves a significant role in the public life of the church, intervening in public issues and winning the ear not only of leading clerics but, in Catherine's case, of the pope himself.

The threat posed by the growing power and prominence of women in the later Middle Ages may be one reason for the proliferation at this time of male-authored literature listing the follies and wickednesses of women. Outright misogyny had been characteristic of some Christian theology at least since patristic times, with Tertullian castigating woman as 'the devil's gateway' through whom sin comes into the world, and Jerome making violent and prurient attacks on sexually active women. In Chaucer's *Canterbury Tales* we hear that the Wife of Bath's fifth husband possesses a collection of such outbursts, a book of 'wikked women', which he insists on reading aloud to her at bedtime. ('By God,' she protests, 'if women had written stories as clergy have within their oratories, they would have written of men more wickedness than all the mark of Adam may redress.'[13])

By the time clerical and monastic authorities had managed to get some sort of grip over women's religious orders and the powerful women within them, however, a new movement had arisen within a quite different social environment. It involved not the women of the aristocracy, but independent women in the new towns and cities. Just as the rise of a new wave of female monasticism had been linked to the rise of the Cistercian order, so the rise of the new forms of feminine piety that are often labelled 'Beguine' may have been linked to the rise of the mendicant orders. Both represented a reaction against the elaborate structures of government that had come to characterise much monastic and clerical life. In place of formalism they exalted poverty, simplicity of life, individual self-dedication, total dependence upon God, and flexible and unencumbered service of the poorest in society. In both their male and female manifestations they were often characterised by an affective piety focused upon the suffering love of Jesus Christ.

Where the friars and the Beguines differed, however, was in their manner of life and their relation to the established church. Though women such as Clare (1194–1253; founder of the Poor Clares) had been closely involved with Francis in the early days of the order he founded, they quickly found themselves relegated to the 'tertiary' or 'third' orders of the Franciscans and Dominicans. These orders were for lay people who supported the friars and wished to imitate their piety within the everyday world of work and domesticity. It would be considered dangerous and improper for single women to travel alone and unsupervised by men, let alone to preach in public. While the friars undertook their work as the new shock troops of Europe with full papal blessing, the laywomen, inspired by the same impulse to dedicate their lives wholeheartedly to Christ, were therefore forging new ways of doing so within the busy towns and cities of the later Middle Ages, particularly in the more urbanised parts of northern Europe. The title 'Beguine' probably disguises enormous diversity, since we are not dealing with an organised or centralised movement like that of the friars. This feminised form of piety took its rise from the actions and desires of individuals rather than from any overarching structure, and it took the form of loose alliances of like-minded women united by common devotion. There is little evidence that such women were hostile to the church, and their piety, which often focused upon the reception of Christ's body in the eucharist, involved attendance at the masses celebrated in their local churches. In several cases we know of local clergy who admired the Beguines and performed such services as hearing confessions and acting as scribes.

Over time, however, the Beguines began to arouse the hostility of the official church, not least because they could not be neatly fitted into any existing structures or categories. Most practised celibacy, though some were married. They took vows, but belonged to no order. Uniquely, they did not beg or live on alms, but supported themselves through their own labour, taking advantage of the new economic opportunities that had opened up in the towns. And they were under no control save that of Christ himself. As the English chronicler Matthew Paris noted in 1243,

> At this time and especially in Germany, certain people – men and women, but especially women – have adopted a religious profession, though it is a light one. They call themselves 'religious', and they take a private vow of continence and simplicity of life, though they do not follow the rule of any saint, nor are they as yet confined within a cloister. They have so multiplied within a short time that two thousand have been reported in Cologne and the neighbouring cities.[14]

Though the name 'Beguine', perhaps derived from 'Albigensian', was invented as a slur, it was hard to make heresy charges stick, for the Beguines did not seem to dissent from theological orthodoxy in any notable way. Their numbers continued to grow. To remain with the example of Cologne, by 1400 there were 169 Beguine homes or convents in the city, and numbers seem to have held steady into the sixteenth century, despite growing ecclesiastical opposition from the late thirteenth century. In 1312 the Beguines as a whole were condemned at the Council of Vienne. In 1318 the archbishop of Cologne required the dissolution of all Beguine associations and their integration into existing orders approved by the pope. The survival of the Beguines in Cologne and elsewhere suggests that such decrees were easier to promulgate than to enforce. There are records of Beguines living in Cologne as late as the eighteenth century, though their numbers had been drastically reduced.

It is to nuns, Beguines and a host of unnamed laywomen that we owe the feminisation of the piety of the later Middle Ages. So far-reaching were its effects that its traces remain in liturgy, art and sculpture, in place names, street names and church names, and in literature of various genres authored by women and men. Until recently medieval women's spiritual writings have tended to be lumped together under the heading of 'mysticism'. While this description can be used to simplify and dismiss, it nevertheless contains some insight. Since women continued to be excluded from theological learning, teaching and debate, none would ever be able to claim the theological, intellectual or clerical authority that was reserved for men alone. The only possible basis on which they could claim the authority to be heard or read was that of spiritual experience, particularly the supernatural experience of dreams, visions, 'showings' or 'hearings'. Men had long believed women less rational than men, and by excluding them from higher education they proved them so. In mysticism women overcame the slur by reminding their hearers that God could speak to the weak and foolish – as they so often characterised themselves – as well as to the wise and learned.

We overhear this modesty and hesitation to speak out in the earliest women's writings. Thus the Beguine who later became a Cistercian, Mechthild of Magdeburg (c. 1207–82), reveals her fear of being condemned and justifies herself in two main ways: first by claiming that her feminine weakness makes her suitable for bearing God's revelations ('For the flood of the Holy Spirit by its very nature flows towards the valley'), and secondly by having God directly sanction her work. Partly because of this different theological as well as sociological basis, much feminised piety was characterised by a focus upon the individual soul in relation to God, and thus by 'interiority'. It also tended to be highly emotional and affective rather than coolly contemplative. Above all, it placed a new emphasis upon intense devotion to the figure of Christ, both as a helpless infant and as the suffering lover of the human soul. It was not only women who developed such piety. Despite their more masculine and martial virtues, especially in public life, the devotional life of Cistercians, for example, was often characterised by an intense love of the human Christ. Yet it is in women's writings that we find some of the most intense and erotic accounts of the soul's relations with Christ. In *The Flowing Light of the Godhead*, for example, Mechthild cries out to Jesus:

> Lord, now I am a naked soul
> And you in yourself are a well-adorned God.
> Our shared lot is eternal life without death.
>
> Then a blessed stillness
> That both desire comes over them.
> He surrenders himself to her,
> And she surrenders herself to him.
> What happens to her then – she knows.[15]

The sexual and bodily imagery used to describe the soul's relation to Jesus stands in contrast to the hostile attitude to the body that some late medieval women displayed in their earthly lives. In the same work quoted above, for example, Mechthild can both affirm that her body was a beast of burden bridled with worthlessness, and insist that she would rather be an embodied woman than a disembodied angel, since only so can she 'entwine her limbs' with God. A similar paradox attends late medieval women's increasing devotion to the sacrament of the eucharist. Whereas male piety tended to focus around the consecration of the host and the gazing upon it, female piety was more interested in its physical reception. The taking into the mouth and body of the body of Christ appears as a frequent theme in women's personal and literary devotion, as does their growing demand for frequent, even daily, communion. Much reflection also focused upon the shedding of Christ's blood. Yet again an earthy, corporeal, sexual emphasis is evident in women's piety, in marked contrast to the extremes of bodily mortification and the embrace of suffering that typified many devout women's earthly lives. The disciplining of the body not only through abstinence from sex, but also by control of the appetite for food, seems to have been common. Catherine of Siena, for example, sought to discipline her body to the point where she could live on the eucharistic host alone.

Given that the Catholic tradition had long insisted that women were more enslaved to the body and its desires than men, it may well be that we find in these medieval women's piety a correspondingly greater urge to destroy their feminine bodies in order to release their soul and spirit for communion with God. Yet not all these women were trying to destroy their sexed flesh in order to release a sexless soul for contemplation of a sexless God, as had been the ideal of some earlier Christian asceticism. On the contrary, the most original contribution to Christian thought is made by those women who experiment with new forms of gender imagery which identify God neither as male nor above sex (the only two options that theologians had previously contemplated), but as both female and male. Similarly fluid use of gender imagery characterises their thought about the soul. Mechthild, for example, characterises God and Jesus not only as bridegroom but as 'Lady Love', the divine lady who was the focus of a knight's aspirations in the medieval literature of courtly love, and the soul as not only bride but as 'Mistress and Queen'.

Even more original was the theological contribution of Julian of Norwich (c. 1342–after 1416). Julian made use of a scribe to record the visions that had been vouchsafed to her by God during a time of intense suffering. The originality of the resulting work, the *Revelations of Divine Love*, lies in the interpretations Julian offers of her visions. Although her theology is in many ways entirely orthodox in its presentation of God as Trinity, it offers a profoundly original interpretation of the trinitarian life of God that applies female language and imagery to both God the Father and God the Son:

> Our life is threefold [as is the Trinity]. In the first stage we have our being, in the second our growth, and in the third our perfection . . . For the first I realised that the great power of the Trinity is our father, the deep wisdom our mother, and the great love our lord . . . Moreover I saw that the Second Person, who is our mother with regard to our essential nature, that same dear person has become our mother in the matter of our sensual nature . . . In our mother, Christ, we grow and develop; in his mercy he reforms and restores us . . . and our separate parts are integrated into the perfect man. In yielding to the gracious impulse of the Holy Spirit we are made perfect . . . Our essential nature is entire in each person of the Trinity, who is one God.[16]

Not only does Julian refer to God the Father and to Christ as mother; she downplays the masculine characteristics of God in favour of love, suffering, weakness and compassion; identifies human and divine power with love rather than with domination; denies that there is any aspect of wrath or anger in God; and speaks of universal forgiveness and salvation.

Before Julian, no Christian writer – with the possible exception of some early gnostics – had ever sacralised the feminine so explicitly. Julian's achievement was to offer a fresh way of thinking about God that, for the first time, brought the divine fully into relation with the female and, in doing so, questioned an identification of God with almighty, male, power from on high. While many male writers had already qualified God's almighty goodness by talk of his mercy and benevolence and even of his 'motherly' qualities, they had never done so in a way that did more than qualify his almightiness. Julian went further, just as the Beguines had done in their reordering of the Christian life. Her obscurity and her classification as a mystic rather than as a theologian may have prevented her ideas from being taken seriously enough to be investigated or condemned.

A final area in which feminisation has been detected in the later Middle Ages is in a flourishing devotion to female saints, including Mary

Plate 11 *Annunciation*, by Antoniazzo Romano (c. 1430–1512)

Depictions of Mary and the female saints were common in medieval times, and the Annunciation (in which an angel declared to Mary that she would bear the Son of God) was a popular subject. In this version by Romano, God the Father watches over the scene from above.

the mother of Jesus. Devotion to Mary took many forms. In the earliest Christianity and in the east, Mary had often been depicted as a powerful goddess, the 'Queen of Heaven'. The affirmation at the Councils of Ephesus (431) and Chalcedon (451) that she was *theotokos*, bearer of God, gave formal recognition to her unique status. Even as a heavenly figure, however, her love and care for humanity were revealed in images such as her sheltering men and women within her cloak. Emphasis upon Mary's tender and motherly love grew in the Middle Ages along with the new devotion to the humanity of her son and his sufferings. The *Pietà*, in which Mary cradles the dead Christ on her lap, became a popular image. Interestingly, however, this particular form of piety appears more in male writings, such as those of Bernard of Clairvaux, than in female ones. Judging by the number of dedications of children, churches and places to Mary in the Middle Ages, however, Marian devotion must have been widespread and popular with both sexes, and her cult seems to have spanned every section of society. Great pilgrimages to the Virgin's shrines at Chartres, Rocamadour, Mont Saint-Michel, Laon, Soissons, Ipswich, Walsingham, and many more, criss-crossed the countries of Europe, while most great churches provided themselves with Lady Chapels. Equally significant was devotion to a plethora of female saints, some of whom, such as Mary Magdalene and St Anne the mother of Mary, attained a peak of popularity in the later Middle Ages. As well as their regular depiction in visual forms, rich and detailed stories and legends grew up around these women. The feminine had never been more visible in Christianity.

Further reading
MEDIEVAL CHURCH AND CIVILISATION
There are many helpful introductions to the medieval church. R. W. Southern's *Western Society and the Church in the Middle Ages* (Harmondsworth: Penguin, 1970) still offers an elegant, informative and incisive introductory survey.

On the centralisation of the western church and the growth of papal power, see W. Ullmann, *The Growth of Papal Government in the Middle Ages: A Study in the Ideological Relation of Clerical to Lay Power* (London: Methuen, 1955), and *A Short History of the Papacy in the Middle Ages* (London: Methuen, 1972). See also Colin Morris, *The Papal Monarchy: The Western Church from 1050 to 1250* (Oxford: Clarendon; New York: Oxford University Press, 1989).

Jacques Le Goff's *Medieval Civilization 400–1500* (Oxford and New York: Blackwell, 1988) offers an engaging survey of medieval history, culture and society from the fifth to the fifteenth centuries.

THEOLOGY

R. W. Southern's trilogy on *Scholastic Humanism and the Unification of Europe* (Oxford and Malden, WV: Blackwell, 1995, 2000, 2003) provides an unparalleled account of medieval scholastic theology, not only analysing its achievement, but setting it in social and historical context. Jaroslav Pelikan's *The Growth of Medieval Theology (600–1300)* (Chicago and London: University of Chicago Press, 1978) offers a clear survey.

Oliver O'Donovan and Joan Lockwood O'Donovan have provided a valuable collection of primary theological texts in *From Irenaeus to Grotius: A Sourcebook in Christian Political Thought* (Grand Rapids, MI, and Cambridge: Eerdmans, 1999). Though it focuses upon political theology, the anthology can also be used as an introduction to the thought of many of the most important theologians of the medieval period.

PIETY

Eileen Power's book on *Medieval Women* (Cambridge and New York: Cambridge University Press, 1975) still offers an elegant short introduction to the topic. Caroline Walker Bynum's books have been influential in helping unlock forgotten aspects of medieval Christian life and piety, particularly in relation to women. A good place to start is with her collection of essays, *Fragmentation and Redemption: Essays on Gender and the Human Body in Medieval Religion* (New York: Zone, 1991). See also her *Jesus as Mother: Studies in the Spirituality of the High Middle Ages* (Berkeley, CA: University of California Press, 1982); and Donald Weinstein and Rudolph Bell, *Saints and Society: The Two Worlds of Western Christendom, 1000–1700* (Berkeley, CA: University of Chicago Press, 1982). Rudoph M. Bell's *Holy Anorexia* (Chicago, IL: University of Chicago Press, 1985) deals with women's spiritual practices centred around food and self-denial. On the medieval spiritual tradition see Bernard McGinn and John Meyendorff (eds.), *Christian Spirituality: Origins to the Twelfth Century* (London: SCM, 1985).

DISSENT

The literature on dissent falls into two broad categories: first, studies such as Emmanuel Le Roy Ladurie's *Montaillou* (London: Scolar, 1978) or Robert E. Lerner's *The Heresy of the Free Spirit in the Later Middle Ages* (Berkeley, CA: University of California Press, 1972) focus upon the nature of heresy (in the former case Catharism in Languedoc); second, studies such as R. I. Moore's *The Formation of a Persecuting Society: Power and*

Deviance in Western Europe, 950–1250 (Oxford and New York: Black-well, 1987) focus on its repression. Both approaches are brought together in the useful collection of essays edited by Scott L. Waugh and Peter D. Diehl, *Christendom and its Discontents* (Cambridge and New York: Cambridge University Press, 1996).

Part II

The modern revolution:
compromises with power

4

The Reformation in context

I shall set down the following two propositions concerning the
freedom and the bondage of the spirit:
A Christian is a perfectly free lord of all, subject to none.
A Christian is a perfectly dutiful servant of all, subject to all.[1]

The reformer Martin Luther (1483–1546) promised freedom. He promised freedom from the burden of the moral law; freedom from fear of
the devil and damnation; freedom from obedience to the pope and his
church. Every infant, he proclaimed, 'crawls out of the font [at baptism]
a Christian, a priest, and a pope'. He himself had been set free by the
belief that no-one and nothing stood between him and God. But Luther
also embraced the role of a servant in relation to his God. He found
freedom in complete, unswerving devotion to the God who had saved
him by sending his Son Jesus Christ. As the servant of the most powerful
master of all, a master who elevates those he loves, Luther could no
longer be enslaved to any earthly power. As he put it in *The Freedom
of a Christian*, he, like his fellow Christians, was not only 'a perfectly
dutiful servant' but 'a perfectly free lord, subject to none'.

What Luther had done, in effect, was to slice out the multiple mediating authorities that had stood between the individual and God in
medieval Christianity. A Christian had to tread carefully, making sure
that the higher powers that controlled his or her destiny were kept sweet.
Luther threw off this mentality. He taught that the one high God was all
that mattered. There was no need to call on the assistance of the saints,
to place faith in relics, to go on pilgrimages, to buy indulgences, to obey
the pope, to structure one's life around the church's complicated system
of confession and penance, to leave the path of perfection to monks and
nuns. In the end, all this amounted to a lack of faith in the power of
God to save. Standing alone before God, the sinner need only throw

himself or herself on divine mercy. No middlemen were necessary. Once you had faith that higher power was on your side, deference to lower powers became unnecessary.

Luther's message did not come out of the blue. It was part and parcel of the reforming ethos that was discussed in the previous chapter, and that had been gathering strength for several centuries. The desire for *reformatio* was shared by people at the highest and the lowest levels of society. In different guises it had been articulated by theologians, friars, bishops, clergy, church councils, monarchs, wandering preachers, peasants, Beguines and mystics. Luther himself was a member of the Observant Augustinian Hermits, and a disproportionate number of those who led the reformation in towns, cities and countryside were preachers and mendicants. They were animated, above all, by a desire to close the gap between the contemporary church, characterised by huge wealth and worldly power, and the church of the apostles, characterised by poverty and service. They contrasted a 'material' church with a 'spiritual' one.

Over three centuries before, the apocalyptic seer Joachim of Fiore (c. 1135–1202) had prophesied that a time would come when *viri spirituales*, 'spiritual men', would arise to lead the world through chaos and confusion to an era of everlasting freedom, love and peace. This would be the era of 'the Spirit' and it would follow on from the present era of the Son and the New Testament, and from the previous era of the Father and the Old Testament. In the era of the Spirit, 'all those wonderful things written about Solomon and Christ will be completed by [these spiritual men] in the Spirit, because in them Christ will reign more powerfully'.[2] Since the calamitous events of the fourteenth and fifteenth centuries, more and more people believed that Joachim's prophecies were coming true. Disasters, ranging from plague to papal schism, fuelled their hopes, as did continuing social and economic upheaval. The time was ripe for a Luther, and the energies of reform erupted across Europe.

This chapter considers the course of the sixteenth-century Reformation, particularly in its heartlands in northern Europe. Beginning with Luther and the Lutheran Reformation, it goes on to consider the development of the Calvinist Reformation and, finally, the course of the multiple movements of reform that are often bracketed together under the heading of 'radical reformation'. The story is continued in the next chapter, which considers the seventeenth-century reformation and the development of later Protestantism. Chapter 6 deals with the Catholic reformation.

Since it was the sixteenth century that proved the crucible in which the future direction of both Christianity and modernity would start to be shaped, it is here that the second part of this volume begins. The 'Christian revolution', which had seen the church win social power in the east and, even more decisively, in the west, gave way to the 'modern revolution', in which the church's power was challenged and taken away. In the sixteenth century the ability of a single church to dominate state and society was fatally undermined by both internal and external forces. Externally, the Catholic church was challenged by increasingly powerful nations and principalities that began to take power from the papacy. Internally, it was threatened by competing versions of Christianity that could no longer be contained or destroyed.

This is not to imply that the sixteenth century witnessed the collapse of the long-standing Christian love affair with dominating power from on high, or that the dream of ecclesiastical control over state and society died. In some ways the Protestant Reformation of the sixteenth century was little more than a minor local difficulty for the Roman Catholic church, which maintained its dominant position in much of Europe and continued its alliance with the Holy Roman emperor (for the crucial part of this period, Charles V). In any case, the most successful Reformation churches, those inspired by Luther (the Lutheran or Evangelical church) and Calvin (the Presbyterian or Reformed church) maintained belief in a God of power from on high and in the necessity of church–state alliance. (Hence the designation of these churches, plus that of Zwingli in Switzerland, as the churches of the 'Magisterial Reformation', because of their alliance with the 'magistrates', the masters of society.) Both Luther and Calvin also followed the example of the Catholic church in appealing to the state for assistance in the coercion, torture and, if necessary, execution of their enemies.

Yet it would be equally false to suggest that the Protestant Reformation represented no more than business as usual under new management. Despite their reluctance to surrender the ideal of ecclesiastical control over the whole of society, the magisterial reformers broke decisively with medieval Catholicism in a number of respects. They allowed the state and 'the secular' more scope; they diminished the distance between clergy and laity; they abolished monasticism; they narrowed women's sphere to the family while giving the family new dignity; they allowed the individual more responsibility and authority in religious matters; they opened up the possibility of a more direct relationship between God and the individual. And in each one of these matters, they anticipated, initiated, reinforced or legitimated key social, economic, political and cultural developments that we associate with the birth of modernity.

The so-called radical reformation went even further. In challenging the whole notion of Christian alliance with power from on high, it anticipated the rise of power from below, which would become a defining characteristic of the modern world. Though a disparate and diverse group, the radical reformers were united in their belief that Christian conviction must be a matter of free, individual, adult choice rather than of coercion or imposition from above. For this reason they wished to cut all ties between church and state. For this reason, too, they also insisted upon the radical equality of all Christians and the inappropriateness of hierarchies of power in church and society. And for this reason they disparaged the 'external' and 'material' aspects of religion in favour of more spiritualised and subjectivised versions of Christianity, whose altar was the heart of each individual. Though fiercely persecuted in the sixteenth century by Protestant and Catholic powers alike, such radicalism would re-emerge in the following centuries to challenge its rivals with new renewed force.

Before proceeding with this account, a note on terminology: the word 'Reformation' with a capital 'R' will be used to refer to the Protestant Reformation of the sixteenth century, which was led by Luther, Calvin and Zwingli (the Magisterial Reformation); 'reformation' with a small 'r' will be used in a much broader sense to refer to any or all of the major initiatives of reform, whether Protestant or Catholic. The word 'Protestantism' is used in an inclusive sense to refer to all those forms of Christianity that flowed from the Reformation and rejected Roman Catholic Christianity. (The original *Protestatio* (protest) was first used in relation to Lutheranism at the Diet of Speyer in 1529 by reforming German princes and cities who were 'protesting' against opponents who wished to halt their innovations.)

The transition to modernity

Religious change in the sixteenth century took place in the context of far-reaching political, social and economic change. Most importantly, two interlinked transitions came together in what is now understood as the take-off to modernity.

First, in relation to economic and social power, came the transition from feudalism to capitalism. In the medieval world, ties of locality, blood and community had been regulative of economic transactions. Land and property were transmitted by both matrilineal and patrilineal inheritance. By controlling land, the few controlled the working lives of the many, who gave their labour in return for benefits in kind – chiefly the use of land and the retention of a portion of its yield. The system was generally stable, except when disrupted by military enterprises, which were usually aimed at seizing or defending land. For most of the Middle Ages, economic growth, which was slow but significant, took place chiefly by improving crop yields. As this happened, some of the more successful peasants grew wealthy enough to create a market large enough to enable others to support themselves by supplying it.

A new manufacturing class was born, which, together with the merchants who traded their goods, gravitated towards the expanding cities. There they began to employ men and women to labour in their workshops. The labour of such employees now became a commodity that could be bought and sold. Very gradually, all that had previously been bound by social and personal ties and obligations became commodified as money became a universal and impersonal measure of value. Those who profited in the new economy could become money-rich through their own achievements. They formed the basis of a new capitalist class of people whose status was dependent not on birth or on land but on their ability to make profits. Composed at first of successful manufacturers ('burghers') and merchants, by the sixteenth century this new middle class was powerful enough to challenge the entrenched and mutually reinforcing power of the nobility and the Catholic church.

The impact of these socio-economic changes on the position of women was significant. The transition from feudalism to early forms of mercantile capitalism might have opened new opportunities to women. In some cities for which records exist, such as Paris, we know that it did. A significant number of women became prominent in various trades, including hairdressing, lace-making, silk-weaving, pharmacy and even working with gold, and did so in their own right. By the fifteenth century, however, their numbers had begun to decline as they were forced out of these occupations by a growing male monopoly. This monopoly was secured by the restrictive practices of the guilds, from which women (and Jews) were excluded. By seizing control of trades and regulating who could work within them, the guilds secured both masculine domination of the new craft economy, and the confinement of women to poorly paid menial work or unpaid labour in the household (or both). Whereas women in feudal society had worked alongside men and had shared many essential tasks, their economic status was now beginning to be degraded relative to that of men. While the franchise of economically successful men gradually expanded as they gained new political power and visibility, that of women shrank to the new sphere of 'the personal' rather than 'the public'. The personal should not be identified with 'the private', however, since the household and sexual relations within it would be matters of profound public significance in the sixteenth century – as we shall see.

Hand in hand with these processes of social and economic change went a second major transition in relation to political and military power: the transition from a loose federation of weak states under the unifying sovereignty of Christendom to powerful, centralised nation states in a diplomatically regulated, secular multi-state system. The medieval 'state' had tended to be small and weak. By the high Middle Ages there were two main forms of polity in Europe: kingdoms, and independent city-states governed by a council. In both, power was in the hands of the landowning nobility, and rulers could rule only through close co-operation with these landowners. Rulers' power was therefore relatively precarious, and could be secured chiefly by kinship alliances and military force. By the fifteenth century, military power was becoming more organised, because of the introduction of firearms and the growth of navies. Both these developments demanded a more highly trained and permanent 'standing' force of men. Those polities with the most effective military forces began to expand at the expense of weaker states. It is estimated that the size of armies relative to the population increased by at least 50 per cent in the sixteenth century, and the evidence from some countries suggests a ten-fold increase.

This military expansion in turn required increasingly centralised, orderly administration and effective forms of capital accounting to maintain it. Since only the state was capable of providing this level of intensive organisation, it grew larger and more powerful. Military power led to greater centralisation, which in turn enhanced military power – and so on. The momentum of growth was such that it virtually brought to an end the rule of feudal states and city-states. By the sixteenth century only the very largest of these could find enough money to maintain their independence in siege warfare. Confederations provided only temporary relief. In the long run, though in some areas it took much longer than others, it was the centralised nation state with an increasingly effective apparatus of control that triumphed right across Europe. At a certain stage, perhaps as early as the seventeenth century, the power of these states began to check one another. Thus through persistent warfare Europe gradually settled down into a more orderly multi-state system in which the actors were more nearly equal, a process that was formalised by the Peace of Westphalia of 1648.

In terms of their internal power relations these new nation states took two forms: absolutist monarchies (such as France, Austria, Spain and Sweden) and constitutional monarchies (such as England and the Netherlands). The power of the nobility had declined since the later Middle Ages, while that of monarchs and of the most successful capitalists was rising fast. The medieval conciliar form of government, with the king meeting in council with about twenty of the greatest men of the kingdom, was no longer appropriate. In absolutist monarchies it was replaced by court offices, and in constitutional monarchies by very limited representative assemblies (parliaments). In either case, by the eighteenth century the nobility and the most powerful burghers were all co-operating with the state. These 'gentlemen', whose power was based on economic achievement as much as on birth, had come to form a new capitalist class who now identified their own interests with those of the nation state, while women were completely excluded from political and civic life. In turn, the state depended on the capitalist class for capital and for maintaining its rule in the provinces. Yet the state was also taking more and more legislative power to itself. By the seventeenth century it had, in many countries, gained active control of class relations through administration of poor-laws, control of labour mobility, regulation of wages and so on. The Crown and the propertied classes were now in control to such an extent that national and class interests fused. In this way, the rise of capitalism and the rise of the modern nation state went hand in hand.

Though this brief summary of the processes involved in the transition to modernity anticipates later developments, the effects were already

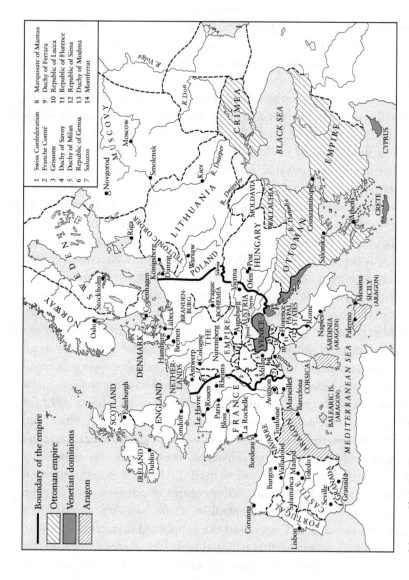

1	Swiss Confederation	8	Marquisate of Mantua
2	Franche Comté	9	Duchy of Ferrara
3	Grissons	10	Republic of Lucca
4	Duchy of Savoy	11	Republic of Florence
5	Duchy of Milan	12	Republic of Siena
6	Republic of Genoa	13	Duchy of Modena
7	Saluzzo	14	Montferrat

Boundary of the empire

Ottoman empire

Venetian dominions

Aragon

Map 4   Christian Europe about 1500

being felt in the sixteenth century. For the Roman Catholic church, they posed a serious threat. The centralised authority of the papal hierarchy of power was threatened by the decentralised decision-making of the market, as well as by the recentralised power of the growing nation states. Newly powerful men – whether monarchs, nobles, merchants or burghers – began to chafe at the church's monopoly of power and to eye its wealth with envy. Growing national sentiment began to undermine loyalty to Rome. Vernacular languages replaced Latin, and increased literacy began to threaten the clerical monopoly on learning. The growing power of northern and western Europe began to shift its economic and political heart away from Rome and the Mediterranean and towards the Atlantic and the Baltic. The Roman Catholic church found it increasingly hard to control the emerging centres of power in Sweden, north Germany, Holland and England. Its diplomatic traditions were largely confined to Italy, Spain, France, southern Germany and Austria. Distance from Rome made it easier to defy the papacy.

For the reformers, by contrast, the changes offered new opportunity. It is no coincidence that Protestantism was centred on the lands most affected by social and economic change. Its origins were in the territories of Germany and Switzerland, and it quickly spread to much of central and northern Europe, including France, Holland, England, Scandinavia and parts of eastern Europe. Not only were these lands harder for Rome to control; they were also home to the new middle classes eager to win more of a role for themselves in society and impatient with the entrenched wealth and privilege of the clergy and the monasteries. The stable, hierarchical society of small-scale communities meshed well with the paternalism of medieval Christianity, but the latter seemed less appropriate in the face of changes that affected individuals' relations to their labour, to their employers and to one another. The subjectivist temper, which had been evident in the later Middle Ages in the desire on the part of individuals to take control of their own spiritual lives and to enter into a more direct and unmediated relationship with the divine, became a more potent force. In some cases clergy and mendicants themselves became disenchanted with Rome and keen to see a reform of the church. They were not the only ones. Ambitious rulers saw in religious reformation the chance to free themselves from Roman interference and take control of ecclesiastical assets – sacred as well as worldly. They could offer reformers shelter and protection from the persecution of

Plate 12 *Martin Luther and his Friends*, by Lucas Cranach the elder (1472–1553)
Luther's patron and protector, Elector Frederick, is at the centre of the painting, with Zwingli on his left and Melanchthon to the left of him. Luther is on Frederick's right. The artist Lucas Cranach was court painter to Frederick, a close friend of Luther, a wealthy citizen and a long-serving burgermeister of Wittenberg.

Rome. Thus religious, economic, social and political change went hand in hand.

Luther's breakthrough

Luther's achievement can be understood only within this context of change. Had he been born in a different time or a different place, it is unlikely that his Reformation would have succeeded. In places such as Italy and Spain he would have been rapidly silenced by Catholic Inquisitions, and control by a single monarch would have led to speedier and more effective repression. As it was, the complicated and fragmented political situation of Germany allowed Luther a great deal of freedom and opened up unique religio-political opportunities. Even to speak of 'Germany' at this time is an anachronism. In the sixteenth century, modern-day Germany was still part of the Holy Roman empire, a loose confederation of several hundred states, ranging from tiny principalities to self-governing cities and large territorial states. In theory, these states owed allegiance to an elected emperor, but in reality they had considerable independence. Not only was Luther protected by a prince of one such state, Elector Frederick of Saxony (1463–1525), but his Reformation spread in cities and states that were willing and able to reinforce their independence from the Holy Roman emperor. (Frederick was the major north German opponent of the emperor.) Luther's use of German rather than Latin helped his ideas spread rapidly in these places. Even more important was the recent invention of the movable-type printing press, which made it possible for him to present his programme in a continuous stream of pamphlets, and which allowed 'news' of the Reformation to spread quickly. Effective use of the media enabled Luther to become one of the first of a long line of male Protestant celebrities.

Though its success depended on its social and political contexts, Luther's breakthrough was religious through and through. He was, above all, a brilliant theologian. He had been trained in theology at the University of Erfurt and had become Professor of Biblical Theology at the University of Wittenberg. His training had been in a late-scholastic mode, and he was heavily influenced by the Augustinian turn, which was discussed in the previous chapter. Like many of his contemporaries he was also influenced by the humanist movement (discussed below), and desired a return to the Bible as the basis of all Christian life and thought. His early theological writings took the form of commentaries on the Psalms, Galatians, Romans and Hebrews. Luther made no clear distinction between his spiritual career and his theological one, and each bore down heavily on the other. As a scrupulous monk he strove for perfection, and found himself distressed and humiliated by his failure to keep God's law. In Augustine he found a theologian who shared his deep sense of sin, and in Paul he found the solution that would finally set him free from its burden.

In later years Luther would mythologise his theological and personal 'breakthrough' as a sudden experience precipitated by reading Romans 1.17, probably in 1518. In a flash he realised that the 'righteousness of God', which he so feared, would not condemn him but save him; for God was a God of love, not wrath. In reality, Luther's breakthrough was probably a dawning realisation, achieved by years of study and reflection on humanity and God. Luther did not share Aquinas' optimistic estimation of 'natural' human ability. A widespread revival of interest in Augustine had taught him that human nature was sinful through and through, and his failures as a monk had reinforced this conclusion. Like Augustine, Luther believed that all human beings were weighed down by a burden of original sin inherited from Adam and Eve, and that the weight was so great that only God's grace could save them. Even then, the sinner would never really be free from sin; even the baptised Christian would sin and sin again. This had led him to a theology of sorrowful humility. What turned its mood from sorrow to joy was a dawning realisation that God is a God of love, not wrath, and that he counts those who turn to him as righteous. Not that he *makes* them righteous, but that he *ascribes* or *imputes* righteousness to them. Luther believed that God's unfathomable mercy lies in the fact that he saves some human beings in spite of what they are and what they do. They remain sinners, but they are justified nevertheless – not because *they* are good, but because *God* is.

It was only later that Luther would understand the pivotal significance of what became called his doctrine of 'justification by faith', and only later that he isolated it as the nub of the difference between him and the Catholic church. To start with, Luther wished merely to reform certain abuses in the church. In 1517 he had written to his archbishop enclosing ninety-five theses 'On the Power of Indulgences', in which he attacked the sale of indulgences by popes and bishops in order to raise cash. Luther believed that the practice was in danger of distorting the true Christian understanding of repentance as an inward change of heart rather than as an external transaction, and of implying that power belonged not to God but to the pope. As the controversy deepened and attitudes hardened, so Luther's invective became stronger and more energetic. In the course of debates with representatives from Rome, two points of difference emerged: Luther's belief in justification by 'faith, not works' and his insistence on the overriding authority of the scriptures.

Between 1518 and 1521 Luther developed the implications of his position. It was Christological through and through. Under the influence of both Paul and late medieval German mysticism, Luther argued that justification comes through Christ because God in his love and grace chooses to gaze upon Christ's righteousness rather than on human sinfulness. Thus we are not to be tarred with the brush of Adam and Eve, but cleansed by the blood of Christ. God, through Christ, has saved human beings from what they were and what they are. All that is left for us is to have faith in what has been accomplished on our behalf and in spite of ourselves – for all the power and the glory are God's, not ours. Thus Luther's doctrine of justification by faith is also correctly called a doctrine of justification by grace. What is required for salvation is the deep, inward, almost mystical sense of salvation in Christ. Individuals no longer have to strive to build up merit and avoid sin, as the Roman Catholic church had so misleadingly suggested. Instead of striving helplessly to be righteous, they may as well 'sin boldly', as Luther put it, confident in the knowledge that salvation is by faith and not by works.[3] With this knowledge comes 'the freedom of the Christian' of which Luther spoke in powerful and compelling terms. No longer a slave to sin, to conscience, to scrupulosity, to monastic rules, to the church or to the sacramental system, the Christian man or woman is set free from anxiety, servitude, sin and death.

This was all very radical, both theologically and socially. As we shall see below, the so-called radical reformation took these ideas very seriously indeed, attempting to establish churches whose constitution would enshrine the priesthood of all believers and, in some cases, fomenting political and social revolution as well. After 1521, however, Luther himself turned away from some of the more radical aspects of his earlier theology. The change was precipitated by his formal break with Rome. Following his condemnation in the papal bull *Exsurge Domine* of 1520, Luther was excommunicated in 1521 and condemned at the Diet of

Worms in the same year. Now he was not simply a prophet, but the leader of a new church, with new responsibilities to match.

When Luther returned to Wittenberg in 1522 to guide and direct the course of reformation there, it was clear from his hostility to many of the reforms put in place during his absence by his follower and erstwhile friend Andreas Bodenstein von Karlstadt (c. 1480–1541) that he was no longer sympathetic to a 'spiritual' reformation centred around mystical union with God in Christ. Instead of abandoning Catholic practice, Luther now became a defender of an objective sacramental religion appropriate for the masses, and of a close co-operation between church and state in the attempt to build a Christian society. The voices of women were silenced, and Karlstadt and the radicals were condemned. Social reform was no longer on the agenda. Faced by large, unprecedented revolts by peasants across the whole area that ran from Leipzig to Trent, and from the border of Lorraine to the border of Upper Austria, Luther condemned the peasant war of 1524–5 in a tract entitled 'Against the Murderous and Thieving Hordes of Peasants'. Showing himself the heir of the persecuting mentality of the late medieval church, he exhorted the princes and nobles to kill the peasants (which they did, in large numbers), and insisted that the liberty of a Christian must be understood as spiritual, not social or political.

Though Luther always insisted that the decisions he took after 1521 were purely theological, there was a pragmatic force to his new conservatism as well. Focused as it was on the individual's inner appropriation of God's grace, his earlier version of Christianity had been purely spiritual. True to this logic, Luther believed that Christianity should not bother itself with material and worldly concerns, but should leave these to the state. Church and state were 'two kingdoms', each with separate concerns and jurisdiction. Yet, as it became clear that Luther's reforms would have to take place independently of the Catholic church, it also became clear that a purely spiritual Christianity was never going to be able to institutionalise itself without some material assistance. Luther himself had survived persecution only because of the protection of Elector Frederick of Saxony. He had also begun to call upon the princes to control radical reformers by force. His church, if it was to develop in the way he wanted, was also going to need political assistance.

It was for similar, partly pragmatic, reasons that Luther also found it necessary to strengthen his spiritual church with material practices.

Luther's followers took over churches that had previously been controlled from Rome, and manned them with their own clergy. (In some cases Roman Catholic clergymen themselves converted, taking their congregations with them.) In matters of liturgy and church order, Luther was generally happy to leave Catholic practices in place unless there was some compelling scriptural reason not to do so. Thus he retained a sacramental system, though he reduced the number of sacraments from seven to two – baptism and eucharist. Instead of fostering a purely inward and subjective Christianity, in the manner of some of the radical sects, Luther thus stamped his branch of Reformed Christianity with an external and objective character. As well as being pragmatic, this expressed Luther's guiding theological conviction that God's grace is externally given to the believer in spite of anything he or she can or should do. Thus Luther retained the practice of infant baptism in recognition of the objectivity of grace and the passivity of its reception. For the same reason, he retained the Catholic understanding that the church must be open to both sinners and saints, for it is not human merit but divine love that makes a church. Thus the two main 'marks' of a true church were, in Lutheran theology, the Word and the sacraments.

Yet this insistence upon the centrality of Word as well as sacrament also helped Luther distinguish his version of Christianity from that of Rome, which placed less emphasis upon the authority of scripture than on that of pope, priests and sacraments. Luther's own theological formation had taken place under the influence of the Bible, and many of his most important theological works took the form of scriptural commentary. His Reformation was guided by his belief that he was returning the church to its scriptural roots. It was through scripture that the Holy Spirit spoke to the believer and gave assurance of salvation. Like Wyclif and Hus before him, Luther was therefore keen that all Christians might have access to the Bible in their own language, and that the reading and exposition of scripture should be central to the worshipping life of the church. Yet Luther did not take a literalistic or fundamentalist view of the Bible. The Bible, he insisted, is not God, and the authority of the Bible is merely derived from God. Likewise, the Word is not identical with the canon. The Word is the living Christ, wherever and however he is communicated. Those parts of scripture that convey the gospel most effectively, such as Paul's letters, have the greatest authority, in Luther's view. Indeed, he was wont to dismiss those parts of the Bible that had little to do with what he believed to be the true gospel message. The letter of James, for example, he dismissed as 'a right strawy epistle'.[4] While many of his followers insisted on the principle of *sola scriptura* (scripture alone), Luther, using a favourite phrase from Augustine, preferred to speak of the authority of 'reason and scripture'.[5]

Luther's biblicism and his concern to put his spiritual gospel on a firm material footing were also manifest in his efforts to provide his followers with the tools necessary to form and sustain their faith. To this end he wrote both short and long catechisms, as well as annotated versions of the Ten Commandments and the Apostles' Creed. Greatly aided by the advances in printing, which meant that such resources could now be widely distributed, Luther was able to lay the foundations for Reformation Christianity to become both a word-based and literate as well as a confessional form of Christianity. Whereas in previous generations Christians had simply been born into the faith and its traditions, which tended to have more to do with practices than with beliefs, they were now schooled to be Christians from the earliest age. And the forum of this formation was to be the home at least as much as the church. For Luther insisted that it was the Christian duty of the *paterfamilias* to bring up his children and household in the faith, a duty every bit as important as that of the priest.

Lutheran Reformation

The spread of Luther's Reformation was due not so much to direct action on his part as to initiatives by those inspired by his ideas. Many people had been waiting a long time for reform; Luther provided the stimulus they needed to take matters into their own hands.

REFORMATION IN THE CITIES

In its initial stages the Lutheran Reformation appears to have attracted the support of a variety of groups: of women as well as men, and of peasants and poor labourers as well as burghers. Though it was disseminated chiefly through urban channels – the sale and discussion of pamphlets and the preaching of clergy, mendicants and dedicated preachers – it won followers in rural as well as urban areas. (The intercourse between the two was greater than is often imagined.) At this stage its appeal seems to have been related to at least three factors: (1) dissatisfaction with the existing state of the church (2), resentment at the multifarious powers, both natural and supernatural, to which the individual was subjected, and (3) desire for a redistribution of this power. Luther's reforming stance, in other words, held out the promise of a realignment of power.

Different people would no doubt be interested in different aspects of this potential. Some women, it appears, were inspired by the promise of greater autonomy within male-dominated church and society, and some peasants, we know, were inspired by the idea that their existing self-governing communities would become the basis of a new society reorganised along gospel lines. Both of these groups would soon grow disillusioned with the course of the Reformation, as Luther and other male leaders turned against them and besought the nobles and princes to do the same.

The main group that remained loyal to Luther and helped his Reformation spread were the city-dwelling burghers who ruled over the small household workshops that were becoming the building blocks of the new economy. Lutheranism became a *petit-bourgeois* movement, giving voice not to the values of expansive entrepreneurial capitalism but to an essentially conservative moralism based on the husbanding of limited resources. It succeeded at the popular level by sacralising the values of the newly successful artisans, and by consolidating their precarious position domestically, economically and politically.

Politically, the Reformation won the burghers new power and status in the cities. Previously, such power had been shared between (on the one hand) the nobles and merchants who dominated the councils, and (on the other) the clergy, monks and friars, who were subject to their own system of law and supported by their own sources of income (accumulated wealth and the ability to levy taxes). Once a city rejected the power of Rome and adopted the Reformation, the power of the clergy was wiped out at a stroke; monastic foundations took just a little longer to dismantle. What this meant was that the role of 'pastor' now opened to burghers, and the wealth of the church could be taken over by the city authorities. The upheaval also gave the burghers the opportunity to raise their status within the cities and to win greater representation on the city councils, particularly those where control was weak.

Economically, the Reformation strengthened the power of the guilds, which increasingly became quasi-religious institutions, with their own (all-male) ritual processions taking the place of Catholic processions such as that of Corpus Christi (in which women had once been able to take part). The Reformation sacralised the work and the values of the burghers. The virtues it applauded were hard work, thrift, honesty, chastity and self-control. To profligacy, insubordination, laziness, drunkenness and sexual licence, it opposed order, simplicity, self-control, obedience and duty. Thus the values of the Reformation proved identical to the values that favoured the burghers against entrenched power (the nobility and the Catholic church) and rival power (poorer workers and women). The consolidation of their position was crucial: fluctuating demand for their products and an over-supply of labour meant that their monopoly had to be preserved at all costs.

At the domestic level, Luther's Reformation greatly strengthened the power of male heads of households over their families and workers. Luther's theology exalted the patriarchal family, legitimated male domination as part of the God-given order of things, and repudiated any form of female independence. God had created women, he wrote, 'for no purpose other than to serve men and be their helpers. If women grow weary or even die while bearing children, that doesn't harm anything. Let them bear children to death; they are created for that.'[6] In any case, Luther believed, it was in serving men that women would achieve happiness and blessedness: 'It is the highest, most valuable treasure that a woman can have to be subject to a man and certain that her works are pleasing to him. What could be happier for her? . . . For all of her works are golden when she is obedient.'[7] Difficulties arose only when women tried to become independent of male control. 'The rule by women', said Luther, 'has brought about nothing good from the beginning of the world. When God set Adam up as Lord over all creatures, everything was good and right, and everything ruled for the best. But the woman came and also wanted to have her hand in things and be wise; then everything collapsed and became a complete disorder.'[8]

In the economic realm the effect of such teaching was to reinforce women's exclusion from positions of power in the new urban, money-based economy. From now on their labour would be largely unpaid (as wives or mothers) or badly paid (as poor workers restricted to the most menial tasks).

In the religious realm the effect was to bring to an abrupt halt the feminisation of Christianity that had been taking place since the thirteenth century. By rejecting monasticism and forcing monasteries and convents to close, the Reformation shut down a vital sphere of female autonomy. By repudiating the veneration of the saints and of Mary it defeminised the sacred realm and created a new situation in which women could express religious feeling only according to rules imposed by men (attending services, listening to male exposition of scripture, singing authorised hymns). By transferring all awe and reverence to a Father God of magnified power, it crushed the possibility of the post-patriarchal revolution in theological understanding that might have been initiated by Julian and her like.

The way in which the Lutheran Reformation served the interests of the burghers is evident in the ways in which it was institutionalised in the cities. Monasteries, nunneries and brothels were closed down, and steps were taken to see that all single women were married off or expelled from the city. Responsibility for the running of churches and the collection of tithes was redistributed, and courts of discipline and marriage were established to give new expression to the churches' juridical function. In Lutheran Augsburg, for example, the city council established institutions of the Discipline Lords and a marriage court in 1537. These bodies (whose operations will be described in more detail in the following section on the Calvinist Reformation) were typical of reformed upper German cities: Basle had introduced a marriage court in 1529, Zurich in 1526, Strasbourg in 1529, and Ulm in 1531. Their aim was to enforce order in both the home and the city. Good order in the one became the image of good order in the other; the 'whore' was Luther's favourite model of wickedness, applied indiscriminately to pope, Roman church, priests and out-of-control women.

This is not to deny that some women, most notably the wives of burghers and pastors, may have benefited from the changes. By abolishing the monastic life and attacking the ideal of celibacy, Luther gave new dignity to the family and to the role of wife and mother. His followers elevated women's labour of love, care and nurture, and turned the home into a site of salvation as important as the church and more important than the cloister. Certainly it was the father who was to have prime responsibility for the moral and religious welfare of his children in the Lutheran scheme, but his wife was to be his honoured and cherished helper, and his family was to be the chief tool of Christian dissemination and discipline.

What Lutheranism did, then, was to take the long-established pater-nalism of Catholic Christianity, but to tie it more closely to the family and the household. It was biological fathers who were now the chief model of godly paternity, not the abbot ('abba') or the priest ('father'). There were massive advantages not only for the burghers, but for Lutheranism itself in this domestic emphasis. Whereas the Catholic church had relied upon the church and the clergy in the vital task of transmission and dis-cipline, Protestantism came to place equal emphasis on the importance of the family. The *paterfamilias* was to assume the role of pastor and teacher to all who lived in his household, both family and workers. He was to be responsible for reading the Word, expounding it, and ensuring moral conduct. His wife would help and strengthen him in discharging his duties, and by faithfully discharging her duty of loving care for hus-band, children and servants she would become a living example of the loving obedience that God required.

REFORMATION OF THE PRINCES

Luther drew on traditional paternalistic imagery in relation not only to the family but also to the polity. Not only was rule by the fathers and obedience by women, servants and children to be the model of civic order; the godly prince was also to understand himself as the 'father of his country', and the lord of the manor as the 'father of the estate'.[9] Together with the Reformation in the cities, the reformation of the princes was the other vital ingredient in the success of Lutheranism, both within the empire and outside it.

Like the burghers, the princes had much to gain by siding with the Lutheran cause. Luther's doctrine of the two kingdoms granted the state and its ruler great power over the church, and almost unlimited power over the people. This involved all the following elements: (1) ideological power, by way of the church's preaching and teaching, which could be mobilised in support of the prince and his state; (2) economic power, for the tithes formerly paid to Rome would now be directed to the ruler, and the existing properties and monies of the church came under his control; (3) freedom from Rome; and (4) assistance in building up new 'national' identities by way of vernacular preaching and teaching and the yoking of sacred power to national identity.

In northern and western Europe a number of princes and monarchs rapidly freed themselves from Roman power, making the church subject to their rule and Christianity the ally of national identity. Within the empire the Lutheran Reformation was established by the late 1530s not only in Electoral Saxony but in a number of other territorial states or Hapsburg dynastic lands, including the Brunswick duchies, Ducal Saxony, Bavaria, Silesia and Brandenburg-Ansbach. Outside of the empire, it established itself permanently in Scandinavia, where it was imposed by the monarchs, who were striving to achieve regional and national independence. By 1551 all of the Nordic countries, including Iceland, had officially become Lutheran and had a national church closely controlled by the Danish or Swedish king. Revolt in the north Netherlands against Catholic Spain and the political opportunism of the king of England took the Lutheran Reformation further afield. But, while the support of the princes was a key factor in the spread of Lutheranism, popular support was also essential to long-term success; in places where it was favoured by the nobility rather than by the people, such as Latvia and Hungary, it would in due course be displaced either by Calvinism or by a renewed Roman Catholicism.

In relation to Lutheranism, then, we can distinguish between a Reformation from below and a Reformation from above, both of which contributed to its success. The two movements that were integral to the beginnings of modernisation were also integral to Reformation: the rise of a bourgeoisie connected with general urbanisation, and the rise of national monarchs in the context of early absolutism and the growth of the nation state. Both went hand in hand with a consolidation of age-old masculine dominance in new circumstances, and with the foundation of the modern family. In the process, the sacred formed new alliances and abandoned old ones. Desacralisation took place as holy spaces, times of year, sacramentals, relics, hosts, images, lamps, rosaries, liturgical vestments and vessels, processions and pilgrimages were denounced by the Reformers. But, above all, the sacred was cut loose from its previous connection with a sacramental priesthood based in Rome and attached more closely to the domestic unit, to the work of men, to the local church and to the nation state.

The Calvinist Reformation
By the late sixteenth century the success of Lutheranism was eclipsed by that of Calvinism, the variant of Protestantism led by the French lawyer and theologian John Calvin (1509–64). Calvinism gained considerable

influence in France in the early 1560s, where it attracted noble as well as popular support against the Catholic monarchy, and in the Holy Roman empire, where it replaced Lutheranism in a number of localities. It became the dominant form of Protestantism in Switzerland, Poland and Hungary, and the state religion of part of the Netherlands, where it played an important role in the late sixteenth-century struggle for independence from Spanish rule. It had a significant impact on the sixteenth-century reformation in England, and extended its influence there during the seventeenth century. It was institutionalised in Scotland, where John Knox (c. 1513–72) led a successful Calvinist Reformation; and it had a major impact in colonial North America, to which European Calvinists emigrated in significant numbers from the early seventeenth century onwards (see next chapter).

Calvinism's success relative to Lutheranism is surprising, given the fact that Calvin had no desire to be anything but a faithful Lutheran. He saw himself as a loyal ally and interpreter of Luther, who wished only to further the cause of a unified Protestant church. To this end, Calvin was even prepared to make concessions to the different forms of Protestant doctrine and practice that were developing in different parts of Germany and Switzerland. Under the influence of the Strasbourg reformer Martin Bucer (1491–1551), he assimilated something of the congregationalist principle of anabaptism, and he was prepared to go further than Luther in purifying worship from Catholic ceremonies. This last move also brought him closer to the Swiss reformer Ulrich Zwingli (1484–1531), who opposed Luther's objective sacramentalism by placing a greater emphasis on the importance of the inner disposition of the believer. Calvin made concessions to Zwingli's symbolic interpretation of the eucharist while nevertheless managing to preserve Luther's sacramentalism intact. All this was done in the hope that a united Protestant body, founded upon Lutheran dogma, would be able to absorb and contain emerging differences and cut off more radical forms of belief and practice at the root. Even when he was directing reformation in the city of Geneva, which would become the cradle of institutionalised Calvinism, Calvin was still willing to make concessions on questions he did not believe to be vital to the essence of Protestantism. His failure to achieve unity was due not only to the schismatic tendencies of the more extreme forms of Protestantism, but to the resistance and independence of Lutheranism itself.

Nevertheless, as we shall see later in this chapter and in the next, the relative success of Calvinism and its Pietist derivatives would increase as time went on. Part of the reason was that Calvinism proved far more adaptable than Lutheranism to the conditions of modernity. Put more strongly, Calvinism provided something of the inner dynamism of the process of modernisation itself. Not only was it able to accommodate such structural changes as the rise of the nation state, capitalism and, in due course, democracy, but under certain conditions it could actually become an engine of such changes. This is not to deny the medieval aspects of Calvinism. To a far greater extent than Lutheranism, which more nearly anticipated the characteristically modern split between church and state, Calvin retained and extended the Catholic ideal of a Christian society ruled over and regulated by the church. Yet in other respects Calvinism abandoned much more of the medieval heritage than Lutheranism. It discarded Catholic supernaturalism and sacramentalism much more wholeheartedly, and along with them the view that the world was under the capricious control of divine and diabolic forces. It had a much more activist temperament than Lutheranism, and tended to embrace rather than to shun change. It was far better adapted to the meaning-structures of a mobile and restless capitalist class than to the traditional paternalistic order of the Middle Ages, or even the basically conservative outlook of guildsmen. And it opened the way to a more democratic constitution in church and state than Luther would countenance – even though participation in the Calvinist revolution was restricted both by sex and by achievement, and the Calvinist church was a male oligarchy rather than a participatory democracy.

If Lutheranism is better read as closing the medieval world than as opening modernity, Calvinism faced in both directions. It moved away from the ideal of paternalistic communalism that had dominated Christianity from the time of Benedict and Gregory the Great onwards, and opened up the possibilities of a more autonomous individualism – at least for adult males. Far from endorsing the potential of a new money-based economy for freeing individuals from communal control, Lutheranism had been just as concerned as the Catholic church with regulating the economy by fixing wages and prices, controlling trade and restricting usury (lending at interest). It had also, as we have seen, strongly supported the attempts of the guilds and the guild masters to hold a free market at bay. While Calvinism was equally concerned with maintaining godly order in society through direct ecclesiastical control, it was nevertheless much more willing to set men free from established control and allow them to rise to their own level. It had much less respect for the established orders of society, and far less reverence for the virtue of obedience, which occupied such a central position in paternalistic communalism.

Much of this difference stems from doctrinal differences between Luther and Calvin. To call them disagreements would be too strong. In all major points of doctrine, Calvin built upon what Luther had established. He too understood the doctrine of justification by faith to lie at the very heart of the gospel and any true interpretation of it. He too believed wholeheartedly in the principle of *sola scriptura* and the power and sufficiency of the Word. He too opposed the sacramental and sacerdotal system of the Catholic church and contrasted externalised husks of the faith with the vivifying inner workings of divine grace. Yet Calvin differed from Luther by imagining God not so much in terms of caring paternalism as in terms of unfettered power and majesty. As he puts it in *The Institutes* (or 'Institution') *of the Christian Religion*,

> Truly God claims omnipotence to himself, and would have us acknowledge it – not the vain, indolent, slumbering omnipotence which sophists feign, but vigilant, efficacious, energetic, and ever active . . . God is deemed omnipotent . . . because, governing heaven and earth by his providence, he so overrules all things that nothing happens without his counsel.[10]

Both Luther and Calvin had been influenced by the nominalist turn in late medieval, post-Thomistic scholasticism that placed emphasis upon the absolute freedom of God and upon his free will as the ground of all order and goodness, rather than upon order and goodness as the ground of his will. But it was Calvin who took the nominalist turn further in his theology than did Luther. Whereas, for Luther, the remarkable, convicting and life-changing fact about God was the depth of his love and mercy, for Calvin it was his transcendent power. Whereas, for Luther, God's love brought the sinner into the closest communion with him, to the extent of his or her becoming caught up in mystical union with the Son, for Calvin the believer maintained a respectful distance from the God who would always be immeasurably greater than any human being. Whereas, for Luther, deification hovered as a possibility at the edges of his theology, for Calvin the thought that man could be caught up into God – even on God's initiative – was the primal blasphemy. For Calvin, God first commanded and humans obeyed, whereas, for Luther, God first forgave and humans rejoiced.

Thus Calvin interpreted the doctrine of justification by faith in a rather different way from Luther. Both began from the same starting point: that all human beings were wretched sinners destined for eternal damnation. In this they agreed with Augustine. But they disagreed with what they believed to be the prevailing Catholic view that the Christian life was a constant struggle to avoid sin and to build up merit, regulated by the church's penitential system. For Luther, the status of a sinner was never wholly banished, but sinners knew themselves to be justified in spite of themselves. Justification should give rise to 'sanctification', to the process by which the lives of redeemed sinners gradually come into line with the fact of their redemption as they are mastered by the Spirit of the God who has redeemed them. Yet there was always the danger of falling back. For Calvin, by contrast, justification consists not so much in being caught up into a joyful sense of the love of God, which may or may not issue in good deeds, but in a more constant and steady conviction of one's 'election' by the gracious will of God, an election that is proved by the way in which one's will is brought into conformity with God's. In Calvin's view, election cannot be lost, and knowledge of election comes through the disciplined and righteous actions of which God's chosen few are capable (plus the earthly rewards that flow from them). For Calvin, salvation is thus a matter of the will rather than of love or of the emotions, at both the heavenly level and the human. Though the perfection of human nature awaits the next life, the foundations can be laid here and now. Those who cannot keep God's commandments are evidently not numbered among the elect. Since nothing happens apart from God's will, they are clearly predestined for damnation rather than for salvation (the so-called doctrine of double predestination). But, since God's will is absolute, there is nothing unjust about this. God wills what he wills; it is his power rather than his love that must win our admiration and assent.

These differences between Luther and Calvin become very evident in their different interpretations of the Decalogue (the Ten Commandments). Following Luther, Calvin made the Decalogue central to his theologico-moral system, and distinguished between the two tables of the law, the first dealing with commandments relating to God, the second with commandments relating to the neighbour. Yet for Luther the first table is about the graciousness and mercy of God – about justification – while the second, less essential, table is about sanctification, the good deeds that might flow from justification but are also there to remind us of the standard of God to which we can only aspire. As such they serve as a constant reminder of our sinfulness (the chief purpose of law, according to Luther). For Calvin, by contrast, both tables contain binding laws that must be obeyed. True, the first table is the most important and has the status of law as much as of gospel – love and obey God, do not worship anything else, keep the sabbath. But the second table is not different in kind. It too contains laws that the elect must keep. What is more, all of these laws must be obeyed by both church and state and enshrined in their systems of legislation. Far from being merely a reminder of what humans cannot do, they must become the basis of what can be achieved in a new Christian society established on the basis of God's law.

For Calvin, then, everything must be subordinated to God and his purposes. The goal of life is to further his will by bringing a godly community into being. Though this is an individual's responsibility, and though individual responsibility was thus greatly heightened in Calvinism, the higher duty is none the less to a community. In this way the individual will of the Calvinist is subordinated both to God and to the godly community, and never allowed to become self-serving. The doctrine lent Protestantism a huge resource of energy and dedication for the cause of building up churches and societies on the Calvinist model. It also heightened a system of virtues rather different from the love, joy and obedience so emphasised in Lutheranism. Here, by contrast, the key Christian virtues were those of self-discipline, self-control, frugality, hard work; the cool, calculating and rational pursuit of objectives; and total dedication to God's cause.

Such a spirit was consistent with the demands of early capitalism, and had a more obvious relevance and appeal to a developing bourgeoisie than had Lutheranism. It fostered not humility and obedience so much as drive, ambition and achievement – albeit in a holy cause. It valued not a passive resignation to the current order of things, but an active drive to improve the world for God. The elect were men whose accomplishments set them apart – and their accomplishments proved their election. Like Luther, Calvin took very seriously Paul's injunction to 'stay in the calling in which you were called' (I Cor. 7: 20). Luther had used it to prove that God had called men to the occupations into which they were born, rather than to some 'higher' monastic vocation. Calvin agreed, but in his hands the injunction took on an active rather than a passive sense – the elect may be called to the very highest tasks, however humble their origins. Calvin interpreted the Old Testament idea of covenant in a related way. Treating the Old Testament as equally authoritative as the New, he noticed the way in which God called Israel out of all nations and made promises of faithfulness and protection, in response to which Israel was to obey his commandments. In the same way, Calvin believed that in the sinful and disobedient world of his time God was calling Christian groups into covenant with him, and ultimately into a worldwide communion of godliness. In this way Calvinism called not only individuals but whole peoples to its cause, and established an internationalist as well as a nationalist dynamic. On the one hand, small, persecuted groups of Calvinist Christians might be sustained by their belief that they had been called into covenant with God; on the other, whole nations might be singled out by the same call; ultimately the whole of human society would be transformed by obedience to God's commands.

True to his own vision, Calvin was tireless, disciplined and rationally active in the cause of social and ecclesiastical reform. Instead of relying upon the Holy Spirit – or territorial rulers – to accomplish what was necessary, he helped formulate the laws and shape the institutions that he thought God demanded. Where Luther had seen in the state and the law only a dyke against sin and a reminder of sin, Calvin believed that natural law could be a faithful reflection of divine law. (In this respect Calvin returned to a more Thomistic position than Luther.) Calvin saw his task not as setting worldly institutions free to perform their own tasks, as Luther had done, but as yoking them to true service of God.

The political and religious upheavals of his day gave him his opportunity to put his theory into practice in the Swiss city of Geneva. A self-governing city-state, Geneva had rejected Catholic leadership in both religion and politics prior to Calvin's arrival. Though Calvin was charged with helping reorganise the city along Protestant lines, he was not, however, given *carte blanche* to turn his vision of a godly society into reality. As in many Reformation cities, the town council was willing to share power with the new church authorities, so long as it retained the balance of that power. In Calvin's theocratic view, however, while both state and church are instituted by God and each has its distinctive and legitimate sphere of authority, and while they must work together in partnership to create a godly society, the church must have ultimate control. In Geneva, Calvin therefore set about not only reorganising the church, but establishing a 'consistory', a court of morals and doctrine, which would be made up of the city's pastors and lay elders and which would have the power to excommunicate – in other words, to cut people off from the church and all its services, including burial. When the civic authorities sought to curb the church's power in the consistory by denying it the right to approve the election of lay elders or to excommunicate, Calvin left Geneva for Strasbourg, where he resided for three years until recalled in 1541.

Political unrest and the threat of Catholic reassertion led to the decision to recall Calvin, and this time he was free to institute reformation on his own terms. Between 1541 and his death in 1564, Calvin set about turning the city into 'the most perfect school of Christ that ever was on this earth since the days of the apostles', as John Knox described it.[11] Calvin was in the remarkable position of being able to write the rules for both religion and politics. The clarity and power of what he achieved would inspire reform long after his death, and in lands far beyond Geneva. In his *Ecclesiastical Ordinances*, Calvin, working from what he took to be a New Testament blueprint, instituted four categories of ministry – doctors (teachers), pastors, deacons and elders – and the institutional frameworks within which each would work. Only the doctors and pastors had clerical status, and together they constituted the 'Venerable Company' of Geneva's pastors. Deacons and elders were lay ministers who were elected to office. The function of the elders was oversight and discipline, while the deacons were responsible for the supervision of charity.

The consistory was to be made up of the elders and the pastors. Its formal charge to its members was to 'oversee the life of everyone, admonish amicably those whom they see to be in error or living a disordered life, and, where it is required, enjoin fraternal correction'.[12] Such correction now included excommunication. In serious charges the offender could also be turned over to the city council which could – and did – inflict a range of corporal punishments, including torture and execution. (The most notorious example was the arrest and burning of Michael Servetus, a critic of Calvin, of orthodox Trinitarianism, and of the doctrine of original sin, in 1553.) Since each of the elders was in charge of one specific district of the city, the consistory had policing as well as judicial functions, and could bring before the court those suspected of disorderly conduct. One estimate finds that in 1569 one out of every fifteen adults in Geneva was required to appear before the consistory. Many of the offences considered had to do with sex and family disorder. They also included relapses to Catholic practices, murmurings against Calvin, unauthorised luxury and display, unseemly dancing and singing, blasphemy and absence from worship.

Part of the success of Calvin's institutional reforms was that they could easily be re-created in different contexts. His system had two further strengths. First, it allowed a partnership of clergy and laymen that enhanced the power of both and avoided the charges of clerical privilege that had so damaged the Catholic church. Second, it could be applied to a single congregation or expanded to cover a whole territory. As Calvinism spread into France, Germany, Scotland, the Netherlands and northern Ireland, both the consistory and the four-fold order of ministry became widely established. Consistories outside Geneva were often arranged in a hierarchy, ranging from those with jurisdiction over only a single congregation to those with jurisdiction over a larger area (often called a synod or classis), which also served as a court of appeal. In places where only a part of the population was Calvinist, such as France, the consistory did not have jurisdiction over the whole polity, as in Geneva, but only over church members. Though power struggles between consistories and secular courts were common, the result was often that the latter took over functions of the former and so turned religious law into secular. During the late sixteenth and seventeenth centuries, for example, the Scots Parliament made witchcraft and adultery capital crimes, and outlawed any activity on a Sunday save that of church attendance.

Calvinist reformation was carried and spread in a somewhat different way from Lutheran reformation. Because it had a much tighter and more self-contained institutional profile and was not dependent upon state support, it was much more easily exportable. To a far greater degree than Lutheranism, it was an international movement carried by refugees from all over Europe who converged on Geneva, were socialised there, and carried Calvinism back to the places they settled. In 1559 the Academy of Geneva was created, primarily to train Calvinist pastors. By 1560 nearly half the population of Geneva was made up of refugees. The city acted as a central hub and resource to which appeal could always be made. In the later sixteenth century, Emden in north-west Germany, close to the Netherlands, performed the same role for northern Europe. Most of the refugees to these cities were highly educated men who were inspired by Calvin and his teaching to organise reformed communities in their own lands. To that extent, Calvinism was carried by a new clerical caste. It was supported by people from a range of social backgrounds, though it spread chiefly in the cities and proved attractive to people of a relatively high level of education. It also won the support of nobles and aristocrats in a number of regions, as in France. There it carried the aspirations of those who opposed the movement towards absolutism in France and who sought to preserve their power against the pope and the monarch. The spread of Calvinism in France was checked only by the royal and aristocratic armies that provoked the bloody religious wars that began in 1562 and ended in 1598, when the royal Edict of Nantes granted a degree of temporary toleration to Calvinism. In the Netherlands, Calvinism spread equally quickly and won the support not only of whole cities but of the Dutch nobility, most notably the House of Orange. Here it carried nationalist aspirations and provoked resistance against Spanish (Catholic) control. Such resistance culminated in the revolt of the Netherlands, which first took shape under the leadership of the Prince of Orange, won control of the northern provinces, and led ultimately to the creation of a Dutch Republic free of Spanish control. (The influence of Calvinism in Britain and later in North America is considered in the next chapter.)

The fact that a large proportion of the cases brought before consistories involved sexual and domestic matters suggests that Calvin's Reformation followed Luther's in its attempt to reform gender relations and place women under tighter male control than had previously been the case. This is not to say that women were as central a concern for Calvin as for Luther, and he had less to say about them than his predecessor. He shared neither Luther's emotional interest in sex nor his outbursts of misogyny. As we have already noted, he also departed somewhat from Luther's paternalistic concerns. Yet in other ways Calvin's system was even more male. His God was more a Father God of power from on high than either Luther's God or the God of Catholicism. The sovereign power of both of the latter had been tempered by paternalism. Calvin's God was more awesome, distant and commanding. Moreover, Calvin's church order was masculine through and through. There was simply no place for women to appear. True, they might in principle be elected to salvation, but there was no sense that they would ever be able to perform the mighty deeds that are the proof of men's election. The best they could hope for was to be the companion and helpmeet of elect men. There was no question of women holding high office in either state or church, and the four ecclesiastical offices were all reserved for men. Calvinism was thus overridingly male in its logic, its symbols and its organisation. The tender, soft, womanly virtues of love and care, which were so central for Luther, sank into the background. Such masculinisation may be related to the fact that, whereas Luther had brought Christianity into closer relation with the personal and domestic realm, the tendency of Calvinism was to push it back out into the public realm with much greater vigour. As we shall see in the following chapter, however, it would not be long before Protestant women would take advantage of both Calvin's and Luther's theoretical insistence that in spiritual terms women were men's equals and, as such, capable of intense personal relationship with the living God.

The radical reformation

The Magisterial Reformation of Luther, Calvin and Zwingli was not the only current of reform that developed in the sixteenth century. And despite their other differences, the Magisterial Reformers were united in their opposition to more radical currents of reform, which they tended to lump together under the heading of anabaptism. Even Zwingli, who moved further than either Luther or Calvin in the direction of a spiritual and subjectivised Christianity, spent a great deal of time opposing anabaptism and denying that his thought had had any influence on the movement. Yet the radical reformation had much closer ties with the earliest phase of the Reformation than the magisterial reformers were happy to admit.

In the early decades of the sixteenth century, reforming voices had been heard in many parts of Europe, each offering its own brand of reform. As Luther became the symbolic focus of opposition to the Roman Catholic church, many contemporary reformers looked to him as their leader. On the basis of his early writings, even the more radical among them were justified in hoping that he would establish a church that was less concerned with accommodating and controlling the world than with

Plate 13　*The Trinity*, by Lucas Cranach the elder (1472–1553)

The masculinist assumptions and agenda of Reformation theology and ethics seem to be reflected in this depiction of the Trinity. The dominant figure is a sovereign male Father God of power, who physically raises the crucified Christ from the dead while the disciples sleep. The Holy Spirit is pictured as a dove.

re-establishing a church worthy of its founder. When Luther declared that Christians should have nothing to do with the affairs of the world, including the world of politics, even his most radical supporters imagined that he was thinking, like them, of establishing a pure, spiritual church on the model of the apostolic church of the New Testament. When he declared his belief in the supreme authority of scripture, they believed that he was rejecting the learned theology of the schoolmen and placing the truth in the hands of all who could read God's word. And when he attacked the pope, the clergy and the entrenched privilege of Christendom, they thought it reasonable to expect that he would support the common man's demands for a greater share of social power. Similarly, when Zwingli began to purge the churches under his control of the material rites, ceremonies and decorations of Catholicism, they hoped that this would be the first step in the creation of a renewed church in which God would be worshipped 'in spirit and in truth' by the pure of heart.

As the Reformation progressed, such hopes were dashed. The success of magisterial reform came to depend upon the support of increasingly powerful political leaders. Not surprisingly, these leaders were unwilling to support a movement that encouraged any form of social or political upheaval. They were also unhappy about reforms that would alter the worshipping life of the Catholic church in dramatic and disruptive fashion. More thoroughgoing reform might be possible within self-governing cities, but even the boldest of the German princes had no wish to pick a quarrel with the Catholic emperor. The magisterial reformers respected these limitations on reform. Their allegiance to the medieval ideal of a perfect Christian society rather than to the more radical one of voluntary, separatist churches had set them on a course that would inevitably lead to conflict with those who refused to give up hope of more thoroughgoing religious and social change. As the latter became more disillusioned by the Magisterial Reformation's accommodations to the world, so the magisterial reformers became increasingly antagonistic towards the radicals.

Yet the radical reformation was not merely a reaction to the Magisterial Reformation. Like the latter, its roots stretched much further back. Humanism, one of the most important of its sources, was a common influence. The intellectual movement that accompanied the Renaissance of the fifteenth and sixteenth centuries, humanism was initially nurtured in the self-governing city-states of Italy, though its influence quickly spread to the cultured urban centres of England, France, the Netherlands and parts of Germany. Renaissance humanism was always an elite, literary and therefore largely male movement. Its advocates saw it as an alternative to scholasticism. Like the latter, its method was one of textual analysis and interpretation. Unlike the latter, however, it did not aim to construct a total system of knowledge, to serve as the basis of Christendom, or to explicate the divine mysteries. Its preference was for reflection on the ways of man rather than on the ways of God, and its overall goal was to serve as a spur to individual human flourishing.

In short, humanism was a set of text-based disciplines with moral improvement as their goal. In general, the Renaissance's preference was for classical texts, both literary and philosophical, since it was here that it found its model of morally persuasive and rhetorically power-ful literature. To the humanists, the dry disputations of scholasticism seemed to have as little literary quality as they had moral force. It was in the classical world, too, that humanists found the inspiration for their political programme of civic republicanism, as we saw in relation to Marsilius of Padua's political philosophy, outlined in the previous chapter. Yet the vast majority of humanists were not opposed to the Catholic church; indeed, they were devout Christians who believed they were serving the Christian cause. They sought to reform and restore the church by getting behind the dusty accretions of medieval scholasticism to the purer sources of Christian truth. Their watchword was *ad fontes* – back to the sources. And the most important of these sources, they believed, were the texts of scripture and the writings of the early church fathers. In order to gain access to the purity of their original form, lead-ing humanist scholars became expert textual scholars and translators. Instead of relying on Jerome's Vulgate Bible, for example, they went back to the Greek and Hebrew texts and prepared new, more reliable translations.

The humanist pursuit of the simple truth was thus as sophisticated an enterprise as that of the scholasticism they attacked. Its results were far-reaching. The rallying cry *ad fontes*, for example, had a direct influ-ence on reformation, as did humanist translations of scripture. Equally, humanism anticipated the Reformation in its biting criticisms of the Catholic church and in its proposals for reform. By far the most influen-tial figure in northern Europe in these respects was the brilliant, urbane, cosmopolitan Erasmus of Rotterdam (c. 1466–1536), who brought many of the advances of the southern Renaissance to the north, and who had a direct influence on many of the reformers. As well as preparing a translation of the New Testament, Erasmus wrote a large number of works, including *The Education of a Christian Prince* and *In Praise of Folly*. In all of these he contrasted the existing excesses and corruptions of the contemporary church with the pure, unsullied truth of Jesus' teachings and the apostolic church built upon them. Simply by going back to these teachings, Erasmus became a champion of causes that seemed extremely radical in the light of subsequent church history. His general preference was for a simple religion of individual piety. As he put it in *The Education of a Christian Prince*: 'Who is truly Christian? Not he who is baptised or anointed, or who attends church. It is rather the man who has embraced Christ in the innermost feelings of his heart, and who embraces him in pious deeds.'[13]

Erasmus is often seen as less radical than the reformers he inspired. In part, this is because of his enduring support for the Catholic church and his failure to support the Reformation. Equally, it is due to the controversy with Luther, in which he opposed the latter's Augustinian belief in the bondage of the human will to sin with a more optimistic belief in human free will. As a Christian humanist, Erasmus opposed the belief that humans were born in helpless bondage to sin. While they always stood in need of God's grace, they were endowed by God with the freedom to choose good or evil. The Christian life was not about passive reception of God's grace – through either Word or sacraments – but about active co-operation with that grace in the living of a moral life. For Erasmus, human beings had genuine responsibility. At their best they could become dignified participants in godliness. Yet he was in fact a good deal more radical, not to say biblical, than Luther in his views on adult baptism, private property and pacifism. And in all these respects he appears to have had a direct influence on the radical reformers with whom Luther would later come into conflict.

What these reformers took from Erasmus, above all, was his interpretation of baptism as instituted in the New Testament as a ritual offered to adults who had received prior instruction in the faith and were therefore ready to receive it. This gave the radicals their basis for supporting adult 'believer's baptism' over infant baptism, and in so doing led to their split with the Magisterial Reformation and to their condemnation as 'anabaptists' (rebaptisers). For the magisterial reformers, as for the Catholics, the church was a divine institution in which God's grace was offered in objective form in Word and sacrament. For the radicals, by contrast, the church was the body of those saints who had received God actively rather than passively into their lives. The sacraments might confirm and consolidate their faith, but they did not create it. In that sense, the radicals were far more 'spiritual' than their opponents. What mattered to them was that each individual had received God spiritually rather than materially – not just in their body but in their soul. Anyone could go to church and receive the sacraments. But only he or she who had received the Spirit of God was truly a child of God, and such a one could no longer make any compromises with 'the world'.

A main reason why Erasmus did not go as far as the radical reformers was that he was a Platonist. As such, he believed that this world was merely an imperfect shadow of the true, divine world that lies above it and draws it forward. Likewise, Christ is the true image of humanity towards which we must always strive, but which we can never attain. To believe that the perfect community can be created on this earth was, for him, to make a category mistake (just as, for Luther, it was to underestimate the power of sin). To the radical reformers, however, this was nothing but a failure of confidence in both God and man. These were, after all, the Last Days, in which God was pouring out his Spirit, and in which men and women could achieve things never previously dreamed of. The radical reformers wanted to create perfect communities here and now. If the world would not be transformed to the heavenly pattern, then so much the worse for the world. Better that a few be saved than that all be damned.

For some radical reformers this meant a withdrawal from the world, and for others an attempt to change the world – to bring in the kingdom by force. It was the latter who would give the anti-radicals their most powerful propaganda. One individual, Thomas Müntzer, and one event, the siege of the radical stronghold of Münster in Westphalia ('Müntzer and Münster') supplied the magisterial reformers with all they needed to discredit anabaptism and justify the ensuing acts of violent repression. Thomas Müntzer (c. 1489–1525) was a spiritualist influenced in early life by the work of German mystics such as Johannes Tauler (c. 1300–61) and Henry Suso (c. 1295–1366). A supporter of the early Luther, in 1520 he became a pastor in Zwickau, where he developed a theology whose emphasis on the authority of the Spirit rather than on that of the Bible began to set him at odds with the developing Lutheran Reformation. After his expulsion from Zwickau, Müntzer travelled to Prague, where he tried to found a true apostolic church, building upon the Hussite legacy. Müntzer's thought became increasingly radical in political as well as in theological terms. Like many radicals, he opposed the bourgeois captivity of the developing Magisterial Reformation and took Luther's belief in the 'priesthood of all believers' more seriously than Luther himself did. At the same time, Müntzer developed an increasingly apocalyptic outlook. In 1524 he travelled to the heartland of the gathering peasants' rebellion in southwest Germany. As the rebellion approached, he put himself at the head of the local troops, convinced that the struggle of the saints in the Last Days had begun. After the defeat of the rebels at the battle of Frankenhausen in May 1525, Müntzer was tortured and executed.

A similarly violent apocalyptic battle was waged by radicals in Münster between 1535 and 1536. Given the fact that persecution against anabaptists had now become routine, the freedom this German town offered for the cause of radical reformation seemed a miraculous sign to scattered radicals. Münster had been led towards radical reform by the preacher Bernard Rothmann (c. 1495–1535), whose considerable support in the city allowed him to carry many with him as he grew more sympathetic to the anabaptist cause. In 1533–4 he bypassed the city council in advocating adult baptism. Very soon, radicals from both Germany and the Netherlands were converging on the city, thus advancing the cause still further. Many of those who came from the Netherlands were 'Melchiorites', followers of Melchior Hoffman (c. 1500–c. 1543), a spiritualist reformer whose ideas had been influenced by Karlstadt and who, after his exile from Strasbourg, had begun baptising adults in Frisia in 1530, whence his influence quickly spread to the Netherlands. Here his teaching won admiration from Reformation sympathisers such as Jan Matthijs and David Joris, who adopted Hoffman's apocalyptic tone. Meanwhile, Melchiorites were also exercising their influence in Münster itself. In March 1534 Matthijs declared that all Christian believers should seek refuge in Münster and await the end of the world. As many as 2,500 people from Westphalia and the Netherlands reached Münster. Radical reforms, including the redistribution of property to create a communion of goods, were instituted. In late February 1534 the prince-bishop of Münster laid siege to the city. When Matthijs was killed in a raid, he was succeeded by his Dutch supporter Jan Beukelsz, under whose leadership much of the behaviour that made the episode so notorious took place. Beukelsz dissolved the city council, instituted twelve elders of his own choosing, declared himself king, and imposed a harsh moral code with compulsory polygamy. On 25 June the city was taken, and its leaders, having been paraded around northern Germany for a number of months, were tortured and executed.

While Müntzer and Münster provided the magisterial reformers, the political authorities and the Catholic church with all the ammunition they needed for repressing any further manifestations of anabaptism, they were in fact relatively atypical of radical reform. For one thing, few radicals had the apocalyptic fervour of a Müntzer or the more extreme Melchiorites, and fewer still advocated violence. While all were critical of the existing state of the world, only a few attempted to change it through direct action. The majority wished only to withdraw from society to form their own small societies of apostolic righteousness. An even more important difference from mainstream anabaptism was the fact that Müntzer, Hoffman and several of those associated with them represented a mystical or spiritualist variety of Christian radicalism.

SPIRITUALIST RADICALISM

As we saw in the previous chapter, Christian mysticism had undergone a revival in the high and later Middle Ages, not only among women, but among some learned and influential male theologians. Important in its origins was the work of Bernard of Clairvaux and the Victorines, who developed a love-mysticism that focused on the communion of the believer with Christ and drew on the Neoplatonist tradition, particularly as that was mediated through the mystical theologian Dionysius the Pseudo-Areopagite (c. 500). From the latter the medieval mystical tradition drew the idea of 'stages' of mystical union in which self-renunciation and purification lead upwards to illumination and then to the final goal of union with God and deification. This mystical tradition entered the German bloodstream through the outstanding contribution of the German Dominican preacher and theologian Meister Eckhart (see ch. 3), who ended his career in Cologne. Eckhart became famous as a powerful vernacular preacher to the laity, especially to the many nuns and Beguines of Cologne. Like them, Eckhart was original in his transcendence of the normal Christian dichotomy of activism and contemplation, worldliness and asceticism. According to Eckhart, God was to be found only in the midst of life: 'Whoever seeks God in some special Way will gain the Way and lose the God who is hidden in the Way.'[14] Above all, God was not mediated through external institutions – even those of the church – but known directly in the sanctuary of the individual soul.

Despite the condemnation of propositions from his work as heretical, Eckhart influenced many early reformers by way of the tradition of German mysticism that developed from his legacy. Particularly important within this tradition were Suso and Tauler, both of whom, like Eckhart, were known for their close association and co-operation with women religious. It was through reading Tauler's work that Luther arrived at his breakthrough. Luther's early theology displayed many features of mystical religion, not least its emphasis upon the inner conviction of grace, the idea of a spiritual church, and the suggestion that this church might be brought into being by the gathering of the pious into *ecclesiolae* (small churches within churches). As we saw above, however, Luther's spiritualism was modified and diluted after his return to Wittenberg; there were enthusiastic fellow travellers with Luther's early theological project who were dismayed by this change of emphasis, and their faithfulness to his original vision put them outside the Lutheran camp.

The most striking example was Karlstadt, who had managed the Reformation in Wittenberg during Luther's exile, but who had pushed the church much further from the Catholic, sacramental model than Luther could now countenance. Driven by a new and passionate hatred of Karlstadt's views, Luther pigeonholed him as a comrade of Müntzer and a dangerous fool, and interned him under observation. Karlstadt eventually regained a partial freedom by fleeing to Switzerland, where he tried to form a new Christian community along the lines of early Lutheran Reform. Yet the two reformers were now irreconcilably opposed to each other in at least three key areas. First, Karlstadt believed that the external Word (or sacrament) can become living only if accompanied by an inner awakening of the Spirit. Second, Karlstadt therefore believed that salvation was not a once-and-for-all conversion but a gradual process in which the life of the believer would gradually be purified as his or her soul grew into union with God. And third, Karlstadt had abandoned the idea of a state-supported church of external authority in favour of that of free, egalitarian groups of laity led by spiritually enlightened souls who had been chosen for their role by the whole congregation.

Karlstadt's version of Protestantism highlights several of the defining features of the more mystical strand of radical Protestantism – perhaps of all Christian mysticism/spiritualism. One of the most important of all is an emphasis on direct, unmediated, personal experience of the divine as the ultimate authority. Such experience is often spoken of as 'spiritual' and as the work of the Holy Spirit, since it is in the Spirit that God is present to the world and to the believer. This spiritual or mystical experience has an authority that overrides even that of church, tradition, sacraments or scripture. Like Karlstadt, most of the more mystical reformers did not deny the importance of these other authorities, particularly the Word. Instead, they saw them as, at best, the external stimulus of the more important inner illumination. As Kaspar Schwenkfeld (1489–1561), one of the most brilliant exponents of Reformation spiritualism, who had been influenced by the early Luther as well as by Tauler and German mysticism, put it: 'Whereas one can neither write nor express with the lips spirit and life, but can only express it in parable, so must one know how to distinguish as is fitting between the scripture and the living word of God (that is, the inward word), and not give symbols that which is reality and truth.'[15] This experiential stress is thus bound up with an emphasis on the possibility of human perfection, deification or sanctification. The radical reformation was highly critical of Luther's and Calvin's doctrine of forensic justification, for they held that believers were transformed by the Spirit from within. The 'good news' was not that the God of Jesus Christ would 'ascribe' righteousness to sinners, but that through the gift of his Spirit sinners could actually become righteous, even in this life.

Spiritualism is thus strongly subjectivised, since it is only in the inner life of the individual, and not in the external life of any social group or institution – not even the church – that God is directly made manifest. This is not to say that mysticism does not produce social forms. It characteristically gives rise to small, intimate, egalitarian, face-to-face groups in which the authority of each individual can be fully accommodated and respected. These are intimate circles for edification. Clericalism is therefore abandoned, and, in theory at least, women stand on a footing of perfect equality with men. Mysticism is also tolerant, since it recognises the possible presence of the indwelling Spirit in other forms of Christianity and even in other forms of religion. Unlike the magisterial reformers, few spiritualist radicals believed that their version of Christianity contained the whole and sole truth, or that that truth must therefore be imposed by the state. For one thing, the spiritualists valued freedom as the only possible ground of true religious conviction. For another, their outlook was relative, since they believed that truth was always higher and greater than any particular expression of it.

In the history of the Reformation, however, each one of these characteristics set the radical reformers of a mystical bent apart not only from Magisterial Reform, but from mainstream anabaptism. The formal similarity between the radicals and the spiritualists derived from the fact that both tended to advocate adult rather than infant baptism and to form themselves into small, non-clerical congregations. In addition, of course, both were opposed to the church type of Christianity and to the direction taken by the Magisterial Reform. Beyond these surface similarities, however, there was a significant and highly important difference between mystical radicals who emphasised the authority of the Spirit, and other radicals who emphasised the authority of the Bible. At the risk of over-simplification, we can refer to the former as spiritualist Christians and the latter as biblicist Christians, and contrast them both with the sacramental Christianity of both the Roman Catholic church and the magisterial reformers.

BIBLICIST RADICALISM

Unlike the mystics, the biblicists located authority in the Word of God, primarily in the scriptures, but also in preaching. The growing availability of Bibles gave this emphasis an indispensable material basis. The translation of the Bible into the vernacular helped make the movement radically egalitarian. Unlike the Catholics, the humanists, the magisterial reformers and even the spiritualists, the biblicists based their faith on the 'plain word' (literal meaning) of scripture accessible to each and every man and woman. This gave biblical radicalism an immediate appeal to poorer, less educated laymen and laywomen who might be able to read and write but who had no higher form of education. Biblical Protestantism would play an important role in the growth of literacy in early modern Europe, and was thus an obvious means by which working people might 'better themselves'. Whereas Luther, following

Augustine, had spoken of the authority of 'scripture and reason', the biblicists believed themselves to be true advocates of the Reformation principle of *sola scriptura* (that scripture contains all that is necessary for salvation), which the more learned reformers had betrayed.

In many ways the biblicist radicals were in fact closer to Calvin than to Luther in their use of the scriptures, for they not only treated the whole Bible as equally authoritative – setting great store by the Old Testament – but interpreted it primarily as a book of *law*. Like the Calvinists, some of these groups regarded themselves as called out of society into a new 'covenant' with God, and, like the Calvinists only more so, they believed that this obliged them to obey the whole law of the Bible. 'More so', because Calvin's attempt to translate biblical law into civil law inevitably led to some compromises. For the biblicists, however, there could be no compromise with the Word of God. In order to keep this law 'to the letter', they therefore separated themselves from the world so that they might set up congregations of 'the saints'. Only thus could they live in strict obedience to Christ's Sermon on the Mount and to his 'harder' teachings against violence and retaliation, oath-taking, adultery in the heart as well as the mind and so on (here the influence of Erasmus again becomes evident). Some practised communion of goods. All believed in 'simplicity' in life and work. Most lived by their own labour, and viewed it as an integral part of their Christian duty. While they did not minimise the power of sin, all these radical groups had before their eyes at all times Christ's injunction to 'be perfect as your heavenly Father is perfect'.

The clearest early outbreak of biblicist radicalism occurred in the city of Zurich in 1525, when followers of Zwingli pushed the ideas of this most radical of the magisterial reformers further than he had done. These were the initial 'anabaptists' (also known as the 'Swiss Brethren'). They opposed Zwingli by performing adult baptism and insisting on the radical equality of all believers, the voluntary principle of church membership, and the importance of separation from the world. Their central doctrines were defined in the seven articles of the *Schleitheim Confession*, which may have been drafted by Michael Sattler (c. 1498–1527), and which was controverted by both Calvin and Zwingli. Anabaptism arose independently in most of the Reformation cities and found intense support chiefly among the lower classes, particularly manual labourers and those outside the guild network. In the early days of anabaptism women also played a more prominent role than in many other forms of Protestantism – a 'criticism' that was frequently made by the movement's opponents. Soon the whole of central Europe was covered with a network of anabaptist communities, with major centres in Augsburg, Moravia and Strasbourg and, later, in Friesland and the Netherlands. The most peaceful and in many ways the most successful form of biblicist radicalism was that which consolidated around Menno Simons (1496–1561) and eventually took the name 'Mennonite'. After the debacle at Münster, Simons firmly rejected the more apocalyptic and mystical elements of radical reformation and established independent, strictly pacifist communities on firm biblical principles. Though persecuted out of existence in Zurich, the Mennonites found an insecure foothold in the Netherlands and survived by making practical compromises with the state and public life.

The differences between biblicist and spiritualist groups of radicals are not hard to see. As well as their emphasis on the authority of scripture over that of experience, the biblicists placed more emphasis on the teaching of the earthly Christ than on union with the mystical Spirit-Christ. Likewise, their religious life had a distinctively moralistic tone and they tended to be far stricter in regulating and enforcing the laws of Christ; the mystics, by contrast, believed that the goal of union with the Spirit would be manifest in a far less clearly defined life lived in the Spirit of love. In sociological terms, the biblicist form of congregation was stronger, more effective at recruitment and transmission, and better adapted to the conditions of exile and hardship in which most radical groups found themselves than were the looser and more individualistic conventicles of the mystics. As we shall see in the next chapter, the latter tended to do best when they sheltered within the structures of a church. This was one reason that groups that began with a more mystical tendency sometimes developed a more sectarian form. At the same time, a number of more biblicist groups allowed their strict emphasis on the law to be nourished by the vivifying experience of the Spirit. As we shall also see in the next chapter, it would be such 'mixed' forms of Christianity that would play a key role in the development of Protestantism after the sixteenth century and give it an easy and influential passage into modernity. This development would first become apparent in the late seventeenth and early eighteenth centuries in the rise of pietism and evangelicalism. In the meantime, the radical reformation clung precariously to existence at the edges of Europe, an exile from persecution by both Protestant and Catholic power.

Further reading

GENERAL

There is no shortage of literature on the Protestant Reformation. Useful general surveys filled with factual information include Euan Cameron's *The European Reformation* (Oxford: Clarendon, 1991), Carter Lindberg's *The European Reformations* (Oxford: Blackwell, 1995; Cambridge MA, 1996) and James D. Tracey's *Europe's Reformations, 1450–1650* (Lanham, MD: Rowman and Littlefield, 1999).

Thomas A. Brady, Heiko Oberman and James D. Tracy have together edited a two-volume *Handbook of European History 1400–1600* (Leiden and New York: Brill, 1996). Consisting of essays by leading Reformation scholars on key topics, both structural and theological, it offers easy access to recent research. Volume I looks at structural and political matters, while volume 2 gives attention to themes, thinkers and outcomes of reformation.

GENDER REFORMATION

Merry E. Wiesner-Hanks's *Christianity and Sexuality in the Early Modern World* (London and New York: Routledge, 2000) offers an informative survey of the period 1500–1750, opening with a chapter on women and sexuality in early and medieval Christianity. Lyndal Roper's *The Holy Household: Religion, Morals and Order in Reformation Augsburg* (Oxford: Clarendon, 1989) shows how central gender reformation was in the early Lutheran Reformation in the cities. Steven Ozment's *When Fathers Ruled: Family Life in Reformation Europe* (Cambridge, MA: Harvard University Press, 1983) offers a more positive account of the Reformation's impact on women.

THE MAGISTERIAL REFORMATION

There is no substitute for reading Luther's and Calvin's own writings, which are accessible and easily available in English translation.

Hans Oberman's numerous books present a fresh portrait of Luther as a larger-than-life character very different from that which later piety constructed, and much more medieval than modern. See, for example, *Luther: Man between God and the Devil* (New Haven, CT: Yale University Press, 1993).

On Calvin, see David C. Steinmetz's *Calvin in Context* (New York: Oxford University Press, 1995), and William G. Naphy's *Calvin and the Consolidation of the Genevan Reformation* (Manchester: Manchester University Press; New York: St Martin's Press, 1994).

THE RADICAL REFORMATION

Erasmus' writings are accessible and entertaining. His *In Praise of Folly* is a good place to start. See also Abraham Friesen's interesting study of Erasmus and his influence on the radical reformation, *Erasmus, the Anabaptists, and the Great Commission* (Grand Rapids, MI, and Cambridge: Eerdmans, 1988).

George H. Williams's *The Radical Reformation* (Philadelphia, PA: Westminster, 1962) introduced the notions of 'radical' and 'magisterial' reformation, and, though his scheme can be criticised, it had an important impact on our understanding of the Protestant Reformation. He also edited a useful collection of radical writings, entitled *Spiritual and Anabaptist Writers: Illustrative Documents* (London: SCM, 1957).

Two informative studies of the Anabaptists are James M. Stayer's *The German Peasants' War and the Anabaptist Community of Goods* (Kingston, Ontario: McGill-Queen's University Press, 1991), and Hans-Jürgen Goertz's *The Anabaptists* (New York: Routledge, 1996).

Robert W. Scribner writes illuminatingly on popular religion in the period, as in *Popular Culture and Popular Movements in Reformation Germany* (London and Ronceverte, WV: Hambledon, 1987).

5

Protestant pathways into the modern world

Now I saw in my dream, that the highway up which Christian
was to go, was fenced on either side with a Wall, and that Wall
is called Salvation. Up this way therefore did burdened
Christian run, but not without great difficulty, because of the
load on his back.

He ran thus till he came at a place somewhat ascending; and
upon that place stood a Cross, and a little below in the bottom,
a sepulchre. So I saw in my dream, that just as Christian came
up with the Cross, his burden loosed from off his shoulders,
and fell from off his back; and began to tumble, and so
continued to do till it came to the mouth of the sepulchre,
where it fell in, and I saw it no more.

Then was Christian glad and lightsome, and said with a
merry heart, He hath given me rest, by his sorrow, and life, by
his death. Then he stood a while, to look and wonder; for it
was very surprising to him that the sight of the Cross should
thus ease him from his burden. He looked therefore, and looked
again, even till the springs that were in his head sent the waters
down his cheeks.[1]

Bunyan's *Pilgrim's Progress*, published in England in 1678, became a
Protestant classic. It offered an allegorical tale of one man's struggle
to overcome sin and win salvation, and succeeded in translating the
objective truths of Protestant theology into the subjective experience of
'Pilgrim', the Protestant everyman. Bunyan later added a second half to
the book, in which he described the spiritual pilgrimage of Christian's
wife, Christiana. Now all of Bunyan's readers could shape and interpret
their spiritual experience by reference to these prototypical pilgrims.

In translating Reformation theology into a different and more accessible mode, Bunyan also reinterpreted. The medium carried a message,
and the message was that true doctrine, ecclesiastical niceties and denominational differences counted for less than an individual's personal relationship with God. What mattered most of all was inward repentance,
assurance of sins forgiven by the work of Christ on the cross, and the
courage and determination to live a holy life thereafter. In that sense,
Bunyan's focus was individual rather than social, and this shift would
be typical of post-Reformation Protestantism more generally.

The Pilgrim's Progress was also a protest. Bunyan was protesting against a cooling of the Reformation spirit. Like many of his Puritan contemporaries in seventeenth-century England, he believed that the sixteenth-century Reformation had not gone far enough. The new Church of England might be Protestant in name, but neither it nor the English nation had turned Protestant in nature. Yet again a distinction was being drawn between the outer and the inner. Outward changes were insufficient. What was needed was an authentic inner reformation, a reformation of the spirit, not just of the letter. This dynamic of constant, cyclical reform was inherent within all forms of Protestantism. Every reformation would eventually go cold as it hardened into merely outward forms, and every reformation would therefore require reform. This was part of the logic of a religion based on intensity of personal experience, and, as such experience became more important to Protestantism, so the need for regular 'revivals' increased. Some reformations and revivals could be contained within existing church structures, while others would lead to schism and the creation of new churches. Luther's initial act of establishing a 'protesting' church dissolved the previously sacrosanct unity of a 'catholic' church, and led to the rapid proliferation of a whole succession of 'protesting' churches. One of the essential tasks of this chapter will be to offer a framework for understanding the plethora of different forms of Protestant Christianity that resulted.

The other main task will be to chart the course of Protestantism from the beginning of the seventeenth century to the end of the nineteenth, and to relate it to accompanying social change. The period witnessed a new phase of modernisation as commercial capitalism slowly gave way to industrial capitalism. In the fifteenth and sixteenth centuries the rise of powerful nation states had been based on superiority in military and political power, but the new absolute and constitutional monarchies remained weak in their infrastructures of control, and still required the assistance of religion to maintain themselves. By the eighteenth century, however, the situation was changing, particularly in Britain. British power was being established on the basis of economic as well as military superiority. Her colonial programme strengthened her position by opening up new markets for her commercial activities, not least in North America. The power of the centralised state, of the capitalist classes and of the nation developed rapidly and in tandem. Social change was evident in the expansion of an affluent middle class or 'bourgeoisie', the breakdown of traditional hereditary forms of power and the rigid social order in which they had been institutionalised, and the growth of new mercantile and commercial occupations in towns and cities.

In the nineteenth century even more dramatic social change would come about through the rise of industrial capitalism and rapid urbanisation. Centralised, large-scale manufacturing, giant corporations and finance capitalism would concentrate economic power in a few expanding cities. While some individuals and families grew fantastically rich through their exploitation of the new means of production, industrial capitalism also gave rise to an expanded professional middle class and produced a new urban working class and lower middle class who sold their labour to socially, and sometimes physically, distant employers. From being recognised members of rural communities, working men and women became cogs in the machine of modern industrial production. Both government and corporations achieved social control through newly extended impersonal, bureaucratic and rationalistic frameworks of control. While Britain was the first nation to experience this transition, the newly independent United States of America followed hard on her heels.

The position of religion altered accordingly. The single most important change was the churches' gradual loss of social power – political, economic and military. As we shall see in the next chapter, the Roman Catholic church clung to such power with greater tenacity than the Protestant churches, and retained significant remnants right through the early modern period. As we shall see in this chapter, the surrender of the dream of state-assisted ecclesiastical control over the whole of society tended to be less traumatic for Protestantism. Although a handful of Protestant state churches (Lutheran, Anglican and Presbyterian) continued to exist, much of the Protestant camp accepted the voluntary principle with relative ease. Rather than viewing Christianity as something to be imposed on people from above by the joint agency of church and state, they now accepted that religion must be a matter of free, individual choice. Though this voluntary principle had always characterised the churches of the radical reformation, both biblicist and spiritualist, it now spread more widely still, and was eventually embraced even by Calvinism. Religion became a matter of 'private' life, while a 'public' sphere of politics, commerce, industry and the law continued on its way free of religious regulation. By the eighteenth century even education and culture – particularly natural science – would begin to break free of Christianity, though in these spheres the divorce took much longer.

The loss of social power did not, however, lead to a widespread repudiation of power from on high in favour of power from below in Protestantism. The high, mighty, all-powerful Father God of the Reformers continued to dominate the Protestant imagination, as did a crushing sense of personal sinfulness and a fear of eternal damnation. If anything, this intensified. As we see already in Bunyan, the message of individual human depravity and inherited sin – the burden Pilgrim carries on his back – became central. As we also see in the passage quoted above, the Protestant solution lay not in the possibility of human self-improvement but in the work accomplished by God-in-Christ on the cross. Jesus' significance was interpreted in terms of 'atoning sacrifice', a self-offering of the Son to the Father, the effect of which was to deflect God's wrath against humanity and lead him to ascribe righteousness to those who accepted the work of his Son with trust, gratitude and lifelong devotion. Salvation was thus achieved though submission to a gracious God who wills to save human beings in spite of their sinfulness. In the main, then, Protestantism remained true to the sixteenth-century Reformers' objective and forensic understanding of salvation, rather than embracing a more subjectivist understanding according to which human beings grow into the likeness of God through the gift of the Spirit. A positive subjectivism that thought in terms of an original goodness rather than of an original sinfulness was even less congenial to the Protestant mind (though we shall note its tentative appearance in liberal Protestantism).

If anything, then, the churches' loss of social power seemed to intensify their efforts to secure dominating power – no longer over society as a whole, but over each and every individual. If they could not control society from above, they could control it from below, by winning each member of society to the Christian cause. Whereas the medieval church had been relatively relaxed about individual piety and more concerned with political and economic power, the post-Reformation churches – both Catholic and Protestant – became far more concerned with policing, regulating and controlling the interior lives of their members. Individuals' 'private' lives became a matter of increasing concern to the churches, as did individual conversion to Christianity. The rise of an evangelistic impulse, with the primary aim of winning the hearts and minds of individuals, became an intense preoccupation of both Catholicism and Protestantism during this period (a topic that will be addressed in the next chapter).

Thus the compensation for the churches' exclusion from power in the public sphere was the rise of a private sphere in which they were able to attain a new intensity of power. A major effect was to bind Christianity ever more closely to women and the family. Though Luther had taken the first steps in this direction, he had insisted that the *paterfamilias* maintain the headship of the household and its religious life. As men increasingly left the home to work in the public sphere beyond it, so the home and the family became women's sphere. And since the churches' sphere of control was increasingly limited to home and private life, this left women with new religious responsibilities, most notably the duty of spiritual care for their household. The churches' teachings on gender difference shifted accordingly: no longer was it men who had to protect women from the snares of sin, but women who had to protect their menfolk from falling into temptation. By the nineteenth century a cult of domesticity had arisen within the middle classes in which women were seen as 'angels in the house' – gentle, spiritual creatures whose vocation lay in the dutiful discharge of their domestic duties. As religion became increasingly identified with women's work, so women turned this situation to their advantage by taking on new responsibilities, not only within the home, but also within the churches and the numerous voluntary bodies associated with them. The latter, as we shall see, became a route by which middle-class and upper-working-class women could enter a public sphere that was otherwise closed to them.

Thus Protestantism's voluntaristic capacities, and the speed and flexibility with which it activated them in response to changing social conditions, made it more adaptable to modern society than Catholicism. The result was that, even though it gradually lost power *over* society, it did not lose power *within* society. In the 'Christian revolution', the church had come to monopolise sacred power and to use it to legitimate the power of emperors and rulers, who, in turn, would support the Christian cause. In the 'modern revolution', sacred power was still needed to legitimate monarchs in the early modern period, but the increasing shift of power to a capitalist class after the eighteenth century gave rise to a new use for sacred power: to legitimate the precarious position of the middle classes. On the one hand, Christianity was used to legitimate the wealth and power of white, male, middle-class Protestants and to sacralise their system of values: hard work, thrift, cleanliness, self-control and so on. On the other hand, it was used to pacify the new industrial and urbanised working classes (whose revolutionary potential was a constant source of fear to the middle classes) as well as the 'other races' on whose exploitation the middle-class prosperity and capitalist success had come to depend (whether these were the subjects or slaves of the British empire or, later, of the North American plantations). Protestant Christianity proved not only compatible with the western capitalist ethos, but an important guarantor and guardian of its values. Movements of challenge 'from below' would still emerge – the Christian anti-slavery movements being an important example – but the broad thrust of early modern and nineteenth-century Protestantism remained supportive of the socio-economic status quo.

Nowhere are these remarks better illustrated than in the United States of America, which became and remains a truly Protestant nation (even when Protestants were outnumbered by Catholics). The fact that the voluntary principle was freely adopted by the Protestant churches in America after Independence in 1776 gave them an unparalleled location at the very heart of the nation and its system of values. Here, by contrast with Catholic Europe, church and state developed side by side in the greatest harmony, and united in a common purpose – the defence of liberty and the support of democratic capitalism and of 'the American way of life'. Just as Protestantism had supported Great Britain in its ascent to world domination in the nineteenth and very early twentieth centuries (and before that had supported the world's first capitalist nation/empire, that of the Dutch), so Protestantism accompanied the American rise to power thereafter.

This chapter traces these developments, beginning with the English Revolution in the seventeenth century and the transformation of Protestantism by the voluntary principle from then through to the eighteenth century (with an excursus on the position of women). It then moves on to consider the rise of American Protestantism and Protestant America. It concludes by looking at the course of Protestantism on both sides of the Atlantic in the nineteenth century, focusing in particular on the role and position of women, and on the development of the 'evangelical' and 'liberal' tempers within Protestant Christianity.

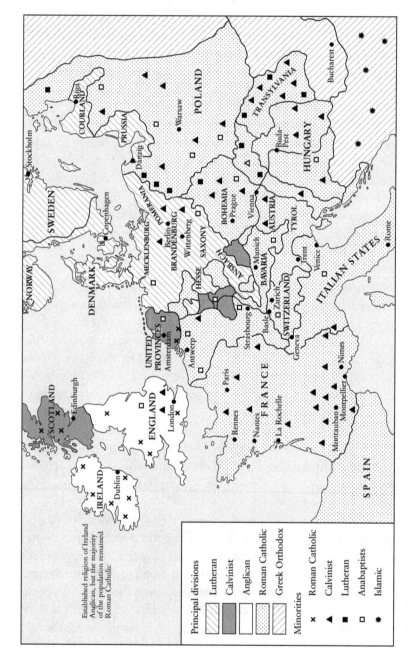

Principal divisions

▨ Lutheran

▨ Calvinist

☐ Anglican

⋰ Roman Catholic

⟋ Greek Orthodox

Minorities

✕ Roman Catholic

▲ Calvinist

■ Lutheran

☐ Anabaptists

✳ Islamic

Established religion of Ireland Anglican, but the majority of the population remained Roman Catholic

NORWAY

SWEDEN
Stockholm

DENMARK
Copenhagen

SCOTLAND
Edinburgh

IRELAND
Dublin

ENGLAND
London

UNITED PROVINCES
Amsterdam
Antwerp

FRANCE
Rennes
Paris
Nantes
La Rochelle
Montauban
Montpellier
Nimes

SPAIN

COURLAND
Riga

PRUSSIA
Danzig

POLAND
Warsaw

POMERANIA

MECKLENBURG

BRANDENBURG
Berlin
Wittenberg

SAXONY

BOHEMIA
Prague

HESSE

ANSBACH

BAVARIA
Munich

AUSTRIA
Vienna

TYROL
Trent

SWITZERLAND
Basle
Zurich
Geneva

Strasbourg

TRANSYLVANIA

HUNGARY
Buda
Pest

ITALIAN STATES
Venice
Rome

Bucharest

Map 5   Christian Europe about 1600

Early modern Protestantism and the development of the voluntary principle

Protestant reformation was not confined to the sixteenth century, but was a continuous and ongoing process. If Germany formed the epicentre of erupting Protestant energies in the sixteenth century, by the seventeenth century that centre had shifted to England. Thereafter, key developments would take place both in England and in continental Europe and then, increasingly, in North America. (The worldwide expansion of Protestantism in the wake of colonial expansion, missionary activity and economic globalisation will be considered in ch. 7.)

Despite important differences, the churches established by the magisterial reformers still exemplified the same basic characteristics as the Roman Catholic church. Not only were they sacramental and 'objective' (regulating sacred power by identifying it with material objects under the control of male clergy); they also sought control over the whole of society, and invoked the aid of the state to help them achieve this aim. In the context of early modern Europe they therefore took shape as national or 'state' churches – such as the Lutheran church in Sweden, the Presbyterian church in Scotland, or the Church of England established by King Henry VIII (1491–1547). The voluntaristic groups of the radical reformation, which sought detachment from political power, were marginalised and persecuted.

After the seventeenth century, however, the voluntaristic principle began to exercise new influence within Protestantism. National churches came under pressure not only from secularising processes that sought to detach worldly power from Christianity, but from alternative, voluntaristic interpretations of Protestantism. That which had been marginal in the sixteenth century gradually became mainstream – albeit in new guises and incarnations. For another effect of the voluntary principle in Protestantism was to give individuals and groups the ability to detach themselves from churches with which they were dissatisfied and to form their own alternative institutions. As a consequence, the period under review witnessed a proliferation of different Protestant groups.

THE ENGLISH REVOLUTION

The process whereby Protestant state churches came under pressure from the voluntary principle and found themselves in competition with alternative forms of Protestantism – some of which reattached themselves to state power – is vividly illustrated by the tumultuous history of seventeenth-century England. This period is also important as the one in which many of the main types of Protestant denomination came into existence.

Henry VIII had thrown off Roman Catholic control and established the Church of England in 1534, when he had Parliament declare him 'Supreme Head of the Church on Earth'. His motives were not so much religious – he considered himself a loyal Catholic in theology – as political and personal. Nationalisation of the English church freed Henry and the Tudor dynasty from Roman interference and gave control over a key source of economic, social and ideological power in the land. An added bonus was that it allowed Henry to bypass the Catholic church's refusal to dissolve his marriage to the well-connected Catherine of Aragon. But, in spite of placing English Bibles in churches, and dissolving the monasteries in 1535 (chiefly for economic and political gain), Henry proved so conservative in religious matters that when a Catholic, Mary Tudor (1516–58), ascended the throne in 1553, she was able to restore Catholicism with relative ease. Her successor, Elizabeth I (1533–1603), realised that the best way to secure her throne, strengthen her nation and avoid the religious turmoil afflicting other parts of Europe was to steer a middle course between Catholicism and extreme Protestantism. Under the Elizabethan Settlement of 1559 the Church of England once more established itself in independence from Rome and adopted a reformed prayer book, while retaining some traditional elements of Catholic practice.

Although Elizabeth's brand of Protestant reform allowed her to consolidate the growing power of the English nation and to hold religious extremism in check, it left the more enthusiastic supporters of reform dissatisfied. These were the 'Puritans', so called because of their concern to purify the Church of England. Puritanism named a broad movement or tendency within English Protestantism, rather than a particular church affiliation. Some Puritans were members of the Church of England, some, like Bunyan, were early Baptists, while others migrated to one of the new forms of Protestantism that arose in the course of the seventeenth century, ranging from Independency to Quakerism. Some of the original Puritans had found refuge in Geneva during Mary's reign, and had been inspired by what they had seen of Calvin's reforms. When they returned to Elizabethan England they campaigned to abolish practices such as the wearing of vestments by the clergy and the retention of

saints' days. They also sought to replace the traditional episcopal structure of the church with Calvin's presbyterian form of church government. They failed under Elizabeth, and they failed under her successor,
James I. Indeed, the Puritan cause in England met with successive rounds
of defeat by monarchs who feared that religious change threatened both
the stability of the nation and their attempts to construct an absolutist
form of rule.

Between 1629 and 1640 King Charles I, set on an absolutist course,
attempted to rule without Parliament. In 1642 civil war broke out. In
the following years of turmoil, huge political and religious upheavals
took place as Royalist and Parliamentary forces opposed one another,
culminating in the execution of the king and the abolition of the monarchy in 1649. Though the war and the regimes that succeeded it briefly
opened up a space for a whole range of radical forms of Protestantism
to flourish, Oliver Cromwell's Republic did not long outlast his death,
and the 'Restoration' that followed saw both the Church of England
and a constitutional monarchy reinstated as the anchors of a stable
English society. In order to protect this stability, however, 'dissent' – as
all non-episcopal forms of Protestantism were now styled – was forcibly
repressed. Bunyan, who had fought on the Parliamentary side in the
Civil War, and who would not cease preaching his Puritan gospel after
the Restoration, was imprisoned in 1660 for twelve years and in 1676
for six months. It was in prison that he began *The Pilgrim's Progress*.

Despite the re-establishment of the Church of England (a church that
remains established to this day, in name at least), and despite the desire
on the part of both state and church authorities to limit the influence of
dissent, it was now felt that the most effective means of doing so would
be by way of limited toleration rather than through active persecution.
The shift towards a relatively tolerant form of licensed state religion
was significant. It reflected a new caution about the destructive potential of religion – a potential witnessed in the English Civil War, the Thirty
Years War (1618–48) on the continent, and the terrible persecutions suffered by those deemed heretical in their own lands, such as the Calvinist
'Huguenot' minority in Catholic France – and a strong desire to suppress this potential. Under the Hanoverian dynasty, which began with
the reign of George I in 1714, England entered an era of relative stability and growing prosperity in which the interests of its expanding
capitalist class were served by the new markets opened up by a growing

colonial empire. The last thing that the constitutional monarchy and the prospering commercial classes wanted was religious or political disruption, which might interfere with economic development. Given its established status and close ties with the powers in the land, the Church of England was well placed to deliver the required stability and cohesion. Its broad, 'latitudinarian', approach was designed to neutralise the destructive potential of different shades of Protestantism by embracing them. Those 'dissenters' who refused this embrace would be tolerated, but in such a way that full citizenship and respectability would always be denied them in English society.

VARIETIES OF PROTESTANTISM

It was in the course of the tumultuous events of the seventeenth century, and its more peaceful aftermath in the eighteenth, that several of the main varieties of modern Protestantism came into being. Some of these embraced the voluntary principle, others did not. Thus it is still necessary to draw a distinction between the non-voluntary state-assisted churches (as we might loosely call them), which preserved the Catholic ideal of ecclesiastical domination of the whole of society, and the voluntaristic churches, which believed in the separation of politics and religion. As we shall see, however, the distinction between the two gradually became less important as the voluntary principle extended its influence.

Though the divide between voluntary and non-voluntary forms of Protestantism became less important during the early modern period, the divides between different forms of voluntaristic church became more so. The most important of all was a distinction that has already been drawn in relation to the radical reformation of the sixteenth century between voluntary biblicist and voluntary spiritualist forms of Protestantism. After the sixteenth century a spectrum developed, with strongly 'objectivist' biblicist forms of Protestantism at one pole, and 'subjectivist' forms of spiritualism at the opposite. For the former, authority and salvation are located outside the believer in the objective Word of the Bible, which must be followed to the letter. For the latter, authority and salvation are located within the believer in the reception of the Holy Spirit. As we shall see, there was also an increasing amount of middle ground between these poles, as some forms of Protestantism joined an objectivist, biblical emphasis with a more subjectivist emphasis on the gift of the Holy Spirit.

*Non-voluntary Protestantism: Puritanism, Pietism, the free
churches and Congregationalism*

Despite the variety of different types of Christianity – both voluntary
and non-voluntary – with which Puritans associated themselves, in its
origins and dynamism Puritanism belonged to the Calvinist family. The
Puritans' ultimate goal was always to convert the whole of society to
perfect godliness, and wherever the opportunity arose they were quick
to try to co-opt the state to assist in this task. Like Calvin, the Puritans
were strongly biblicist, and often took the Old Testament as seriously as
the New. They placed enormous stress upon the importance of education, and continued the Reformation tradition of family worship, prayer
and catechetical instruction led by the male head of the household.
Like Calvin, the Puritans read the Bible as a book of laws by which
the whole of life, both individual and social, should be regulated. They
regarded the performance of godly deeds as essential to the pursuit of
holiness, and generally placed less emphasis on the moment of conversion – important though that was – than on the sanctified life that
should grow out of this conversion. This is why Bunyan places the story
of Christian's conversion, quoted above, very early in narrative of *The
Pilgrim's Progress*. Most of this 'progress' comes after conversion, and it
is then that salvation is won. Bunyan was typical of Puritanism in seeing
the Christian life as a dramatic and continuous struggle between good
and evil, a gruelling combat in which the prize was eternal life. Puritans
were known for their severe personal self-discipline and their systematic
approach to the cultivation of inner holiness – to which the vast number
of autobiographies, spiritual diaries and journals they produced bear
witness.

Pietism developed later than Puritanism, in the late seventeenth and
early eighteenth centuries, and its epicentre was the western provinces
of a Germany that was not yet a unified nation state. Like Puritanism,
Pietism's main affinities were with non-voluntary, state-assisted Christianity, but with Lutheranism rather than with Calvinism. Pietism arose
as a reforming movement within the Lutheran churches, just as Puritanism had arisen as a reforming movement within the Church of England. In some German states, as in Württemberg, Pietism was relatively
easily incorporated into the established church, whereas in others, such
as the increasingly powerful eighteenth-century Prussian state, it ended
up in opposition to established Lutheranism. Generally speaking, Pietism

Plate 14 *Interior of St Odolphus Church*, by P. J. Saenredam (1597–1665)

Saenredam's famous paintings of the interiors of Dutch churches helped shape an ideal image of Protestantism – 'cleansed' of all Catholic paraphernalia, pure and unsullied. In this painting pulpit and preacher replace altar and sacrament as the focus of attention.

was politically opportunistic. If it could best influence society through alliance with the state church (as in Württemberg) it would do so, but if it was offered independent support by the state (as in Prussia) it would avail itself of that opportunity even if in so doing it became set on a collision course with the established church. In and of itself, Pietism did not favour absolutism, constitutionalism or democracy. Its chief concern was not to win political power and shape society but to shape individual souls, and it would make use of whatever form of political backing would best enable it to achieve this aim.

German Pietism spread quickly through a number of states after about 1680, taking both moderate and more radical forms. The latter, heir to the German mystical tradition, emphasised the work of the Holy Spirit in the hearts of men and women, and sometimes took anti-establishment and millenarian forms. The former tended to work for moderate reform within the Lutheran churches, and won support from many clergy as well as from many lay people. Under the patronage of Frederick the Great, king of Prussia, a Pietist university was founded at Halle, which became the intellectual hub of the movement. A body of younger theologians and pastors trained at Halle helped carry Pietism throughout Protestant Germany in the eighteenth century. In Herrnhut in Saxony, in the experimental religious settlement established by Count Nicholas von Zinzendorf (1700–60), Pietism, allied with Moravianism, took the form of an intense, affective Christ-mysticism, a 'religion of the heart' that would later influence the birth of Methodism.

In its concern with a personal ethic rather than a social one, Pietism showed its allegiance to Lutheranism rather than to Calvinism. Its Lutheran origins were also evident in the greater stress it placed on conversion and the inward conviction of conversion. For Pietism, as for later evangelicalism, the once-and-for-all experience of conversion became the central and defining event of the Christian life. Though it rejected neither Word and sacrament nor the importance of good deeds, Pietism developed a strongly subjectivist stress. What mattered were not only the external means and evidences of salvation, but their inner appropriation. If anything, Pietism went even further than Puritanism in this direction, though the ability to hold together something of the 'objectivism' of both the Magisterial Reformation and biblicist Protestantism with something of the 'subjectivism' of the more mystical forms of reformation was common to them both – as it would later be of Methodism and of evangelical Protestantism more generally.

Both Puritan and Pietist preaching were noted for their practical and hortatory force; their aim was not merely to educate individuals about God but actively to draw them into the path of holiness. The Puritan view of theology, as summarised by William Perkins, was 'the science of living blessedly forever'.[2] The most influential work of German Pietism, Philipp Jakob Spener's *Pia Desideria, Heartfelt Desires for a God-Pleasing Improvement of the True Protestant Church* (1675), outlined a resolutely practical programme of personal as well as ecclesiastical purification. It involved the creation of small groups within the established church for Bible reading, repetition of the sermon, prayer and discussion, their aim being the cultivation of a more perfect practice of personal piety in all aspects of everyday life. Pietists argued that, while Luther had initiated a revolution in doctrine, there had not been a corresponding 'reformation of life'. Far more optimistic than Luther, they believed in the possibility of active transformation of this world and the achievement of the kingdom of God on earth. It would be brought about, however, not by a revolution from on high but by a revolution from below – not by the actions of state or state church but by the trans-formation of ordinary lives, one by one. In keeping with this optimistic and activist spirit, Pietism inspired not only numerous charitable activi-ties but many notable missionary initiatives both at home and overseas.

If Pietism represented an outcome of the voluntary principle working within Lutheranism, then the rise of the 'free churches' represented the outcome of the voluntary principle working on Calvinism. In order to make this transition, Calvinism had to overcome both the idea that the (Calvinist) church was the sole possessor of truth and the belief that the state should be an instrument in the creation of a society conformed to this view of truth. Calvinism, in other words, having been a natural sup-porter of religious and political non-voluntarism, had to abandon both. Within the context of early modern Europe and, above all, of North America, it slowly made this transition, becoming a tolerant and vol-untaristic church whose members were there by choice – albeit based on election – and who would respect the right of other Christians to attend different churches of their choice. As such, Calvinism became increasingly conformed to the democratic ideal in which each and every individual becomes sovereign over his or her own life choices – a remark-able migration from its starting point in Geneva.

Though it drew on elements internal to primitive Calvinism, includ-ing its potential for an intensely individualistic development of activist holiness, such free-church Calvinism did not, however, develop without a struggle. It was shaped not only by the modernising contexts in which it found itself, but under the influence of more clearly voluntaristic and tolerant competing forms of Christianity, both biblicist and humanist. Its natural reversion to a more absolutist stance was evident in all the main centres of its development – in England, Holland and North America. In each one, when the opportunity of forming an established Presby-terian state or territorial church briefly arose, it was quickly seized. In America, for example, the earliest free churches, though they did not compel membership, would admit no other churches in their territory and offered full civil rights only to their own members. Here, as in Pres-byterian England immediately after the Civil War, it was only gradually that toleration was extended to other groups, largely under the influ-ence of Pietism and voluntaristic forms of Christianity. In other words, Calvinism came to adopt the voluntaristic stance only slowly and some-times less than wholeheartedly. In some situations, as in the Netherlands, a free-church Calvinism would be forced to distinguish itself from the official state-church Calvinism.

By the eighteenth and nineteenth centuries, however, many Presbyterian churches had come to identify much more wholeheartedly with the cause of democracy and the rise of secular states. Given their powerful theological tradition, some Calvinist thinkers were able to contribute to the theoretical and ethical basis of these developments. In the Netherlands, for example, Johannes Althusius (1557–1638) argued for the independence of politics from ethics, theology and philosophy, while still attempting to defend a close agreement of church and state. Hugo Grotius (1583–1645) and John Locke (1632–1704) went much further, the latter, in particular, helping to lay the foundations of the modern theory of natural law. In cutting loose the first table of the Decalogue (duties to God) from the second table (duties to fellow humans) and insisting that only the latter could be the basis of state legislation, such Protestant thought, flowing side by side with classical influences, aided the development of a wholly secular natural law that did not depend in any way on religious principles. (In general, however, the principles of modern political theory and democracy were derived as much from ancient classical and modern rationalistic sources as from Protestant Christianity.)

Congregationalism, which arose in late sixteenth-century and early seventeenth-century England, did not wholly abandon the ideal of a territorial church sovereign over the people, and wished to see the whole of society shaped by the gospel. Unlike the Baptist churches (see below), it had no inclination to abandon infant baptism in favour of adult baptism, or to depart from any other of the established church's traditional rituals and forms of worship. Like the Puritans, with whom they shared so much, Congregationalists sought to purify the existing church rather than to create a new one. Yet the voluntary principle was more integral to the outlook of Congregationalism, rather than an adaptation to necessity as in the case of the free churches. Congregationalist churches exhibited the democratic principle far more clearly than Calvinism did, by insisting on the strict equality of congregational members and by electing preachers and officers, who remained at all times accountable to their congregation.

Many Congregationalists began as separatists who believed that the kingdom of God would be hastened not by political or ecclesiastical action from above, but by the gathering of the pure in heart into communities of the saints. This sometimes encouraged the desire to effect a separation between state and church, and to work towards independent self-government within congregations. These simple principles were laid down by the founders of Congregationalism, most notably Robert Browne (c. 1550–1633) and Henry Barrow (c. 1550–93), by the late 1580s. They developed in both separatist and nonseparatist directions under conditions of persecution and exile: early Congregationalists fled to both the Netherlands and North America, and strengthened their movement in the process. In the context of the English Revolution and its aftermath prior to the Restoration, Congregationalism developed in two different streams. Independency (the allegiance of Oliver Cromwell) supported both the state-church ideal and the independence of each congregation. This movement died out after the Restoration. The wider body of Congregationalism developed in a more co-operative direction in which congregations, while retaining their independence, nevertheless recognised a bond of common faith and order, and would extend help and fellowship to one another.

Voluntarist biblicism: the Baptist churches and Methodism

The Baptist churches belong so clearly to the biblicist, voluntarist form of Christianity that they can be said to define the type. With its origins in Erasmian humanism and the radical ideals of early Lutheranism, the movement first took shape in the anabaptists' protest against the dilution of the Reformation. As we saw in the previous chapter, this early Baptist movement was defined by its practice of adult baptism, which served as a vivid ritual marker of its voluntarist status. Immersion in water marked the transition of the believer from the world to the company of the saints – 'the baptised' – and has been a mark of Baptist identity ever since. Later Baptist communities also retained anabaptism's strict adherence to biblical teachings and rejection of the Catholic theory of ecclesiastical sacraments. For Baptists the 'Lord's Supper' was mainly a symbolic enactment of congregational fellowship and an expression of personal faith in Christ. In the course of a partial adjustment to the conditions of the world, however, Baptists gradually relaxed their attempt to live in conformity with the perfectionist morality of the Sermon on the Mount. By the eighteenth century the early anabaptists' refusal to bear arms, to countenance violence, to take oaths and to occupy official positions within the state was becoming less common. The concern for strict standards of personal holiness and discipline enforced through excommunication was retained, but such holiness now had more to do with standards of private, domestic and sexual conduct.

The Baptist movement in the sixteenth and early seventeenth centuries survived in moderated form, having also abandoned the enthusiastic and apocalyptic tendencies of earlier anabaptism. Its stronghold was in the Netherlands under the leadership of Menno Simons. Its next phase of development took place in England, where it was drawn into close contact with Puritanism and exercised a significant influence upon Congregationalism and Independency. Despite the schism of 'Particular Baptists', who adhered more strongly to Calvinist principles, the 'General Baptist' churches (so called to differentiate them from the former group) were opposed to many doctrines of Calvinism, including predestination. More egalitarian in organisation, Baptist churches were independent or congregational in polity, though they gave regular expression to their inter-church relationships through 'Associations'. Egalitarianism was strengthened by the movement's location of authority not in dogma or theology but in the plain text of scripture, accessible to all who could read. Some of the socially and politically radical potentials of Baptist belief were released in the Civil War period in England. Oliver Cromwell's disavowal of the radical Parliament of 'saints', which included Baptist tendencies, in favour of a more moderate Protestantism helped strengthen this tendency. Baptism also developed in a democratic direction in the equally vibrant religious context of colonial North America (see below).

While all the varieties of Protestantism reviewed above had their birth in the sixteenth or seventeenth century, Methodism's origins in the eighteenth century made it the first and most important early modern form of Protestantism – in roots as well as in development. Though it was influenced by Pietism, its context was that of Hanoverian England and established, moderate Anglicanism. It presented itself not as a form of dissent but as an attempt at reform of the Church of England from within. Its leaders, John Wesley (1703–91), his brother Charles (1707–88) and their friend George Whitefield (1714–70) were all members of the Church of England who had founded a 'Holy Club' in Oxford in their student days in order to pursue salvation; they earned their nickname because of the 'methodical' way in which they pursued this goal. Under the influence of Pietism, John Wesley, the organising genius of British Methodism, later established a conventicle system whereby those members of the Church of England who wished to pursue holiness would band together in small groups to meet for weekly prayer, Bible reading and mutual exhortation. They would be ministered to by an itinerant preacher who would move around a 'circuit' of such groups. Those served by this system would not leave the Church of England or cease to receive its sacraments, but would vivify their objectivist faith with a more subjective appropriation and systematic application of its graces.

Even in the face of mounting hostility from the clerical leaders of the Church of England, the Wesley brothers remained concerned to cultivate the approval of Anglican, monarchist and Tory circles. They preached violently against Catholicism and dissent, and were deeply dismayed at the loss of the American colonies. Yet the Wesleys' social and political conservatism was belied by the religious forces that John's preaching and Charles's hymns managed to unleash. Particularly during the first phase of Methodism, roughly 1740 to 1770, the movement at grassroots edged towards a mystical-spiritualist form of voluntarism, as the brothers unleashed the 'enthusiasm' that Hanoverian religious and political leaders so feared and deplored. John Wesley described his own conversion in 1738 in subjectivist terms, laying stress upon the importance of feeling, albeit a gentle warming rather than a burning or rushing flame. As he famously recorded in his journal:

> In the evening I went very unwillingly to a society in Aldersgate Street [London], where one was reading Luther's Preface to the Epistle to the Romans. About a quarter before nine, while he was describing the change which God works in the heart through faith in Christ, I felt my heart strangely warmed. I felt I did trust in Christ – Christ alone for salvation; and an assurance was given me that He had taken away my sins, even mine, and saved me from the law of sin and death.[3]

In the itinerant preaching ministry that dominated Wesley's life thereafter he tried, with much success, to induce a similar experience in his hearers. Conversion, for Wesley, was a second baptism in which people were born again. The person who has not been 'born of God', he wrote, 'is not sensible of God. He does not feel . . . Hence he has scarce any intercourse with the invisible world.'[4] But when he is born of God, then 'the Spirit of or breath of God is immediately inspired, breathed into the newborn soul' and, by this direct agency, 'spiritual life is not only sustained but increased from day to day'.[5]

Methodism's critics were alarmed not only by this strongly experiential, subjectivist strain, but also by its doctrine of human perfectibility ('Arminianism'). Wesley believed in individual responsibility and free choice in the drama of salvation. He rejected the Calvinist idea of election, which, he believed, encouraged complacency and backsliding – for why, if you know yourself to be saved or damned in spite of anything you can do, should you make an effort to change your life? In Wesley's theology, no-one was predestined either to salvation or to damnation. God would save all who turned to him, received his Spirit and abandoned sin. More than that, he would reward them with direct experience of the divine and with gradual progress towards perfection and sanctification. Wesley's thoroughgoing biblicism, the counterbalance to his more subjective spiritualist tendencies, led him to take texts such as 1 John 3.9, 'Whosoever is born of God doth not commit sin', at face value. Yet Wesley also held that even those who have been saved may backslide. Their entire life must therefore be devoted to strenuous cultivation of a biblically based perfection in order to avoid the ever-present danger of losing hold of grace. Both the rewards and the dangers were high, and, however routine their outward circumstances might be, the inner lives of Methodist Christians were transformed into high drama. Whereas, for Calvinists, salvation or damnation seemed to be all up to God, for Methodists they could seem to be all up to them.

By contrast with the measured, tolerant, reasonable tones of established Anglicanism, Methodism seemed fanatical, irrational and dangerous to its critics, and exciting and empowering to its converts. It attracted people from all levels of society, but did particularly well among women – including some wealthy women who supported the movement – and the working classes. It had particular success in areas where the Anglican parochial system had not penetrated and where economic change had swept the vulnerable into new conditions of hardship and danger – in mining communities and later in industrial towns, for example. This constituency gave Methodism a politically subversive potential that was feared by its critics, particularly after the danger of revolution had been 'proved' by the French Revolution of 1789 and ensuing events. Yet Methodism never realised this potential. Its appeal certainly seemed to lie in the fact that it offered the socially disempowered direct access to divine power – as well as to social support from fellow Methodists – and so held out some chance of coping with the difficult or even desperate conditions they faced. Yet the energies it released tended to be turned towards individual self-perfection rather than towards social reform. Moreover, the values Methodism embraced – of hard work, cleanliness, self-discipline, honesty, personal integrity, dutiful submission to higher power – were directly supportive of the industrial-capitalist enterprise and made Methodists reliable and hard-working employees. By the nineteenth century, British Methodism had become a means by which the lower middle classes achieved social respectability and worked for social change within established structures, rather than an impetus for revolutionary change.

In North America, to which it was quickly exported, Methodism developed its democratic potential more quickly, helped by the brilliant leadership of George Whitefield. Such potential was realised within its own ecclesiastical structures as well as more widely in society. In England, where the Church of England refused any form of incorporation of the Methodist movement and so forced Wesley to turn Methodism into a voluntarist denomination, Wesley nevertheless organised the Methodist church along semi-hierarchical lines. By establishing an ordained ministry, he not only excluded women from positions of leadership, but turned the Methodist ministry into a route for social advancement among those who lacked the resources, including a university education, to become clergy in the Church of England. In North America, Methodism – like the Baptist churches – remained somewhat more flexible, more able to draw on the talent of those attracted to its teachings, and somewhat more critical of 'establishments' in both religion and society.

Voluntarist spiritualism: mysticism and Quakerism

Though harshly persecuted in the sixteenth century, the spiritualist tendency within Protestantism survived. Given its voluntarist and individualist basis, it is hardly surprising that mysticism/spiritualism found many different expressions, gave rise to different sorts of social formation, had widely varying political tendencies (or none), and appealed to very different constituencies. For example, in some instances – as in the Civil War period – the spiritualist tendency might take an apocalyptic form, with its followers believing that they were standing on the threshold of the final, spiritual age of society in which peace and brotherly love would replace coercion and all external forms of religion. In others it might appeal to a highly educated philosophical elite – such as the Cambridge Platonists or Baruch Spinoza (1632–77) in Holland.

The three main sites of spiritualist activity during the early modern period were also the main sites of Protestant energy: Germany in the sixteenth century, Holland in the late sixteenth and early seventeenth centuries, and England in the seventeenth century. In many cases mysticism represented a reaction against the external and objective elements of contemporary forms of Christianity, Protestant as much as Catholic. In sixteenth-century Germany not only Karlstadt and Schwenkfeld but also Hans Denck (died 1527) and Sebastian Franck (c. 1499–c. 1542) gave written expression to their disillusionment with an inadequately spiritualised Lutheran Reformation. Calvinism was similarly criticised by the French scholar Sebastian Castellio (1515–63), who eventually broke off his previously close relations with Calvin and became known for his defence of religious toleration. Castellio's writings had an influence in the Netherlands, where the Dutch humanist and politician Dirck Volckertszoon Coornheert (1522–90) criticised the exclusivism of Dutch Calvinism and championed tolerance born of a piety based on an internal experience that unites, rather than on external rituals and dogmas, which divide.

By the seventeenth century, many spiritualist Christians had entirely despaired of the first, abortive, attempt at reformation and called for a true, spiritual reformation to take its place. They disagreed about the ways in which their inner faith should take external form. Schwenkfeld, Franck and Coornheert had no interest in forming new churches and tended to think that like-minded, spiritual Christians would gather together in purely voluntary groups of mutual edification. The seventeenth-century Dutch Collegiants, by contrast, institutionalised their version of Christian spiritualism in the 'colleges' from which they derived their name. Other spiritualist communities, such as the Familists, the members of the Family of Love, founded in Holland by Hendrik Niclaes in 1540, gathered around a spiritual leader. Despite being outlawed in their own country, the Familists survived in England until the end of the seventeenth century, and had some influence upon Quakerism and its founder, George Fox (1624–91). By Fox's time there was such an international confluence of mystical ideas that it was possible for a writer such as John Everard to translate and make accessible the ideas of a whole range of Christian mystics, ranging from Plato to Dionysius the Pseudo-Areopagite to Tauler to Hans Denk. Everard appears to have been another influence on Fox, as was the German mystic Jakob Boehme (1575–1624), whose writings generated considerable interest in the seventeenth century.

The success of Quakerism or 'The Society of Friends' owed a great deal not only to the charisma of its leader, George Fox, but to the organisational and strategic ability of Margaret Fell (died 1702), later Fox's wife. It also benefited from the way in which the movement, following Fox's lead, managed to control the inherently uncontrollable impulses of spiritual individualism by supplying it with a biblical and Christological basis. Robert Barclay (1648–90) supplied the movement with a systematic theological basis in his *Apology for the True Christian Divinity*, usually known as *Barclay's Apology* (1676).

A weaver's son who had looked, in vain, for spiritual satisfaction in existing forms of Christianity, Fox began to witness to an inward spiritual faith based on the direct revelation of Christ in the heart of the believer. Christ would be known in his 'light', which would illumine directly. As Fox put it, 'I was sent to turn people from darkness to light, that they might receive Christ Jesus, for as to as many as should receive Him in His light, I saw he would give power to become the sons of God.'[6] Such Christological spiritualism – which did not deny the authority of the Bible, but regarded its authority as derivative of the light that shone through it – found institutional embodiment in local meetings at which 'Friends' gathered together and witnessed if moved by the Spirit to do so. Gradually elders and overseers were appointed to make administrative arrangements and to organise poor relief; and monthly, quarterly and yearly meetings were convened in order to bind the local meetings together in a broader organisational framework.

So far as possible, Friends kept the 'externals' of religion to a minimum. An ethos of simplicity, plainness and lack of external adornment grew out of an emphasis on the importance of the inner rather than the outer life. External differences, including those of gender and social class, were to be disregarded in the life of the Spirit. Friends were neither to practice 'hat honour' (the doffing of hats to superiors) nor to dress in showy garments. Even their gravestones were to be identical. Quaker women were allowed to speak in meetings as well as to preach, and a sizeable number published books. (In the decade 1651–60, for example, Quaker women's writings amounted to roughly half of the total publications by women in England.)

Not surprisingly, the Quakers attracted intense hostility in England from both church and state. In the face of Restoration, they maintained their strong defence of the voluntary principle. As Margaret Fell put it in a letter of 1660 to the king 'On Persecution', Quakers were obedient to the established authorities 'so far as they do rule for God and his truth, and do not impose any thing upon people's consciences, but let the gospel have its free passage through the consciences of men'.[7] The Quakers' refusal to swear oaths, to bear arms and to pay the compulsory tithe to the Church of England led to the imprisonment of many of them. The effect was to heighten Quaker suspicion of the world and worldliness and, in Britain, to push Quakerism into a quietist direction – though some Quakers, such as John Bellers (died 1725), proposed schemes of socialistic social reform unthinkable in more established forms of Christianity. The different conditions of North America, in which Quakerism was quickly established, allowed greater latitude to experiment with social and economic reform. Though their overall numbers always remained relatively small, Quakers of all countries would exercise a disproportionate influence in philanthropic, humanitarian and pacifist initiatives.

Prophetesses, witches and wives

If the sixteenth century witnessed a crisis in male–female relations, to which the Reformation represented one response, there is little sign that early Protestantism satisfactorily resolved the crisis. Protestantism encouraged women to believe that they could seek God on equal terms with men, but the terms were dictated by male authority, both human and divine. Even Quaker women found they had constantly to justify their speaking in public, and tended to do so not in terms of their natural dignity but in terms of a weakness that could be overcome by the Spirit of Christ. (As one Quaker woman put it when rebuked by her male audience, 'No, you are all women, but I am a man.'[8]) The religion of the early Reformation tended to identify God with mastery, and mastery with men. Women, promised so much in theory, found themselves confined in practice (to the home and domestic labour, above all).

This unstable 'solution' to the gender crisis was bequeathed to later forms of Protestantism. On the one hand, women were told that they had souls and that these souls could soar to God; on the other, they were exhorted to obedience, self-sacrifice and domesticity. This tension between spiritual freedom and domestication is very evident in the neglected second half of Bunyan's *Pilgrim's Progress*. On the one hand, its message is almost feminist: Christiana is not only the spiritual equal of Christian, who sets out on the same path and reaches the same goal, but she does so with greater ease. Whereas Christian suffered greatly in the Valley of Humiliation, for example, Christiana, humble already, passes through with no difficulty at all. On the other hand, the differences between the two pilgrimages are telling. Whereas Christian leaves his family behind and beats a lonely path to his God, Christiana travels with her friend, Mercy, and her two sons. Her achievement lies in bringing her whole family to God. The guidance and support she receives on the way come from wise male guides. And her victory consists in submission to the divine King, who rules the Celestial City.

It was because it offered women more in theory than it would allow in practice that early Protestantism's solution to the gender crisis proved so unstable. Very occasionally we hear a woman voice her complaint, as in the English Revolution, when the times made it possible for some women's words to be put into print. One of them, Margaret Newcastle, mourned that 'Men, that are not only our Tyrants, but our Devils, keep us in the Hell of Subjection, from whence I cannot Perceive any Redemption'.[9] Long before this, however, the records of the marriage and discipline courts established by the Reformation allow us to see that the sixteenth-century reformers' 'solution' to the gender problem was unstable from the start. Far from submitting willingly to male mastery and the ideal of godly household and marriage, women and their husbands clogged the courts with their marital disputes. In the end, women were indeed contained, but only by virtue of superior force, both legal and physical. Husbands and civil authorities supported one another in administering discipline. The former could beat disobedient wives, so long as their instruments of violence did not exceed the width of their thumb (the 'rule of thumb'), while the latter could intervene with the ultimate threat of execution, if marital violence did not prove sufficient. Calvin went so far as to say that a woman must not leave a physically abusive husband unless her life were in danger, and his consistory in

Geneva only once awarded a temporary separation in the many cases of abuse that came before it.

But the more that women resisted their domestic captivity, the more troublesome and unstable they seemed, and the more they had to be controlled. For John Knox in Scotland, the solution was simply to deny women any autonomy whatsoever. In his *First Blast of the Trumpet against the Monstrous Regiment of Women* (1558), Knox attacked the Catholic queens of the day (Scotland's Mary, Queen of Scots, and England's Mary Tudor, in particular), and argued that women were unfit for any position of authority.

> For who can denie [he argued] but it repugneth to nature . . . that the foolishe, madde and phrenetike shal governe the discrete, and give counsel to such as be sober of mind? And such be al women, compared unto man in bearing of authoritie. For their sight in civile regiment, is but blindness: their strength, weaknes: their counsel, foolishenes; and judgement, phrensie, if it be rightlie considered.[10]

Women's proneness to 'phrensie' was considered by many in the early modern world to be not only a moral weakness but a biological one. Knox drew on both Aristotle and Aquinas to prove the point, for both considered that woman was biologically underdeveloped in comparison to man. The scientific view accepted by early moderns was that women had been subject to less 'heat' in the oven of the womb and were therefore more moist, spongy, passionate and unstable. Lacking the strong inner scaffolding of a man, and having no reliable ordering core, either mental or bodily, they were therefore much more prone than men to being blown about by internal or external drives and forces. The necessity of external male control was correspondingly greater.

This view that women were more likely than men to be possessed by both divine and diabolic forces was one factor behind the witch hunts and trials that became such a striking feature of early modern history. Although the earliest witch trials date from the fifteenth century, the most active period was between 1450 and 1750, and involved both Catholics and Protestants. During the sixteenth and seventeenth centuries, when the persecution was at its height, it is estimated that between 100,000 and 200,000 people were officially tried, and between 50,000 and 100,000 executed.[11] Given the size of the European population at the time – around 81 million in 1500, rising to around 140 million in 1750 – the numbers involved were considerable. Accusations and trials were not evenly spread across Europe, but tended to be concentrated in the smaller territories of the Holy Roman empire, Switzerland and parts of France, particularly those in which a bishop or other church official was head of both church and state. In Spain, Portugal and Italy, where cases of witchcraft were handled by official Catholic inquisitions, most witches were dismissed as stupid or deluded old women. Broadly speaking, then, the disruptive power of women appears to have been considered far more of a threat north of the Alps and Pyrenees. What was fairly consistent across Europe, however, was the fact that women were the focus of the witch hunts; between 75 and 85 per cent of those questioned, tried and executed after 1500 were female. Of these, the vast majority were middle-aged or older single women.[12]

What we see in the post-Reformation era is a shift not in the persecuting mentality of church and society, or in its methods, but in its object. The chief enemies of Christendom were no longer heretics, Jews or lepers, but witches. Witchcraft accusations had a long history in Christendom, and the witch was understood to be a person who manipulated sacred power to the disadvantage of others. Now, however, the images of diabolical liaison, gruesome crimes, sabbath gatherings and plots to overthrow the true church, which had previously been applied to heretics, were applied instead to witches. Instead of exhibiting womanly virtues of love, care, humility and nurturance, witches were women who had sex with the devil, killed babies, dried up mothers' milk, poisoned food and rendered men impotent.

Just as medieval persecution had been driven by genuine fear of the loss of precarious privilege to rival groups, so the witch hunts and witch trials seem to have had a rational basis. Mobilised by both men (who took charge of the whole process) and women (who sometimes informed against 'witches'), a major factor appears to have been the attempt to secure and defend a hierarchical pattern of gender relations in early modern society. Some of the women accused were undoubtedly involved in magical or spiritual practices in which they laid claim to a sacred power over which an exclusively male religious hierarchy (both Catholic and Protestant) wished to maintain its monopoly. Other accused women may have been wholly innocent, but they too tended to be women who were peripheral to male supervision yet had power in their own right – widows, single women, midwives, healers.

As with heresy, the charges gained credence from the fact that a number of those interrogated admitted to their crimes – including consorting with the devil. Whether doing so absolved them of a sense of responsibility for that of which they were accused, or allowed them some sense of empowerment, is not clear. In some cases it may simply have been a way in which they could articulate their deepest feelings and desires. This could happen even among the respectable women who never came near a court. Thus Thomasine Winthrop, wife of John Winthrop, the early Puritan leader in America (see below), confessed on her sickbed to doubts about her conversion, telling her husband that the devil had wanted her to cast off her 'subjection' to her husband.[13] Such incidents suggest that the symbolic universe of witchcraft and diabolism perhaps allowed women to give voice and substance to otherwise unspeakable fears, sufferings and desires, while at the same time providing men with a powerful means of controlling them. It is obviously significant that even here some sort of resolution could be found only when women were placed, either by themselves or by their accusers, under male control – whether that of the devil or that of the male authorities who tried to keep evil at bay. At some level this must have seemed to most of those involved a more satisfactory solution than admitting the possibility of genuine female autonomy and rebelliousness.

Yet the same 'phrensie' that led women to consort with the devil also allowed some Protestant women in the early modern world to be taken very seriously by their male contemporaries, not as witches but as 'prophetesses' who had been in direct contact, not with the devil, but with God. While mystical forms of Protestantism granted women the greatest opportunities in this regard, even more socially respectable and politically established forms of Protestantism could permit seventeenth- and eighteenth-century women to participate in the drama of salvation and to have spiritually eventful lives, at least in the privacy of their own chambers. Judging from their spiritual diaries, an internal spiritual pilgrimage not unlike Christiana's was undertaken by many Protestant women, despite the fact that in externals they were increasingly confined to the routines of domestic life. In private they developed absorbing personal relationships with God that could, in some cases, lead to friction with husbands and families.

By the late eighteenth century, however, the balance was already tipping heavily away from an emphasis on women's natural divine and diabolic potentialities to an identification of female godliness with faith-ful fulfilment of domestic duties. As this new solution to the gender crisis and the danger of independent women presented itself, witchcraft accu-sations began to die down. Gradually women came to be seen not as more frenzied, unstable and sexually active than men, but as gentler and less sexual. When John Wesley spoke of the suitability of one particular candidate as his wife, he began his argument by commenting that as a housekeeper 'she understands all that I want done', that as a nurse she was just what his 'enfeebled carcase' needed, that as a friend she 'sympa-thized . . . in all', and that as a fellow evangelist she was 'both teachable and reprovable'.[14] Women's godliness was now being identified with obedient fulfilment of their domestic roles. A good Christian woman was a good wife and mother, who would find fulfilment in serving her family rather than in communing directly with God.

One reason that this solution seems to have proved more effective than the earlier one was that, whereas Reformation theology had promised women much in theory and allowed little in practice, later Protestantism offered little in theory but more in practice. This was no carefully worked-out strategy, but an accident of history. As modernisation accel-erated along with rapid industrialisation, religion was increasingly rel-egated to a private, domestic sphere. As this happened, men began to vacate the religious sphere and left it for women. The domestic and reli-gious spheres began to overlap and reinforce each other, just as in earlier times the political and religious spheres had done the same. This allowed women a good deal more autonomy and control in the spheres that were now given over to them than had been possible in earlier centuries. As the household became a sphere of private life, so the *paterfamilias* del-egated the duties of spiritual care for the family to his wife. Similarly, churchgoing and charitable activities became more female than male concerns. Though men retained ultimate clerical power, women were able to assume considerable responsibility for voluntary activities in the church. As power drained from both the religious and the domestic spheres, women were left to inhabit them and, to some extent, to create their own religious worlds. The doctrine of separate spheres for separate sexes had finally won the day. The penalty was that the public power of both women and religion were much diminished. Both the witch and the prophetess were banished to history. The reward – as we shall see at the end of this chapter – was that after the eighteenth century both the family and religion opened up to women as spheres in which they could, for the first time, operate with greater autonomy.

The American experiment

Before following the story of Protestantism into the nineteenth century, it is necessary to move from Europe to North America, where colonial expansion provided reformation with another key site of development. In many ways such development took place in parallel with what was happening in Europe, rather than independently of it. Influence flowed in both directions, lending early modern Protestantism a cross-Atlantic, and increasingly Anglo-Saxon, profile. As in Europe, so in North America, Christianity in both Catholic and Protestant forms moved from the non-voluntarist ideal of ecclesiastical control over society and politics only slowly and under the pressure of external events. So wedded to the voluntarist model of religion did the United States of America become after Independence, however, that a voluntaristic and democratic tendency is often projected back to the very beginnings of American religious history and the story of the 'Pilgrim Fathers'.

THE ORIGINS OF AMERICAN CHRISTIANITY

The men and women who landed at Cape Cod and travelled to Plymouth, Massachusetts, in 1620 were English Congregationalists who shared a typically Puritan disillusionment with what had been achieved by way of reformation in Europe. Disappointment at the failure of the Elizabethan Settlement led them to migrate to Holland. But what they were 'fleeing' was not so much European intolerance as Dutch tolerance. They disliked both the materialism and the religious pluralism of Dutch culture – no place to bring up children – and chose to emigrate to America in order to keep themselves free of such contamination. Securing the sponsorship of English merchants, the pilgrims set sail on the *Mayflower* for Virginia, the centre of early English settlement on the eastern seaboard. They ended up in Cape Cod by accident, having been blown off course, and it was from there that they travelled to Plymouth. Far from being voluntarist in orientation, they made little distinction between religion and politics, and aimed to create a settlement in which their brand of Protestantism would control social life in every detail.

The freedom to preach and organise soon attracted many more Puritan settlers. In 1628 a group of English Puritans, again mainly

Congregationalists, purchased a controlling interest in the New England (trading) Company and secured a royal charter that allowed them a considerable degree of self-rule. The first migration to Massachusetts Bay, of more than 1,000 settlers, took place in 1630. During the next decade over 20,000 more followed. Though not all of these later settlers were Puritans, their destination was the well-organised Puritan colony, whose leaders, such as the first governor, John Winthrop, were deeply committed to the project of creating a godly society. Like Calvin in Geneva, and with a motivation that owed much to his pioneering example, the early settlers found themselves in an unusually favourable position to turn their dream of a 'holy commonwealth' into a reality. Not only were they few enough to be able to discipline and regulate their members effectively, even in their private lives, but they had both the will and the political power to do so.

To an even greater extent than Calvin, the leaders of New England Puritanism were working in virgin territory. The metaphor is deliberately chosen, for they saw themselves as called to master not only the soil but also the souls who were placed under their stewardship. Their God, like Calvin's, was still a commanding male God, and they were to be his deputies in bringing godly order into chaos. They viewed the land to which they had come (and the peoples who inhabited it) not so much as an innocent paradise but as a wilderness of ungodliness that had to be disciplined and tamed. It was both uncivilised and fallen, as were the souls in their care. Yet their aim was not the paternalistic one of mastering others – certainly not other white men – but that of fostering individual self-mastery. They were, after all, Congregationalists who believed in the priesthood of all believers and their equality before God. Any man could become a full member of the colony with what we would now call full civil rights. Since membership entailed membership of the 'covenant', initiation was by religious means. Every man who would join must prove that he had had an authentic conversion experience. This could be done only by way of a spoken 'testimony' before the congregation. Before long, such testimonies, which would later have a central place in almost all American evangelicalism, came to assume a fairly set form in which men told first of their pre-conversion sins, their travails under sin, and their eventual release through submission to God, who, through the atoning work of his Son, offered the sinner forgiveness and set him on a new, godly, path of life. The sincerity of this conversion would be tested not only by the speaker's emotional tone, but by the nature of his post-conversion conduct.

Only men could testify before the congregation, and only men could become full members of the covenant. The mastery of women through strict implementation of the typically Protestant ideal of the godly household was a central part of the American Puritan experiment. As the later New England leader John Cotton (1595–1652) put it, God had appointed humans to 'live in Societies, first, of Family, second, Church, thirdly, Common-Wealth'.[15] While it was accepted that women could also have conversion experiences, these experiences would be written down in private and judged by the elders of the community. Whereas male testimonies tended to stress men's independent action, their struggle with God and their eventual partnership with him, women's were more often couched in terms of their lifelong submission to God. Women were allowed no public roles in these early societies, either in church or in politics. Where they did try to claim them by preaching to mixed groups, as in the mid-seventeenth-century cases of Anne Hutchinson (1595–1643) and Mary Dyer (c. 1611–60), both of whom claimed the authority of the Holy Spirit and eventually became Quakers, they were tried and exiled. If they persistently returned, as in Dyer's case, they were executed. New England experienced its own witch hunts, culminating most notoriously in the trials and executions in Salem Village, north of Boston, in the 1690s. It was not only disobedient women who were excluded from the colony, however. So too were all those who did not share its Puritan ideals. The settlers fought with the Native Americans, who had first occupied the land, and insisted that immigrants who practised other forms of Protestantism settle elsewhere.

The godly communities continued for several generations, producing such outstanding leaders as John Cotton and his descendent Cotton Mather (1663–1728). The tumultuous events in contemporary England gave them an occasion to consider and confessionalise their separate identity in the 'Cambridge Platform' (1648), in which they reaffirmed their Reformed theology and their 'non-separating' (between church and state) form of Congregationalism. They constructed an effective educational system for the transmission of this faith, from Harvard College for the training of ministers at the top, to *The New-England Primer* (which taught reading and writing to all children by way of the Lord's Prayer, the Ten Commandments and the Apostles' Creed) at the bottom.

While the American myth of origins identifies the Pilgrim Fathers and other early Puritan colonists as the founders of America and of the American religious tradition, there were, of course, others who had preceded them. These included not only the original inhabitants of the land, the Native American population, but other European Christians.

Europeans' motives for the colonisation of North America had always been mixed. Trade, commerce, land, adventure, politics and a host of personal reasons all played a role, even for the Puritans. The English had made their first permanent settlement at Jamestown, Virginia, in 1607, and, while trade and national glory were part of what drove them, they would certainly not have viewed their motives as purely secular. They made the Church of England their colony's established church, and Anglicanism (later called 'Episcopalianism' in North America) was quickly established more widely. Yet the English were newcomers compared to the Spanish Catholics, who had been in North America since the sixteenth century (see next chapter). The latter's missionary efforts in 'New Spain' resulted in a significant number of Native American conversions in the areas of what are now called New Mexico and California. There were also large numbers of Catholics in Quebec, a French colony from 1608 until its conquest by the British in 1759.

And then there were all the other Protestants who, by the end of the eighteenth century, had established a significant number of Christian alternatives to the New England Way. A significant number of these were immigrants from Europe, including Dutch and German Reformed Christians, Mennonites, German Baptists, Schwenkfelders, French Huguenots and German Lutherans. Like the Catholics, however, such groups appear less prominently in later popular versions of American history than do the multiplying English-speaking Protestant groups. Of the latter, the church that had the most in common with the Puritans was undoubtedly the Presbyterian church, home to growing numbers of English-speaking Scottish and Irish immigrants (who played a major role in spreading Calvinism right round the globe). It was from this original Presbyterian root in America that the Calvinistic free-church movement, discussed above, would eventually develop.

Even more important in terms of the history of American church–state relations, at least in terms of historical influence, were the settlements established by Roger Williams (c. 1603–83) in Rhode Island and William

Penn (1644–1718) in Pennsylvania. Both men were English, the former a Puritan, the latter a Quaker. What distinguished their politico-religious experiments was their voluntaristic insistence, against the Puritans, that state and church should be kept separate. In Williams's case this conviction sprang from a Baptist voluntarism that believed that, since genuine conversion and godly acts must be free and uncoerced, the state should not have any influence in religious matters. He also opposed what he regarded as the Puritan theft of native lands. Under Williams's direction, Rhode Island became the first of the North American colonies in which freedom of worship was defined as a right for (almost) all groups. As such, it became something of a refuge for a variety of forms of religious confession. Penn's motivations were not dissimilar. Though his chief purpose was to found a refuge for Quakers, his 'Holy Experiment' was characterised by a toleration and a pluralism that were decidedly liberal for his times, not least in the community's relations with Native Americans.

In terms of subsequent American history, these colonies have greater significance than those of the Puritans, for it is here, particularly in Philadelphia, that we see the earliest anticipations of democracy and, most important of all, of secular governments allowing freedom of religious choice to their citizens, while nevertheless favouring Christian civilisation. But these colonies were unusual. It would be some time before the voluntary principle would make headway against the prevalent model of Christianity established 'from above'.

RELIGION FROM ABOVE

The century or so leading up to Independence was a period in which the slow and intermittent growth of voluntaristic forms of Protestantism was vastly outpaced by that of non-voluntary forms of Christianity – Puritan, Presbyterian, Lutheran and, most importantly, Anglican. This was an era in which 'religion from above' established a dominant presence not only in the religious life of the emerging nation but in its visual landscape as well. The growing importance of the established Anglican church intertwined with the growth of a more hierarchically ordered American society, whose developing social and political elite were becoming evident in rural as well as in urban society. The elegant churches erected by Anglicans and other major denominations symbolised their growing power in the land. The increasing status of the clergy was also noticeable. And the

237

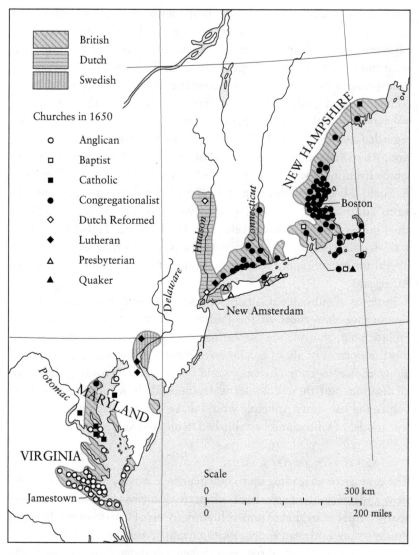

Map 6   The church in North America, 1659

message that they tended to deliver from their pulpits was of obedience not only to the governing authorities, imperial as well as colonial, but to the Almighty God, who ruled over all. Far from being a grassroots religion of sturdy independents, this was a religion *for* rather than *of* the people, which encouraged deference rather than revolution.

There is little evidence that 'the people' disliked or shunned these churches. While it is true that Christianity was established only slowly in late colonial America, it was nevertheless established. The spread of Anglican Christianity was, of course, greatly aided by its position as the established church of the ruling power, Great Britain. Not that the British, or even the Anglican, authorities in Britain were particularly efficient at organising their church in the middle and southern colonies. Their failure to appoint a bishop for America was the most telling example. Yet Anglicanism did spread, due not only to the energy of many individual clergymen but also to the support of imperial authorities and colonial society. From the turn of the century it was also greatly aided by two voluntary associations, the SPCK (the Society for Promoting Christian Knowledge) and the SPG (the Society for the Propagation of the Gospel), established in Britain with the express purpose of supporting and financing mission in the colonies. Wherever an Anglican church was established, it brought with it the parish system, according to which it had care of all the souls in the local territory for which it was responsible. This meant that an Anglican pastor would concern himself with all who lived in his parish, particularly by baptising, marrying and burying them, but also by dealing with their troubles and needs as well as he could. Generally speaking, attendance in Anglican churches seems to have been fairly representative of the whole social spectrum. Existing clergy records of those who took communion on a Sunday list their congregants in a descending order from the most to the least socially prominent, and it was sometimes the ones at the bottom of the list who were the most faithful.

In many ways, then, religious life in late colonial America came to resemble religious life in England. This was true not only in relation to the pre-eminence of the Anglican church, but also in the subordinate position of dissenting forms of Protestantism. Just as in England, the latter were extended a grudging toleration in the eighteenth century, which nevertheless left them in a position of weakness. This was true even of the churches of the early Puritan settlers, despite the fact that they were greatly privileged in comparison to their counterparts in England by virtue of being the only established church besides that of the Anglicans (i.e. a church supported by their semi-independent colonial states through taxation). When it became apparent that growing numbers of settlers were keeping their distance from these churches, many of them eventually shifted to a model of ministry and organisation somewhat closer to that of the Anglicans. In New England, for example, Puritan congregations created a new parish system after 1680, and appointed 'presbyteries' to strengthen clerical power through association. Other denominations exhibited the same tendencies. The Presbytery (later Synod) of Philadelphia, established in 1706, was both a symptom and a cause of growing Presbyterian success. It was a centralised clerical organisation rather than a lay one, and it proved extremely effective in co-ordinating Presbyterian growth, order and discipline.

Like its English counterpart, eighteenth-century American religion from on high, particularly Anglicanism, tended to downplay God the Holy Spirit and God the Son in favour of God the Father. Its tone was moralistic. Jesus was invoked chiefly as a moral teacher and exemplar. The preacher's aim was not to stir individuals to spiritual enthusiasm or great emotion, but to encourage, exhort and command them to live better – more moral and more orderly – lives. The ethical message was, of course, modulated to the different condition of its hearers, in terms not only of their social position but of their gender. As a form of paternalism, such Christianity offered masters a message different from that offered to those in subjection to them. To masters it commended love, patience, gentleness and kindness towards those over whom they had authority – virtues intended to temper rather than to dilute the authority and strength of leadership to which masters were called. To their subjects, who included women, children and servants, it enjoined obedience, trust, self-sacrifice and humility.

While there were to be some limits to the obedience that was commanded by religion on high (for it was wrong to obey an ungodly command even from a parent), these limits were fairly faintly drawn. In the case of slaves they were not drawn at all. As Bishop William Fleetwood, an SPG activist, insisted in *The Relative Duties of Parents and Children, Husbands and Wives, Masters and Servants* (1705), 'no one has Authority against Justice' – except slave-holders. Whereas servants may resist an unjust command, the slave must practise absolute obedience, with 'compliance and submission'.[16] As well as justifying this in terms of the trading needs of the English nation, Fleetwood turned to Augustine's and Luther's teachings on 'the freedom of the Christian' in order to justify the view that such freedom was to be understood as 'entirely Spiritual'. For this reason even the slightest disobedience on the part of a slave would count as insurrection and be punishable accordingly. So long as this was understood, however, all would be well in the relations between masters and slaves. The former were still exhorted to the paternalistic virtues.

In this way Christianity proved an important ideological support both for the increasingly prosperous and powerful American middle classes and for the increasingly important institution of slavery in colonial America. It certainly did not bring the institution of slavery into existence, for it had been found in most pre-modern societies, including Christian ones. More immediately, slavery was introduced to North America from the English West Indies. By 1660 the law in each colony established slavery's elemental forms: the slave-owner possessed the slave, the slave's labour and the slave's progeny. The trade in slaves was driven by purely commercial interests, on the part of both those who traded them and those who owned them and their labour. Between 1680 and the Revolution, half a million African slaves were brought into America, transforming the colonies and their economy in the process. All the southern colonies and several of the northern ones exploited this captive, coerced labour force.

Yet though the motive force of slavery was economic, paternalistic Christianity found itself naturally adapted to legitimate and normalise the institution, through its message to both slave-owners and the slaves themselves. This was particularly true given the unique form of slave-holding in most parts of America, where, rather than a single plantation-holder maintaining very large numbers of slaves, a single slave-owner, typically a farmer, would usually own from ten to twenty slaves, many of them young males. A paternalistic message was much better adapted to such an institution of family size. The slave-owner was encouraged to treat his slaves as 'children', tempering discipline with kindliness. Indeed, a great deal of Christian literature placed strong emphasis on the heavy burden of responsibility the slave-owner had to carry. Rather than being morally judged, he was encouraged to view himself as something of a moral hero. But he was also exhorted to have his slaves baptised and to allow them to worship regularly.

The winning of slave souls for Christianity was the other important element of Christian influence upon the institution of slavery in America. In the early days of slave-owning, many masters appear to have been reluctant to bring slaves into contact with Christianity. This may have been because they themselves were not churchgoers, or because they thought black slaves unworthy of contact with Christianity. Even more likely was their fear that contact with Christianity might undermine the institution of slavery. Christianity, particularly Protestantism, was by this time associated in some minds with freedom rather than with slavery. Thus we find clergy having to reassure slave-owners that slave baptisms will not abolish slavery, and slave-owners worrying that further conversion to Christianity will make their slaves proud and 'uppity'.

In the event, however, they need not have worried, for Christianity served to disempower rather than to empower the first generations of slaves. It did so not only by preaching obedience and submission, but by playing some part in the destruction of the native cultural and religious systems on which Africans might otherwise have been able to draw. Whereas other 'foreign' peoples who came to America were able to sustain their identity through their religio-cultural traditions, the slave trade led to what one historian has called the 'death of the African gods' in America.[17] The wide dispersal of slaves between different plantations was one factor, as was the active hostility of slave-owners to collective slave activity of any kind. The churches reinforced this, condemning any 'heathen' practices on the part of those they baptised, including 'feasts, dances and Merry meetings'. This is why the history of America tells us of the English Puritans, Scottish Presbyterians and German Lutherans in America, but not of the religious systems of the Akan, Ashanti, Dahoman, Ibo and Yoruba societies. By 1760 public African religion had been all but destroyed in the mainland colonies. What survived were the 'portable' religious practices that an individual might practise alone, such as traditions of magic and healing. When African religious practice was reconstructed after Independence, it would be in a Christian mode.

RELIGION FROM BELOW

With the exception of the Quakers and, in a few cases, the Baptists, all the American Protestant churches in the eighteenth century tended to support a slave-holding economy. They did so because of their broadly paternalistic worldview, their belief in the sinfulness of that which had not come under the influence of the Protestant faith, and their suspicion of all 'heathen' peoples. (At this time unequal treatment was still based on religio-cultural, rather than pseudo-scientific 'racial', grounds.)

But there were also wider structural reasons for the support of slavery. Slavery was good for the economy. What was good for the economy was good for the nation, whether Britain or America or both. And the American churches' generally co-operative relations with the state meant that what was good for the nation tended to be viewed as pleasing to God. Of course, both the Congregationalists and the Presbyterians had good reasons to be hostile to English nationalism and the English national church, but the effect of this hostility was to bind them more tightly to an emerging American nationalism. Thus they shared the broad civic and economic orientation of Anglicanism, but switched the object of their loyalty. They did not disagree with the fundamental principle that church and nation should support each other, but they took the nation to be America rather than England.

The struggle for American independence and the establishment of the American republic after 1783 illustrate these general remarks very clearly. Organised religion was not a direct cause of either development. Indeed, many Christians were deeply uneasy about the war against the British. Having preached loyalty and obedience to one's masters for so long, it was difficult suddenly to support armed insurrection. Many clergy railed against the chaos and disorder that were likely to result. The Anglican Samuel Seabury, who later became the first Episcopalian bishop in the United States, believed that royally appointed delegates had been displaced by 'congresses, committees, riots, mobs, insurrections [and] associations'. 'If I must be devoured,' he wrote, 'let me be devoured by the jaws of a lion [the king] . . . not *gnawed* to death by rats and vermin.'[18] Loyalist clergymen could be found in every colonial denomination: most Anglicans, various New England Congregationalists, many Presbyterians. Yet the 1775 letter of the Philadelphia Synod indicated the torn loyalties of the latter: while instructing the laity in loyalty to King George III, it also noted 'the revolution principles' on which his own throne had been established.[19]

In the event, large numbers of middle-colony Presbyterians and Virginia Baptists came to support the struggle for independence. Other 'dissenters', including the German Lutheran and Reformed churches, simply kept quiet. In fact, the most common denominator among pro-Revolution clergy was the possession of a state-church pulpit. Even tax-supported Anglican ministers supported the Revolution in significant numbers, as did many Congregationalists. There is thus no easy link to be made between dissenting Protestantism and the rise of republicanism, as if a straight line connected the Pilgrim Fathers with the American Constitution. Those who gave their support to the Revolution, however half-heartedly, tended to do so not because they believed in abstract principles of liberty and democracy, but because they felt that their greatest loyalty was now with the emerging American nation.

Because most American churches had not obstructed independence, there was no reason for the founders of the new American republic to seek to crush or reform them in the way that there would be in revolutionary France (see next chapter). The most committed loyalists, mostly Anglicans, simply left the country after the war was over, many of them settling in Canada. Conversely, because religion had not played a central political or ideological role in the Revolution, there was no reason why it should suddenly attain a high profile in the new American Constitution. Nor did it. The Declaration of Independence of 1776 laid down the natural rights of man, but made no mention of religion. None of those who drafted it had any straightforward loyalty to organised religion, and the most important religious influences upon the constitution were broadly liberal and deistic ones, as we shall see in the final section of this chapter. When religion was mentioned, in the famous First Amendment to the Federal Constitution passed in 1791, it was in order to make explicit what had already been implicit in the constitution: that the state would not interfere in religious matters.

The vagueness of the wording led to considerable public debate about what was intended. Some took it to mean that a single established church should give way to 'multiple establishment', whereby a number of different churches could be supported by the state. In the end, however, public debate swung away from this to the conclusion that no church should gain state support by way of taxation. Yet the idea that the state supported Christianity was never dispelled. While the constitution refused support for any particular denomination, there were good reasons in theory as well as in developing practice to believe that it was broadly supportive of America conceived of as a Christian, even a Protestant nation. Few, if any, yet thought in terms of complete religious freedom or pluralism where that involved equal treatment and toleration for all forms of religion and belief.

The American Revolution thus played a key role in the formation of a distinctive American form of Christianity in at least two ways.

First, by abolishing any formal religious establishment it allowed a free-for-all among any and all forms of Christianity, unleashing an exuberant era of religious ferment and evangelical activity even more extensive than that which is encompassed by the notion of a 'Second Great Awakening'. In that way it gave rise to a pluralism and diversity that were unknown in any single state within Europe. What was also unusual in America was the extent to which these new forms of Christianity could grow up from the grassroots. This is not to say that each and every individual could or did now found his own church. Even though some important new forms of religion, such as Mormonism and Spiritualism, came into existence at this time, they tended to adopt a denominational form of organisation. But even if denominational forms of Christianity remained the norm, their success would now depend upon their ability to appeal to their grassroots members. In that more limited sense, religion from on high was indeed being replaced by religion from below.

Second, the American Revolution helped reshape Christianity by reshaping the nation. America was no longer to be made in the image of Britain. Instead of being part of a constitutional monarchy supported by a state church, it became an independent republic supported by God and by reason. While its polity was founded on 'natural' and 'reasonable' laws, it was happy to agree that ultimately these laws were underwritten by God. Though it no longer had need of an established church to bolster its still fragile power, it was content to let the churches in general lend it their support. Thus the nation and Christianity (in general) entered into a relationship of happy though informal mutual support. The churches allowed the state to take over the main sources of social power, in return for which they were allowed a fairly free operation in relation to the realm of individuals' private and domestic lives. As the churches renounced social power, so they in effect renounced the right to have any direct control, or even any say, over economic, political or military matters. These now belonged to a public realm, controlled by the state. What the church gained in return was the opportunity to control the private sphere. In so far as it would shape society, it would now do so by shaping individual hearts and minds. In that sense too, religion would work from below rather than from above. The reason the churches accepted this situation so happily, apart from their lack of choice, was that much Protestantism, as we have seen, was already internally adapted to this concentration upon the private and domestic realms. The forms that were not so well adapted, most notably Congregationalism, Presbyterianism and Lutheranism, though they quickly adjusted to the free-church model, lost ground to more naturally privatised forms of voluntaristic Protestantism.

In 1790, when the first federal census was taken, the most numerous congregations in the original thirteen states had been the Anglicans, Congregationalists and Presbyterians. In the census of 1850 the three most populous religious communions in America were the Baptists, the Methodists and the Roman Catholics. Even the latter, who had risen to prominence chiefly because of the large numbers of Catholic immigrants from Europe, would quickly develop a free-church form, much to the consternation of Rome (see next chapter). Baptists had their beginnings in the earliest colonies, as in Rhode Island, where Roger Williams himself became a Baptist in keeping with his voluntarist convictions. Such voluntarism made the Baptists extremely well adapted to the conditions of republican America, and their biblicism and anti-intellectualism made them highly effective missionaries to America's unconverted, especially on the western frontier. The typical Baptist preacher did not require a college education, and found himself naturally equipped to evangelise fellow farmers and ordinary working people. In antebellum America he enjoyed enough denominational support to uphold him in his missionary activities, but not so much that it hampered the free exercise of his ministry or lifted him too high above his audience. Methodism also proved spectacularly successful in the American religious free market. Like the Baptist churches, Methodism spread through itinerant preaching, spearheaded by George Whitefield. Independence brought to an end its potentially damaging alliance with the Church of England by causing a decisive split between American and British Methodism. Like the Baptist churches, Methodist experiential biblicism managed to appeal to the unlearned and uneducated, while simultaneously playing a major role in the spread of literacy. It also played an important role in 'civilising' rural society, especially on the frontier, not least through inculcating the womanly virtues of domestic piety and the manly virtues of hard work, honesty and independence.

The rapid growth of the Baptist and Methodist churches in the eighteenth century was part of a wider shift towards a voluntaristic, anti-elitist, experiential 'Christianity of the heart' whose origins are often discussed under the blanket heading of the first 'Great Awakening' (a notion given currency by its major theological spokesman, Jonathan Edwards (1703–58)). The beneficiaries were all those denominations that supported a Christianity rooted in personal experience. Neither the Baptists nor the Methodists were immune to enthusiasm and miracles; wonder-working, prophecy, dreams and visions formed a part of their evangelistic stock in trade. This emotionalism and 'orality', together with the ease of forming new independent congregations, made both denominations particularly attractive to poor white and black Americans, both slave and free. Immediately after the Revolution, separate black congregations began to form in both north and south, often with the approval of the white congregations from which they split. Separate congregations and denominations of black and African Baptists, Methodists, Episcopalians and Presbyterians were formed by this means.

Miracles, supernatural interventions and wonder-working were also characteristic of other mystical religions on the fringes of the American religious establishment, including the Universal Friends, the Shakers, the Mormons and the Spiritualists. Despite their widely divergent religious and social ideals, all represented revolts against the bourgeois ideal of the Jacksonian age, and all rejected the nuclear and isolated family and the Protestant ideology of separate spheres for men and women. With their roots in the Second Great Awakening, both the Universal Friends and the Shakers were led by women who established separatist communities that rejected the domestic ideal of Protestantism in favour of celibacy. Women were also attracted to the Mormons, whose founder, Joseph Smith (1805–44), claimed to have received visions from heavenly beings, culminating in the revelation of *The Book of Mormon* to him by the angel Moroni. On the basis of this scripture, published in 1830, Mormonism appeared to many of its followers to be the definitive American religion, replacing the complexities and excrescences of European Christianity with a gospel of simple truth. Spiritualism, founded by the Fox sisters in 1848, centred around techniques for establishing communication with the dead (the spirit world). While it remained a largely white movement, it too was notable for the prominent place occupied by women.

At one level, then, the republic opened the door to an unprecedented religious pluralism in America. At another, the overall effect was a gentle homogenising of American religion, which, for all its important and often bitterly contested internal differences, now tended to witness to a common Protestant identity based around voluntarism and loyalty to the Bible, the family and the nation. Each of these authorities was understood to reinforce the others, and a threat to one would be perceived as a threat to the others. A strong millennialism was another common feature. Millennial belief gave expression to the powerful Protestant sense that God was literally on America's side, and that destiny had chosen the American nation to fulfil his purposes for mankind. Rather than dwelling on a coming apocalypse, America looked forward to a coming millennium, in which Christ would rule for a thousand years. The nation's manifest destiny was to prepare for this consummation.

If asked to explain the distinctiveness of this destiny, many Americans would now speak in terms of a love of liberty that lay at the heart of American religion and politics and distinguished the 'new world' from the 'old'. This was not, of course, democracy in any full sense. The 'public' whom the Revolution enfranchised did not include women, Africans or poor whites. Yet, even with these omissions, sovereignty had been greatly extended from the English model, in which it had lodged in a Parliament made up of Lords, Bishops, and Commons elected from a tiny franchise of property-owners. American liberty, limited though it may have been, was a source of national pride, and one that the churches could embrace without too much disruption to their traditional patriarchal teachings. When parts of the nation and the Protestant establishment in the north started to move towards a more extended democratic ideal at a different speed from the south, the result would be civil war.

Evangelicalism and liberalism in the nineteenth century

The fact that both sides in the American Civil War invoked Christianity in their support is some indication of the extent to which it had saturated the American consciousness by the mid-nineteenth century. 'The prayers of both [north and south] could not be answered', said Lincoln as the war neared its close; 'that of neither has been answered fully.'[20] Each side believed that the war was a punishment for the nation's sins; but the south, more loyal to a paternalistic form of Christian culture, believed that the sins were those of greedy and avaricious Yankees, while the north, now more wedded to voluntaristic and progressive ideals, laid the blame on reactionary southern slave-holders. At Gettysburg in 1863 Lincoln made it clear that victory must belong to the liberal ideal, resolving on behalf of his countrymen 'that this nation, under God, shall have a new birth of freedom'.[21]

Even if freedom for blacks and women was deferred in practice, liberty now reigned supreme in theory. The outcome of the Civil War was to bind both politics and religion to the liberal ideal. If the war had been a punishment for neglect of this ideal, then the nation's rapidly growing power in the postbellum period must be a sign that it had returned to God's favour. Never before had America made such rapid economic progress. When in the closing decades of the eighteenth century Alexander Hamilton, the far-sighted Secretary to the Treasury, had argued that the newly independent American economy must be shaped in such a way that it could take advantage of 'industry', few really understood what he meant. America's economy was still based largely on trade and agriculture, and even the most advanced industrial country in the world, Britain, was still in the early stages of its industrial revolution. What Hamilton realised was that the emerging technologies based around steam and mechanisation offered a power so vast and unprecedented that they could revolutionise the economies of the countries that were able to exploit them. By the later nineteenth century, Britain, still the most powerful nation in the world, had proved his point. But America was not far behind. The postbellum years witnessed an extraordinary upheaval as railways, canals and new forms of industry transformed the country, shifting its economy away from agriculture to industrial production, and uprooting its population from the countryside to the growing cities. Rapid population growth and immigration supplied the labour needed for new industries and their service sector. As in England, an industrial working class and a professional middle class developed, the former squeezed together in poor housing near their places of work, the latter dwelling in larger villas in more salubrious areas. Karl Marx predicted an inevitable clash between these two classes. Though there was in fact no general uprising of 'the proletariat', there were indeed some serious riots and disturbances in America's cities in the 1870s and 1880s.

It was against this background that Protestantism in both Britain and America entered into what some have called its 'golden age'. On both sides of the Atlantic, churchgoing reached new levels. In Britain, for example, the 1851 national religious census indicated that around 40 per cent of those over the age of ten in England and Wales were in church on census Sunday (though this number can be adjusted downwards if multiple attendance is discounted). On both sides of the Atlantic, churchgoing appears to have reached a peak around the 1870s. Protestantism's triumph within the radically altered socio-economic circumstances of the nineteenth century was by no means assured, and was due to many factors including the remarkable energy of its highly motivated followers, among whom women assumed a prominent place.

For the first time we have records reliable enough to know for sure that women outnumbered men in the churches. While a very few were now allowed to enter the ordained ministry, the vast majority had to content themselves with a vocation of domestic care. In a complete reversal of the medieval and Reformation understanding of women, they were no longer regarded as vortexes of barely contained sexual and emotional energy that must constantly be mastered, but as 'the weaker sex' – kind, gentle, submissive, passive, self-sacrificing and asexual. Men, who were now more likely than women to be regarded as only a step away from being 'beasts', must be protected from their baser instincts by women's ministrations and good example. Women must save them. Such ideals were communicated not only by male preachers and teachers, but by the thousands of evangelical journals and magazines that were avidly devoured by nineteenth-century women readers. They took particularly vivid shape in the stories of virtuous womanhood that figured largely in such literature, in which tales were told of women who, by sheer moral and spiritual force, saved the men they loved from the sinful lives into which they were falling. Their reward, in many cases, was not only a sense of spiritual triumph, but the love of the man they had saved.

The separation of sex roles was bound up with the creation of separate spheres for men and women in industrial society. In earlier centuries, when household and workplace were not differentiated, men and women had often worked together. Now that men left the home to go to work and women stayed in, the idea that the sexes had different capabilities became more plausible. The creation of separate spheres for men and women reinforced the idea that each sex had different capabilities, while the idea that each sex had different capabilities justified the creation of separate spheres. The churches played a key role in this process, not least in making this contingent state of affairs seem natural and God-given. Just as rapid socio-economic change in the late Middle Ages had opened up new opportunities for both sexes and precipitated a gender crisis, so the rise of industrial society led to a similar situation in the nineteenth century. In both cases mainstream Christianity allied itself with patriarchal interests to develop an ideological justification for male exclusion of women from the new economic and spiritual opportunities that presented themselves. Now middle-class women were instructed that their Christian duty was to remain within the household and serve husbands and children without pay, while working-class women had to do this and engage in menial paid employment as well. Though they had little choice but to conform, women nevertheless found ways of partially subverting the situation in which they found themselves. As before, the religion that held them in subjection also provided their chief means of escape. In early modern Protestantism such escape came through laying hold of the opportunities presented by the Reformation doctrine of the priesthood of all believers and of women's ultimate spiritual equality with men. In nineteenth-century Protestantism, escape came through an exploitation of the new opportunities for spiritual leadership in home, church and, increasingly, society.

The significance of this strategy, and the importance of women's contribution to the triumph of Protestantism in the nineteenth century, have sometimes been obscured by the high public profile of male Christian leaders, several of whom attained celebrity status. As we have already seen, Protestantism had given rise to male celebrity figures from the very start, not only because the Protestant creed lent itself to the creation of individual heroes of the faith, but because Protestantism was always adept in making use of the latest media of communication to bring its message to the masses. In the nineteenth century, Protestantism made good use of mass-circulation journals, while retaining the now time-honoured method of itinerant preaching. Whereas earlier preachers would stop to address the men and women they happened upon in the streets and fields, however, the destination of nineteenth-century preachers was more likely to be large, organised gatherings and rallies. In the earlier part of the nineteenth century these gatherings tended to be camp meetings held under canvas and lasting anything up to a week. By the later nineteenth century large theatres, lecture halls and stadiums were available, and evangelical rallies might consist of a series of 'lectures', with audiences present for far shorter periods of time. Whereas eighteenth-century celebrities such as John Wesley and George

Whitefield had expected men and women to struggle with a sense of sin and damnation for long periods, often years, before finally coming to a sense of 'assurance', late nineteenth-century celebrities such as Dwight L. Moody (1837–99) came to expect their hearers to be won for Christ during a single rally.

The evangelical experience changed accordingly. Although it retained the outlines that were already present in *The Pilgrim's Progress*, there were also some significant changes in the postbellum period. Bunyan's Pilgrim had had to leave behind family and community to seek God, pass through a lifetime of temptations, shun all worldly wealth and power, and face suffering and martyrdom. His reward came only after death. By the time Billy Sunday (1863–1935) brought the evangelistic message to huge crowds in America and Britain, the demands had been much relaxed. His invitation on the final day of his New York campaign was typical. 'Do you want God's blessing on you, your home, your church, your nation, New York? If you do, raise your hands . . . How many of you men and women will jump to your feet and come down and say, "Bill, here's my hand for God, for home, for my native land, to live and conquer for Christ?"' The basic structure of Christian's pilgrimage was still there, but stripped to its bare essentials. Dwight L. Moody, Sunday's immediate predecessor as celebrity evangelist to America and Britain, managed to distil the evangelical message to 'the Three Rs': Ruin by Sin, Redemption by Christ, and Regeneration by the Holy Ghost. The immediacy of the rewards that were on offer also became more apparent. As Moody, who had made his fortune as a shoe salesman, put it, 'I never saw the man who put Christ first in his life that wasn't successful.' No longer did these evangelists, unlike their Methodist predecessors, speak of supernatural gifts and display miraculous supernatural powers. Their gospel was far more businesslike. They dressed in suits, modelled success-through-stability in their own lives, and taught that Christians were known by good works that brought rewards. Thus middle-class lifestyles were sanctified, and Christ became a personal saviour and dependable helpmate in the travails of modern life. Though such American evangelicalism was thoroughly nationalistic, it was also highly individualised. Moody and Sunday backed American greatness, but they did not back a particular church. They instructed their converts to go to church, but they did not mind which church – so long as it was Protestant. Nor did they try to change society. Given their thoroughly moralistic outlook, they sincerely believed that society would advance when individual behaviour improved.

Not all nineteenth-century evangelicals supported such a narrow approach. While they never advocated far-reaching structural reform of society, and while they steered clear of intervention in general economic or political policy matters, they were often willing to campaign on single issues, particularly those with a clear moral, humanitarian or philanthropic dimension. At the start of the century some evangelicals in both Britain and America had been involved in anti-slavery movements. The British evangelical Member of Parliament William Wilberforce (1759–1833) and his supporters had played a key role in the campaign to abolish the slave trade in Britain and her colonies (made law in 1807) and to abolish the institution of slavery completely (made law in 1833). In America, where the abolition of slavery took longer, the most famous preacher of his day, Charles Grandison Finney (1792–1875), also combined the evangelical message with a concern for social reform. During the 1830s, Finney had broken from traditional Presbyterianism in protest at its organisational rigidity and low view of natural human ability. Finney believed that Christianity could transform both individual and society, and, though he always put the missionary task of converting the individual first, he also involved himself in campaigns for the abolition of slavery, (limited) co-education, temperance, peace, sabbatarianism, care for the retarded, and even dietary reform. Evangelicals also tried to right social wrongs through personal contact with influential public figures. On both sides of the Atlantic, evangelicalism made close links with big business, sometimes through the conversion of leading magnates, in an attempt to work from the top down for an amelioration of the condition of workers, particularly women and children. In this way a pattern was set for evangelical reform in the modern world. Many Christians were motivated both by concern to help all individuals for whom Christ had died, and by a desire to preserve social order in industrial society and in the colonies. As Wilberforce explained to his middle- and upper-class readers, '[Christianity] . . . renders the inequalities of the social state less galling to the lower orders, whom also she instructs, in their turn, to be diligent, humble [and] patient'.[22]

Given many male evangelicals' view that the gospel was effective in keeping not only the lower orders but also women in their place, it is ironic that it should be the evangelical Protestant concern with social reform that helped many women escape total domestic captivity. Nineteenth-century women soon began to found voluntary societies for moral reform with even more zeal than their male counterparts. As long as they remained faithful to the cult of true Christian womanhood and appealed to evangelical moral priorities, it was very hard for Christian men to oppose their work. Though voluntary work allowed women to enter into 'the world' as active campaigners and charity workers, they were therefore careful not to make direct or aggressive incursions into public space, or to appear to be meddling in public affairs. Their social protests always took the form of campaigns on moral issues, particularly those that were of obvious concern to an evangelical ethic. When women, particularly white women, championed the abolitionist (anti-slavery) cause, for example, they appealed to the moral welfare of black women and children under slavery and the depredations suffered at the hands of callous, violent and sexually aggressive slave-owners; Harriet Beecher Stowe's enormously successful novel *Uncle Tom's Cabin* (1852) provides a good example of this popular strategy. While being largely unobjectionable to male evangelicals, this method allowed female campaigners to attack not only the institution of slavery, but the unjust rule of men more generally. A similar proto-feminist strategy emerges clearly in other forms of female-led evangelical reform movement, including those against alcohol and prostitution. Both quickly widened their brief to a more general critique of male behaviour and 'brutishness'. Why should women continue to suffer the effects of a macho culture that celebrated hard drinking and promiscuous sexual activity? By raising such questions, organisations such as the Women's Christian Temperance Union and the New York Female Moral Reform Society rose to national prominence. The latter, founded in 1834 in the wake of Finney's revivals, generated 445 auxiliary meetings, and its weekly journal, *The Advocate of Moral Reform*, grew into one of America's most widely read evangelical papers, with 16,500 subscribers. Its aim was to unite women into a general union that might ultimately control the behaviour of men and boys. Such control would be achieved, however, not through political reform but through women's influence in the home and in the education of children.

Some resistance was encountered. When male evangelicals founded an anti-prostitution society in New York in the wake of the success of the New York Female Moral Reform Society, for example, they wrote to

Plate 15   *Sunday Morning in Virginia*, by Winslow Homer (1836–1910)
   The home as a scene of religious nurture, and the mother's role at the heart of it, became a popular subject of nineteenth-century art. Though most depictions were of white families, here the American artist Winslow Homer, painting in the immediate aftermath of the Civil War, shows black children gathering around their mother and the Bible in a scene of domestic harmony.

the organisers of the latter suggesting that they could now close down. (The suggestion was ignored.) Warnings that activist women might over-step the mark of female propriety were frequent. Thus the *Free Church Magazine*, discussing 'Female Methods of Usefulness' in 1844, cautioned women against 'zeal and activity . . . lest they sacrifice those meek and lowly tempers which are so calculated to adorn and promote the cause they love and advocate'. While it admitted that there were 'certain duties which sometimes call women out of their quiet domestic circles', it instructed that such duties should not be motivated 'from any desire of a more public sphere', but out of 'obedience' to Christ's commandments to serve others. Likewise, when Sarah Grimké, a 'notorious' Quaker feminist, contributed an article to *The Advocate of Moral Reform* that attacked women's captivity in the home and criticised the way in which the Bible was used by clergy to justify female subservience, it was felt

255

that she had overstepped the mark.[23] The suffrage movement, while having important Christian roots, had to break from mainstream Protestantism in order to campaign for women's rights (most notably, the right to vote). Thus Lucretia Mott (1793–1880) remained a Quaker in good standing throughout her whole career, the Grimké sisters moved from Episcopalianism to Presbyterianism to Quakerism, and Elizabeth Cady Stanton (1815–1902), converted by Charles Finney, later turned against evangelicalism.

In the subsequent history of nineteenth-century Christian social thought and action the significance of women's voluntary societies has been overshadowed by that of the male-led social-gospel movement. In theological terms the latter was certainly more radical than most evangelical social reform, whether male or female, since it aimed not just at an amelioration of existing conditions, but at more far-reaching social change. The movement dates from 1848, a year of social revolution, protest and unrest in many parts of Europe. In that year the English Anglicans F. D. Maurice, Charles Kingsley and John Ludlow met to plan a Christian response to Chartist agitations for democratic political reform. Maurice's social gospel was based on an incarnational Christ-mysticism. Starting with the premise that 'every man is in Christ', Maurice argued that every individual and the whole of human society must therefore be the object of Christian concern. Christians must seek fellowship with 'everyman', not just with their fellow Christians or with God. Preaching brotherhood and co-operation, Maurice and his fellow Christian socialists attacked as 'a lie' the principle of individual competition that underlay *laissez-faire* capitalism. Rather than advocating a radical social or economic revolution, however, they favoured small-scale practical initiatives that included education for working men, and the establishment of producer co-operatives.[24]

These European influences quickly fed into the developing social-gospel movement in America, which is usually dated from the 1870s. As in Europe, it arose in response to a stage of industrialisation in which large corporations, their owners and political allies were seen to be profiting excessively at the expense of the new working classes. Here too the social gospel often commenced with an attack on individualism, which it challenged with a Christian-based social vision. As the most influential American spokesman of the social gospel, Walter Rauschenbusch (1861–1918), put it: 'We are emerging from the era of individualism. The principle of co-ordination, cooperation and solidarity is being applied in ever-widening areas and is gaining remarkable hold on the spirits of men.'[25] Rauschenbusch based his theology on Jesus' preaching of the kingdom of God, a kingdom that could not be confined to another world but must involve the 'harmonious development of a true social life' here and now. By making use of a class analysis inspired by the new social sciences, and by advocating selective public ownership, Rauschenbusch exemplified the development of the social gospel into a more radical socialist tradition than before.

With the social gospel, we find ourselves squarely in the territory of liberal rather than evangelical Christianity. By the end of the nineteenth century, the division between liberals and evangelicals or, even more broadly, between liberals and conservatives, was becoming sharper. As we shall see in chapter 7, the gulf between them would widen in the early part of the twentieth century to become even more significant than other intra-Protestant denominational divisions. For much of the nineteenth century, however, most Anglo-Saxon Protestantism tended to converge in a broad, triumphant stream in which differences were subordinated to a broader sense of common purpose. The unity of nation (the *United* States) and the might of empire (*Great* Britain) went hand in hand with the unity of the Protestant religion, which was believed by many to seal their triumph. It was only when cracks in national and imperial cohesion could no longer be papered over that divisions within and between religions also started to become more apparent.

For much of the nineteenth century, however, that which united Protestants, both liberal and evangelical, was greater than that which divided them. The common ground can be captured in three main points.

First, they shared a voluntaristic approach that viewed religion as a matter of individual free choice, that was happy to tolerate the coexistence of different Protestant churches and the differences between them, and that willingly embraced the separation of church and state and the increasing autonomy of political and economic life from religious control. One symptom of this was a withdrawal of ecclesiastical intervention in the public sphere in favour of intervention in the private, domestic sphere. The latter was particularly evident in a concern with the morals of the individual, the relations between the sexes, and the welfare of the domestic unit. Increasingly, Protestantism became a religion of 'the family'.

257

Second, they shared a growing optimism about human choice and ability, which was expressed in a 'rugged Christian individualism' that assumed that each person was free to resist or to embrace divine grace, and that this choice would be reflected in their actions. (The Calvinist emphasis on the utter depravity of the human will and the passivity of human beings in their own salvation was criticised by many, as was the Lutheran separation of faith and works.) Individuals were now felt to be responsible for their own salvation and destiny, as well as for those of the nation. Some even believed that righteous human activity could hasten the kingdom of God on earth, an optimism that was sometimes expressed in postmillennialism, that is, the belief that a truly Christian society was being prepared in the USA, fit for the coming of Christ.

Third, the Protestant churches had in common a willingness to identify 'Christian (Protestant) civilisation' with 'western civilisation' more broadly and with 'the American nation' more particularly. In the USA, Protestant churches were generally willing to sanctify the nation and its social, political and economic arrangements as God-approved. Above all, they allied themselves and their religion with the values of liberty, democracy and progress. The effect was first and foremost to support the interests and values of the white, male Anglo-Saxon middle classes, though social concern and charitable initiatives and outreach to the 'less fortunate' were also a feature of the Protestant ethos. The belief that western civilisation was at the leading edge of human history, and that Protestantism had propelled it to that position, also gave Protestants the confidence to impose that civilisation more widely, thus strengthening the Protestant missionary impetus (see ch. 7).

Given all this, the division between liberal and evangelical Protestants in the nineteenth century often amounted to no more than a slight difference in doctrinal emphasis. Generally speaking, evangelicals placed more emphasis on human sinfulness, and liberals on natural human goodness. From this flowed a greater emphasis on human dependence on the part of evangelicals, and on human independence and autonomy on the part of liberals. Likewise, evangelicals would place more emphasis upon human need of revelation, particularly through the Bible, while liberals would place more emphasis on the natural ability of human reason. In some cases, as we have seen above, liberals would reject an evangelical emphasis on individual morality in favour of concern with a more wholesale Christian reform of society at the structural level – though only a minority of liberals ever supported the social-gospel movement. Structurally, both liberalism and evangelicalism were pan-denominational ideological movements that were not exclusively associated with any particular form of Christian denomination and did not give rise to a distinctive new form of ecclesiastical institution. Yet evangelicalism had a natural and genealogical affinity with voluntarist biblicism and the free churches, while liberalism had an affinity with the non-voluntaristic historic churches on the one hand and with voluntarist spiritualism on the other. Such differences help explain why liberalism could arise in both Catholic and Protestant Christianity, but evangelicalism could never take a Catholic form (see next chapter).

Though Christian liberalism had its golden age in the late nineteenth century, and though that century saw its greatest triumphs – not least success in assimilating the potentially devastating findings of natural science into Christian theology – it would be wrong to give the impression that its origins were exclusively modern (or that its expressions were exclusively Protestant; see next chapter). The idea that liberalism simply represents an accommodation to modernity is too simple, for it ignores not only liberalism's historic roots but the extent to which other forms of Christianity were also decisively shaped by the modern context.

If liberalism is defined in terms of its belief in human free will and responsibility for salvation, and in its relatively positive estimation of human ability and dignity ('humanism'), then liberalism is probably as old as Christianity itself. In the west the Augustinian tradition fought and conquered this tradition, but did not destroy it completely. Its periodic renaissances tended to come about under the influence of classical thought, as in the work of Erasmus and, most importantly, in the work of scholastic humanists such as Aquinas. Each time it arose, it tended to be attacked by representatives of the Augustinian tradition, as in Luther's battles with Erasmus over free will (which echoed Augustine's earlier struggles with Pelagius).

What distinguished modern liberalism was probably its desire not merely to 'reform' by returning to 'the sources' of Christianity, but to move forward and advance on what had gone before. As such, post-seventeenth-century liberals allied themselves with the forces of reason, progress and 'enlightenment', and turned their backs on the 'superstition' and 'darkness' of previous eras, including Christian ones. Such liberalism could take both secular and Christian forms. Generally speaking, it took the former in parts of Europe, where it found itself engaged in lethal struggles with the church – with Calvinism in seventeenth-century Scotland and with Catholicism in seventeenth- and eighteenth-century France.

In America, because of its very different religious and political history, liberalism tended to take a less militant form, and atheism was rarely avowed. Here, as in Europe, liberalism often took shape as a reforming movement within existing churches, but it was in the USA that liberal Christianity also found its most significant independent institutional manifestation, in the Unitarian church. Championed by a newly confident republican New England bourgeoisie in the immediate aftermath of British defeat, Unitarianism took over something of the tolerant and latitudinarian spirit of the Anglicanism that – in the case of some congregations – it replaced. Its great foe was 'enthusiasm' and the whole experiential, pietistic and populist emphasis of the first Great Awakening. The growth of Unitarianism came about organically as previously existing congregations, some Episcopalian and some Congregationalist, gradually switched allegiance. Its emphasis on the importance of moral, social and rational order was in deliberate contrast to the more popular revivalist piety of the day, as was its open and tolerant attitude, its scepticism about election, predestination and a God of hellfire and damnation, and its calm confidence in the abilities and destiny of humankind. Such confidence was reinforced by the exhilaration of American independence and an accompanying sense of America's manifest destiny. Unitarian worship was focused on a benevolent Father God, who commanded self-discipline and charity towards one's fellow men. Rather than being explicitly anti-trinitarian, most Unitarians practised a strongly ethical religion in which Christ was revered as an exalted and even supernatural moral teacher rather than worshipped as a pre-existent divine being. Above all, Unitarianism enshrined the liberal sense of human beings' natural affinity with divine truth. As the great Unitarian leader Theodore Parker explained, the truth of Christianity did not depend upon Jesus' divinity, since 'the great truths of morality and religion, the deep sentiment of love to man and love to God, are perceived intuitively and by instinct'.[26]

Above all, liberalism in America stood for the cause of liberty against superstition, irrationality and intolerance. As such, it can be argued to lie at the very root of modern American society, not least through its direct influence upon the founding of the republic. For the American Declaration of Independence and the American Constitution give expression, not to any denominational form of Christianity, but to the broadly liberal-deistic beliefs of those who drafted it. Their authors were part of a commonwealth of like-minded men and women from both sides of the Atlantic, and the mutual influence between French and American deism and republicanism has always been acknowledged. In this way, theistic liberalism can be said to have its greatest influence in America, not at the level of organised religion, but within the developing politico-cultural liberal mainstream. Indeed, some scholars have argued that by the twentieth century the most pervasive religion in modern America was not Protestant Christianity, but a vague, theistic and nationalistic civic religion. In that sense, liberal Protestantism's triumph can be said to lie to some extent in its disappearance; it dissolved into the blood-stream of American culture. Evangelicalism, by contrast, would give rise to more militantly counter-cultural movements, of which fundamentalism would be the most striking example. But this story belongs to the twentieth century, and to the final chapter of this volume.

Further reading

THE ENGLISH REFORMATION

Patrick Collinson's *The Birthpangs of Protestant England: Religious and Cultural Change in the Sixteenth and Seventeenth Centuries* (Basingstoke: Macmillan, 1986) is an elegant introduction. Christopher Hill's *The World Turned Upside Down: Radical Ideas during the English Revolution* (London: Temple Smith, 1972) offers a classic treatment of radicalism in the English Revolution.

VARIETIES OF PROTESTANTISM

Ernst Troeltsch's classic study of *The Social Teaching of the Christian Churches* (London: Allen and Unwin; New York: Macmillan, 1931) still offers one of the most helpful analyses of the varieties of post-Reformation Protestantism.

Patrick Collinson's work on Puritanism is clear and insightful. See, for example, *The Elizabethan Puritan Movement* (London: Cape, 1967). On Pietism, see Mary Fullbrook's account of Pietism in three different national contexts, *Piety and Politics: Religion and the Rise of Absolutism in England,*

Württemberg, and Prussia (Cambridge and New York: Cambridge University Press, 1983), which teases out the movement's sociopolitical potentials. Patricia Caldwell's *The Puritan Conversion Narratives: The Beginning of American Expression* (Cambridge and New York: Cambridge University Press, 1985) looks at subjectivist aspects of Puritanism in an American context.

On Methodism see David Hempton, *The Religion of the People: Methodism and Popular Religion 1750–1900* (London: Routledge, 1996); John Kent, *Wesley and the Wesleyans: Religion in Eighteenth-Century Britain* (Cambridge and New York: Cambridge University Press, 2002); and Dee Andrews, *The Methodists and Revolutionary America: The Shaping of an Evangelical Culture* (Princeton, NJ, and Oxford: Princeton University Press, 1996).

On the radical reformation groups, including the Quakers, see Michael Mullett's *Radical Religious Movements in Early Modern Europe* (London and Boston, MA: Allen and Unwin, 1980), which is particularly useful in placing them in their wider politico-economic contexts.

PROPHETESSES, WITCHES AND GODLY WIVES

There are two useful, wide-ranging accounts of women and religion in the early modern world: Merry E. Wiesner, *Women and Gender in Early Modern Europe* (second edition, Cambridge and New York: Cambridge University Press, 2000), and Marilyn J. Westerkamp, *Women and Religion in Early America 1600–1850* (London: Routledge, 1999).

On the witch hunts, see Brian Levack, *The Witch-Hunt in Early Modern Europe* (London and New York: Longman, 1987); R. Kieckhefer, *European Witch Trials: Their Foundations in Popular and Learned Culture 1300–1500* (London: Routledge and Kegan Paul, 1976); Christina Larner, *Witchcraft and Religion: The Politics of Popular Belief* (New York: Blackwell, 1984); and Lyndal Roper's thought-provoking collection of essays, *Oedipus and the Devil: Witchcraft, Sexuality and Religion in Early Modern Europe* (London and New York: Routledge, 1994). See also Keith Thomas, *Religion and the Decline of Magic* (London: Weidenfeld and Nicolson, 1971).

Barbara Welter's account of 'The Cult of True Womanhood' is contained in essays collected together in *Dimity Convictions: The American Woman in the Nineteenth Century* (Athens, OH: Ohio University Press, 1976). On women and religion in nineteenth-century America, see also Carroll Smith-Rosenberg, *Disorderly Conduct: Visions of Gender in Victorian America* (New York: Oxford University Press, 1985), and Lori D. Ginzberg, *Women and the Work of Benevolence* (New Haven, CT: Yale University Press, 1990).

THE AMERICAN EXPERIMENT

Sydney E. Ahlstrom's *A Religious History of the American People* (New Haven, CT, and London: Yale University Press, 1972) offers a magisterial survey of religion in north America. Nathan Hatch's *The Democratization of American Christianity* (New Haven, CT, and London: Yale University Press, 1989) accounts for the success of American evangelicalism in terms of its ability to throw off power from on high and harness the energies and commitments of ordinary people. John Butler's *Awash in a Sea of Faith: Christianizing the American People* (Cambridge, MA: Harvard University Press, 1990) is a work of revisionism that argues (among other things) that Protestant Christianity in America has always been less democratic than its supporters would like to claim. On slavery and American religion see Albert J. Raboteau, *Slave Religion: The 'Invisible Institution' in the Antebellum South* (New York: Oxford University Press, 1978).

EVANGELICALS AND LIBERALS

Boyd Hilton's *The Age of Atonement: The Influence of Evangelicalism on Social and Economic Thought, 1785–1865* (Oxford: Clarendon; New York: Oxford University Press, 1991) is a classic. David Bebbington's *Evangelicalism in Modern Britain* (London and Boston, MA: Unwin Hyman, 1989) is a major historical survey that treats evangelicalism as an Anglo-American movement and sheds a great deal of light on its relation to the wider culture. See also George M. Thomas's *Revivalism and Cultural Change: Christianity, Nation Building, and the Market in the Nineteenth-Century United States* (Chicago, IL: University of Chicago Press, 1989).

There is surprisingly little literature on liberal Christianity, and no general introduction to the subject. Most histories of liberal Christianity deal primarily with its American manifestations. Conrad Wright's *The Beginnings of Unitarianism in America* (Hamden, CT: Archon, 1976) remains the standard account of the Unitarian movement. See also Henry F. May, *The Enlightenment in America* (New York: Oxford University Press, 1976); Kenneth Cauthen, *The Impact of American Religious Liberalism* (New York: Harper and Row, 1962); and William R. Hutchison, *The Modernist Impulse in American Protestantism* (Oxford: Oxford University Press, 1982). For a more general portrait of liberal religion, see Linda Woodhead and Paul Heelas, *Religion in Modern Times: An Interpretive Anthology* (Oxford and Malden, MA: Blackwell, 2000).

6

Catholic and Orthodox negotiations with modernity

Syllabus of the principal errors of our time . . .
   1. There exists no Supreme, all-wise, all-provident Divine Being, distinct from the universe . . .
   15. Every man is free to embrace and profess that religion which, guided by the light of reason, he shall consider true . . .
   24. The church has not the power of using force, nor has she any temporal power, direct or indirect . . .
   44. The civil authority may interfere in matters relating to religion, morality and spiritual government . . .
   77. In the present day it is no longer expedient that the Catholic religion should be held as the only religion of the State, to the exclusion of all other forms of worship . . .
   80. The Roman Pontiff can, and ought to, reconcile himself, and come to terms with progress, liberalism and modern civilisation.[1]

Simply by dissolving the unity of Christianity, the Reformation had a profound effect on the Catholic church. It was not that post-Reformation Christians were left with choice of religious affiliation, for in most cases their faith would still be determined by the society and family into which they were born. But after the Reformation, Europeans were no longer simply born 'Christian'. However dim and distant the threat of Protestantism might seem to, say, an Italian peasant, he would now be aware that he possessed a 'Catholic' identity that set him apart from some other so-called Christians north of the Alps. This inevitably resulted in a new self-consciousness about religious identity not only on the part of individuals but on that of whole societies as well. Whereas, before, the cultural world into which a Catholic was born could be received simply as 'the world', 'the truth', 'the way things are', there was now an awareness that other Christians occupied different worlds and had different accounts of the truth. This did not necessarily destabilise Catholic or Protestant worldviews, but it made people more aware that they belonged to a particular tradition, and more sensitive to its distinctive features. Increasingly the churches articulated their separate identities by way of 'confessions'. 'No faith is firm which does not show itself in confession,' wrote Philipp Melanchthon, the author of the Lutheran *Augsburg Confession*. 'We believe, teach and confess . . .' began the Lutheran *Formula of Concord*; 'This holy synod confesses and believes . . .' said the Catholic Council of Trent.

The 'confessionalisation' of Christianity was bound up with other factors too. One was the growth of absolutism in Europe. Just like the papacy centuries before, the national monarchs of Europe strove to achieve unconstrained sovereign power – political, economic and military. The power of the church was inevitably compromised by the emergence of such higher power in Europe, and many national monarchs were keen to appropriate as many of the church's temporal and spiritual resources as possible. Since the church retained some control over these resources, however, it was in a position to do deals. It formed a series of alliances with political absolutism that helped it safeguard its interests in a challenging situation. Sacred power was still a valuable resource in the creation of sacred nationhood and sacred monarchies, and confessionalisation helped the church safeguard this asset. Such power became bound ever more tightly to the papacy and priesthood and to the official offices, teachings and structures of the church. The effect of the reform, rationalisation, centralisation and doctrinal definition that took place in Tridentine Catholicism (i.e. Catholicism after the Council of Trent) was to regulate the sacred more tightly than ever before.

Thus the Catholic church took steps to secure a power that was now threatened not only by the rise of Protestantism, but by competing forms of secular power. It responded to the former by differentiation and attack and to the latter by differentiation and alliance. As we have seen in the preceding chapters, the strategy of many Protestant denominations in the context of the early modern revolution was not dissimilar. They too confessionalised (Luther's *Confession concerning Christ's Supper* of 1528 and the *Augsburg Confession* of 1530 being the first confessions of all), and they too made alliances with nations and nationalism. This led to a paradox that will be explored in this chapter: that, while confessionalisation was intended to mark the difference between Catholic and Protestant, the fact that both forms of Christianity pursued the same strategy of doctrinal self-definition meant that what united them was actually as important as what divided them.

Without in any way underestimating the hostility that Catholics and Protestants often felt for one another, or the seriousness of their attempts to differentiate their confessions, this chapter will show that early modern Catholicism and Protestantism actually had much more in common than is often acknowledged. Both became increasingly 'ecclesiastical' and clericalised, both placed a new emphasis on human sinfulness and incapacity, and both put a new stress on the need for divine grace mediated through the church. Both, in other words, tended to swing in the direction of power from on high. The strategy provoked protest not only from defenders of power from below within the ranks of the churches themselves (religious liberals), but from advocates of power from below in the political realm as well (political liberals). When political events shifted dramatically in favour of the latter constituency, most notably in the French Revolution of 1789, the churches in Europe found themselves in grave danger of being identified with the causes of tyranny and reaction rather than with liberty, fraternity and equality.

Constrained by its intensified commitment to power from on high in its doctrine, internal organisation and political alliances, a confessionalised Roman Catholic church was unable to evade this danger. It sided with the opponents of freedom, democracy and progress in Europe – of whom there were many. As the *Syllabus of Errors* issued by Pope Pius IX in 1864, and quoted above, indicates, it did so not only in the eighteenth century, but through the nineteenth and into the twentieth. While Protestantism also tended to side with the cause of social order and national stability against revolutionary change, its greater internal pluralism and voluntaristic potential, and the more varied social locations in which it found itself, lent it greater flexibility and prevented it from being so uniformly identified with the cause of reaction. In North America, as we saw in the previous chapter, the Protestant and Roman Catholic churches took a route different from the one they took in Europe by allying themselves with the causes of liberty and democracy rather than with conservatism.

There are also complicating factors, which smudge the lines of this neat analysis. The internal variety of the confessions, both Catholic and Protestant, is one. The importance of the suppressed voice of liberalism within the Catholic church is another. Likewise, the different sociopolitical locations of Catholic and Protestant confessions complicate the picture – for where a confession helped defend the identity of a threatened political or ethnic group, as with Catholicism in Ireland or in Poland, for example, it could have revolutionary and liberating rather than reactionary potential. Finally, revolutionary upheaval in both sacred and secular realms did not necessarily have the same effect or mean the same things for men as for women, and the two genders did not necessarily react in the same ways. While the early modern revolutions won greater political liberty for many men, they did not effect a similar change for women, who continued to be disenfranchised and excluded from public power. After the eighteenth century, women appear to have remained more loyal to the Catholic church than men, and to have become more active in the transmission of the faith. Some scholars have gone so far as to argue that, in the nineteenth century and the first part of the twentieth, it was women rather than men who saved the churches from rapid decline.

As far as the development of the Orthodox churches in the modern world is concerned – the subject of the final part of this chapter – there are some interesting parallels with the course of the Roman Catholic tradition from which it was now so decisively separated. In both cases the dominant motif was a continued proclivity for alliance with higher power, and in both cases competing Christian traditions of power from below arose, on occasion, to challenge and protest. Both churches had to face the challenges of modernity, albeit in rather different guises, and both had to make compromises with competing forms of secular power.

But there were significant differences as well. For one thing, as we have seen in earlier chapters, Orthodoxy inherited a tradition of alliance with political power from on high that was different from that of Catholicism. Both were non-voluntary churches that sought control over the whole population. But, whereas Catholicism claimed superiority over all secular power, including the state, Orthodoxy sought partnership and co-operation rather than control and domination. This model had governed relations between state and church in the Byzantine empire, and it continued to shape such relations into the modern period. Just as Orthodoxy tended to resist the lure of absolute power, so it also tended to resist concentrating power in a single place and a person. Unlike Catholicism, it supported a conciliar rather than a monarchial ideal, and, while patriarchs would hold power over the church in their own territory, they did not have power over one another. Even though the 'ecumenical' patriarch in Constantinople claimed to be first among equals, he never claimed the authority of a 'pope'. Indeed, the tendency was rather the opposite: to the creation of increasing numbers of autocephalous (self-governing) Orthodox churches.

The main effect of these differences, as we shall see, was to make the Orthodox encounter with modernity somewhat more diverse and less confrontational than the Catholic one. Rather than entering into a protracted struggle with secular power, Orthodoxy tended to revert to its traditional posture of subordination to the state.

Reform in head and members

If the previous two chapters were taken in isolation, the reader could be forgiven for thinking that after about 1520 the western world turned Protestant. In fact, the overall numbers of Protestants remained small compared with those of Catholics, and the Catholic church retained most of its vast wealth, some of its pan-European legal functions, and its massive political reach. The most powerful polities of the Reformation period – Spain, France and Austria – remained Catholic. And the Roman church continued to view itself as the one, true, universal church of Christ, whose dominion had been secured by God himself for the last millennium and a half. Catholicism was a Goliath that for some time refused to be threatened by a small, upstart Protestant faction. It had to take notice only when the latter started to win political backing and, particularly in the German territories, to become a threat to Catholic power, both political and papal. Political and ecclesiastical power could not be easily separated, not only because the emperor was still the 'Holy Roman' emperor, but because the pope was a political ruler in his own right, with control over the Papal States in Italy. Rome was not just a religious power but a territorial one, and the church remained a 'temporality' or a 'property' as well as a 'church' in a more spiritual sense.

The fact that modern men and women tend to think of a church as a spiritual power rather than as a temporal or political one, and to assume that when a religion becomes political it has ceased to be authentically religious, is a measure of just how much Christianity has changed in the last five hundred years, dragging common-sense assumptions with it. This is a measure of the ultimate success of the reforming voices that had been calling for a 'spiritual' reform since the thirteenth century. Powerful among these, as we saw in chapter 3, were the mendicant orders, particularly the friars, and associated theologians and lay groups. In the late medieval period some 'spirituals', such as the more moderate

Franciscans, were absorbed into the life of the church, while others were attacked as heretics. They did not disappear. In the sixteenth century, for example, *spirituali*, men and women inspired by the poverty of Jesus and the apostles, criss-crossed Italy preaching a gospel of repentance and calling for reform of the church. They seem to have come from all classes. Some were radicals and prophets with a millenarian emphasis in their preaching. Some spoke of a *papa angelicus*, an angelic pope, who would purify the church and inaugurate a new spiritual era. Others who called for a spiritual reform of the church 'in head and members' were from more exalted circles. We have already mentioned the theologico-political expression of spiritualist views in the work of men such as William of Ockham and John Wyclif. In the sixteenth century their opinions were being echoed by powerful men closer to Rome. When in 1529 Pope Clement VII protested to the Venetian republic (which had become powerful through trade) about its occupation of two cities of the papal state, Ravenna and Cervia, the Venetian Catholic ambassador, Gasparo Contarini, replied that the pope should not care, since his power was properly confined to the spiritual realm, and a papal state was in any case a distraction from the church's true activity: the care of souls. Contarini's arguments could be dismissed by Rome as politically expedient, but his point of view carried theological weight.

At the institutional level the desire for spiritual reform found expression in the new confraternities that sprang up across Europe, including the Oratories of Divine Love founded at the end of the fifteenth century. These were mainly urban-based voluntary brotherhoods of male Christians, both lay and clerical, who met together in order to encourage charity, personal sanctification and reform of the church from within. Their piety often centred around frequent communion and confession. Equally, the spiritualising impetus was institutionalised in the remarkable number of new monastic orders founded between 1524 and 1540, chiefly in Italy. These included the Camaldolese, the Theatine order, the Capuchins, Barnabites, Somaschi and Ursulines. Like the confraternities, these orders display continuity with medieval ideals and piety, rather than representing anything new that might be labelled 'counter-reformation'. Their aim was to return to a purer, more spiritual form of Christianity modelled on the early church. In that sense, they were backward-looking rather than forward-looking. The ideal of voluntary poverty and a closer personal relation with God was often prominent.

The Capuchins, for example, wished to return to the pristine Franciscan ideal of uncompromising poverty. A number of existing orders also developed 'Observant' movements, which sought a return to the simplicity and purity of their founders' original ideals. (We noted that Luther was an Augustinian Observant.) While many of these initiatives won papal blessing, none came about as a direct result of papal action, and none arose as a direct response to Protestant reform.

It is the gradual seizing of initiative by the papacy and centralisation on Rome that distinguishes the reform that began to reshape Catholicism after about 1540, during the papacy of Paul III. Some of the first moves were largely defensive, provoked by news of Protestant growth transmitted by papal nuncios from across Europe. One of the most important initiatives was the reorganisation and strengthening of the Roman Inquisition after 1542. While the Spanish Inquisition was an office of state, its Roman counterpart was under the control of a committee of cardinals responsible to the pope. Another step was censorship. A list of prohibited books was first drawn up by a nuncio in 1549, and an official Roman *Index of Forbidden Books* followed in 1557. The latter was wide-ranging in scope, and even prohibited the reading of vernacular Bibles.

A certain defensiveness is also evident in the early sessions of the Council of Trent, convened in 1545. Unlike several previous councils, Trent was called by the pope, who kept control of proceedings through his papal legates. (Trent is located in the Alps, far north of Rome, and the council was situated there in order to make it easier for northern European bishops to attend.) By this time there was no question of rapprochement with Protestantism. In the pope's eyes the chief purpose of the council was condemnation of heresy and the formulation of rebuttals of Protestant attacks on the church. The council would help Catholic Europe regroup in the face of attack. It was politically expedient, not only because it brought church leaders together, but because it satisfied widespread and long-standing calls for a church council, not least by the Holy Roman emperor of the time, Charles V (ruler of both Spain and Austria).

The first two sessions of the council, in 1545–7 and 1551–2, reflect this largely defensive agenda. Though some delegates hoped for more constructive reforms, particularly in relation to the church's own life and organisation, it is clear that the pope did not share their enthusiasm. The call for 'reform in head and members' was by now centuries old, and carried an implicit recognition that serious change would come about only if the theory and practice of papal power ('the head') were addressed. A few of the humanist cardinals at the council shared this agenda. Though he was somewhat less radical, Charles V also hoped for swift and decisive action to rid the church of its more obvious 'abuses' and to impose discipline in its life. Both would be disappointed at what transpired in the first two sessions, for it quickly became clear that Pope Paul III had no clear or systematic agenda for reform, and was certainly unwilling to consider change 'at the top'. He was engaged in a pragmatic attempt to strengthen and defend the church against its enemies, and was concerned to vanquish reform, not to give in to it.

The most constructive outcome of these first sessions was a clear statement of the Catholic church's teaching on the doctrine of justification, which clarified the nature of the disagreement with Protestantism through a confident assertion of the Catholic position. As with other definitions and decisions, the council first set out an explanation, followed by condemnations of the opposing view:

> If anyone says that man can be justified before God by his own
> works . . . apart from the grace of Jesus Christ, let him be anathema.
>   If anyone says that the free will of man, moved and aroused by God,
> does not co-operate at all by responding to the awakening call of God,
> so as to dispose and prepare itself for the acquisition of the grace of
> justification, nor can it refuse that grace, if it so will, but it does nothing
> at all, like some inanimate thing, and is completely passive, let them be
> anathema.[2]

At a stroke, the council defended itself against Protestant accusations that it taught a doctrine of justification by works, while affirming a more positive view of human abilities than Protestantism's by insisting that human beings are free to resist or to co-operate with divine grace. In what would become the 'official' Catholic view, human beings were represented as capable of an active relation with God, rather than a merely passive one in which they can do no more than become channels of the divine will. A broadly humanist position had triumphed over a more Augustinian one. Trent also clarified a number of other points of doctrine and church order. It affirmed the position of holy scripture as worthy of equal reverence with the tradition that is 'preserved in unbroken succession in the Catholic church'; the validity of the Latin mass and of the seven sacraments rather than two; the presence of 'the whole Christ' in both the bread and the wine of the eucharist; and the power of the ordained priesthood to consecrate the sacraments, and its origin in the New Testament.

Trent's most constructive proposals for reform stemmed from its third and final session, convened by Pope Pius IV in 1562–3. Rather than looking over its shoulder at Protestant criticism, Catholicism was now looking forward, constructing a programme for the reform and revital- isation of the church. The desire to re-form the church on the model of the earliest Christian communities was gradually being supplanted by the desire to create a church capable of meeting the challenges of present and future while remaining true to its heritage. Catholicism's horizons were also expanding geographically. Improved navigation and the imperial conquests of Spain and Portugal had opened up new lands to Catholic mission, and with them the idea of Catholic expansion across the globe. There were souls to be won not only in Europe, where the church hoped to win Protestants back to the true faith, but overseas. The task of the final session of the council was to help shape a disciplined and revitalised church capable of taking advantage of these apparently God-given opportunities. It was almost like the preparation for a vast onslaught on the world, and it is perhaps not surprising that martial imagery became increasingly popular in Catholic circles. The universal horizons of Catholicism were opening up once more.

In moving from defence to attack, the council sponsored measures for reform that would have far-reaching effects. Two were particularly important: those that had to do with reforming the clergy and those that had to do with reforming the institution of marriage. Both had the effect of strengthening the church's hold over the individual lives of the faithful in the two spheres where the church's power remained unchallenged: in church and home. Both also had to do with the means of transmission of a revitalised faith. In relation to the clergy, the aim was to turn an undisciplined and badly prepared body of men into a highly trained army of dedicated professionals. One vital step was to propose new measures for clerical training, most importantly the establishment of seminaries in every diocese. Another was to attempt the reform of the office of a bishop so that, instead of being an absentee landlord and grandee, he became a dedicated officer resident in his diocese and engaged in regular review of his clerical troops. In relation to marriage, the council took steps to control an institution that had previously been somewhat peripheral to the Roman Catholic church. Before the Reformation, marriage had been treated as a secular as much as a religious institution, in which the power of making vows lay in the hands of the man and woman who were marrying each other. Weddings often took place outside the church, and were valid even if contracted without the presence of a priest. One reason for this relative neglect of marriage was, of course, the higher status of the celibate life in Catholic eyes. Now, however, the church took steps to align the sacred more securely with marriage and the family, just as the Protestant churches had done. The sacramental and indissoluble nature of the marriage bond was re-emphasised, and the definition of what constituted a valid marriage was tightened up. All marriages were now to be contracted in the presence of a priest and before two or three witnesses. In both an actual and a metaphorical sense, marriage was brought inside the church.

Another important issue of transmission related to the decrees of the council itself. It was all very well for bishops and cardinals to make decrees, but what influence would they have on the church once Trent was over? Pius IV made a decisive move by giving all the decrees his approbation, but forbidding their interpretation without papal approval. He created a commission of the cardinals, the future Congregation on the Council, on which he conferred the sole authority to interpret the decrees. The voluminous proceedings of Trent were not published until the nineteenth century, and the pope retained overall control of the nature and the pace of reform. The process would be long and complicated. There were too many powerful, independent political actors for the papacy merely to impose its will on the Catholic world. European rulers, especially the mighty kings of France and the Holy Roman emperors, exercised a great deal of control over the church in their respective lands, and regarded themselves as independent spiritual as well as secular rulers. In France the decrees were not published at all and had no legal standing, but were implemented piecemeal by bishops. In Spain, by contrast, the decrees were published with the general approval of the then emperor, Philip II (1527–98).

Although reform of the 'members' gathered pace, that of the 'head' lagged behind. Catholic ecclesiology (doctrine of the church) remained unexamined. The hierarchical model that had developed throughout the medieval period, which viewed the pope as supreme in both temporal and spiritual power over bishops, clergy, rulers and people, persisted by default. Nevertheless, a succession of reforming popes instituted changes aimed at rationalising the growing bureaucratic apparatus in Rome. The process began with the establishment of 'congregations' led by standing committees of cardinals, each responsible for control of a particular aspect of church activity (a development paralleled or perhaps copied by the creation of departments of state in increasingly secular states). In 1588 Pope Sixtus V undertook the most thoroughgoing reform of the Roman curia by creating fifteen congregations, which together formed a system of government for the church as a whole in both its spiritual and its temporal dimensions. Papal nuncios became ambassadors of Rome in every part of the Catholic world, and acted as 'line managers' between Rome and local rulers and clerics. In the process, power became centralised upon Rome to a greater degree than ever before. A series of educational, liturgical and disciplinary innovations, all emanating from Rome under Pius V, reinforced this trend. Most notable were the publication of *The Roman Catechism* in 1566 and that of the revised *Roman Breviary* in 1568, the codification of liturgy in *The Roman Missal* in 1570, and the completion of a revised Roman Bible in 1593 (the so-called *Vulgata Clementina*).

Such measures left the political and economic power of the church and the pope not only intact but enhanced. The office of the papacy had been debased in the late Middle Ages by its residence in Avignon and by schism. Its restoration was held back by a succession of popes who concerned themselves more with dynastic politics and defence of the Papal States than with the spiritual functions of the papacy. There was a serious danger that Rome would decline to become no more than a minor European state. The administrative reorganisation of Rome, with an eye to the spiritual conquest of the world, signalled a return to universal as well as to local concerns. The pope was a universal leader, not a local magnate, who would speak *urbi et orbi* – to the city (of Rome) and to the world.

The claim to universal sovereignty would also be signalled in more symbolic ways. Even before Trent, steps had been taken in this direction. One was to give greater emphasis to the spiritual, sacramental role of the papacy. Efforts were made to project the saintly charisma and mystique of the papacy. Some popes associated themselves closely with monasticism and the ideal of apostolic poverty, chiefly by becoming protectors of religious orders. The ritual ceremonies surrounding the papacy were also elaborated and codified, and a new 'cult' of the consecrated host was encouraged, with the festival of Corpus Christi becoming a universal festival of the church centred on Rome rather than on a local shrine. Equally important was the rebuilding of Rome. This grand project became a vital element in the reconstruction of the papacy. Its aim was to give architectural expression to the fact that Rome was not merely one episcopal city among others, but the centre of gravity of the whole of an expanding Christendom. To signal this, its heart would shift from the old Lateran palace and cathedral to a new basilica built over St Peter's tomb. St Peter's and the Vatican palace would become the architectural focus of a new, ideal city centred on the person and the sacramental function of the pope. Rome would be revived not only as a diplomatic and legislative centre, but as a centre of pilgrimage for all the faithful.

Begun by Pope Nicholas V in the mid-fifteenth century, the reshaping of Rome was completed only in the seventeenth. Its patrons were all popes, cardinals and other high-ranking ecclesiastics, deeply imbued with the political and spiritual values of Tridentine Catholicism, and anxious that these should be properly exhibited. The architects and artists employed in the creation of the new Rome were supremely successful in interpreting the desires of these patrons. The great 'Baroque' artists presented a unified and hierarchical vision of the world, in which the power of God flows down from the heavens to the earth by way of the church, and in which human beings can be caught up into the heavens by participation in the beauty of truth and the truth of beauty. Like the early Byzantine churches, the new Catholic churches aimed to bring heaven down to earth. Domes and cupolas representing the heavens became the central feature in their church designs, culminating in Michelangelo's dome of St Peter's, completed in 1590. The intention was to provoke emotion – to overpower, overawe and inspire. Above all, the Baroque draws the believer upwards, to the heavens. Its figures tend to be superhuman, their eyes raised towards heaven, their bodies floating upwards, mingling with angels and clouds as they approach God, their progression like a pillar of flame.

Plate 16 *The Triumph of the Chair of St Peter* (*Cathedra Petri*), by Giovanno Lorenzo Bernini (1598–1680), St Peter's, Rome

There could hardly be a more powerful image of the reassertion of papal power than Bernini's mighty monument in the apse of St Peter's. The throne from which St Peter was thought to have preached is encased in bronze and held aloft by the 'doctors of the church' Ambrose, Augustine, Athanasius and John Chrysostom. The Holy Spirit in the form of a dove pours down inspiration from above.

Confessionalisation

It is easy to draw the contrast between Catholic and Protestant, using architecture as a focus. Protestants favoured simple and unadorned buildings for worship. God was present in Spirit and in Word – rather than in material objects – and the visual focus would often fall on the pulpit. Worshippers would sit in ranks of pews, normally in order of social class, and face the preacher. The walls of the building would usually be unadorned, and the glass plain. The sacred was to be heard rather than seen, and sensual distractions were to be avoided. It was, in any case, ridiculous to think that God could somehow be brought down to earth by human artefacts. God could never be contained in a temple built by human hands, and costly decoration did more to glorify those who commissioned it than to glorify the living God. True worship consisted in contrite hearts and changed lives, not in splendid ceremonies and ostentatious adornments.

For many Protestants, the interior of a Baroque Catholic church smacked of idol worship rather than Christianity. Bright colours, statues of the saints, the flickering lights of candles, reliquaries, gilt and stained glass and the smell of incense launched an assault on the senses. At the heart of it all was not the pulpit but the altar, the site of Christ's repeated unbloody sacrifice in the eucharist, and the sphere of operations of a priest decked in costly vestments. Behind it a reredos depicting heavenly figures and perhaps Christ himself invited the worshipper to join with the company of heaven in the celebration of the holy mysteries. What the Protestant found gross, blasphemous, gaudy and vulgar, the Catholic found moving, reverent and celebratory. For the Catholic the church was not a mere auditorium, but the place where the divine and the human drew close and where the most precious gifts of man were rightfully dedicated to the praise of God.

Such differences are important – but perhaps not as important as they seemed to contemporaries. Viewed from a longer perspective, it is the similarities between post-Reformation Catholicism and Protestantism that stand out as much as the contrasts.

The most significant commonality, a shared emphasis on confession, has already been mentioned. In both Catholicism and Protestantism, it was manifest in the new emphasis given to literacy, education and theology, and it gave rise to a wealth of catechetical, educational, instructional materials. Both clergy and laity became better educated in their faith and more concerned with points of doctrine. Faith became a matter of correct propositional belief, not merely of feeling, intention, behaviour, ancestry or social belonging. The clergy became better educated, and the period given over to theological training before ordination steadily lengthened for both Catholic and Protestant throughout the seventeenth century. Religion became more codified, more rationalised, and in the process more internally uniform. The vast range of beliefs that the medieval church had encompassed were narrowed down in order to eliminate confusion and establish a clearer sense of identity. Confessionalisation helped ensure a new uniformity within each confession, while in the process underscoring and accentuating difference between Catholic and Protestant. That which they had in common was that which divided.

Though confessionalisation also involved a rationalisation of religion, an increase in internal coherence and organisational effectiveness, it did not necessarily make it more rational. Individual reason was not to be excised, but it was to be subordinated to the teachings of the church. The latter were now designed, in both confessions, to offer coherent world-views (see ch. 7). It was these, rather than the use of unaided individual reason, that dictated what was rational for their followers. Christians were to have faith so that they might understand, rather than the other way around. New attitudes of loyalty, obedience and party spirit were called for. In some Protestant denominations, especially those with a tradition of some local independence, confessional uniformity would be maintained chiefly at the congregational level. In larger denominations it would be enforced 'from the top', as organisational structures became more wide-ranging, centralised and efficient.

The same process was visible in post-Reformation Catholicism. Increasingly the truth was defined by the magisterium, disseminated by schools, colleges, seminaries and official publications, and preached by the clergy. False belief was reported by those on the ground, investi-gated by the Holy Office, condemned by the magisterium, proscribed by the *Index* and, if necessary, punished by excommunication – or worse. One of the most notorious examples concerned the Catholic condem-nations of Giordano Bruno and Galileo for claiming that the Earth revolved around the Sun rather than vice versa. After a trial lasting seven years, Bruno was burnt in Rome in 1600. Galileo ended his life under house arrest. This would be the beginning of a battle between

Plate 17   *Victory of Catholic Truth over Heresy,* by Pierre Legros II (1666–1719)
Situated in Il Gesù church, Rome – the first church of the Jesuit order – the spirit of
confessional Catholic self-confidence finds full expression in this sculpture by Legros.

confessional Catholicism and 'scientific rationality' that would last until the mid-twentieth century. One of its most important effects was to alienate many supporters of science and reason from the Roman Catholic church and to ensure that the rationalist movement of the late seventeenth and eighteenth centuries, which we call the Enlightenment, would take on an increasingly anti-clerical and secular form, especially in Catholic Europe. Another was gradually to push to the margins of Catholic life the more moderate forms of Christian liberalism that sought to reconcile faith and reason.

An intensification of power from on high was another characteristic shared between post-Reformation Catholicism and Protestantism. In both, God became more powerful, more transcendent, more dominating. We have already seen this mechanism at work in Reformation Protestantism, where it reached the logical limit of its development in the theology of Calvin. Despite their apparent opposition, both Calvinism and the art and architecture of Baroque Catholicism were making a similar point: God was above, humans were below. The gulf between the two appeared wider than ever before. Not only was God greater, but the world was more sinful. Calvin had spoken of the 'total depravity' of humankind. Sin, he said, was not merely a defect but an active force for evil working in the heart of everyman. While the confessional Catholicism outlined at Trent was careful to distinguish itself from this position by insisting on the reality of human freedom, it too placed a new emphasis upon sinfulness. Post-Reformation Christianity was characterised by 'hyperculpabalisation', a new intensity of emphasis upon the guilt of each human being and the necessity of expiation by way of regular self-examination and confession. This emphasis upon the necessity of self-scrutiny and an internalisation of self-discipline became common to both Protestant and Catholic. Even though Luther had abolished the sacramental status of confession, he continued to believe in the importance of supervised penance, as did most other forms of Protestantism. Though the practice of confessing before a clergyman might be abandoned, some social or 'fraternal' mode of examination and confession – such as the Calvinist consistory – would often take its place.

A new austerity and a new emphasis upon self-mortification, self-sacrifice, and self-abnegation were thus evident in Catholicism as well as in Protestantism. It was evident even in the version of mysticism that spread across Catholic Europe from Spain in the seventeenth and eighteenth centuries. Inspired by the writings of Teresa of Avila (1518–82) and later by her disciple, John of the Cross (1542–91), this was a mysticism that believed that total detachment from the world and self-annihilation were the necessary preconditions for the vision of God. Pierre de Bérulle (1575–1629), who, above all others, was responsible for spreading Teresian mysticism in France, insisted that 'we must consider our being to be finite and imperfect, like an emptiness that needs to be filled'. At the close of the seventeenth century, Madame Guyon (1648–1717), a disciple of François de Salignac de la Mothe Fénelon (1651–1715), rediscovered St John of the Cross and advised spiritual people to tread 'the way of death', of 'annihilation and denudation'.[3] In Jansenism Catholicism drew even closer to a more Calvinist form of austerity. While some of the Jansenists, most famously Blaise Pascal (1623–62), were also subject to mystical transports, the defining mark of the movement was its emphasis on human sinfulness and justification by faith alone. These views were spelt out by Jansen, bishop of Ypres in the Spanish Low Countries (Belgium), in his posthumous homage to Augustine, *Augustinus* (1640). Though Jansenism became embroiled in bitter controversy with the Jesuits (see below), who favoured a more positive, Thomistic, view of human nature, and who were less austere and, in the eyes of the Jansenists, too 'lax' in their moral instruction, Jansenism managed to avoid full condemnation from Rome until 1713, when the papal bull *Unigenitus* condemned 101 propositions drawn from the *Moral Reflections* of the Jansenist Pasquier Quesnel. The difficulty was not so much the Jansenists' view of human nature and divine power (after all, Trent had affirmed that nothing can be done without grace), as Jansensist advocacy of 'Protestant' initiatives such as greater lay participation in the church and translation of the scriptures into the vernacular. 'The reading of scriptures by women' was particularly condemned by Rome. Jansenism was also attacked, both politically and spiritually, because it had come to serve as a rallying point in France for opponents of the monarchy and the papacy, and for the 'Gallican' supporters of a national church.

An intensified emphasis on God's power and human sinfulness went hand in hand with an intensification of the power of his church and clergy. This may seem more obvious in relation to post-Reformation Catholicism than to Protestantism. After all, was not this what Protestants recoiled from when they considered 'papist' practices – the worship of man, not of God? And was not this what the reforms of Trent had been designed to secure – the power of the pope and his clergy? The churches of the Protestants were plainer because their ecclesiology was plainer. They needed no priest to stand between them and God. Their church was the gathered faithful, not a body of clergy who presumed to interpose themselves between the believer and God. All this is true, in theory. But in practice the difference between Catholic and Protestant was again somewhat less stark. Not even the most extreme radical Protestant would dispense with the social dimension of Christianity, with some sort of church. None really imagined that personal salvation could or should be pursued independent of the body of the faithful. In practice the lowest Protestant chapel was just as important to its members as was the highest Catholic church to its flock.

Likewise, although Protestants might protest that they had no priests, and while some genuinely believed the pope to be the Antichrist, their 'pastors', 'ministers', 'leaders' or 'preachers' would normally have as much authority over their flock as a Catholic parish priest would, and as high a standing within the local community. Though Protestantism often shunned episcopacy and allowed congregations (or at least their male 'elders') some power over their pastors, the rising standards of clerical education for both Protestant and Catholic clergy served to differentiate both from their flocks. By the eighteenth and nineteenth centuries, both Protestant and Catholic clergy were becoming identified with the new professional classes, and were more likely to associate with doctors, lawyers and successful businessmen than with the average member of an average congregation. In both cases, all the clergy were male.

The clericalisation of the church was a central aspect of the modernisation of both Protestantism and Catholicism. The rising status of the clergy and the new openings for clerical ministry that reformation had brought into existence in both Protestantism and Roman Catholicism may well have been a major factor in the proliferation of churches in the early modern period on both sides of the Atlantic. In the clerical profession more and more talented and intelligent men, both Catholic and Protestant, found an escape from employment that would otherwise have been less demanding and less well rewarded. In societies that still had limited openings for education and stratified social systems, clerical office offered an obvious and important route to self-advancement. This, in turn, reinforced the growth of the church. As more and better-qualified men became pastors, so the faith was transmitted more effectively, and, as the faith grew, so more pastors were required. For Catholics, as we shall see below, the same was also true of the religious orders, who experienced a similar period of vitality in the early modern period. Unlike the clerical office, the latter opened opportunities to women as well as to men.

The widening gap between the divine and the human, the clerical and the lay, did not, however, mean dissociation. On the contrary, post-Reformation Catholicism and Protestantism were both characterised by their emphasis on 'condescension'. Though a gulf had opened up between creature and creator, the latter, in his unfathomable mercy, had chosen to breach it. The agent of mediation was Jesus Christ. Both Catholic and Protestant art tended to depict his divinity rather than his humanity. Though he walked on earth, he clearly belongs to the heavens. He is God rather than man. Yet he came to earth to save wretched sinners. New forms of Catholic piety focused on the Sacred Heart of Christ and the Man of Sorrows. Christ's suffering was often emphasised to the point of mawkishness. Yet the outcome tended to be not passive devotion but an activist charitable impulse. ('Quietism', in the form of the mystical passivity encouraged by Fénelon and Guyon, was condemned by Rome in 1699.) Increasing numbers of Catholics devoted their entire lives to care of the poor, the sick, the despised – sometimes to the point of exhaustion. Just as Jesus had poured out his life for others, so Christian men and women strove to follow his example and obey his command. No-one was excluded from the burden of care: saintly bishops organised relief for the poor, and noblemen from the most exclusive confraternities wiped the sores of beggars and prepared their corpses for burial.

Thus the early modern era witnessed a realignment of the sacred. The pattern was common to both Protestantism and Catholicism, despite more superficially important divisions between them. Above all, the sacred became more tightly regulated and more closely aligned with the church (or rather, confessions) than ever before. This did not represent a new impulse within Christianity. As we have seen throughout this volume, Catholic Christianity had always been concerned to control the sacred and to direct it along authorised sacramental and sacerdotal channels. What were novel were the more effective means of achieving this goal, means that were eagerly seized upon by both Catholic and Protestant authorities. The result, in both confessions, was to reinforce

Plate 18 *The Burial of Count Orgaz*, by El Greco (1541–1614)

Both confessional Catholicism and Protestantism emphasised the gulf between God and humanity, heaven and earth, but held out the promise that faithful sons and daughters of the (true) church might cross over. Here El Greco depicts the death of a wealthy and devout Spanish noble and the ascent of his soul from earth to heaven, where Mary, John the Baptist and other saints intercede with Christ for his salvation.

denominational rather than democratic forms of church organisation and to strengthen the power of the clergy. (This, as we saw in the last chapter, was true even in relation to American Protestantism.) The ecclesiastical and clerical captivity of the sacred went along with a new emphasis upon the importance of other-worldly salvation. When the sacred had floated more freely, it was more easily harnessed by individuals and small communities and used for personal projects – for survival, success, healing, cursing, blessing. In so far as these uses continued, they were increasingly frowned upon by the church, and condemned as 'magical' and even 'diabolical'. The range of activities under attack is indicated by a Westphalian ordinance of 1669 against

> putting leaves in water on St Matthew's eve, putting pigs' hair on the fire, binding trees on New Year's day, driving out spirits by putting St John's wort on the walls, Easter bonfires accompanied by all sorts of songs that take the name of the Lord in vain while a great deal of devilry goes on, soaking meat in water tied up with bread, butter, lard and the like, hanging up St John's wreaths or crowns, making sacrifices.[4]

The previous chapter considered the way in which tighter religious and political regulation of the sacred led to the so-called 'witch craze'. In the early modern period, the sacred was aligned ever more closely with the church and the next life, rather than with the individual, the world and this life. Christianity became a religion of salvation rather than of amelioration. Rather than sacralising this life, it denigrated the self and the world relative to what would come after. Charitable action was directed at heavenly rather than earthly goals, and the missionary impulse was stimulated by the hope of saving souls from non-Christian cultures and customs in this life, and from hell and damnation in the next.

Catholic mission

The preceding bird's-eye survey of some main characteristics of confessional Christianity telescopes time. In reality these characteristics developed at different paces in different locations between the sixteenth and the nineteenth centuries, and were carried over into the twentieth, as we shall see in the next chapter. This is also true of the centrally important mission impulse in confessional Christianity. Missionary activity can be divided into two phases, each with a different religio-political profile: the sixteenth and seventeenth centuries and the nineteenth and twentieth centuries. The political and ecclesial disruptions of the eighteenth century disrupted foreign missions and created a break between the two phases. In the first phase Catholicism took the lead; in the second, Protestantism. The first will be considered here, the second in the following chapter.

In both phases domestic and overseas missionary activity went hand in hand, but this was particularly true in the first phase of mission, when the attempt was made to root out 'superstition' in both Europe and the wider world. Lasciviousness, idolatry, boisterousness, drunkenness, magic, local religious customs and lay appropriation of the sacred were the objects of evangelical hostility at home as much as abroad. An English traveller commented in 1655 that the Indians of the New World found it 'inwardly hard to believe that which is above sense, nature and the visible sight of the eye'. Much the same comment would be made by many mission-minded Christians of their own brethren back home. 'There is another Indies waiting to be evangelised here in Spain,' Teresa of Avila's celestial voice told her.⁵

DOMESTIC MISSION

Catholic mission at home pioneered methods more often associated with evangelicalism, before Protestantism had even come into existence. In the earliest phase of mission, Europe hummed with the activity of travelling missioners. It was the 'regular' clergy (i.e. members of monastic orders) rather than 'secular' clergy who spearheaded the first phase of Christianisation. Some orders, such as the Lazarists, founded by Vincent de Paul (c. 1581–1660), were brought into being in recognition of the fact that the secular clergy were not up to the job. With their headquarters at the former priory of St Lazar in Paris, the Lazarists, or Vincentians, who won papal approval in 1632, fanned out across France and even further afield to Christianise rural parishes. Their prime target was, in Vincent de Paul's words, the 'poor people of the fields'. They were joined in their work by the Eudists, founded in 1643 by John Eudes (1601–80). The earliest, most active and most widespread of all the early Catholic evangelists, however, were the Jesuits or Society of Jesus (SJ), founded by Ignatius of Loyola (1491–1556) and approved by Pope Paul III in 1540. Though the prime purpose of the Jesuit order was mission abroad (see below), such activity was quickly supplemented by mission at home, and Jesuits were active missioners across the length and breadth of Europe.

Their activities in newly or partially Protestantised areas won some souls back to the Catholic fold, but they were also active in missionary activity in Spain, Italy, France and other Catholic areas. Unlike the Lazarists and Eudists, the Jesuits tended to concentrate their activity in urban settings rather than rural.

The methods used by the Catholic evangelists were adapted from late medieval practice, particularly from the public preaching of the Franciscans and Dominicans. Some fifteenth-century preachers had carefully evolved mission strategies. When they arrived in a town they might head for the marketplace, set up their 'stall' – which might include a painted board with what was in effect the preacher's logo – and begin their 'routine'. In the sixteenth and seventeenth centuries techniques became more sophisticated. Mission manuals, offering strategies for converting crowds, appeared in large numbers. Missionary work might now be undertaken by teams of four, six or eight evangelists, who would tackle whole areas parish by parish, and remain there for anything up to six weeks. Their aim was to reach every person in the area, to teach them the basics of the faith, to convince them of sin and the need for repentance, to hear each person's confession and to offer the sacrament of penance. Catechetical instruction would be given with the aim of teaching the basics of the faith, including the creed, the Our Father and the Hail Mary. The focus of missionary activity was on individual piety and change of heart, not merely on corporate obedience. The intention was to encourage an examination of individual conscience in the light of Christian doctrine, with special emphasis, to quote one Lazarist, 'on repentance . . . man's last end . . . the enormity of sin, the severity of God on unrepentant sinners . . . hardening of the heart . . . final impenitence . . . remorse, relapses into sin . . . gossip . . . envy, hatred and enmity, oaths and blasphemies . . . intemperance in food and drink and other similar sins which are usually committed by country folk'.[6] The intention, as in Methodist preaching a century later, was to induce fear and a lively sense of sin. For Catholics, however, the remedy was available not in an unreliable inner sense of assurance, but in the objective sacraments of the church. Once the missioners had left, the 'converted' would return to their parish church with new gratitude and understanding and a lively sense of the protective and reassuring agency of the sacraments. The piety of the cloister was being brought into the world.

Education became an increasingly integral element in mission. Parish missions were emergency measures that could achieve only so much. More settled and lasting results could be achieved through educating children in the faith from the earliest age. Again it was the new and revived Catholic orders that took the initiative in establishing schools, colleges and universities in unprecedented numbers. In some cases they used their own resources; in others they were supported by the state or local people. The rate of educational expansion was astonishing, and tended to be demand-led. Ignatius, for example, had not initially regarded education as a major Jesuit ministry, but it grew to become the most important of all the order's activities. It began with the success of a Jesuit college for lay students established in Messina in 1548, which led to mounting requests for the foundation of schools from across Europe. There were 144 Jesuit colleges by 1579 and 372 by 1615, and their numbers continued to grow until the suppression of the Jesuits in 1773. The Jesuits published their definitive educational programme, the *Ratio Studiorum*, in 1599, and it governed their schools for three centuries. Most Jesuit colleges offered a humanistic secondary education for boys, but some were fully fledged universities. The entry requirement of some knowledge of Latin meant that the schools tended to attract the children of the elite, and in the seventeenth century the Jesuits began to provide boarding schools for the sons of the nobility.

Education for girls was left to the women's religious orders. While several women's orders were founded in the post-Reformation period with the intention of engaging in active mission work, like contemporary male orders, Tridentine Catholicism was insistent upon the cloistering ('claustration') of nuns. As in Reformation Protestantism, the new energies and independence of women and their desire to take a more active role in church and society were viewed with suspicion. Where magisterial Protestantism responded with an ideology of separate spheres for women that insisted upon women's domestic captivity, official Catholicism ruled that women needed the protection of either a husband or a cloister wall: *aut maritus aut murus*. The most determined efforts to establish active women's orders with a public ministry, such as that of the Englishwoman Mary Ward (1586–1646), were forcibly suppressed. Ward's English Ladies or Institute of Mary was modelled on the Jesuits and undertook missionary and educational work. Despite initial papal approval in 1616, Ward refused to compromise her belief that 'there is no such difference between men and women that women may not do great things', and was condemned as a heretic. Other isolated groups of 'Jesuitesses' were also dissolved.

> We have learned [wrote Urban VIII in 1631], not without great displeasure, that in several parts of Italy and beyond the Alps, certain women or virgins take the name of Jesuitesses without any approbation from the Holy See . . . and that they are accustomed to undertake and exercise works very little in conformity with the weakness of their sex and their spirit, with feminine modesty and above all with virginal shame, works which many highly distinguished in the science of sacred letters by their experience and their innocence of life [i.e. men] would only undertake with difficulty and with the greatest circumspection.[7]

The female orders that survived were the ones that compromised. In relation to education, the most influential were the Ursulines, founded by Angela Merici (c. 1474–1540) in Brescia in 1535. Though they originally took no formal vows, they were later transformed into a cloistered order that followed the *Rule* of Augustine, and their work was restricted to teaching girls in their convents. The same progression to claustration was the fate of the Visitandines or Visitation nuns, founded at Annecy in Savoy by Jane Frances de Chantal (1572–1641), working closely with Francis de Sales (1567–1622). Their original intent was a simple lifestyle, visiting the sick and the poor in their homes. Papal approval of the cloistered order was granted in 1618. The only 'order' to evade claustration was the Daughters of Charity, founded by Vincent de Paul and Louise de Marillac (1591–1660). Their members were drawn from women across the social classes, and their ministry was to the poor. Because their founders were careful never to refer to them as 'nuns' or an 'order', because they confined themselves to charitable work, and because their members were not drawn from the elite and there were consequently no worries on the part of relatives about dowries and muddled inheritances, they managed to survive as an active order modelled on a confraternity. They diversified from assisting the poor to working in hospitals, from teaching catechism to running orphanages.

Domestic mission was not, however, solely in the hands of religious. Some of the key practical reforms instituted by Trent had been designed to turn the secular clergy into more effective agents of evangelisation. The starting point of these reforms was the reform of the episcopal office – for only if bishops were resident in their dioceses and conscientious in their pastoral duties would they be able to discipline their clergy and set them a good example. Reform of the episcopacy was greatly aided by the example of saintly Tridentine bishops such as Charles Borromeo (1538–84), bishop of Milan, who became a model of what a modern Catholic bishop should be. By the seventeenth century, bishops had generally become far more conscientious about their diocesan roles, and many did not merely visit their clergy on an annual basis, but organised regular conferences and retreats for their edification. The process was regularised by the gradual establishment of seminaries in each diocese. Seminaries, confraternities of the clergy, and colleges for what would now be called in-service clerical training were also established by reformers. The pioneers were the Oratorians, a community of priests organised in Rome by Filippo Neri (1515–95) and approved in 1575. In France, Bérulle took the lead in developing Oratorian communities whose chief purpose was to staff seminaries and colleges.

The status of parish clergy was also raised and 'purified' by making the secular clergy resemble more closely the 'regular clergy' (monks). Celibacy was enforced more strictly. Clergymen were to wear cassocks. They should not attend dances, taverns or local revelries. They were to be examples of sobriety, morality and charity to their flocks. The changes were largely effective. Though the long-standing rivalry between secular and regular clergy never wholly disappeared, the former won a victory not by beating their opponents but by joining them. After the seventeenth century they played an increasingly central role in the task of Christianising and confessionalising Europe.

OVERSEAS MISSION

Christian mission abroad was most successful when it had European colonialism as a travelling companion. Much the most extensive Christianisation in the early modern period took place in what would later be called 'Latin' America, where Christian preachers accompanied Spanish and Portuguese explorers, adventurers, traders and colonists. A whole (mainly male) society was exported, its religion along with it. Motivations were complex and muddled. The quest for enhanced political and economic power was central. After the discovery of new techniques of navigation and new technologies of shipbuilding, the westward expansion of the Spanish and Portuguese empires seemed a natural geographical expression of their political expansiveness. Gold and silver were needed for trade with the east, but it was soon realised that an abundance of fertile land and slave labour could also be exploited to supply cheap spices, sugar, tobacco and other luxury items. But motivations for conquest and settlement were also religious. The idea of crusade was still alive, and a new hope arose of an assault on 'the Turk' from another direction. Late medieval apocalyptic hopes fed this dream, for Joachim had prophesied that the kingdom of God would be established when the New World was conquered and Jerusalem restored. During the fifteenth century, in a series of crusade bulls, the Holy Office granted the Portuguese sovereign temporal and spiritual jurisdiction over the lands in the west. The discovery of the 'West Indies' by Christopher Columbus in 1492 led to the intervention of Pope Alexander VI in the following year. He divided the area to be colonised: the west to the Spaniards, the east to the Portuguese (a line of demarcation that resulted in Brazil's becoming a Portuguese possession), and left the responsibility for organising the church in these places to the Spanish and Portuguese monarchs.

Thus the earliest Christian activity in what would become Latin America took place within a late medieval framework, rather than in a Tridentine, organised, confessionalised mode. The first Christians on the scene were the Dominicans, Franciscans and Augustinians. Their concern was with extensive rather than intensive Christianisation. Some were spurred on by a desire to baptise as many as possible before the imminently expected end of the world. As disease (brought in by the newcomers) began to ravage the native peoples, it became imperative simply to baptise the people before they died. The pioneer in Mexico, Peter de Ghent, is supposed to have administered 14,000 baptisms a day at the height of his ministry. Within a generation of the military conquest a million souls were said to have been saved. The motivation of those who received baptism is not entirely clear. There may have been a desire to win access to the powerful God(s) of a powerful people, and it was in that sense that military conquest eased the way for religion. Yet there is little indication that those who were baptised had any deep understanding of Christianity, or any intention of abandoning their existing forms of religious belief or practice. Later generations of missionaries would despair at the superficial nature of the 'conversion'.

Despite the obvious association of mission and colonialism, not least in the minds of the native peoples, the two were not always allies. Some of the regular and secular clergy in the Americas became sharp critics of European exploitation of the Indians. The Spanish *encomienda* system, which granted settlers control over blocks of land and the peoples living on them, and which was in effect a disguised form of slavery, was attacked by a number of Christians, most famously Bartolomé de Las Casas (1474–1566), a settler who became a Dominican. It may have been under his influence that Pope Paul III issued a bull, *Sublimus Deus* (1537), which affirmed that Indians were free men and must not be converted by force. Las Casas was also the indirect inspiration of the *New Laws* (1542) by which Charles V of Spain attempted to abolish *encomienda*. In theology, the debate was taken up by Spanish Thomism, whose moral and theological achievements would later feed the modern tradition of 'human rights'. This 'second scholasticism' was largely the achievement of the Jesuit tradition, and is discussed in the next section.

The first Jesuit missioners reached Mexico in the 1570s, and their arrival marked the end of the medieval phase of mission and the introduction of a new, more intensive style. They too came into conflict with the settlers. The Jesuits' most famous achievement was the establishment of 'reductions', Christian villages of native peoples gathered together under Jesuit control, protected from slave-hunting Europeans. After 1609 the Jesuits began to settle a whole people, the Guarani Indians, in an experimental Christian republic situated in an area that encompasses parts of what are now Paraguay, Brazil and Argentina. Despite violent attacks from Portuguese and Spanish settlers, Madrid recognised the frontiers of the Guarani republic in 1649. In some ways the experiment may be likened to Calvin's in Geneva, for here, too, an attempt was made to create a pure Christian society under the control of the clergy. In other ways the Jesuit model looked back to feudal society rather than forwards to capitalism, and was distinctly paternalist. The beginning of the end of the Guarani experiment came in 1750, when the king of Spain, breaking the promises of his predecessors, ceded part of the republic to the Portuguese. It took the Spanish and the Portuguese six years of bloodshed finally to defeat the Guaranis, and this led to a souring of relations between the colonial powers and the Jesuits. Between 1767 and 1769, 2,337 Jesuits were expelled from Spanish colonies. Their suppression in other parts of Europe, and eventually by the pope himself, was a measure of just how powerful they had become.

As will be made plain in the next section, the clash between Jesuits, national rulers and the papacy was one between competing forms of expansive centralised, rationalised religio-political power. The same conflict occurred in Latin America, where Rome came to regret giving patronage over the church to Spain and Portugal. The action had made the Spanish and Portuguese monarchs directly responsible for missionary work, for nomination of the higher clergy including bishops, and for setting the boundaries of dioceses. Though Rome was quite slow to recognise the importance of its overseas missionary duties, and Trent said little directly about the matter, the church's counter-offensive came eventually in the foundation of the Congregation for the Propagation of the Faith ('the Propaganda'), in 1622. Even then, the Congregation was initially involved in domestic rather than overseas evangelisation. Once established, however, it began to put into place a programme for more efficient and centrally controlled missionary endeavour. It undertook such work as the production of catechisms in many languages, but most importantly it took upon itself the task of co-ordinating mission around the world. In order to get around the problem of patronage, it introduced the subterfuge of 'vicariates', sending 'vicars apostolic' (clergy with episcopal status by another name) around the world to govern the churches of mission territories in the name of the pope.

The Jesuits were a rival organisation of a kind rather different from an absolutist monarchy. Their leader, Ignatius Loyola, was a Basque ex-soldier, and his military and organisational genius is apparent in the constitutions he drew up for his new order. Much longer and more detailed than earlier *Rules*, they dispensed with time-consuming communal activities such as fixed hours of worship, and marshalled their members into an effective evangelistic force with eight 'ranks' and a chief commander, the 'superior general', residing in Rome. Like an early modern army, Jesuits were to obey their superior officers – including the pope – without hesitation, and to conform their will to that of the church and the order. As Ignatius puts it in the Constitutions:

> Let us with the utmost pains strain every nerve of our strength to exhibit this virtue of obedience, firstly to the Highest Pontiff, then to the Superiors of the Society . . . by rejecting with a kind of blind obedience all opposing opinion or judgement of our own . . . as if [each one] were a corpse which suffers itself to be borne and handled in any way whatsoever.[8]

To ordinary Christians too, Ignatius in the *Spiritual Exercises* had commended not just filial but 'servile' fear, and suggested that if the church define anything as 'black which to our eyes appears to be white, we ought in like manner to pronounce it black'.[9] All of this was, of course, fully acceptable to Rome, and led to great support for the Jesuits in the early post-Reformation period. It was they who became the 'shock troops of the Counter-Reformation', and they who took the initiative in a good deal of missionary work overseas.

The original goal of Ignatius and his companions, following a crusading logic, had been mission to Palestine. When this proved impossible, Ignatius' student roommate, Francis Xavier (1506–52), sailed for India in 1541. He worked in India, Malaysia, Indonesia and Japan, establishing networks of Jesuit missioners. Though he made few converts, his work attracted great interest in Europe. In Asia, the Jesuits gradually became the most important religious order. Matteo Ricci (1552–1610) established a toe-hold in China, winning the favour of the Chinese emperor. By the end of the seventeenth century, despite a period of persecution, it is estimated there were 200,000–300,000 converts, and 120 missionaries. But a quarrel over rites, and increasing Chinese suspicion, weakened the church's position. In Japan the number of Christians grew to 300,000, until Christianity was outlawed in 1616. In India Robert de Nobili (1577–1656) sought conversions among the higher castes, and in Indo-China Jesuits worked alongside vicars apostolic, with increasing friction between the two. Only in Korea was Christianity established by indigenous means, when lay Koreans discovered Christianity through books that had come from China in the seventeenth and eighteenth centuries.

Though the growing power of the Jesuits was undoubtedly the main cause of friction with Rome, the immediate occasion of the conflict between them was a controversy concerning missionary methods. This was the so-called dispute over rites. Xavier, Ricci and de Nobili had pioneered a method of Catholic 'adaptation' in Asia. They would make contact with the educated elite among the native population where they settled, learn their language, try to understand their customs, and then attempt to translate and adapt the Christian message in a way that would make sense to its new audience. They communicated their ideas with respect, as one spiritual and intellectual elite to another. Their intention was to raise up an indigenous clergy as soon as possible. Some Jesuits even believed that the Chinese had retained elements of a natural religion or a primitive revelation. Such ideas provoked opposition in Europe, not least among the Jansenists, whose suspicion of the lax ways of the Jesuits seemed to be confirmed by the latter's toleration of 'superstition'. The Jansenists, like many confessional Catholics, and, increasingly, Rome itself, believed that Christianity could not be allowed to co-exist with any 'merely human' – and therefore sinful – non-Christian culture. The acceptance of the one must mean the rejection of the other. In any case, a uniform church demanded uniformity of practice. Matters came to a head in 1693, when the vicar apostolic in China forbade some of the Jesuit practices, and the Holy Office upheld his position. Papal condemnation of Chinese and Indian rites came in 1715 and again in 1742 and 1744, as the controversy rumbled on. Even the suppression of the Jesuits by the pope in 1773 and the waning of missionary activity in the eighteenth century did not end the debate, and the issue of 'enculturation' would continue to be a live issue in the next, modern, phase of missionary activity.

Absolutism and anti-absolutism

If the remodelling of Rome gave architectural expression to the growing ambitions of the papacy and the Catholic church, the erection of grand palaces by the monarchs of early modern Europe bore witness to similar claims to 'absolute' power. Given the nature of their claim, there would inevitably be competition between different 'absolutisms'. Yet mutually beneficial alliances would also be possible.

In 1595 Philip II of Spain consecrated a new palace on the hills outside Madrid: the Escorial. It had taken twenty-two years to build, and its scale was vast: 205 × 160 m (224 × 175 yds), it had 2,673 windows and 1,200 doors. Yet this was not merely a secular building; it was also a religious one. Some say that Philip modelled it on Solomon's temple. Certainly, the six kings of Judah have pride of place in its central courtyard, the Patio of Kings. And the central focus of the whole complex is a vast church dedicated to St Laurence, its cupola constructed by the same man who had worked on St Peter's in Rome. Alongside the state apartments and the offices and lodgings of Philip's civil service, the Escorial incorporated a monastery, a library and a vast collection of holy relics. Philip himself chose to live in monastic simplicity in his whitewashed private apartments, and his personal oratory looked down directly on to the high altar of St Laurence. He dubbed his palace-monastery 'a hovel for a king and a palace for God', and desired that it should express 'simplicity of form, severity in the whole, nobility without arrogance, majesty without ostentation'.[10] This was one model of the relationship between church and state in an era of absolutism, a relationship of close alliance in which the sacred was nationalised and the monarchy sacralised. Philip's own piety is not in doubt. But he had much more to gain from a close relationship with Rome than personal salvation. In just a few generations Spain had been transformed from an agglomeration of second-rate powers with divided interests, whose population included Jews, Christians and Muslims, to a unified kingdom with a dominant position in Europe, and had acquired a vast empire beyond it. The achievement would not have been possible without the assistance of sacred power. Catholicism provided a unifying culture that was imposed by a range of persuasive and downright coercive measures against Jews and Muslims. The fragility of the achievement required continuing measures to preserve a clear Catholic identity centred around power from on high. In due course the late medieval movements of mystical lay piety of the *alumbrados* (the illuminated ones), among whom women were very active, would be suppressed by the Spanish Inquisition. Monasticism was regulated and policed by the state authorities, and the monastic reform movement of observance was gradually imposed on all orders.

The power of the Spanish monarchy was also underwritten by Roman support. The king was not merely a secular ruler, but a religious figurehead who embodied a 'Catholic monarchy', a 'national Catholicism' or, to his enemies, a 'Spanish papacy'. What is more, Rome supplied the mantle of religious legitimacy to the Spanish colonial empire. The power that accrued to the monarchy was not merely spiritual but also temporal, and little by little the Spanish Crown would win almost complete control over the church and its possessions within its territories. It appointed clergy, required their submission to its laws, presided over councils and synods, and administered and shared the church's wealth. Even papal bulls were referred to the king's council before publication in Spain. It has been estimated that the church's contribution to the state as a whole made up about a third of what came into the treasury – far more than the claimed fifth that came from American bullion.

While the church might have looked, even to itself, like an independent and equal partner in the relationship with the absolute monarchy

Plate 19   The Escorial Palace (El Real Monasterio de San Lorenzo de El Escorial)

of Spain, it was, therefore, the weaker partner and in some ways the loser. A secularisation was taking place whereby the state took over many of the church's former functions and prerogatives. Sacred power leaked away from the church to the nation and its ruler. The problem was that, compared with the medieval situation, Rome was now negotiating from a position of weakness. As the empire of the Ottoman Turks expanded its reach into Europe and began to threaten Italy and the western Mediterranean, the papacy was left with no choice: Spain was its only powerful and reliable ally. The Hispano-Roman alliance allowed the unified Spanish monarchy to consolidate its power over Italy and within the Holy Roman empire. A truce with the Ottomans after the Battle of Lepanto (1571) allowed a reorientation of the alliance against the rebellious Dutch heretics as pope and king collaborated in a *reconquista*, both spiritual and temporal, of Protestant Europe.

Outmatched by secular power, confessionalisation helped the church hedge and preserve as much of its sacred power as possible. Given that its monopoly over such power had already been lost with the rise of Protestantism, it was now imperative to prevent any further leakage, and to bind sacred power to the church and the papacy as tightly as possible.

Even the religious orders, which could and should act in partnership with the church, must be carefully controlled lest they become independent conduits for sacred power – as the Jesuits threatened to be. The Catholic church's main task in relation to secular power was to make sure that absolute rulers remained as favourable to Catholic power as possible, and to this end the church became increasingly skilled in the art of diplomacy. Though Rome might sometimes be backed into a corner by its close alliance with one particular political power, such as Spain, it nevertheless retained a certain freedom of manoeuvre, and it was always possible for it to make new alliances with rising powers. The fact that sacred power transcended any particular political alliance allowed the church to move on when the political circumstances required it. Its aim was always to secure as much space as possible for the church within the jurisdictions of the European states, and to protect as many of its traditional functions as possible. Papal diplomats were concerned to safeguard the church's control of law and education, its revenues, its control over clergy and clerical appointments, freedom for Catholic worship and instruction, and continued possession of ecclesiastical 'temporalities'.

In some ways Rome was fighting a losing battle, for absolute rulers sought to take control of as much of the power traditionally reserved to the church as they possibly could. Yet the church continued to have its uses for absolute rulers, even the most despotic. In the east in the eighteenth century, the 'enlightened despots' Frederick the Great of Prussia, Catherine the Great of Russia and Joseph II of Austria-Hungary consulted with the 'Enlightened' thinkers of their day – including Kant and Voltaire – and attempted to institute rational reforms in their respective societies. Yet even they sought, not to abolish religion altogether, but to curb its destructive potential and make use of its potential for social welfare and stability. Frederick, for example, introduced a policy of religious toleration into his confessionally mixed territories, but gave particular support to Pietism, recognising the usefulness of its educational, charitable activities and its willingness to subserve the state. By supporting the Pietists he could secure social welfare cheaply, along with the benefits in social pacification that accompanied it. Joseph II, by contrast, was willing to accept the title of Holy Roman emperor and to support Catholicism in his territories, but was quick to bring Christianity almost wholly under his personal control. He reorganised Catholic parishes, schools and seminaries in order to effect a thoroughgoing Christianisation of the population, which, he believed, would serve the cause of national unity and social stability.

What the enlightened despots did not do, in spite of their vaunted conference with Enlightenment thinkers, was to attempt any serious social reform that might improve the position of the masses – many of whom still suffered under conditions of serfdom in the east – or take any steps that might lose them some of their 'absolute' power. Neither did the kings of an increasingly populous and powerful France. Louis XIV (1638–1715) established himself as a model of royal absolutism, ruling with authority and increasing ostentation. His palace at Versailles embodies a power, centred on his own person, that had lost any trace of the austerity and asceticism of the Escorial. Instead of presenting the king as a servant, Versailles presented Louis as the Sun King, a new Apollo. The throne room, where he sat on a silver throne beneath a canopy of state, was the Salon d'Apollo, and depictions of Apollo and his chariot riding across the sky ornament both palace and garden. Power was now veiled and dignified by aesthetic rather than by religious means, by obedience to the canons of wit and good taste rather than by charity and the commandments of God. Yet even Louis did not ignore the benefits of alliance with the Roman Catholic church. There is a grand chapel at Versailles, even if it is not at the very centre of the complex, and Louis and his successors were assiduous in maintaining their status as Catholic monarchs. Some of the higher clergy held key positions in court, and the church was closely identified with what would soon come to be seen as the *ancien régime* – the old order of things.

For, even as absolute power reached new heights, opposition was mounting. Different currents of thought and argumentation converged in what amounted to a wide-ranging attack upon power from on high, both sacred and secular. These currents were both Christian and anti-Christian. Some drew on classical sources, including traditions of republicanism and humanism and their scholastic or Renaissance mediations. Some were inspired by the increasing prestige of science and the empirical method. All were stimulated by the growth of an educated elite in Europe (female as well as male), a new cosmopolitanism, and an increase in the number of public spaces in which ideas could be discussed – not only court circles, but universities, salons, coffee houses, clubs and societies. At least three different trajectories of thought fed anti-absolutism.

The first emphasised the importance of universal law and its ability to regulate absolute power, whether of pope or sovereign. Here the foundations were laid by Christians, both theologians and jurists. The question whether supreme authority in the state belonged to the people or to their sovereign leader had already been addressed in relation to spiritual power in the debates between conciliarists (ecclesiastical constitutionalists) and papalists (ecclesiastical absolutists) in the fourteenth and fifteenth centuries. It was revived and extended to the issue of temporal power in the sixteenth century. Particularly influential was the flowering of moral and political theology in Spain, referred to above as 'second scholasticism'. This revived Thomism was tempered by humanism, and stimulated by contemporary debates related to Spain's expanding empire. The latter provoked questions about the rights of subjects and the duties of rulers, to which both Dominican and Jesuit scholars in the flourishing universities of Spain sought answers by making use of an approach inspired by Aquinas.

Both Francisco de Vitoria (1483–1546) and Domingo de Soto (1494–1560) insisted that all rights come from God, but that because man is created in God's image he is the source and measure of the law. Positive laws established by rulers are therefore subordinate to natural human rights, and must never override them. This theocentric humanism was developed in the next generation by the Jesuits Francisco Suarez (1548–1617) and Luis de Molina (1535–1600). Both stressed the reality of human freedom. Molina, in particular, provoked a storm of opposition in Christian Europe with his view that God in his mercy allows human beings the freedom even to turn away from him, and that divine grace becomes effective for salvation only through the concurrence of human free will. Molina's views were echoed by both Arminian Protestants and anti-Jansenist Jesuits in seventeenth-century debates over free will and divine determinism.

The second influence on anti-absolutism was a new 'scientific' analysis of society. In many ways this had been anticipated by Vitoria's and Suarez's reflections on the state and divine right. Instead of arguing that power flows from God on high to the pope and thence to the rulers he anoints, the second scholastics believed that it was not the church but the people, constituted as a political community, who mediated divine power: 'All power comes from God through the people.' Sovereignty is therefore delegated to the king by the people, and the delegation is conditional upon the ruler's just use of power.[11] A tyrant can be legitimately overthrown. The role of the church in Vitoria's and Suarez's view is as a kind of constitutional court that guarantees human rights without being able to administer them or make laws. The pope is seen as the moral conscience of the political sphere. As a model of the rational criticism of existing political institutions, this approach took a major step towards the rational analysis of society and politics. Second scholasticism was not, however, fully empiricist in method. That is to say, it worked with a hierarchy of sources in which revelation and tradition were still at the top, and natural reason and the new sciences below them.

The methodological revolution that accompanied the modern revolution was a reversal in this hierarchy of authority, whereby reason and experience become the standards against which revelation must be judged. The difference can clearly be seen by comparing the scholastic project with the dictionaries and encyclopedias that were first produced in the seventeenth century: Denis Diderot and Jean-le-Rond d'Alembert's *Encyclopédie ou dictionnaire raisonné des sciences, des arts et des métiers* (1751–77) and William Smellie's *The Encyclopaedia Britannica* (1768–71). Whereas the scholastics began from divine knowledge and attempted to form it into a universal scheme of knowledge, the encyclopedists began from empirical observation and attempted to form it into a universal scheme of knowledge. Knowledge from above gave way to knowledge from below.

This scientific method was applied to society by supporters of absolutism (such as the political philosophers Machiavelli and Hobbes and the jurist Jean Bodin) as well as by those who wished to moderate absolutism, such as Locke and Gerson. In France, one of the most influential books in the first part of the eighteenth century was Montesquieu's *The Spirit of Laws* (1748), which placed existing governments in two categories, 'despotic' and 'balanced'. In the former the power of the ruler was unrestricted. In the latter, separation of powers and the rule of law prevailed – as they did in Hanoverian Britain. Jean-Jacques Rousseau (1712–78) went furthest in *The Social Contract* (1762), where he argued that all political power derives from the people – 'the sovereignty of the people'. Here God, instead of undergirding political right, as in Vitoria, Suarez, Locke and Gerson, becomes marginal to political theory. All that is left is power from below (the power of the people) without needing power from above (the power of God) to secure it.

Finally, anti-absolutism was fed by increasingly positive evaluations of human ability and dignity, and by a new appreciation of the importance of human well-being and happiness. In some ways this was the most anti-Christian trajectory of all, for confessionalised Protestantism and Catholicism had swung to an opposite extreme in placing emphasis upon human sinfulness and wretchedness and the importance of total self-abnegation and unremitting austerity, if not misery. Both the pious Catholic and the Pietist were caricatured in the eighteenth century as men who walked with eyes downcast, sighing and groaning as they went. The reaction, as much emotional as philosophical, was a countervailing optimism and cheerfulness. It took two forms. The more austere was the rationalist version, associated with Enlightenment thinkers. Bolstered by rapid scientific progress, it stressed man's innate powers of reasoning and his ability, through proper use of them, to penetrate the mysteries of physical nature, human nature and human society. If man would cut himself loose from priestcraft and superstition and, in Kant's famous phrase, 'dare to think', then who knows what he might achieve? The more light-hearted doctrine of human ability was that of the Romantics, pioneered in the work of Rousseau. The Romantics stressed not human reason, but human beings' natural, pre-social, creative, artistic, intuitive, mystical abilities. Both rationalism and Romanticism favoured a 'natural' religion, and, though they conceived it in very different ways, their visions had more in common with each other than with confessionalised Christianity, whether Protestant or Catholic.

The church and the French Revolution

Radical and anti-absolutist ideas were not confined to an intellectual elite, and writers such as Tom Paine, the English author of *Common Sense* (1776) and *The Rights of Man* (1791), helped popularise them on both sides of the Atlantic. But what really moved such ideas from the margin to the mainstream were the revolutionary upheavals in North America in 1776 and in France in 1789. The American and French Revolutions meant different things to different people and inspired different hopes and fears among different social groups, but few would deny that in some sense they embodied the revolt of power from below against power from on high. 'Liberty' was the favourite slogan of revolution on both sides of the Atlantic, and it was 'the people' who rose up to claim power for themselves and to oppose 'tyranny'. Because the Roman Catholic church had become so closely identified with power from on high – monarchial, social, masculine, ecclesiastical – it inevitably began to find itself identified with tyranny rather than with liberty.

The wider causes of the French Revolution have been much debated; its immediate cause was national bankruptcy. In the course of the seventeenth and eighteenth centuries, France, engaged in almost ceaseless warfare with its rivals, rose to a position of political and cultural pre-eminence in western Europe. The economic cost was huge. In 1789 the monarchy found itself buried under mounting debts. After a long series of failures to deal with the problem, the medieval institution of Estates General was convened. This ancient framework, composed of deputies of the 'three estates' of the realm – clergy (particularly bishops), nobility and commoners – quickly proved unequal to the task of representing the interests of the new social groups of a modernising nation. The third estate turned itself into a National Assembly, drafted a new constitution, and gave voice to the revolutionary idea that the people could and should govern themselves. Approved in 1791, this constitution abolished many old institutions and social privileges, contained a declaration of individual rights, and gave political power to groups not hitherto involved in public life. The French Revolution was under way.

One of the institutions whose power and rights were redefined by the new constitution was the church. In France, as in newly independent America, it quickly became apparent that constitutional democracy sat uncomfortably with an established state religion. If citizens were to be free to shape their own destinies, and if their first loyalty was to the nation state, then established religion must go. The modern state must be secular in the sense that it must not impose a particular faith on its people. Toleration must be extended to all religions, and even to unbelief. What is more, the church must be subject to political control. Since Rome should not be able to control the religion of the French, the remaining powers and prerogatives of the church should be placed under the authority of the state. To this end, the new National Assembly quickly asserted its authority over the church. Monasteries were closed, church lands seized and tithes abolished. The general aim of the 'Civil Constitution of the Clergy', enacted in 1790, was to rationalise the church in

France, abolish all forms of Christianity that were thought to have no social or civil use, and cut ties with Rome to a minimum. Dioceses and parishes were reorganised, clergy were to be elected on the same basis as civil officials (i.e. by the male property-owners of their district), and their salaries were to be paid by the state.

To begin with, then, the new government of France aimed to maintain the church but curb its independence. As the revolution unfolded, however, it became clear that this uneasy form of state–church alliance would not work. To begin with, many clergy would not co-operate, with some – the 'non-jurors' – refusing to swear allegiance to the new constitution. Then in 1792 Pope Pius VI condemned the measures in France, and threw in a condemnation of the revolution and its liberal and egalitarian principles for good measure. Shortly after, persecutions and humiliations of the church and clergy began as a strong anti-clerical temper took hold among many supporters of the revolution. This intensified as France found itself at war with the absolutist monarchies of Europe, and as revolution itself came to be seen as a religious cause, serving not the God of Christianity but the new gods of Reason and Liberty. The antagonism between church and state intensified in some rural parts of France, where peasants, who had gained much less from the revolution than the bourgeoisie had, arose in rebellion against the revolution, wearing badges depicting the Sacred Heart of Jesus, and marching with non-juring priests at their sides.

In France, then, the church and the modern state became increasingly polarised. The pattern was gradually repeated elsewhere in Europe where the Catholic church was in alliance with secular power from on high. In many ways the papacy's hands were tied, not least by its position as absolute ruler of the Papal States in Italy. The modern popes repeatedly defied democratic and nationalist hopes of a unified Italy by refusing to surrender control of these territories. At the same time, because the papacy was unable to defend its territories itself, it was forced into alliance with some of the most conservative regimes in Europe because they were able to lend it military assistance. The earlier failure to reform the papacy and to deal with the church's temporal possessions now had the effect of linking it to the forces of reaction and conservatism against those of liberty, democracy and modernisation. The opposition would still be being played out as late as the 1930s, when Republicans fought unsuccessfully against Catholic monarchists in the Spanish Civil War.

As the political landscape of Europe changed in the nineteenth century and the categories of 'right' and 'left', 'conservative' and 'revolutionary' emerged, there was therefore little doubt about which side the Catholic church represented. It had become the enemy not only of many on the political left, but also of the social classes that had most to gain from the political changes affecting Europe. Of these, the most important were the lower-middle-class urban bourgeoisie, and, as the century wore on, the new industrial working classes. In most parts of France and Spain, for example, a pattern developed whereby the rich went to mass and the urban workers stayed at home – a pattern that still persists today. Only in rural areas was the pattern different, with the (gradually shrinking) peasantry often maintaining an alliance with the church and tradition against a rapidly changing world. As we shall see in a moment, women were also more likely than men to remain loyal to the church, whatever their class, and many remained loyal supporters of the faith.

Fortress Catholicism

While the minority of individuals and movements within Catholicism that are reviewed in the next section allied themselves with the cause of liberty and tried to take the church with them, the papacy and its by now highly effective centralised administration reaffirmed its commitment to power from on high with renewed vigour. The church became a 'fortress', opposed to the modernisation taking place outside its walls, pulling up the drawbridge, standing firm by its own confessional principles. In 1864 Pope Pius IX issued the encyclical *Quanta Cura* and with it the *Syllabus of Errors*, quoted at the start of this chapter. They stand as testimony to the siege mentality of fortress Catholicism and its continuing opposition to modernisation. Also referred to as 'ultramontane', because it looked for authority beyond the mountains (the Alps) to Rome and the pope, this stance would be maintained from the time of the French Revolution right up to the Second World War by a succession of modern popes, only really coming to an end in the 1960s after the reign of Pius XII (1939–58). The Second Vatican Council (Vatican II), held between 1962 and 1965, marked the end of this distinct, late confessional, phase in the church's life.

Table 6.1 *Papal reigns since 1789*

Pius VI (Giovanni Angelo Braschi)	1775–99
Pius VII (Gregorio Barnaba Chiaramonte)	1800–23
Leo XII (Annibale della Genga)	1823–9
Pius VIII (Francesco Saverio Castiglione)	1829–30
Gregory XVI (Bartolomeo Cappellari)	1831–46
Pius IX, 'Pio Nono' (Giovanni Maria Mastai-Ferretti)	1846–78
Leo XIII (Gioacchino Vincenzo Pecci)	1878–1903
Pius X (Giuseppe Melchior Sarto)	1903–1914
Benedict XV (Giacomo della Chiesa)	1914–22
Pius XI (Achille Ambrogio Damiano Ratti)	1922–39
Pius XII (Eugenio Pacelli)	1939–58
John XXIII (Angelo Giuseppe Roncalli)	1958–63
Paul VI (Giovanni Battista Montini)	1963–78
John Paul I (Albino Luciani)	1978
John Paul II (Karol Jozef Wojtyla)	1978–2005

The watchword of fortress Catholicism was unity. As the *Syllabus of Errors* indicates so well, ultramontane Catholicism saw itself as a unity set over against the divisions of the modern world. It was a total system that required nothing from outside. The Roman Catholic church was the only true church. It had one Lord (Jesus Christ), one leader (the pope), and one faith, timeless and unchanging. For ultramontanism, truth was more important than freedom, and the church was sole guardian of the truth. Though the Catholic church's alliance with the forces of reaction in modern Europe lost it the support of many progressives, it also won it a new sort of loyalty. Those who made a commitment to fortress Catholicism did so with a new and self-conscious dedication, in defiance of other choices – for modernity, secularism, socialism, the nation state, and so on. In Europe the pope became an alternative leader for those disillusioned with modernisation and fearful of change, for those anxious to preserve a Catholic identity against the encroachments of the modern state, and for those who did not wish to exchange the glories of the past for the baubles of the present.

The church also won and retained the loyalty of many women. Though it was still ruled by men and a male God, it could provide support for a feminised culture based around the values of love, tenderness, self-sacrifice, humility, care for others and nurture of the family. For women uprooted by the disruptions of industrial capitalism, whether by a move to a city or emigration to a new country such as the United States, it could also help preserve ethnic identity through connection with 'traditional ways' of doing things – some of which dated back to medieval rather than confessional Catholicism. Such piety often centred on home as much as church, and had a distinctly feminine flavour. Mexican women in North America, for example, might maintain in the home a shrine that would bear a statue of the Virgin of Guadalupe (the protectress of Mexico), the miraculous Santo Niño de Atocha, his mother Santa Maria de Atocha, a Nuestra Señora de San Juan de Los Lagos, and Saint Anthony of Padua. Flowers, and important family documents such as a marriage certificate or letters, might be placed with the statues. Candles would be lit to signify the continuing devotion to the saints, or to make special intercession. A rosary, novena cards, commemorative medals and crucifixes might be placed on the altar, and pictures of the saints hung on the walls. Souvenirs from old Mexico might also be put on the shrine.

In the course of the nineteenth century, the sanctification of the home would be increasingly encouraged by the official church – both by individual writers, often clergy, and by the magisterium itself. A distinctively Catholic form of domestic piety came into being, which encouraged the link between family and church. In terms of its historical resources, fortress Catholicism was well placed to sponsor a feminised, domesticised piety, for, unlike Protestantism, it had not abolished its links with Mary and a host of female saints. In other ways, however, the Catholic church was at a disadvantage relative to Protestantism, particularly because of its emphasis on the higher calling of celibacy – an emphasis that tended to devalue the more mundane routines of family life and women's work outside the cloister. As we have seen, the invention of domestic piety lay at the very heart of the Protestant Reformation, in a way it never had in Catholicism. While Catholicism was equally anxious to attract and retain women, to harness their energies for the church and to discourage them from swapping domestic roles for paid jobs that should be reserved for men, it also had to be careful not to discourage the growing number of women who were entering into religious orders in the nineteenth century. As teachers, missionaries, charity workers and parish assistants, the latter would have an important role to play in the survival of fortress Catholicism. Indeed, the number of female religious overtook that of male religious in the course of the nineteenth century.

Initially, then, the church proceeded by likening the domestic vocation of women to that of nuns. The mother, particularly the middle-class mother, should be retired and secluded, cloistered in her home. She should be modest and chaste, performing her sexual duties purely for the purpose of procreation. Her calling was to obey God and serve others. Such advice dated right back to Francis de Sales's advice to French women in the seventeenth century. It was revived by Paul Lejeune, who created a 'rule' for women that was translated in 1913 as *Counsels of Perfection for Christian Mothers*. Lejeune advised women to pray and to read the Bible and pious books, but to avoid the mystical writings of Teresa of Avila because women's imaginations were too sensitive to 'the extraordinary phenomena recorded in the works'.[12] By the later nineteenth century, however, an alternative trajectory of authorised female piety had emerged, which conformed much more closely to a Protestant exaltation of the domestic role as angelic and God-given. Domestic advice books (often written by clergy) and magazines and novels (often written by laymen and laywomen) exalted the wife and mother as an unsung heroine, whose worship consisted chiefly in serving husband and children and encouraging their faithfulness. Mary became the model of domestic piety. Though she was superior in dignity to St Joseph, explained the *Catholic Girl's Guide* of 1905, she allowed him to rule the family. And when he returned from work he was pleased to see 'his evening meal ready and everything as orderly as possible'.[13]

The concentration on family, sexuality and women's piety would become increasingly important for fortress Catholicism. As other, more public roles of the church were taken over by the state and secular agencies, this tendency would increase. But it would not be at the expense of any diminution of male, paternal, papal and clerical power. The strengthening of the latter, which had been a central aspect of the confessionalisation of Catholicism since the sixteenth century, would continue. If the reinforcement of the male and the authoritative was one side of the achievement of fortress Catholicism, the validation of the female and the affective was the other. And the two went hand in hand. From Pius IX to Pius XII, a line of modern popes reinvigorated the church both by strengthening centralised male control and by encouraging a new and intense form of feminised devotional piety with a strongly Romantic flavour.

MASCULINISED AUTHORITY

It was the concern for unity and control that lay behind the promulgation of papal infallibility at the First Vatican Council (Vatican I) of 1869–70. The council, attended by 700 bishops, had time to produce just two documents before being broken up by the Franco-Prussian war and the invasion of Rome, but their topics are significant. The first, *Dei Filius*, defined the unity of God and the Catholic faith against the errors of the time. The second, *Pastor Aeternus*, defined the doctrines of papal primacy and infallibility. The pope, the latter declared, has 'full and supreme power of jurisdiction over the whole Church' in matters of faith, morals and discipline. This power extends over 'each and every church' and 'each and every shepherd and faithful member'. Moreover, when acting in the office of teacher of all Christians, the pope possesses, by virtue of his apostolic authority, 'the infallibility with which the divine Redeemer willed his Church to be endowed'. While the doctrine of infallibility has been invoked only once since Vatican I, in relation to the promulgation of the doctrine of the Assumption in 1950, the more important consequence of this definition was the symbolic centralisation of power and authority in the papacy and in the curia that served it. The move was resented by some Catholics: by those bishops who found their powers curtailed, for example, and the by church in places such as America, which were widely separated from Rome not just geographically but by virtue of their very different social and political contexts. The effect of papal centralisation, however, was to make possible a uniformity of belief and practice within the church that made the claim to possession of absolute and unchanging truth more plausible and less subject to the acids of modern pluralism and relativism.

The continuing reform of clergy training and the standardisation of Catholic doctrine and teaching were also important in this process. Throughout Europe and America in the nineteenth century, new seminaries were opened where boys would be admitted when young, sheltered from the wider culture, and socialised within a tightly controlled Catholic ethos. Uniformity of curriculum had been established by Leo XIII's encyclical *Aeterni Patris* of 1879, which had confirmed Thomas Aquinas as the 'official' theologian of the Catholic church. From then on, Thomistic texts and manuals were used to provide arguments and certitudes that would have to be rigorously memorised by seminarians. Under Pius X, any hint of deviation from these truths became

punishable by suspension or dismissal. In order to root out all traces
of 'modernism', Pius introduced an 'Anti-Modernist Oath' in 1910, to
which every clergyman from the highest to the lowest had to subscribe.
(The Oath remained in force until the 1960s.) Pius X also attempted to
ensure uniformity in Catholic teaching both through the introduction
of a new catechism and by bringing forward the age of confirmation,
thus ensuring that young citizens of Catholicism would be able to recite
its propositions even before they reached puberty. (It was through Pius's
efforts that first communion became a key rite of passage for young
Catholic boys and girls, who would dress up in best suits, white dresses
and lacy veils for this important day.)

Equally important in the standardisation of Catholic culture were the
Catholic church schools, which flourished across Europe and America
into the first half of the twentieth century. The church's educational programme was greatly assisted by a huge increase in the number of religious teaching orders, an increase that was part of the wider monastic
revival that characterised nineteenth-century Roman Catholicism. One
of Pius VII's first acts was also the restoration of the Jesuits in 1814.
They resumed their role as the papacy's personal army, police force
and ministry of information, helping spread the teachings and pieties
of fortress Catholicism to Catholic communities throughout the world.
The Dominicans and Benedictines were also reformed, the Redemp-
torists reorganised, and numerous new orders and congregations established. The most phenomenal growth, however, was in religious orders
for women; between 1862 and 1865 Pius IX approved seventy-four congregations for women religious alone.

The standardisation and centralisation of Catholicism helped reinforce the pope's personal authority and turn him into a focus of
Catholic devotion. The process was aided by new methods of communication: photography enabled the image of the pope to be widely
circulated; the railways brought the faithful to Rome; Vatican Radio
(established by Marconi in 1931) enabled the popes to speak directly
to the faithful in Europe. Now pictures of the pope might appear on
the walls of the faithful alongside those of the saints. Not surprisingly,
many of the modern popes became personally autocratic: Pius XII, for
example, insisted that staff at the Vatican kneel to receive his telephone
calls. In many ways the popes of fortress Catholicism remained absolute
monarchs in an age of rapidly spreading democratic constitutionalism.

Plate 20   The signing of the Lateran Treaty between Italy and the Papacy (1929)
  The Lateran Treaty regularised relations between the papacy and the 'secular' nation of Italy by declaring Roman Catholicism the state religion and recognising a new state, called the Vatican City, as fully sovereign and independent.

Their belief in strong leadership, the patriarchal family and social discipline naturally led them to sympathise with right-wing politics and even with fascism. This tendency was reinforced by the papacy's dislike of socialism and, even more strongly, of communism. In his encyclical *Quadragesimo anno* (1931), for example, Pius XI spoke of Bolsheviks as 'missionaries of Antichrist'. The increasing persecution of the church under Soviet communism, the savagely anti-Catholic regime that developed in Mexico, and the attacks on Catholics by communists in the Spanish Civil War served only to strengthen this attitude.

  Gradually, however, the modern popes were beginning to take a more detached attitude to European politics, and to try to avoid identification with any one regime or form of government. The loss of the Papal States in 1870 aided this process. As the political map of Europe was divided into increasingly secular nation states, the popes gradually abandoned the battle to assert political control, and devoted their energies instead to securing concordats that would preserve Catholic freedoms, particularly in relation to education and worship, within these new states. Indeed, so concerned did the papacy become with maintaining political neutrality in Europe that it came under heavy criticism during the First and Second

World Wars for refusing to take sides. In the run-up to the Second World War, for example, Pius XI issued a famous encyclical, *Mit brennender Sorge* ('With Burning Anxiety'), in which he denounced German actions against the church, idolatrous nationalism and Nazi racial theory. Just five days later it was followed by another encyclical, *Divini Redemptoris*, in which he attacked communism and 'amoral liberalism' in even fiercer terms than he attacked Nazism. When Pius XII became pope in 1939, he tried to maintain a similar policy of even-handedness. His now notorious hesitation to condemn German policies against the Jews seems to have been motivated less by anti-Semitism than by a fear of condemning the Nazis when Stalinist atrocities seemed to him equally reprehensible.

FEMINISED PIETY

As the papacy gradually withdrew from the struggle for political control in Europe, its struggle for control in matters of religion, and over its own faithful, intensified. Not only did this involve a struggle to wrest control of church affairs from national governments; it also involved a struggle to control the lives, beliefs and emotional loyalties of Catholic clergy and laity. What the modern popes sought was the development of a more unified Catholic culture that would shape and form Catholics from the cradle to the grave. If the fortress was to survive, its confession must be internalised and its laws engraved on the minds and hearts of Catholics. The promulgation of a clearer and more unified system of doctrine was one element in this policy. Equally important was the encouragement and licensing of an intense, emotive, feminised piety with symbols such as Mary and the Sacred Heart of Jesus at its centre.

As well as establishing uniformity of belief, the modern papacy was therefore active in the attempt to establish a powerful Catholic devotionalism. Pius IX played a key role in establishing such piety by attempting, in Romantic style, to restore the grandeur and splendour that were thought to characterise the medieval church. Key features of medieval piety that had been mocked by the Enlightenment were restored: veneration of Mary and the saints, their shrines, medals and statues. Particularly important was Pius's dogmatic definition of Mary's immaculate conception in 1854 (the dogma that Mary was conceived and born without original sin), and his endorsement of a number of miraculous visions of the Virgin in France (the visionaries were often young women).

Pius IX also helped revive the late medieval cult of the Sacred Heart of Jesus, instituting in 1856 a feast of the Sacred Heart to be observed throughout the church, and reinstituting the associated practice of novenas (the granting of indulgence to all who received holy communion on the first Friday of nine consecutive months). Pius IX's measures were carried forward by his successors, particularly by Pius X, whose particular concern was with worship and the life of the parish. He reformed canon law, tightened up clergy training and introduced a number of liturgical changes, including more frequent communion for the laity and the introduction of plainsong in worship.

Though men orchestrated and implemented many of these changes, some, such as the cult of the Sacred Heart and new cults of Mary based on visions, stemmed from women's piety. It was also women who played the key role in implementing them in church and home. Like Protestantism, fortress Catholicism managed the tension between male leadership and female devotion by developing a doctrine of separate spheres and roles for men and women. Whereas early and medieval Catholicism had tended to view women as lesser creatures than men, able to be saved only by transcending their sex, women were now seen as divine creatures made by God for a role different from men's. This tied women more closely into domestic roles and prevented the mystical escape that had previously been open to them – in Catholicism as well as in Protestantism. Women's duty was not so much to serve God as to serve their families. 'Your Catholic family', wrote a New York parish priest, 'symbolises in miniature the Mystical Body of Christ. The father is the head of the body and represents Christ. The wife represents the Church, and the children, as members of the body, represent the faithful.'[14] Of course, Catholic women still had the escape of the cloister, but the religious life was changing as well. If the family became more sanctified, the nunnery became more domesticised. Nuns were to be supervised and spiritually serviced by a male priesthood – their 'fathers in God' – and, instead of devoting themselves to mystical adoration of God, they were to be more actively engaged in caring, nurturing and self-sacrificing activism. The majority of women's orders established in the nineteenth century were founded for a particular task, a 'service' – teaching, nursing, caring for orphans, caring for elderly priests, and so on.

The growing activism of women's religious orders now offered women opportunities and responsibilities that many found highly attractive. Not only did some women religious achieve considerable authority within their own orders, but they were also able to claim social power in some of the roles they undertook in 'the world'. Their vocations gave them a chance both to serve the Lord and to improve the lives of his children. Even those women who remained in the home may have appreciated their change of status from daughter of Eve to angel of the home. Though there was absolutely no question of women's ordination in the Catholic church, the teachings of Rome and the clergy now ascribed to their domestic activity a new dignity, with some Catholic writers going so far as to suggest that they were playing priestly roles within the home. This provoked something of a backlash from male authority. In his encyclical *Summi pontificatus* (1939), Pius XII insisted that it was the father who should fulfil the position of priest in his own house. The feminisation of religion seemed to be going a bit too far.

Thus, by virtue of an intensification of male authority that nevertheless allowed room for female piety, the Catholic church managed not only to retain its hold over the lives of many of its followers, but to recruit new ones. Those within the fortress found themselves shaped and formed by an intense and all-embracing religious culture that claimed them at birth and refused to let go even at death. The Catholic faith was reinforced through a powerful visual, symbolic and sensual culture in which Gothic architecture, stained glass, colourful statues and paintings, sacred hearts, rosaries, lace, vestments, candles, plainsong, bells, incense, holy water and intense personal devotion to a male pope and female saints would all play a part. It was still inseparable from a system of belief in which the fear of sin and damnation assumed a central place, and in which salvation was taken to depend upon regular attendance at mass and regular confession and penance. In that area and many others, the legacy of early modern confessionalisation – and more ancient Christian tradition – lived on. Rather than abandon this legacy as incompatible with changing modern mores, the church retained, strengthened and added to much of what had been established in the early modern period. Its counter-cultural stance was intensified, not relaxed.

Liberal Catholicism

Not all Catholics agreed with the stance of the modern papacy and the 'official' church. While many of those hostile to Catholic reaction simply turned their backs on Rome, some critics remained within its ranks. Throughout the 'fortress' period the term 'liberal' was applied to these dissenters, normally as a term of abuse. It was imprecise, for it encompassed a whole range of opinions and views. It is helpful to distinguish at least three. *Political* liberalism was sympathetic to some of the developments associated with the rise of the modern state, and was particularly concerned to attempt a reconciliation between Catholicism and democracy. *Social* liberalism reacted in indignation to the socio-economic inequalities and injustices thrown up by the rise of industrial society, and drew on Christian resources for solutions. *Theological* liberalism sought greater freedom in relation to theological enquiry, and a greater openness to modern scholarship and a more empirical approach. While some forms of Catholic liberalism combined two or more of these different strands, others pursued one in total isolation from the others. Here some of the most important manifestations of liberalism within eighteenth- and nineteenth-century Catholicism will be briefly surveyed, each illustrative of a different aspect of the struggle between power from on high and power from below in modern Catholicism.

LAMENNAIS AND LIBERAL CATHOLICISM

In retrospect, the political liberalism championed by Félicité de Lamennais (1782–1854) and his supporters appears remarkably mild, yet it led to a notorious excommunication and condemnation that helped inhibit similar bursts of Catholic enthusiasm for liberalism and democracy for decades. The French Catholic Lamennais became an advocate of the liberty the Revolution had proclaimed. The church must seize such liberty, he argued, and fight for freedom of action and expression, which was fundamental to the gospel. As he put it, 'the liberty which has been called for in the name of atheism must now be demanded in the name of God'. In a short-lived but influential periodical, *L'Avenir* (1830–1), Lamennais called for 'a free church in a free state', and argued that the church must champion the true freedom that Christianity alone offered, siding with the people against the forces of both reaction and revolution.

Lamennais was inspired by the Roman Catholic church in places such as Belgium, Poland and Ireland, where it existed under non-Catholic regimes, allied itself with the cause of political liberty and appeared to flourish. Since Pope Gregory XVI was actively fighting for the restoration of Catholic control over the states of modern Europe, however, he was in no mood to respond favourably to Lamennais or to his suggestion that the church needed liberal reform. Despite the fact that Lamennais became an ultramontane who championed the institution of the papacy, Gregory condemned his liberalism in the encyclical letter *Mirari vos* (1832) and, two years later, in *Singulari nos*. Lamennais, forced out of the church, dedicated himself to the service of the working class, became a socialist, and chose to be buried in a pauper's grave.

THE AMERICANIST CONTROVERSY

American Catholics were enthusiastic supporters of the First Amendment's separation of church and state. Throughout the nineteenth century, when the church in Europe was still involved in a struggle against modern democracy, Catholics in America worked willingly with the American state and affirmed their loyalty to a democratic context in which they believed the church could flourish. Some even pressed for greater democracy in the running of the church's internal affairs.

A number of American Catholics, such as Isaac Hecker (1819–88), attempted to combine political liberalism with theological liberalism. Hecker was a convert from transcendentalism (see next chapter), who founded a new missionary religious order, the Paulist fathers. Hecker's interpretation of Catholicism diverged from ultramontane traditionalism by placing emphasis on the authority of the Holy Spirit, and urging a morality that emphasised active virtues rather than avoidance of sin. Hecker was also a powerful defender of 'a free church in a free state'. However, some more conservative Catholics in America – particularly German, French and Italian Catholics – resented the views and influence of Hecker and the other so-called 'Americanist' Catholics, and tried hard to turn Rome against them. They succeeded only after Hecker's death, when a biography of him by a fellow Paulist reached Europe. In 1899 Leo XII issued a letter, *Testem benevolentiae*, which criticised a constellation of ideas he termed 'Americanism'. These ideas included not only Hecker's but, more generally, the view that the church in America 'could be different from that which is in the rest of the world'. It was not until the later twentieth century that the American Catholic attempt to pioneer a new relationship with modernity would eventually win the sanction of Rome (see next chapter).

THE MODERNIST CRISIS

In 1907 Pope Pius X issued the decree *Lamentabili* and the encyclical *Pascendi*, which condemned 'modernism' every bit as fiercely as *Mirari vos* had earlier condemned liberalism. In these documents Pius X characterised modernism as a unified movement of political and theological liberalism ('a synthesis of all heresies'), which questioned the absolute authority of scriptural revelation, tradition and the magisterium and taught (1) historical relativism based on belief in the inaccessiblility of divine truth to human reason; (2) that the origins of all religion lie in the development of a 'religious sense' that detects a 'vital immanence' at the heart of all things; and (3) that church and state must be separate. Despite Pius's fears, it is clear that modernism did not in fact constitute a unified movement, and that its concerns were almost exclusively theological. If the modernists had a unifying concern, it was simply to offer a fresh presentation of Catholicism that would take account of modern scholarship.

In fact, the so-called modernists were intellectuals, both clerical and lay, who had been encouraged by a slight softening of the condemnation of modern scholarship under Leo XIII, and who were influenced by developments in modern scholarship in general, and in Protestant theology and biblical study in particular. Many of the modernists worked within the institutional spaces opened up for free theological reflection by modern universities within non-Catholic states, particularly in England, Italy, Germany, Belgium and America. In many ways, however, France became the epicentre of the modernist movement, and the French biblical scholar Alfred Loisy (1857–1940) became its most important spokesman. A biblical scholar as well as a theologian, Loisy accepted the conclusion of historical scholars that the New Testament is a record not of historical fact but of the opinions and interests of the early church. His conclusion, however, was a conservative Catholic one: that a Protestant reliance on scripture as the basis of Christian faith must be abandoned in favour of a Catholic understanding of the church as the authoritative interpreter of truth. Loisy's argument, however, was not welcomed by a church that still maintained that Moses was the author of the Pentateuch and believed that any scepticism about biblical 'facts' would open the door to subjectivism. After Loisy's excommunication in 1908, modernism was suppressed for a generation.

SOCIAL CATHOLICISM

The only area in which a gradual loosening in official, papal Catholicism's attitude to liberalism was discernible was in relation to social liberalism. The social teaching of the Catholic church had long maintained that the different 'estates' of mankind were part of a natural and God-given order. The fact that some people were born poor and others rich was providential. Both must accept their station in life, and the rich (who often included the clergy) must honour their God-given duty to care for the poor. As we have seen, even the Franciscans did not really question this view; St Francis's witness was against riches, not poverty, and neither he nor any other constituency of the official Catholic church contemplated a truly redistributive justice. In 1891, however, Leo XIII published an encyclical, *Rerum novarum* ('The Condition of Labour') which marked a new departure for Catholicism. Instead of merely advocating charity as a balm for social and economic injustice, *Rerum novarum* considered the evils of unbridled capitalism as well as of socialism and communism, and insisted that the state must treat the worker with justice and equity and take responsibility for regulating wages and conditions of work. Most significantly of all, the encyclical even supported the right of workers to form trade unions and to take strike action if situations demanded it.

While *Rerum novarum* was radical within the context of fortress Catholicism, however, it was hardly so within a world in which socialism and communism were now active forces. The Anglican theologian Henry Scott Holland described the encyclical as 'the voice of some old-world life, faint and ghostly, speaking in some antique tongue of things long ago'. The underlying social conservatism of the papacy was clearly revealed by the suppression of some imaginative attempts to put social Catholicism to work: the Sillon movement, condemned in 1910 by Pius X, for example, and the worker-priest movements, suppressed by Rome in 1954.

Papal suspicion did not, however, prevent the rise of an important and influential manifestation of Catholic political and social liberalism in the late nineteenth and early twentieth centuries: Catholic political parties. In contrast to earlier Catholic attempts to suppress political democracy, these parties represented an attempt by the church – and particularly by lay Catholics – to influence the democratic process from within. Such parties developed in most European countries, and were located on both the right and the left of the political spectrum. Negatively, the Catholic parties defined themselves against existing socialist, liberal or right-wing traditions; positively, they aimed to mobilise Catholic social and political teachings in the context of modern Europe. All were characterised by a commitment to the defence of the Catholic church and religion; most were also committed to a communitarianism intended to moderate the excesses of individualism and capitalism. After the Second World War, Christian Democratic parties became more open, ecumenical and non-confessional. They enjoyed considerable electoral success in the early post-war period, and played an important role in reconstruction and the development of welfare provision. Gradually, however, as both the papacy and the laity retreated from the idea that there could be any direct correspondence between the Catholic faith and a particular political programme, the Catholic inspiration and composition of these parties dwindled. Today the parties that still exist tend to be politically centrist and religiously non-aligned.

Rerum novarum and later papal directives also encouraged the widespread and many-headed movement of political and charitable activism within Catholicism that came to be known as 'social Catholicism'. Its twin motivations were a growing awareness of the extent to which late nineteenth-century society had become secularised (prompted in France by the official separation of church and state in 1905), and a growing concern with 'the social question', the problems of industrial society in general and the working class in particular. Social Catholics were concerned both to identify social problems and to attempt direct interventions to solve them. Attempts were made to bring the church into closer relation with various aspects of modern life by forming organisations such as co-operatives, youth clubs and credit associations. One of the distinctive features of the movement was the involvement of both clergy and laity, men and women. While the magisterium expressed concern that lay initiative should not run ahead of clerical authority, the movement allowed Catholics a freedom of action within society analogous to that which Protestant charitable societies allowed lay Protestants.

For women this was particularly significant. *Rerum novarum* had maintained a firmly patriarchal stance. In defending the right to private property, it taught that the right applied chiefly to 'a man in his capacity of head of the family', and insisted that 'paternal authority can neither be abolished by the state nor absorbed', and that 'a woman is by nature fitted for home work'. Ironically, however, social Catholicism allowed women to enter into the public world and contributed to their politicisation. In France, for example, a number of Catholic social-action groups for women banded together after the First World War to form the *Commission d'éducation sociale civique de la femme*, which, with over a million members, became the largest female organisation in France, and campaigned vigorously for women's suffrage. While the magisterium continued to defend power from on high, power from below was asserting itself within the body of the church.

Orthodoxy

Orthodoxy and Catholicism related differently to the modern world not only because their churches were different, but because each encountered a different 'modernity' as western and eastern Europe followed different paths of modernisation. While both shared a history of feudalism that gave way partially and patchily to absolutism, the east was dominated by imperial rather than national powers (Russian, Austrian/Hapsburg and Ottoman) right up to the First World War. The transition from rural to industrial economy took far longer, and when it did come about it did so under the central control of socialist and communist governments rather than of free-market democracies. The attempt to establish the latter was made only after the collapse of communism in the 1980s. Thus the political regimes with which the Orthodox churches had to negotiate in the modern period proved to be significantly different from those with which the Catholic church had struggled.

THE EARLY MODERN PERIOD: FROM BYZANTIUM
TO RUSSIA

The fall of Constantinople to the Turks in 1453 brought to an end a Greek Christian empire that had lasted for eleven hundred years. Yet the eclipse of Byzantine imperialism by Ottoman imperialism did not prove as disastrous for the patriarch and his church as might be supposed. Given that the Ottomans tolerated non-Islamic religious groups within their territories, Orthodoxy could simply transfer allegiance from one imperial regime to another. Of course, the church and the patriarch could not hope to enjoy such close relations with a Muslim ruler as with a Christian one, or to exercise power over the whole of the population, but the authority of the patriarch was nevertheless extended over a wider territory than before. The administrative power of the Orthodox ecclesiastical authorities under Ottoman rule was greater than in the Byzantine empire. All Orthodox, whether Greeks, Bulgars, Serbs, Arabs or Albanians, were classified by the Ottomans as *millet-i-Rum* (the religious community of the Roman empire) and taken to be under the leadership of the patriarch in Constantinople.

The expansion of Greek authority was resented by many Orthodox, and hostility generated by ethnic rivalry and cultural difference was intensified by anger at ecclesiastical corruption under the Ottomans. It became increasingly common for clerical offices to be bought and sold, for the highest ones had become lucrative and influential positions under the Ottomans, and the lower ones had to be bartered by the bishops and patriarchs in order to finance their own positions. Despite their subordination to Greek and Ottoman authority, the separate identities of the different Christian peoples within the empire continued to develop, and Orthodox churches played an important role in consolidating separate ethnic identities in places such as Bulgaria, Serbia, Montenegro, Romania and Armenia.

In Russia a political vacuum caused by the collapse of Mongol rule allowed Orthodoxy to do even more (see ch. 2). As well as helping to unify a Russian people, the church would ally itself with the emerging empire centred on Moscow to regain its ancient role as champion of expansive imperial power. A crucial step was taken in 1472, when Grand Prince Ivan III (1462–1505) married the niece of the last Byzantine emperor, proceeded to use the title 'tsar', and adopted the symbol of the Byzantine two-headed eagle. Just as the Frankish kings in the west had dignified their imperial ambitions by claiming the mantle of the Roman empire, so the Russian emperors did the same – though it was the eastern empire they had in mind. In both instances the churches proved willing allies, happy to endorse the rulers' claim, and happy to claim the power to do so. The doctrine of Moscow as a 'third Rome' (after Constantinople) was first expounded in a letter written in 1510 by the abbot Filofei to Vassili III (1505–33). The church in Russia would, he said, illumine the whole world and last for ever – and with it the empire that had its support.

Yet the church's alliance with power from on high was not without its Christian critics in Russia. There, as in the west, Christian expansion

Map 7   The world of Eastern Orthodoxy

had come about in part through the spread of monastic foundations. In Russia as in Byzantium, the monasteries could serve as alternative centres of Christian thought and life, independent of the church (and empire). Unlike western monasticism, Russian monasteries were never brought under a single rule, and the ancient eremitic tradition continued alongside more social forms of monasticism. The tradition of

322

Hesychasm, inspired by the ideal of deification through illumination that had been articulated by Simeon the New Theologian and Gregory of Palamas (see ch. 2), continued to flourish in Russia, and it was some of the followers of this tradition who began to criticise the direction being taken by the 'imperial' church. Most prominent in the protest were holy men such as Nil Sorsky (1433–1508), who embraced the ideal of apostolic poverty and powerlessness. The 'Non-Possessors', as they became called, objected not only to the church's alliance with political power, but to its vast and growing wealth. Leading churchmen such as Iosif of Volokolamsk (1440–1515), who defended the church's possessions and supported a centralised monarchy, became known as the 'Possessors'. In 1503 a church council decided in favour of the Possessors. The Non-Possessors retreated to their communities away from Moscow, but were persecuted and destroyed by the mid-sixteenth century.

The Possessors also favoured a monastic ideal, but understood it quite differently from the Non-Possessors. In their hands it became a tool of ecclesiastical domination over the whole of society, which they tried to regulate along monastic lines. Unlike the Non-Possessors, who regarded the pursuit of godliness as a matter of devotion and experience, the Possessors regarded holiness chiefly as a matter of obedience to rules. The book *Domostroi* ('Household Management'), by the monk Silvestr, written in 1556, reflected this attitude and laid down detailed instructions on how a Russian should run his life and his household. Its themes were ritualism, formalism, piety and patriarchalism. The alliance between state and church tightened, with the head of the Russian church receiving the title of 'patriarch' in 1589. The so-called 'Council of the Hundred Chapters' of 1551 laid down the ideal of a partnership in state–church relations, with the tsar and the patriarch the two heads of a single Christian kingdom.

In practice, however, the state began to dominate the church, particularly after the seventeenth century, when the model of absolute rule and subjugation of the church took hold in Russia as in western Europe. The 'Russian Hildebrand', Patriarch Nikon (1652–58), attempted to reassert the power of the church, and in doing so adopted a western model of ecclesiastical higher power. Taking *The Donation of Constantine* as his authority, he asserted the absolute sovereignty of the church

Plate 21   *The Holy Trinity*, by Andrei Rublev (c. 1370–1430)

   In this scene, created in or near Moscow within the context of monastic revival, Rublev depicts the Old Testament story in which three angels visit Abraham to represent the mysterious nature of God-as-Trinity. Compared with many western depictions (e.g. plate 13), the three persons of the Trinity are presented in a relatively non-hierarchical fashion. God the Father is thought to be the figure on the left, towards whom the others incline their heads.

over the state, and claimed for himself the title 'Great Lord', hitherto reserved for the tsar. He also attempted to expand the power of the Russian church outside Russia by proposing reforms that would conform Russian Orthodox doctrines and practices more closely to Greek ones. The policy of Hellenisation was fiercely opposed by many of the clergy, such as the archpriest Avvakum, who wished to reassert Russian distinctiveness in the face of renewed contact with the west. Nikon and Avvakum were both condemned at a church council of 1666–7, and the supremacy of the tsar affirmed. But in practice many of Nikon's ecclesiastical reforms were adopted, and the party of 'Old Believers' was defeated, though the schism continued to divide the faithful.

When Peter the Great (1682–1725) took power in Russia he took pains to ensure the complete subordination of the church. His *Dukhovny reglament* ('Church Regulations') abolished the office of patriarch, and instituted a new church council under the control of a civil servant. As part of his programme of westernisation and modernisation, Peter placed the more westernised clergy of the Ukraine in positions of power. As we noted above, Catherine the Great (1762–96) continued the policy of absolutism and westernisation, and maintained the subordination of the church. In the nineteenth century, enthusiasm for western-style reform waned, and governments adopted more conservative policies designed to protect the ruling elite. The church became a supporter of this policy, defending the interests of 'Orthodoxy, autocracy and nationality'. Its reward was continued financial and legal support from the state, and protection against religious rivals.

THE MODERN PERIOD: COMMUNISM AND AFTER

Both church and state in Russia faced a crisis of legitimacy in the nineteenth century, which took place in the context of a broader debate about Russian identity. Dissatisfaction with the current order of things was widespread, but what was to be done? Could Russia forge a distinctive path of modernisation that would abolish present injustices without abandoning cultural distinctiveness? Such questions gave rise to a period of fertile intellectual exploration, in which religious ideals were championed by some and 'materialism' by others. 'Slavophiles' such as Aleksei Khomyakov (1804–60) supported a conservative, communitarian model of modernisation that opposed western 'individualism' with the model

Plate 22 *Allegory of the Russian Church and State*, by I. Szczyrsk

In this allegorical engraving of 1683, heavenly power vindicates earthly power and destroys its enemies. While Christ blesses the young co-emperors Peter (later the Great) and his half-brother Ivan, their enemies are defeated by angels.

of *sobornost* ('individual diversity in free unity'), which echoed the conciliar tradition in Orthodoxy. In literature, writers such as Leo Tolstoy (1828–1910) and Fyodor Dostoyevsky (1821–81) attempted to represent the finer as well as the more corrupt aspects of Orthodox and Russian life. Both were influenced by the Hesychast tradition. Tolstoy celebrated the simple piety of the Russian peasant, and repudiated the formal structures and inclination towards violence of both state and church. Dostoyevsky portrayed the ambiguity of Orthodoxy in his day – its spiritual richness embodied in its hermits and holy men (*startsy*), and its corruption by leaders of church and nation who sought to secure control over the lives of others.

A new generation of theologians also arose. Influenced by western theology, but keen to recover and revive their own heritage, they turned to the fathers and the traditions of Orthodoxy as well as to western philosophy to articulate an authentic Orthodox theology in the context of the modern world. Sergei Bulgakov (1871–1944) developed a metaphysical theology that owed much to the work of Khomyakov and Vladimir Soloviev (1853–1900), as well as to western philosophical Idealism. His thought is based around the notion of the interdependent harmony of all things in *Sophia*, the creative Wisdom of God, which forms the basis of creation as it empties itself in perfect love. His colleague and friend Nikolai Berdyaev (1874–1948) developed a stronger emphasis on the value of the unique creative 'personality', while insisting on the necessity of developing individuality in communion. Georges Florovsky (1893–1979) abandoned philosophical Idealism in favour of a return to the 'objectivity' of Greek patristic thought, while maintaining Bulgakov's and Berdyaev's theme of individuality-in-communion. Vladimir Lossky (1903–58) developed the same themes in dialogue with the thought of Gregory of Palamas, emphasising the mystical tradition of Orthodoxy, and expounding the theme of individual deification through the realisation of individual uniqueness. In Lossky's view the kenotic (self-giving) Spirit of Christ inspires the development of a unique form of holiness in each person. (On the revival of Greek theology later in the twentieth century, partly under the influence of the Russian émigrés, see next chapter.)

The flowering of modern Orthodox theology was interrupted by political events that it proved impotent to influence. All the theologians mentioned above were eventually forced into exile in Europe (chiefly in Paris). The Bolshevik Revolution of 1917 had divided Russian Christians. Some allied themselves with the communist cause; others opposed it. From the early 1920s a movement called the 'Living Church' attempted to constitute an Orthodox church that would be acceptable to the communist regime, but the 'conversion' of Patriarch Tikhon (elected in 1917) to the Soviet regime rendered the Living Church redundant. Tikhon's eventual successor, Sergi, issued a Declaration of Loyalty in 1927. Despite the capitulation of ecclesiastical authority, the communist authorities sought to emasculate and, if possible, to destroy the church completely. What soon became apparent was that communism was based on an ideology every bit as absolute, totalising and exclusive as that of the church, and that their harmonious co-existence was impossible. Stalin's war on religion was unprecedented in its ferocity, and savage persecution throughout the 1930s reduced the 46,000 churches of pre-revolutionary Russia to a few hundred. Only four bishops remained at liberty.

The church in Russia was saved by the Second World War. For one thing, Stalin needed it to take control of religion in the newly annexed territories. For another, Stalin was aware that the church could be useful in mobilising the Russian people to defend the motherland and make the enormous sacrifices that would be called for. 'Patriarch' Sergi, as he became in 1943, was happy to oblige. Limited toleration was continued after the war, in so far as the church could be helpful in furthering the state's post-war agenda – as in extending Russian ecclesiastical jurisdiction over churches in the countries of eastern Europe coming under Soviet control. Yet the Khrushchev era saw further religious repression and more church closures. Relief came only after 1985, when Mikhail Gorbachev's policies of *glasnost* and *perestroika* led to the relaxation of restrictions on religion. The millennium celebrations in 1988, for the thousandth anniversary of the acceptance of Christianity in Kiev, marked a turning point for the church.

For other Orthodox churches under communist rule, a similar sequence of events took place: a period of active persecution gave way to ongoing suppression and then to a partial relaxation and limited tolerance. Ecclesiastical leadership failed to oppose the state not only because its freedom of manoeuvre was so limited, but because certain advantages could accrue from collaboration with communist rule. Above all, the state secured Orthodoxy's monopoly over all other forms of religion; in the Ukraine, for example, all Greek Catholics were placed under Orthodox control. The Orthodox church's long-standing tradition of alliance with political power may also have played a part, for it is noticeable that the churches that did offer resistance to communism tended not to be the Orthodox ones. In Bulgaria as in Russia, Orthodoxy lost credibility through submission to the communist authorities, whereas, in Romania, East Germany and Poland, Protestant and Catholic churches proved their ability to mobilise opposition as well as support for the state. The 'western' churches' opposition to communism, however, was helped by the support given by their brethren in non-communist lands – including the pope himself.

Just as communism carried some benefits as well as terrible costs for Orthodoxy, so its collapse proved a mixed blessing for the church. The certainties of its status ended abruptly after the 1980s, as did its privileges. In the Ukraine, for example, the Ukrainian Catholic church was re-legalised, and millions of nominal Orthodox Christians returned to their true faith. Equally threatening was the law of Freedom of Conscience passed in 1990 in Russia, which granted complete freedom of religion. The Russian Orthodox church reacted by accusing Catholics and Protestants of 'sheep-stealing', and condemned even long-established faiths such as Baptism as dangerous 'sects' that were threatening the purity of Russian culture. Its lobbying led to the passing of new laws in much of the former Soviet Union, designed to restrict the activity of 'foreign' or 'harmful' sects. The nationalistic tendency of Orthodoxy became increasingly apparent, not least in countries such as Serbia, where the church proved unable to distance itself from civil war in the former Yugoslavia and unwilling to make a principled stand against the atrocities associated with 'ethnic cleansing'.

In many ways Orthodox ambivalence about 'modern democracy' is interestingly reminiscent of that of the Roman Catholic church two centuries before. In post-communist societies both churches now display qualified support for democracy, but often ride roughshod over democratic sensibilities when it comes to imposing Christian priorities on culture and society. In both churches conflict between conservative and liberal tendencies has intensified, and in both the conservative tendency currently appears to have the upper hand.

Further reading

CATHOLIC REFORMATION, CONFESSIONALISATION AND MISSION

Michael Mullett's *The Catholic Reformation* (London and New York: Routledge, 1999) offers a comprehensive introduction to Trent, its antecedents and its aftermath. See also H. O. Evennett, *The Spirit of the Counter-Reformation* (Cambridge: Cambridge University Press, 1968). There is an excellent short introduction to Catholic reformation by Elisabeth G. Gleason in Thomas A. Brady et al. (eds.), *Handbook of European History 1400–1600* II (Leiden and New York: Brill, 1995). Hubert Jedin is the most influential interpreter of Trent. Many of his works are in French, but see Hubert Jedin and John Dolan (eds.), *History of the Church* V: *Reformation and Counter Reformation* (New York: Seabury, 1980).

Jean Delumeau's *Catholicism between Luther and Voltaire* (London: Burns and Oates, 1977) offers an influential account of the development of post-Reformation Catholicism in France, and of early modern Catholic mission activities. John Bossy's *Christianity in the West 1400–1700* (Oxford and New York: Oxford University Press, 1985) offers a rich portrait of popular late medieval Catholicism and a less sympathetic account of the impact of Reformation. See also Louis Châtellier, *The Europe of the Devout: The Catholic Reformation and the Formation of a New Society* (Cambridge: Cambridge University Press, 1989).

There is very little on early Catholic mission in English, besides mission histories that offer minutely detailed narratives of key events and individuals but little social analysis. There are some books that shed light on particular missions, however, such as Jacques Gernet's *China and the Christian Impact: A Conflict of Cultures* (Cambridge: Cambridge University Press, 1985). See also A. D. Wright, *The Counter-Reformation: Catholic Europe and the Non-Christian World* (London: Weidenfeld and Nicolson, 1982). Felipe Fernández-Armesto and Derek Wilson's *Reformation: Christianity and the World 1500–2000* (London: Bantam, 1996) is an insightful popular account that draws attention to the similarities between post-Reformation Protestantism and Catholicism.

THE CHURCH, ABSOLUTISM AND REVOLUTION

John McManners's *The French Revolution and the Church* (London: SPCK, 1969) offers a clear historical account. A more sociological approach can be found in Ralph Gibson, *A Social History of French Catholicism 1789–1914* (London and New York: Routledge, 1989). On the modern papacy see K. O. von Aretin, *The Papacy and the Modern World* (London:

Weidenfeld and Nicolson, 1970); Paolo Prodi, *The Papal Prince: One Body and Two Souls: The Papal Monarchy in Early Modern Europe* (Cambridge: Cambridge University Press, 1987); and Owen Chadwick, *The Popes and European Revolution* (Oxford: Clarendon; New York: Oxford University Press, 1981).

FORTRESS CATHOLICISM AND LIBERAL CATHOLICISM

Jonathan Sperber's *Popular Catholicism in Nineteenth Century Germany* (Princeton, NJ: Princeton University Press, 1984) offers a portrait of fortress Catholicism on the ground. See also Mary Heimann, *Catholic Devotion in Victorian England* (Oxford: Clarendon; New York: Oxford University Press, 1995). The history of American Catholicism is told in Jay P. Dolan's *The American Catholic Experience* (Notre Dame, IN: University of Notre Dame Press, 1992). Karen Kennelly (ed.), *American Catholic Women: A Historical Exploration* (New York: Macmillan; London: Collier Macmillan, 1989) is a useful collection, and I have drawn on the excellent chapter on 'Catholic Domesticity, 1860 to 1960' by Colleen McDannell.

On liberal theology see Bernard Reardon, *Liberalism and Tradition: Aspects of Catholic Thought in Nineteenth-Century France* (Cambridge and New York: Cambridge University Press, 1975); and Alex Vidler, *A Century of Social Catholicism 1820–1920* (London: SPCK, 1964) and *A Variety of Catholic Modernists* (Cambridge: Cambridge University Press, 1970). On Catholic social teaching and political Catholicism, see M. P. Fogarty, *Christian Democracy in Western Europe, 1820–1953* (London: Routledge and Kegan Paul, 1957).

The *Catholic Encyclopaedia* is a useful general resource, and it is interesting to compare the current edition with earlier editions in order to see how significant the changes in Catholicism's self-presentation have been over the last century. The papal encyclicals can be found on the web at <http://www.vatican.va>.

ORTHODOXY

Philip Walters offers a clear and helpful survey of Orthodoxy since 1453 in Adrian Hastings (ed.), *A World History of Christianity* (London: Cassell, 1999). Steven Runciman's *The Orthodox Churches and the Secular State* (Auckland: Auckland University Press; London: Oxford University Press, 1971) is an accessible short history of Orthodoxy in relation to secular power.

On the recent history of the Russian Orthodox church see Jane Ellis, *The Russian Orthodox Church: A Contemporary History* (London: Croom Helm, 1986); and Nathaniel Davis, *A Long Walk to Church* (Boulder, CO: Westview, 1995). On the churches of Russia and eastern Europe under communist control see Sabrina P. Ramet's *Nihil Obstat: Religion, Politics and Social Change in East-Central Europe and Russia* (Durham, NC, and London: Duke University Press, 1998).

The history of Russian theology and spirituality is addressed in Georges Florovsky's *Ways of Russian Theology* in *The Collected Works of Georges Florovsky* (Belmont, MA: Nordland, 1979).

7

Twentieth-century fortunes

Historians of the twentieth century in the third millennium will probably see the century's major impact on history as the one made by and in this astonishing period [its second half]. For the changes in human life it brought about all over the globe were as profound as they were irreversible. Moreover, they are still continuing.[1]

Though a final verdict will be possible only when the passage of time allows us to take a longer perspective, the final part of the twentieth century may be judged one of the most momentous in the history of Christianity. For in just three decades, between 1970 and 2000, Christianity collapsed in parts of the northern hemisphere, and gained new vitality in much of the south.

It was not just Christianity that changed; the world changed too. Eric Hobsbawm is not alone in noting the historical significance of the changes that took place in the second part of the twentieth century. The widespread sense that something of such magnitude had occurred that it constituted a break with what had gone before was signalled by the use of terms such as 'postmodern', 'post-industrial', 'post-Christian' and 'post-colonial'. Though these terms are much debated, few disagree that the last part of the twentieth century witnessed an erosion of long-established forms of social order and moral control. Negatively, such collapse involved a dissatisfaction with established, hierarchical orders, and may be characterised as a 'flight from deference'. Positively, it was born of a sense of the sovereign right to freedom and self-determination of each and every unique individual human being, and may be characterised as a 'turn to the self' or 'subjective turn'. In the language of this volume, power from on high was decisively challenged by power from below. The impact on Christianity was far-reaching.

But, however significant the change, it was not wholly unprecedented. What happened after the 1960s was that a turn to the self, which had been in train since at least the eighteenth century, finally became a widespread social priority. Until then its progress had been most advanced at the cultural level. The Enlightenment rationalists had championed the rights of the individual in the eighteenth century; Romanticism had spread the cult of self-reliance, individual creativity and authenticity in the nineteenth; from the end of the nineteenth century, feminism and socialism had attacked the reign of bourgeois male power and extended the rights of the sovereign individual to women and the working classes; the rise of the psychoanalytic movement in the twentieth century had given the enterprise of individual self-development new prominence, new vocabulary and new tools. At the socio-economic level, however, the attainment of sovereign individuality had remained a privilege reserved largely for a white, male middle-class elite – the businessmen, professionals and opinion-formers of capitalist society. Middle-class women remained confined to domestic roles that encouraged relational and self-sacrificial virtues, while working-class men and women had neither the time nor the resources to seek personal empowerment. For the working class the only hope of gaining greater social power was by way of organised activity (party politics, trade unions) rather than by way of individual assertion. The empowerment of working-class women was simply unthinkable (as, indeed, it still is). Outside the west, those under colonial rule, whatever their class, condition or level of personal attainment, had to defer to their foreign masters.

The upsurge of power from below came about by way of a set of unprecedented changes that gathered speed after the Second World War. Their precondition was the destabilisation of the power of the male capitalist elite, who had monopolised social power since the breakdown of feudal society, and who had greatly extended their position after the seventeenth century by taking advantage of the opportunities opened up by industrial capitalism. Their power was shaken, above all, by the Great Depression of the 1930s, which undermined the operation and certainties of *laissez-faire* (free-market) capitalism. The weakness opened up space for opposition: for working-class strikes and protests, for some triumphs on the part of organised labour, for the spread of communism after the Bolshevik Revolution of 1917, and for movements of colonial independence outside the western world. Some European countries embraced fascism in the attempt to restore order. In those that did not, on both sides of the Atlantic, threatened socio-economic elites made far-reaching concessions to the previously disenfranchised by granting a universal franchise that allowed even women the right to vote, and by regulating the market through the nationalisation of key industries and the creation of a welfare state.

But it was only after the 1960s that the old authorities lost authority. Whereas, before, the authority of the 'higher ups' in society – the bank manager, the vicar, the schoolteacher, the factory manager, the doctor, the local landowner – had seemed interlocking and mutually reinforcing, it now collapsed like a pack of cards. Those 'below' were no longer willing to defer. The younger generation rebelled first, with students in the vanguard of public protest, and the baby-boom generation (those born between about 1946 and 1964) leading the way. Individuals now felt themselves to be more important than existing forms of entrenched privilege and the institutions that supported them – from family to factory to university to colonial power. What mattered was not duty but integrity, not conformity but authenticity. No longer willing to be told what to do and what to think by outside authorities, or to live life in prescribed roles (as a wife, a mother, a student, a worker, etc.), individual women and men wished to be set free to live out their own unique lives in their own unique ways. What was involved was not just a subjective turn in the sense of the empowerment of the individual agent, but a subjective turn in which self-development and inner well-being become the main focus of concern. Whereas the former has to do with the individual's becoming autonomous and self-reliant (external power), the latter has to do with each person's experiencing, understanding, integrating, enhancing and enriching his or her unique experiences, feelings, bodily sensations, dispositions, hopes, desires and moods in his or her own unique way (inner power). Subjectivisation in the first sense, in other words, has more to do with Enlightenment values of freedom, self-determination and individuation, while subjectivisation in the second sense has to do with Romantic values of affectivity, self-expression and harmonious relationship within oneself and with others. Since both forms of subjectivisation treat the self as sovereign, and authorise each individual subject to become the highest authority in the living of his or her own life, they have a common basis. Unless otherwise indicated, 'subjectivisation' and 'the subjective turn' will therefore be used inclusively in what follows to embrace both senses.

The upsurge of power from below was linked to a number of fundamental social changes. The most important had to do with economic change and the shift to what is sometimes called 'late capitalism'. After the 1950s, for the first time in the history of the human race, the majority of the population ceased to be tied to the land. The peasant disappeared altogether in the west, and became less common even in Third World economies. In the space of a generation, human life shifted its focus from the natural environment to the man-made environment of the town or city. Tertiary knowledge-based and service-based industries increased dramatically, at the expense of both rural labour and industrial manufacture. Though neither of the latter disappeared, much production shifted to the Third World, as the economy became more truly global than it had been before. (Colonial economies had been expanded national economies rather than global economies.) The power of production and supply was now balanced by that of demand and consumption, with some commentators speaking of the rise of 'consumer capitalism'. The power of the consumer was bolstered not only by increased and more widespread affluence but by an explosion of credit stemming from the loosening of restrictions on lending by financial institutions after the 1970s. Economic change was accompanied by change in the social structure as the middle class expanded rapidly to incorporate all but the unskilled. The massive expansion of higher education in many parts of the world reinforced this shift, and equipped increasing numbers with a high level of specialised skills. As affluence spread, the majority of the western population found itself cut loose from the anxiety about securing the basic necessities of life, and in this sense the baby-boom generation experienced the luxury of becoming 'post-materialists'. The concern with subjective well-being that became increasingly evident from the 1980s onwards, and was catered for by a growing 'well-being' industry (from spas to spiritual retreats), was the most visible result.

Thus the last quarter of the twentieth century proved an age of unprecedented affluence that re-established capitalism as the dominant economic mode worldwide. (For much of the Cold War period, it was unclear whether capitalism or communism would emerge as the dominant socio-economic system, and the struggle between them was intense right through to the 1980s.) Though increases in wealth were most stupendous in the 'developed' west, national and individual incomes rose across the world. The impact was less than it would otherwise have been in many 'developing' countries, however, not only because of structural weakness and disadvantage relative to the west, but because an explosion of population meant that increased wealth had to be distributed among twice, sometimes three times, as many people. So significant were the changes wrought by capitalism in the last quarter of the twentieth century, however, that by the early twenty-first century the distinction between 'First', 'Second' and 'Third' World economies that had been drawn since the 1950s was having to be rethought. It now seemed as if both the globe and individual societies within it could be divided into a majority, whose wealth was growing, and a discarded minority, whose poverty and problems seemed chronic. In western societies, economic deprivation went hand in hand with ethnic and gender marginality, as the service needs of the wealthier middle classes were increasingly tended to by an 'underclass' of women, non-whites and immigrants.

Unprecedented changes also took place with regard to women, the family and gender roles. Many were the outcome of allowing women access to higher levels of education and access to the workplace alongside men, albeit not on terms of perfect equality. Women's entry into the public sphere was made possible by the huge expansion in the number of jobs available; for the first time in history it was to men's advantage rather than disadvantage to allow women into the workplace, at least in the west (so long as the most powerful jobs could still be retained by men). The invention of effective forms of contraception added momentum to the 'sexual revolution'. Culturally, new opportunities for women were defended largely in terms of secular ideologies of human rights and human equality. Yet women's roles changed more slowly and painfully than some had hoped. What happened was not so much that women shed their old roles as wives and mothers, but that they gained additional ones in full-time or part-time paid employment. The struggle to manage not only twice as much work as before, but an identity that fell uncomfortably between the roles of thrusting career woman and caring wife and mother, led to some disillusionment with feminism. The dual burdens of childcare and of labour that was less well remunerated than that undertaken by men began to weigh on women outside the west. Nevertheless, the post-Reformation ideal of the patriarchal family, in which men and women occupy separate spheres and carry out different functions, was decisively challenged, particularly in the west.

Finally, the post-1960s revolution involved the political emancipation of the colonial world, as decolonisation took place with astonishing rapidity after the Second World War. The reason was not simply that many western countries now found their extensive empires a financial burden, but that growing demands for independence made them increasingly difficult and costly to rule. It was no longer possible for whole societies to be controlled by a handful of white men and their native collaborators. In any case, the growing western commitment to autonomy and self-governance undermined the will of western people to retain their colonial empires. The supreme confidence in the superiority of 'western civilisation' that had reached a peak at the beginning of the twentieth century had virtually disappeared by its end, undermined in part by the barbarity of which such 'civilisation' had shown itself to be capable during two world wars. It was also undermined by a growing appreciation of cultural difference, which again stemmed in part from the awareness of the atrocities to which racist and utopian ideologies had given rise in Nazi Germany and, to some minds at least, in Vietnam. The west's image of the non-western world changed accordingly. Images of an exotic 'orient', the wily 'Turk', or heathen peoples crying out for the benefits of civilisation, gave way in some quarters to a new global vision in which all human beings were imagined as common occupants of a single 'blue planet' (the image of planet Earth taken from space). Within this single 'global village', however, 'the west' still tended to think of itself as more developed than 'the rest'. The latter were therefore in need of at least the material benefits of capitalism and democracy, if not of the cultural. But 'the rest' proved to have voices and minds of their own, and to be more internally differentiated than the west had assumed. To the alarm of western governments, religions that had been dismissed as archaic provided rallying points for countries and peoples that pioneered forms of modernisation different from that prescribed for them by world banks and north Atlantic foreign policy.

This chapter traces the impact of all these changes on Christianity, and its role within them. It explores the way in which Christianity's long-standing alliance with power from on high proved a serious handicap in the late modern context, particularly for those forms of Christianity in which the alliance had been strongest. In its opening section it considers the massive loss of social power suffered by many western churches, and the decline in individual commitment to Christianity that often accompanied it. Since challenges to theology were felt long before challenges to the institutional church really began to bite, the middle section of the chapter traces the clash between theological knowledge 'from above' and modern empirical knowledge 'from below' over a more extended period – from the late eighteenth century down to the start of the new millennium. The chapter ends with a discussion of the fortunes of Christianity in the southern hemisphere in the post-colonial period. Here, too, real change became most visible after the 1960s. Prior to that time, Christianity had been identified, however informally, with colonial power. Independence changed that, as it had done almost two hundred years earlier in North America. It allowed Christianity to indigenise in analogous ways, becoming a religion *of* rather than *for* the people, and helping to ease the transition to capitalist modernity. Nowhere was this alliance with emergent power from below more obvious than in relation to the charismatic forms of Christianity, which not only were established by non-elite men and occasionally women, but offered empowerment through the Holy Spirit to each and every individual. Though the fates of Christianity in north and south might appear to be opposite – with secularisation (the decline of religion) characterising the former and sacralisation (the growth of religion) the latter – the decline of deference and the subjective turn may therefore be identified as influential to both processes.

Social and personal secularisation

Secularisation appears to have characterised most western societies since the late nineteenth century, but to have accelerated dramatically after the 1970s. Two different forms or aspects of secularisation may be distinguished. 'Social secularisation' names the process whereby religion loses its power and influence over and within society, while 'personal secularisation' has to do with the decline of individual allegiance and commitment to religion. Here we shall consider personal secularisation first, before moving on to look at social secularisation and the links between the two.

PERSONAL SECULARISATION

Where Christianity is concerned, levels of personal allegiance may be gauged by a variety of indicators relating to personal belief and practice, such as church membership or attendance. Since reliable records of such things have been kept only in the latter part of the twentieth century, it is extremely difficult to compare secularity (or 'sacrality') in different eras in Christian history. In relation to the west, however, our sketchy evidence suggests the following picture of secularisation and sacralisation in the modern era.

Confessional Christianity, both Protestant and Catholic, had been deeply concerned to establish a more sincere Christian commitment on the part of individuals, a commitment that would be nurtured and signalled by frequent church attendance. In much of Christendom up to the early modern period, men and women seem generally to have received the eucharist no more than once a year, at Easter (though we know very little about medieval patterns of attendance). The confessional churches took steps to monitor church attendance more closely and to discipline those who did not appear regularly, and we know that this had some effect. We do not know exactly when and at what rate patterns of more regular, particularly weekly, churchgoing were established, but we do know that by about 1870 levels of weekly church attendance reached a peak in many western societies. At this time somewhere around 40 per cent of the population on both sides of the Atlantic might be in church on a typical Sunday, some attending more than once in the same day.

Over the course of the next hundred years, church attendance declined steadily. In much of Europe it had roughly halved by 1970, though in the USA the decline was less steep. Between 1970 and 2000 it halved again in many European countries, where weekly attendance by the end of the millennium was as low as 8 per cent of the population in Britain and 4 per cent in Sweden.[2] (France and the Netherlands had become the other two most secular countries in western Europe, with both Catholic and Protestant churches affected.) In the USA, post-1970s decline was somewhat less dramatic. Estimates of levels of regular churchgoing in North America at the end of the twentieth century vary from 40 per cent to 20 per cent of the population.[3] (There is heated debate about which figure is correct, though the evidence to support the lower figure is more compelling.) Patterns of churchgoing have also shifted on both sides of the Atlantic since the 1970s, with fewer people attending weekly, and more attending irregularly – once a month or even once a year. In some ways, then, it looks as if churchgoing in the new millennium may be reverting to a more medieval pattern, with the post-Reformation confessional period representing not the norm, but the more unusual episode in between.

SOCIAL SECULARISATION

Though levels of personal secularisation thus show some significant variation between different western countries, social secularisation has been much more uniform. From the sixteenth century onwards Christianity has gradually been pushed out of the many public spheres over which it once had influence or control – politics, the economy, education, welfare and so on. This is the process that is sometimes called 'functional' or 'social' differentiation, and it refers to the way in which a society's main functions gradually separate into distinct, autonomous spheres. For religion it means, quite simply, a loss of social power. Yet this loss has not always been as rapid and inexorable as is sometimes implied. In tracing the way in which the churches became more marginal to western societies, the second part of this volume has identified a number of stages in the process, which may be summarised as follows.

We begin with the peak of Christian social power that had been attained by about the twelfth century. Thereafter, although the medieval church's political and economic power was repeatedly challenged in disputes with powerful secular rulers, it was not until the sixteenth century that a handful of monarchs began to take much fuller control of the church in their territories. Though this weakened the universal power of the church, it did not undermine non-voluntaristic Christianity. The church, whether Protestant or Catholic, was simply nationalised. Early modern rulers needed Christianity almost as much as their medieval predecessors had done. They needed it to legitimate their power and to unify the often fragmented peoples of their territories into a single nation state. They needed it to provide education and welfare, to help administer law, and to channel revenues to the Crown and charitable bodies. Above all, they needed a national church as an intermediate structure that could bring power from on high to bear, by way of local churches and their clergy, on every soul in the land. For the church, unlike any other institution in the land, was capable of reaching into the fabric of each individual life – into the 'soul of the nation'.

By the seventeenth and eighteenth centuries, however, early modern states were beginning to take over many of the functions that had formerly been carried out by the church. As their power became more extensive and more intensive, their need of ecclesiastical power diminished accordingly. In many ways modern states overtook the confessional churches by imitating them. They too became increasingly centralised and bureaucratised; they too extended their infrastructure of control over individuals' lives; they too became effective agents of propaganda on behalf of their own power. Not that rulers now jettisoned the sacred and the services of the church, but they became more selective about what they required. They continued to make use of the churches' services in education and social welfare. But in law, politics, taxation and other economic matters, they were rapidly taking power into their own hands. Constitutional monarchies were in an even stronger position relative to the church than absolute monarchies were, since they had the support of the new and expanding capitalist classes. Since the latter dwelt in every part of the land, they could take responsibility for local pacification and the mediation of political power to the local level. In addition, the support of this powerful and increasingly extensive section of society meant that constitutional monarchs had less need of the sacred to legitimate their power.

Where monarchial rule gave way to more democratic or republican forms of polity after the eighteenth century, the situation changed yet again. A more severe form of ecclesiastical marginalisation resulted, in which the state withdrew its formal ties with non-voluntarist Christianity altogether. Now an individual's primary allegiance was to nation, not church, and his or her sense of identity might alter accordingly. In most cases the change was willingly embraced, as modern men and women rejected the churches' right to control their belief and their 'private' lives. (Indeed, the creation of the modern 'individual' was bound up with the freeing of a private sphere from outside interference.) Since state power was no longer seen as imposed from on high, but as flowing from 'the people', and since in most countries those people were confessionally variegated, the state could no longer support just one form of Christianity or even one form of religion. To do so would be to privilege one group over another, and thus lose the votes of the others. Thus the sacred and the political became detached from each other, and the state took over the majority of the public functions formerly associated with the church – control of politics, the economy, the law and, more gradually, social welfare and education. Even non-voluntary forms of Christianity were forced to adopt the voluntarist mode (a shift sometimes referred to as that from 'church' to 'denomination').

Finally, after the 1960s, the churches' control of social power was further eroded by the changes sketched at the start of this chapter. Widespread urbanisation undermined the close links between religion and society that had often existed at the local level in small-scale rural communities. At the national level, states continued to sever their remaining links with Christianity. Many communist countries waged active war against religion, both Christian and non-Christian. Democratic regimes tolerated religion, but gave it little active assistance. With the growth of pluralism and multi-culturalism among their citizens, they became increasingly concerned to treat all religions, both Christian and non-Christian, with an equal hand. Toleration often amounted to secularisation as states and legislatures strove to keep religion and politics separate and to guarantee the right of each individual to freedom and self-determination in the spheres of 'private life' and 'personal belief' (with which religion would have liked to be concerned, since it was now denied access to the public sphere). Religion also became more marginal to economic power, as consumer capitalism cut itself free from as many restrictions and controls as possible (including that of the state, to an unprecedented degree). The 'market' threatened the churches by changing the ways in which people worked and played – by undermining the sabbath day of rest, for example, and by providing alternative forms of entertainment and spirituality.

CONNECTIONS BETWEEN SOCIAL AND
PERSONAL SECULARISATION

The churches' loss of social power does not necessarily lead directly to a decline in individual commitment to Christianity, for the connections between social and individual secularisation are complex and sometimes indirect.

Where political power is concerned, the most obvious connection occurs where the state becomes actively hostile to religion and tries to destroy it. This happened in many communist states, and had a major impact on individual commitment. Estonia, the former East Germany and the former Czech Republic are now the most secular countries in Europe, if not in the world. The withdrawal of state support for the church on the part of modern democracies has more mixed results. It certainly makes it impossible for the church to impose itself on populations as it once did, and it certainly means that allegiance to Christianity is unlikely to be tied up with desire for personal advancement in society as once it might have been. Yet, as we saw in relation to the USA in chapter 5, the disestablishment of religion and the consequent shift to voluntarism on the part of the churches does not necessarily lead to a dramatic decline in individual commitment. Indeed, continuing state support for a particular church can seem to be a positive disadvantage in the conditions of the late modern world, as we shall see below. Nor does the political marginalisation of the churches necessarily lead to a 'privatisation' of religion that sees it withdraw from political activity entirely. Such activity simply has to take place in new ways, in keeping with the churches' new position relative to the state and public space. For example, the previous chapter noted the role played by the churches in the overthrow of communism and the support of modern democratic and human rights. Within longer-established democracies, such as the United States, the churches have also spoken out on a number of political issues, ranging from nuclear disarmament to control of the worst excesses of free-market capitalism, with the American Catholic bishops making important interventions on both issues.

In many ways the area of public life over which the churches have struggled longest and hardest to maintain control, and in which their loss of power has perhaps had the most direct impact on individual commitment, has been that of education. The connection between social and personal secularisation in this area is obvious, for the survival of Christianity depends on its transmission to the next generation, and such transmission depends on the church's ability to form and shape young people. Where Christian influence can be secured in schools and colleges, therefore, Christianity has a better chance of survival than where it is solely dependent on the initiative of churches and parents. In so far as Christian control over education shrank after the 1960s, social secularisation can therefore be expected to lead directly to personal secularisation. The effects are already becoming apparent, and the situation is further complicated by the gathering pace of a general 'deregulation' of knowledge. This involves not so much the state's wresting control of knowledge and education from the churches, as a loss of control over knowledge on the part of both church and state. Such deregulation is partly the result of the privatisation of the media, and partly

Plate 23   God Bless America: Evanstown, Indiana, 2003

This wayside photograph, taken at the time when US troops were attacking Iraq, illustrates the way in which Christianity can be used to legitimate the modern nation state, its actions and interests.

Plate 24   *The Holy Family*: in the grounds of the Crystal Cathedral, Los Angeles
The defence of the family and of so-called 'traditional' male–female relations has become a major preoccupation of much modern Christianity. Here a sculpture of the 'Holy Family' in the grounds of a Protestant mega-church helps reinforce the legitimacy of the modern nuclear family.

the result of the rise of new technologies of communication such as the internet. The effect is to allow consumers to design their own packages of entertainment and information, rather than to be 'programmed' by those in control of the mass media (many of whom, in the early days of broadcasting, had had very clear educational strategies, which sometimes had a Christian basis).

The churches' struggle to maintain control over the transmission of the faith has also centred round the issue of control of the family. As previous chapters have indicated, the family became a major focus of Christian concern after the sixteenth century, partly out of a recognition of its importance in socialising the next generation of Christians. As the church's control over public life waned, its concern to regulate domestic life increased. The result has been an intensification of the relationship between Christianity and the family. So tight has the bond become that the western churches' claim to wider sociopolitical significance has now come to rest in large part upon their self-presentation as defenders of 'family values' against the acids of modernity. The results in terms of individual commitment to Christianity have been mixed. On the one hand, more conservative forms of Christianity have benefited from the retention or even the recruitment of those who support the values of domesticity and wish to uphold the 'traditional family'. On the other hand, the identification of Christianity with family values may have alienated subjectivised selves who believe in 'freedom of choice' in relation to sexual and 'lifestyle' choices. The churches' defence of the family also prevented them from giving support to the cause of women's enfranchisement (until it was a *fait accompli*), thereby rendering them unattractive to some of those who accept and support this change.

The varying fortunes of different types of Christianity

Secularisation has not been uniform within modern Christianity, and different types of church have experienced significantly different rates of growth and decline since the 1960s. Broadly speaking, it is the non-voluntarist churches which have suffered most, while the voluntarist churches have fared rather better. The varied fortunes of the churches appear to relate quite closely to the extent to which they have been able to adjust their long-standing commitment to power from on high to accommodate the subjective turn.

NON-VOLUNTARY CHURCHES

The decline of non-voluntarist Christianity of both Catholic and Protestant forms in the west has been greater than that of any other variety of Christianity. Indeed, the decline of the 'mainline' churches (a category that largely overlaps with that of the historically non-voluntarist churches) has been so dramatic that it accounts for a good part of the total decline of Christianity in the west since the 1960s.

Of all the non-voluntary churches, it is the state churches that have in many ways suffered the most. When a state church loses its central role in society it loses something of its soul. After the 1960s, the remaining privileges of state churches, such as the Church of England and the Church of Sweden, came to be widely criticised, from within as well as without. If the protest was muted, that was simply because it was increasingly apparent that the power such privileges secured had become vestigial. Given the rapid decline of the state churches after the 1960s, the

347

retention of established status began to appear counter-productive. They suffered not merely from the fact that the alliance between religion and politics that was their birthright was now widely viewed as unacceptable, but because their equally close and long-standing alliance with the social status quo proved a liability once the latter came under attack. For those baby-boomers who embraced the ideals of the counter-culture, the churches appeared to be part of the 'square', 'respectable', 'straight', 'uncool' society against which they were rebelling. Attendance figures suggest that, once baby-boomers stopped being brought to church by their parents, many simply ceased to attend. Given that deference to God, to the political authorities, to the established social order, to the clergy and to one's elders and betters had always been central for these churches, the decline of deference hit them head on.

But the state churches were not the only ones to suffer. Decline was as severe for many non-established mainline churches in Europe and the USA, including the Methodists, Presbyterians, Congregationalists and – increasingly after 1980 – the Roman Catholics in countries where they did not enjoy a religious monopoly. What all these churches had in common was that they had non-voluntaristic histories, especially in Europe, but did not enjoy the benefits of formal or informal political establishment. Like the state churches, they were perceived by the post-1960s generations as belonging to an 'old order' from which many people now dissociated themselves; but, unlike the state churches, they did not even have the benefits of residual establishment to fall back on. For, although state churches might now have few active members, they still retained vast historic wealth, access to public power and publicity, a virtual monopoly on life rituals such as baptisms and funerals, and a residual civic role in many towns, cities and villages. To some extent, they were therefore cushioned from the harsher effects of secularisation and could afford to stay open, even if few attended.

This is not to imply that non-voluntarist Christianity remained internally unchanged during the twentieth century. While retaining a broadly conservative stance in their respect for established hierarchies of authority in both church and society, many mainline churches nevertheless liberalised to such a degree that they are now often referred to as 'liberal' or 'liberal-mainline'. Such liberalisation involved, above all, 'humanisation' – a turn away from divine transcendence to 'the human' and human values. God was humanised, and his forbidding severity thoroughly transmuted into a warm, fatherly love; Jesus became a personal friend and saviour; and human goodness and dignity attracted a good deal more emphasis than human sinfulness. (The development of liberal theology is considered in more detail in the section that follows.) In the process, mainline Christianity ceased to be confessional and dogmatic and became broadly ethical in emphasis. To be a liberal Christian now had less to do with adherence to dogmatic formulations than with living a loving, caring and unselfish life. Traditional liturgies were revised in order to reflect these changes, not least by giving more space for 'human' participation. Even Roman Catholicism liberalised in a humanistic fashion, most notably through the innovations that were introduced by the Second Vatican Council (1962–5).

Though it has sometimes been claimed that the liberalisation of non-voluntarist Christianity has been the cause of its rapid decline after the 1960s, it is equally plausible to suggest that the problem lies in the limited and qualified nature of such liberalisation. The mainline churches' continuing attachment to power from on high is evident not only in aspects of their historic liturgies and in the architecture and decoration of their buildings, but in their residual alliances with social power, and their own institutional arrangements. In the latter, for example, a hierarchy of priests continues to dominate 'the laity', with women either being excluded from ordination altogether or allowed access only to the lower rungs of the clerical ladder. The claim to treat all human beings as equals and to defend human rights is undermined by such limitations. What is more, while the mainline churches have partially embraced the subjective turn's commitment to individual autonomy and rights, they have not embraced the turn to inner freedom, self-development and well-being. They have not, in other words, been able or willing to place the unique individual centre stage and devote their energies to catering for individual spiritual growth. They have allied themselves with the more self-sacrificial ideal of service to every member of humanity, but not with the self-empowering ideal of helping each person explore his or her own unique spiritual path.

Thus mainline Christianity may have suffered so greatly because it has fallen between two stools. On the one hand, it has remained too allied with power from on high to attract those subjectivised selves who came to maturity during or after the 1960s, while on the other it has alienated a potentially sympathetic socially and morally conservative constituency by becoming too liberal in its teachings. Nevertheless, some of the entrenched advantages of many state churches, mentioned above, continue to work to their advantage. In addition, the mainline churches' record of public service, care in and for the community, and ability to make significant political interventions is impressive. The latter relates, of course, to the historic role and self-understanding of these churches as responsible not only for the welfare of their own members, but for that of the whole of society.

VOLUNTARIST BIBLICISM

During the same period that the non-voluntarist churches were experiencing precipitous decline, many voluntarist biblicist churches were holding their own or even growing. What is more, it was some of the more conservative forms of biblicism that seemed to be doing the best, despite the fact that they consciously set their faces against liberalism, humanism, 'secular modernity' and the general direction of late modern society.

The obvious conclusion was that their success was the result of their opposition to the subjective turn, but closer examination of the evidence suggests that this is only half the story. For in many ways voluntarist biblicism has proved extremely compatible with late modern society, not least in its voluntaristic stance. The idea that each and every individual is directly responsible for his or her religious commitment and must make a free choice for or against God has proved immediately congenial to the modern democratic ethos. So too has the idea that each individual is responsible for his or her own salvation and has direct and unmediated access to saving truth via the Bible, without the need of priests, theologians or other experts. In addition, evangelicalism (the most important trajectory of voluntarist biblicism in the modern west) has proved wholly compatible with the capitalist ethos of late modernity. Far from objecting to this economic system, many forms of evangelicalism promised to aid their followers in reaping the rewards it could offer (whether directly, by way of 'material blessings' from God, or indirectly, by inculcating capitalist virtues of hard work, honesty, thrift, self-help, responsibility, enterprise and so on). Evangelicalism also proved itself compatible with both nationalistic sentiment (particularly in the USA) and a more international, globalised ethos (pan-evangelicalism). Perhaps most importantly of all, voluntarist biblicism accommodated the subjective turn in its fullest sense by offering believers direct, subjective experience of God and the promise that this would stabilise, vivify, enhance and reconstruct their inner lives.

Yet, far from capitulating to late modernity, voluntarist biblicism also offered its followers a refuge from some of the most challenging and destabilising aspects of late capitalist living. In the face of rapid change it offered the security of a God and a religion that were said to be timeless and unchanging – for evangelicalism presents itself as based solely and directly upon the timeless truth of God presented in the Bible, and as an instantiation of the pristine form of early Christian community exemplified in the New Testament. In a 'postmodern' age, which claimed to be sceptical of absolute truth and bound to accept the value of all cultures, voluntarist biblicism therefore offered certainty and security about truth and falsehood, right and wrong, and a basis on which white, Anglo-Saxon culture could assert itself against multi-cultural alternatives. So far as the individual was concerned, the evangelical belief that God has a 'plan' for each and every person, and that everything that happens in life happens for a reason, provided a framework for containing the risks and anxieties that accompany the collapse of traditional social structures and secure employment prospects. By offering very clear and direct ethical teachings about the proper roles and duties of individual men and women, voluntaristic biblicism also offered a clear road map for dealing with moral complexity, and a reassuring alternative to the highly demanding subjectivist ideal that each and every individual should be responsible for discovering his or her own life path.

Such moral direction was clearest in relation to the family and gender roles. Building on its Reformation heritage, twentieth-century evangelicalism identified family values with gospel values and affirmed the sanctity of marriage and the necessity of male headship. Building on its nineteenth-century heritage, however, it denied that women should simply be mastered and dominated by men, and affirmed a doctrine of separate spheres and roles for the sexes, in which women have prime responsibility for domestic matters and an equal share in responsibility for the spiritual well-being of their household. Opposition to sex outside marriage, homosexuality, promiscuity, feminism, abortion and the confusion of gender roles became an increasingly important aspect of evangelical identity and its 'witness' against wider society.

The evangelical defence of the family intensified after the 1970s, in response to the challenges to traditional gender roles that were noted at the start of this chapter. So serious was the threat felt to be that the most socially withdrawn form of evangelicalism, fundamentalism, was provoked to take a public, political stand. As Jerry Falwell, the founder of the Moral Majority, explained in the central section of *Listen, America!* (1980):

> In the past twenty years a tremendous change has taken place [in the structure of the family] . . .
> The Equal Rights Amendment [1972] strikes at the foundation of our entire social structure . . .
> Most Americans remain deeply committed to the idea of the family as a sacred institution. A minority of people in this country is trying to destroy what is most important to the majority . . .
> Feminists are saying that self-satisfaction is more important than the family . . .
> The Domestic Violence Prevention and Treatment Act could establish a federal bureaucracy to intervene in matters relating to a husband and wife . . .

In its concluding part, the book states the positive goals of the Moral Majority movement:

> We must stand against the Equal Rights Amendment, the feminist revolution, and the homosexual revolution . . .
> Right living must be established as an American way of life . . . The authority of Bible morality must once again be recognized as the legitimate guiding principle of our nation.

Falwell's words were addressed to 'moral Americans' who 'still believe in decency, the home, the family, morality, the free enterprise system, and all the great ideals that are the cornerstone of this nation'. The defence of American values and the defence of family values went hand in hand. Subsequent rallying points for evangelical campaigning and direct action have included the continuing practice of abortion, the introduction of marriage services for gay couples, and the ordination of homosexuals.

Fundamentalism

Though it emerged on the public stage in the 1980s, fundamentalism had been gathering strength throughout the twentieth century.

Its origins date back to a series of widely circulated publications on 'The Fundamentals: A Testimony to the Truth', written by conservative Protestant theologians and biblical scholars in Britain and America between 1910 and 1915. The first leaders of fundamentalism tended to be well-educated Christian scholars and theologians from colleges, universities and seminaries in North America, whose interests were being threatened by a number of interlinked developments, including the dominance of liberalism in the churches, the rise of the 'secular' university, the discoveries of science, the widening of the franchise, the rise of multiculturalism and the campaign for women's rights.

The fundamentalists made their stand on the 'plain truth' of scripture. Far from rejecting science *tout court*, they sought to establish the Bible as a book with scientific dependability. Where scientific discovery deviated from the 'literal truth' of scripture, the latter must prevail. It was this belief that led fundamentalists to defend 'creationism' (the belief that God created the world in seven days, as reported in the book of Genesis) against Darwinian evolution, and that led to the notorious Scopes Trial of 1925, in which an attempt to ban the teaching of evolutionary theory in schools was defeated. In practice, the 'plain truth' of scripture was scripture interpreted according to a very particular understanding transmitted by authorised preachers, commentators and teachers in the churches and schools and colleges that developed throughout the twentieth century to support what became a distinctive fundamentalist subculture in the United States.

Central to the fundamentalist scheme of interpretation was a framework of 'dispensational premillenialism', whose origins can be traced back to the work of the British writer and church leader John Nelson Darby (1800–82), leader of the proto-fundamentalist group commonly known as the Plymouth Brethren. Darby's scheme was consolidated by Cyrus Ingerson Scofield (1843–1921), whose immensely influential Bible with dispensationalist commentary (the *Scofield Reference Bible*) was published in 1902. Premillenialism represented a clear break with the optimistic 'postmillenial' views of much nineteenth-century Protestantism that maintained that continuous improvement on earth would lead to the return of Christ and his glorious reign on earth for a thousand years. By contrast, premillenialists took a much more pessimistic view of the world, predicting that Christ would return to earth before the millennium and gather the saved into heaven in the 'rapture' before defeating the forces of evil that remained on earth. Thereafter the saints would reign with him in glory for a thousand years (the millennium). By reading the Bible in terms of this scheme, fundamentalists treat both Old and New Testaments as equally authoritative parts of a unified historical narrative in which world history is divided into a succession of seven 'dispensations'. They secure a totally encompassing ethic and metaphysic in which every aspect of reality receives an explanation, every event of history gains meaning, and every aspect of public and personal life is understood as under God's direct control.

Twentieth-century evangelicalism

Despite the publicity it has received, fundamentalism has remained a relatively small movement within Christianity, largely confined to North America. Its voice continues to be heard and to exercise an important influence within American Christianity, not least by turning the dial of what counts as authentically 'biblicist' Christianity to an extreme setting. But it is the much broader and more moderate trajectory of evangelical Christianity, whose origins were traced in chapter 5, that has proved the more successful form of voluntaristic biblicism – indeed, the most successful of all varieties of Christianity in the twentieth century.

The most remarkable feature of evangelicalism has been its ability to reinvent itself without appearing to sacrifice its integrity. The icon and the undisputed, though unofficial, leader of a revivified twentieth-century evangelicalism was Billy Graham (1918–). Graham's evangelicalism was significantly different from that of his nineteenth- and early twentieth-century predecessors: less individualistic, more socially engaged, and more open to the findings of modern science. It was pragmatic, relatively unconcerned about denominational, national and racial difference, and chastened in its optimism about western superiority and inevitable progress. All this was new. Yet traditional emphases remained, including a reliance upon scripture, an emphasis on the importance of conversion, evangelism and the atoning work of Christ, and a belief in family values. Graham's method of evangelism by means of huge rallies held across the globe was also in continuity with that of his evangelical predecessors, though it made use of the latest technology and techniques. Like his predecessors, Graham called participants to 'come forward' and give their lives to Jesus. His achievement was to make the old new without obvious compromise.

Such evangelicalism survived and flourished throughout the tumultuous closing decades of the twentieth century (though there is some emerging evidence of a serious slowdown in growth and even of decline after the late 1980s). It has done well not only in North America, but in much of Europe as well. In both places it has managed to appeal to all sectors of society but, above all, to the middle classes – from the relatively poor to the extremely affluent. It has also managed to adapt to the needs of some baby-boomers' children, 'Generation X', not least through the establishment of 'new paradigm' mega-churches such as those of the Vineyard Christian Fellowship, founded by John Wimber. Such churches openly welcome 'seekers', and allow debate and discussion about the gospel. They minimise all traces of power from on high, reducing clerical hierarchies and liturgical formalities to a minimum. (Small groups play a key role.) There is even some relaxation of teaching relating to gender roles, with a broad acceptance of women's entrance into the workplace and of sexual equality – so long as the family does not suffer. Yet, while making the individual the focus of its proclamation and its offer of salvation, evangelicalism continues to situate the self very firmly and securely within the context of God, the church community and the family. It offers far more by way of guidance, shelter and support than more fully subjectivised forms of religion and spirituality (see below). Thus the success of much voluntarist biblicism in late capitalism appears to lie in its ability to combine 'the best of both worlds' – a world of power from on high and a world of power from below. In direct contrast to liberal Christianity, which 'falls between two stools', evangelicalism has managed to accommodate the subjective turn, and to reconcile it successfully with a framework of power from on high.

With regard to subjectivisation, evangelicalism speaks directly to the individual, offering him or her intense, healing, soothing, empowering, life-changing experiences of the divine. Such experience comes to a climatic point in conversion, but is sustained thereafter by the ever-present experience of the Spirit of Christ guiding and sustaining life in every detail (even to the extent of providing parking spaces). This experiential stress has intensified since the 1970s, largely under the influence of the movement of 'charismatic renewal', which is reviewed at the end of this chapter. The most successful forms of evangelicalism in the west are now those that have accommodated such 'Holy Spirit' Christianity and have become charismatic-evangelical rather than simply evangelical.

355

Plate 25 Willow Creek Community Church, suburbs of Chicago
'New paradigm' evangelical churches such as Willow Creek abandon many of the traditional features associated with churches in order to become more accessible and welcoming
to modern men and women. In this central meeting area people gather before or after a
Sunday service to chat, eat brunch, or grab a coffee.

They have also accommodated the subjectivist turn of post-'60s culture,
not least in the adoption of a therapeutic language and ethos and in their
increasing stress upon the provision of personal spiritual well-being.
The former is evident in the growth of 'biblical counselling', and in
the proliferation of small groups in evangelical churches, many of them
catering explicitly for a range of personal problems (from sexual abuse to
lack of self-confidence). The latter is evident in the increasingly common
evangelical offer of enhanced health and well-being for body, mind and
spirit.

Yet this emphasis on empowerment from below does not displace a
wider framework of power from on high. The evangelical God remains
a male God of supreme power, the maker and disposer of all things, who
controls every event and the whole course of history from moment to
moment. He still provides very clear guidelines and roles for those who

follow him, all of which must be obeyed. True, he waits for his will to be voluntarily embraced, but it is still he who gives the grace to obey and he who overwhelms the sinful individual will. Salvation consists in surrender, and humanity remains mired in sin. Thus evangelicalism still supports a negative rather than a positive subjectivism, and remains highly suspicious of individual self-authorisation. Ultimately the rules of God and the rules of the Bible are there to be obeyed, not to be argued with. Evangelicalism also tends to remain wedded to patriarchal imagery, reinforcing the idea of fatherly leadership through its invocations of God, even when it relaxes its more explicit teachings about male headship.

Though this ability to combine the best of both worlds has served evangelicalism well, it has not been successful enough to stem the overall decline of Christian churchgoing in the west since the 1970s. It may be that both evangelicalism and fundamentalism appeal to niche markets. Those who reject external authority in a more thoroughgoing way are not likely to be attracted. Those who are disillusioned with the 'traditional' family and sympathetic to feminism are likely to be hostile. Such 'subjectivists' have at least three options: they may reject religion altogether, they may embrace some form of 'alternative' spirituality, or they may turn to a more intensely subjectivised, spiritualist form of Christianity.

VOLUNTARIST SPIRITUALISM

Despite long decline throughout the confessional period, often under conditions of persecution or social and political disadvantage, spiritualist forms of Christianity staged something of a revival in the late twentieth century. Since the 1980s, for example, attendance at Quaker meetings in several western countries has registered a sharp increase, though the total numbers involved remain tiny. Generally speaking, it is those forms of radical Christian voluntarism that have subjectivised the most that have tended to do best, while those that have merely humanised (such as some Unitarian congregations) have done less well. Of all the main varieties of Christianity, it is voluntarist spiritualism that can most easily accommodate the subjective turn, since its historic resources predispose it to privilege inner, experiential authority over outer, external forms of authority. Given its historical marginalisation, however, this spiritual option remains highly under-resourced within the Christian domain.

357

Particularly since the 1980s, those seeking personal spiritual growth and wary of authoritarian forms of religion have been more likely to embrace 'alternative', post-Christian forms of spirituality than to pursue Christian ones. There has been an explosion of such spirituality since the 1980s, in both Europe and America, and growth is continuing. In some cases such spirituality is institutionalised in small groups; in others it is offered on a one-to-one basis with a practitioner offering spiritual guidance to a paying client. Such spirituality ranges from New Age to indigenised eastern religions, to yoga or reiki. (The menu of options changes regularly, keeping pace with changing fashions.) The common denominator in such alternative spirituality is its highly subjectivised nature. The individual is the focus of attention, and the object of the advice, rituals and techniques on offer is to help each person discover his or her unique spiritual profile and path. Authentic spirituality can be based only on the subject's own authentic experience, not on anything imposed from outside. Far from being individualised or atomised, however, such spirituality is 'holistic' at two levels: first, it treats the 'whole person', composed of body, mind and spirit; second, it aims for a harmonious relationship not only between the separate elements of the person, but between self and others. 'Holistic relationship' is thus the ultimate goal of all such contemporary spirituality.

Particularly in the United States, there appears to be some significant overlap between alternative spirituality and more spiritualised forms of Christianity. The overlap became clear at the start of the twentieth century in the revival of interest in 'mysticism', where personal experience of union with the divine was taken to be the common denominator in all religions, both Christian and non-Christian. Books such as Evelyn Underhill's *Mysticism* (1911) sold well, as did William James's more scientific exploration of *The Varieties of Religious Experience* (1902). In this early phase the revival of interest in Christian spirituality was most evident among members of the mainline, non-voluntarist churches, including the Roman Catholic. In the latter, one of its most influential spokesmen was Baron Friedrich von Hügel (1852–1925), who published *The Mystical Element in Religion* in 1908.

After the Second World War spiritualist versions of Christianity became less concerned with the past than with the present, and less interested in the corporate and liturgical dimensions of spiritual experience than in spirituality as a form of individual self-development. A notable expression was Norman Vincent Peale's *The Power of Positive Thinking* (1952), which remains one of the best-selling books of all times. While Peale, an evangelical minister, was concerned with the ways in which spirituality could improve both the external and internal aspects of an individual's life, later books have tended to place more stress on achieving inner spiritual serenity and well-being. Recent best-selling examples of such subjectivised quasi-Christian spiritual guidance include *A Course in Miracles* (1975) and M. Scott Peck's *The Road Less Travelled* (1978). Other best-selling authors, such as Deepak Chopra, draw on both Christian and non-Christian spiritual resources and ideas and offer a universalist form of spiritualism.

Most 'official' Christian churches remain hostile to or dismissive of subjectivised spirituality, whether Christian or non-Christian. The Vatican has issued repeated denunciations of New Age, for example, condemning it as a modern variant of the gnostic heresy. Nevertheless, it is interesting to note the development of a number of successful 'pockets' of spiritualist Christianity within both voluntarist and non-voluntarist forms of Christianity in the late twentieth century, all of which direct attention to individuals' unique spiritual growth. One of the best examples is the increase in the popularity of spiritual retreats and one-to-one spiritual direction. The rise of small groups connected to evangelical (and other) churches has already been noted, and such groups are well adapted to individual spiritual self-expression and growth-in-relationship. Both cathedral worship and Orthodox worship are also doing well in the west. They offer a highly aesthetic liturgical context in which individuals are free to think their own thoughts, pray their own prayers and experience God in their own ways. Similarly, the number of people who say that they visit churches and cathedrals to 'find some space' for themselves and to get in touch with the spiritual dimension of experience also appears to be growing. In these and other ways, individuals are making use of a selective range of aspects of traditional Christian practice in order to support personal spiritual pilgrimages. They would rather 'do it my way' than be told what that way should be, but their belief in the sacred remains.

The fact that women are over-represented in subjectivised forms of religion and spirituality is undoubtedly significant. In the milieu of holistic spirituality, for example, recent evidence suggests that women make up around 80 per cent of both practitioners and clients. Women's

Plate 26   Statue of Norman Vincent Peale in the Crystal Cathedral, Los Angeles

The Crystal Cathedral in Los Angeles keeps Peale's gospel of self-help alive, promising that God will reward those who help him, themselves and one another. Here the Christian message helps sacralise prosperity, capitalism, the self – and the 'American dream'.

long-standing preponderance within spiritualist forms of Christianity has also been noted several times in the course of this volume. The reasons are not hard to find, for, while women have traditionally been excluded from positions of power in the majority of the Christian churches, and continue to be so in many of them, such restrictions are absent in the realm of 'the Spirit'. Here women achieve empowerment on equal terms with men, both in theory and in practice. What is more, in the realm of holistic spirituality in particular, the widespread Christian sanctification of women's domestic role is generally absent. Women are freed to 'be what they want to be', and to draw upon sacred power in the difficult task of reconstructing their individuality outside the supportive but constricting confines of traditional female roles. In some forms of mystical spirituality, God is also spoken of in a female register, and imagined in ways that subvert established expectations of male power from on high.

The displacement of theology

As well as losing social power in modern times, Christianity lost cultural power. At the same time that the churches were becoming more marginal to political and economic affairs, theology was being sidelined in modern culture. Where once Christianity had been central in shaping western thought, it now had to take its place alongside a growing number of competing cultural influences. Its loss of status was evident in its reduced institutional space. In the medieval system of higher education theology had been 'the queen of the sciences'. In the modern university it sometimes had to fight even to be admitted into a liberal curriculum. The status of theologians fell accordingly. Where once a degree in theology had opened doors to the most lucrative and powerful careers in the land, now it was the theologians' old rivals the lawyers who were more likely to enjoy such privileges – as well as holders of new technical-managerial degrees. By the twenty-first century the adjective 'theological' was used in popular parlance to refer to something arcane and irrelevant.

THE CHALLENGE TO THEOLOGY

The displacement of theology was serious for Christianity not only because it has been a deeply theological religion from the start, but because the early modern, confessional phase of its history made it more so. Theological definition became central to Christian identity. The more the churches lost social political and economic power, the more cultural power and precision became important to them. Since being a Christian could no longer mean simply belonging to a Christian society, it must now mean believing certain things. So closely did the churches identify with their theological confessions that an attack on the one constituted an attack on the other (see ch. 6).

From the seventeenth century through to the nineteenth, both Protestants and Catholics produced systematic works of dogmatic theology that were central to the tasks of teaching, training and articulating confessional Christianity. This was knowledge from on high with a vengeance. One of the earliest systematic statements of the Lutheran position was that of Abraham Calovius (1612–86), professor of theology at Wittenberg. He began to produce his twelve-volume *System of Theological Themes* in 1655. An equivalent expression of Calvinist orthodoxy was made by the professor of theology at Geneva, Francis Turretin (1623–87), whose extensive *System of Polemical Theology* defended the doctrine of double predestination and other elements of Calvinist thought. Equally influential for the Reformed tradition was the *Compendium of Christian Theology* published by Johannes Wollebius (1586–1629) in 1626.

The Catholics, sheltered from attack by the protective walls of a defensive church, produced systematic works of confessional theology right up to the twentieth century. Though there was often little variation in substance between them, manuals of theology were produced by Catholic theologians in colleges, universities and seminaries across the world. Some of the earliest, such as Juan de Torquemada's *Summa de Ecclesia* (1450), were written to prove Catholicism's superiority to other religions (in the Spanish context). After the Reformation a host of others, such as Robert Stapleton's *Principiorum Fidei Doctrinalium Demonstratio* (1579), were written to defend Catholic truth against Protestant critics. As atheism as well as Protestantism began to launch an attack on the Catholic church, *summa confessorum* became increasingly common, sometimes under the heading of 'fundamental theology'. There was also a massive production of manuals of moral theology, for which the Jesuit Juan Azor's *Institutiones Morales* (1600) provided a model. Under fortress Catholicism the production of manuals of confessional theology reached a peak. Some of the more widely used included Ignatius Ottiger's *Theologia Fundamentalis* (1897), Adolfe

Tanquerey's *Synopsis Theologia Fundamentalis* (1896), and the manuals and compendia of moral theology produced by such nineteenth- and early twentieth-century authors as Jean-Pierre Gury, Jerome Noldin, Albert Schmitt, Friederike Heinzel, Benoît-Henri Merkelbach and Dominic Prümmer.

Today such works are largely forgotten. They are read neither by Protestants nor by Catholics, and certainly not by non-Christians. They are not referred to by contemporary theologians, and they have been excluded from most textbooks of Christian theology. What was once central to the post-Reformation theological enterprise has now become marginal. The enormous confidence that underlay these works of systematic theology – that each confession possessed the truth in its essentials, that this truth could be given clear and systematic expression, that it could furnish an impregnable worldview, and that the faithful must submit to it – faltered in the face of growing challenges.

The most important challenge came from what may broadly be called the empirical method. Confessional theology was done 'from above' rather than 'from below'. Its method was to begin with revealed dogma, as that was embodied in scripture and authoritative confessional statements, and to draw out in systematic fashion its implications for understanding God, man and the world. After the seventeenth century this approach was threatened not only by direct attack but by the growing prestige of alternative, empirical methods. The latter reversed the scheme of understanding, so that thought began with human experience and worked upwards towards higher truths. The confessional theological method began with faith and explored it by way of reason, whereas the empirical method began with reason and tested faith. In philosophy, René Descartes (1596–1650) has become the symbol of this reversal. Instead of beginning by trusting in revelation, he began by doubting everything. From this starting point he built up a scheme of knowledge on the basis of what he found to be the one indubitable truth, the truth of his own cognitive activity: *cogito ergo sum*. Having established his own existence to his satisfaction, he then worked back up to establish the existence of the world and of God. The final scheme of knowledge that Descartes offered turned out to be fairly conservative. What was new was the method by which he arrived at it.

Descartes was a rationalist; that is to say, he worked with a method that privileged human reason and treated clear and distinct 'ideas' as the building blocks of knowledge. Rationalism was challenged by a more radical method still, that of philosophical empiricism. The Scottish Enlightenment philosopher David Hume (1711–76) developed the position, well aware of its implications for religion. He questioned the status of 'ideas' by arguing that they were nothing more than the impressions left in the mind by repeated sensation. Far from being an elegant rational mechanism filled with universal ideas, the mind was a *tabula rasa* whose concepts were built up by the constant impact of sensation. The repeated experience of seeing and feeling a chair, for example, built up the idea of a chair. Since all true knowledge came by way of experience, all true knowledge must be tested by way of experience. The consequences for traditional religion were ominous. If we work solely on the basis of our experience of the world, Hume argued in the *Dialogues Concerning Natural Religion* (1752), we cannot possibly infer that a wise and good deity created it, since it contains far too much suffering and evil. Likewise, we can never believe a miracle such as the resurrection, since a miracle is a violation of a natural law, and what we speak of as a natural law is simply a repeated experience of a regular connection between two events. A single experience of a lack of connection can never overturn the repeated experience of connection that established the 'law' in the first place.

The empiricist challenge was vastly strengthened by the rapid growth in the power and prestige of the scientific enterprise after the sixteenth century. This, combined with technological progress, gave a practical rather than a merely philosophical demonstration of the efficacy of the empirical method. For modern science was based on an approach that began with observation, developed a hypothesis to explain an observed regularity, and tested the hypothesis by way of experiment. And it seemed to work. Science delivered not only new ways of understanding the world, but more effective techniques for living in the world. It was hard to argue with Newton's laws, or with smallpox vaccination, the steam engine, or electricity.

Both science and philosophy therefore challenged the very basis of confessional theology. Their challenge was primarily methodological and epistemological. They made knowledge from below seem the norm, and knowledge from above the anomaly. In many ways this methodological challenge was more significant than the substantive challenge to Christian belief posed by particular scientific discoveries such as heliocentrism or the vast age of the Earth. Such discoveries might cause an initial flurry of Christian disquiet, but most could be accommodated without too much difficulty. Thus a pattern emerged whereby theology would cede a little bit of its former territory to science, then move on. Christians still believed science and theology to be compatible enterprises, the one dealing with the laws of nature, the other with the laws of God. But with each threatening discovery there was always the possibility that some Christians would be left behind, unwilling to concede to science a particularly important element of biblical or doctrinal belief. As we have seen above, the Darwinian theory of evolution led to such an outcome when those who refused to abandon belief in the biblical account of creation separated themselves off from the 'liberal' mainstream. Most theologians, however, accepted Darwin with relative ease by viewing the Genesis stories as mythological – vivid, poetic presentations of deep spiritual truths – and by arguing that God must have created the world by means of evolution.

It was not only the natural sciences that challenged theology. The human sciences and the social sciences also had an impact. In relation to the former, it was the new methods of 'modern', 'critical' history, developed after the seventeenth century, that first posed a threat. Whereas church history since Eusebius had been written from above, the new historians began to write history from below. The former had assumed that the prime mover in history was divine action. The new historical method gradually abandoned this hypothesis without any apparent loss of explanatory power. Events could be just as well, perhaps rather better, explained solely in terms of this-worldly factors. The most controversial application of this new approach was to the scriptures themselves. The 'historical critical' method of biblical interpretation, as it came to be called, was slowly accepted by many Protestant denominations over the course of the nineteenth century. In Roman Catholicism it was banned until the 1940s.

By the later part of the twentieth century, theology was also being challenged by the so-called scientific study of religion, an approach that encompassed the sociology, anthropology and psychology of religion, and gave rise to the umbrella discipline of 'religious studies'. This was yet another symptom of the ever-widening application of the scientific method. With the rise of the social sciences in the late nineteenth century, theology's domain shrank yet again. At the start of the modern revolution it had still been the authoritative voice on God, man and the world. Now the world was claimed by the natural sciences. Humanity was first claimed by 'the humanities', particularly by history, and then by psychology as well. And to top it all, the social sciences now staked their claim to expertise in relation to human society. In the process they also turned their attention to 'religion'. Indeed, Max Weber (1864–1920) and Emile Durkheim (1858–1917) – as well as some of their predecessors – were centrally concerned with religion, not least with the decline of the churches in modern societies. The Christian religion and Christian theology became objects of scrutiny from a variety of angles, many of them hostile.

THEOLOGICAL RESPONSES IN THE EIGHTEENTH AND NINETEENTH CENTURIES: THE LIBERAL TURN

The empirical challenge left theology with a number of options. One of the most attractive was to accept that knowledge from below had its place – in relation to the natural world – but to maintain the right of theology to deal with the more important questions about God and man. This broadly 'liberal' approach recognised the validity of the new sciences, but sought a harmonious co-existence between them and theology. The liberal position was worked out in a number of different ways, some of which retained conservatism in relation to the core theological enterprise.

Ethical liberalism

One of the most influential attempts to separate religious from scientific knowledge in order to protect both parties was that of the philosopher Immanuel Kant. In a famous passage in his *Groundwork of the Metaphysics of Morals* (1785), Kant raised the question of the authority of Jesus Christ. 'Even the Holy One of the gospel', he argued, 'must first be compared with our ideal of moral perfection before we can realise him to be such.'[4] In a single sentence Kant isolated the nub of the issue that would separate what would come to be thought of as the liberal theological position from the conservative one. For the latter, the truth of Christianity was based on the authority of God, before which human reason had simply to submit in faith. For the former, human reason must judge even the authority of God, for how else could authority be recognised as such? Those of a conservative bent viewed the liberal position as arrogant: who was man to judge God? Those of a liberal frame of mind might reply that they had no intention of comparing man to God; they were simply pointing out that human beings must use their God-given reason to distinguish between truth and mere superstition.

Kant's own position arose as much from his understanding of the limitations of the human mind as from an over-confidence in its abilities. Like Hume, from whom he had learned a great deal, Kant believed that the human mind was reliable only when it was processing sense data. Kant disagreed with Hume, however, by suggesting that the mind contained innate ideas – such as those of time and space – that allowed it to attain reliable knowledge of the world. When it came to the supernatural rather than the natural world, however, Kant believed that the human mind was not qualified to deliver knowledge, since no sense data were available. Here human beings had to walk by faith, not by knowledge. But although 'pure reason' would find itself out of its depth, the 'practical' or moral reason could still serve as a guide, for Kant believed that human beings had an innate moral sense, and that it was this that pointed them to the existence of a divine being who must be the ultimate source and guarantor of the moral law. Jesus was worthy of reverence not because he founded a religion – for that was there already in the moral law, engraved on the hearts of men – but because he founded the true church, which was composed of those who recognised and obeyed this law. For Kant, this church was 'invisible', an 'ethical commonwealth' that had no essential connection with the visible religious institutions of mankind.

Kant was attempting to secure faith by distinguishing it from empirical knowledge. If Christianity was primarily a matter of morality, then nothing in this world and nothing that science might discover could touch it in any way. Hume's criticisms could have no purchase, for Christianity had to do with the moral law within rather than with the natural world without. The main strategy of liberal theology, as it developed in the course of the nineteenth century, was to maintain some such division of territory, and the Kantian attempt to reserve the sphere of ethics for theology became a common move. Even for those who never read Kant, the 'moralisation' of Christianity had clear precedents. Pietism, for example, naturally took a moral turn, and placed its emphasis on good deeds and holy lives rather than on metaphysical speculation or dogmatic conformity. (Kant was himself influenced by the Pietist tradition.) In the English-speaking world, the latitudinarian position of the Anglican church had long emphasised morality rather than dogma, believing that the former delivered social cohesion while the latter encouraged dispute and disorder. In the USA, the confident rationalism of the Unitarians delivered a similar message. And the more that modern states distanced themselves from any particular confession and sought the assistance of Christianity in developing national identities based on inclusivism and civility rather than on exclusive identity, the more this ethical liberalism was likely to find itself in a congenial social location.

In the nineteenth century this moralising tendency found expression in a number of *Lives* of Jesus. The pioneer of the genre was Hermann Reimarus (1694–1768). He was followed by D. F. Strauss (1808–74), J. E. Renan (1823–92), Johannes Weiss (1863–1914), Albert Schweitzer (1875–1965), and a host of more popular writers. Influenced by the rise of the modern historical method, all worked not from above, beginning with the Jesus of orthodox Chalcedonian belief, but from below, starting with the documents of the New Testament. Employing a modern historical method, they attempted to strip back to the 'true' historical Jesus, buried behind layers of accretions. They believed that the latter were not limited to the additions of later Christian history, but were built into the New Testament itself by the early communities and writers who produced it. The tendency to discover a teacher of a pure moral gospel behind these sedimentary layers was clearest in Renan, for whom the 'true' Jesus emerged as a man who showed the human race the nature of *la religion absolue* (pure religion) for the first time. This was a purely ethical-spiritual religion, with no external elements whatsoever, whether churches, priests, rituals or dogmas. It found its perfect expression in the Sermon on the Mount, and had been betrayed by the church ever since. For Renan there was no warrant for calling Jesus divine in a Chalcedonian sense. He was, however, divine in the sense that he enabled the human race to take its biggest step towards the divine by imitating him in lives of moral purity.

Like Renan, few liberal theologians were willing to reduce Jesus to a merely human moral teacher. Like Kant, they identified the moral law with the supernatural, and believed that in some way, however vaguely it might be expressed, Jesus transcended this world. Even Albert Schweitzer, who attacked the writers of the liberal *Lives* of Jesus for seeing nothing but their own reflections at the bottom of the historical well, took refuge in a Jesus who was spiritually born in the hearts of men and continued to offer supernatural moral leadership. Though they might be willing to surrender many aspects of the supernatural, liberal theologians were not prepared to detach the sacred from morality. In many cases this led to a drastically reduced faith centred around individual moral sensibility. Another writer of a *Life* of Jesus, Matthew Arnold (1822–88), abandoned belief in miracles, prophecy, atonement, a benevolent creator God, the doctrine of the Trinity, and the ability of the church to deliver the truth, but clung to the 'sweet-reasonableness' of the Jesus of the gospels and the latter's ability to point sincere individuals towards an 'eternal power, not ourselves, that makes for righteousness'.

But the quest for the historical Jesus led some thinkers out of the Christian fold altogether. In his *Essence of Christianity* (1841), Ludwig Feuerbach (1804–72) had argued that God was merely man's ideal of himself projected into the heavens. The most iconoclastic of all the writers of *Lives* of Jesus, Friedrich Nietzsche (1844–1900), went further by pouring scorn upon Christians' refusal to admit that 'God is dead' and that 'we have killed him', and by asserting that individuals must now have the courage to live moral lives without any external support except the affirmation of life itself.

Quite apart from the criticisms of Feuerbach and Nietzsche, the difficulty of formulating an ethical liberalism that could escape the captivity of the individual moral consciousness becomes evident in perhaps the most influential attempt, that of the German Lutheran theologian Albrecht Ritschl (1822–89). The latter focused his theology around the idea of the kingdom of God interpreted as an ethical community. For Ritschl, it was the kingdom, not merely individual righteousness, that was the object of the historical Jesus' proclamation. But what did this kingdom actually amount to? At one level, Ritschl's kingdom was a kind of ideal international ethico-religious spiritual community that would express a worldwide consciousness of human solidarity. Such solidarity, however, could be established only on the basis of a European, Christian and indeed Lutheran culture. That is not to say that Ritschl endorsed nationalism, for, even though he supported Bismarck's creation of a unified German nation, he envisaged the kingdom of God as a check on national sentiment, and advocated an alliance of the sacred with humanity rather than with nationality. Yet in practice Ritschl believed that the nation state would help usher in the moral integration of humanity in the kingdom of God, and that a Lutheran theology of individual moral vocation was its indispensable basis. The effect was to sacralise the existing German socio-economic and political order, and to set it upon a foundation of individual moral endeavour understood in conservative Lutheran terms.

The attempt to reclaim 'society' as an arena of proper theological and Christian concern proved fraught with difficulty. The sociological roots of this difficulty were uncovered by Ernst Troeltsch (1865–1923) in his *The Social Teaching of the Christian Churches* (1912). Taking Ritschl's endeavours as his starting point, Troeltsch pioneered a sociological approach to Christianity to show how the churches' social teachings – or absence of such teachings – related to its shifting relations with social power. Troeltsch argued that there was no such thing as 'Christianity' – only a set of different sociological types, each of which was related to a distinctive social location. If Troeltsch's work made the approach of thinkers such as Ritschl look naive, or at least one-dimensional, that of Karl Marx (1818–83) and his disciples made it look impotent in analytic and practical terms. In their very different ways, both Troeltsch and Marx suggested that the starting point of social analysis must be humanity, not God; empirical data, not dogma; society, not theology. The results of such analysis, immensely more powerful in the hands of a Marx or an Engels than in the social theology of the Protestant or Catholic churches, may have done more to discredit the latter than any explicit critiques of theology did.

Romantic liberalism

The ethical turn was not the only strategy of liberal theology. Ethical liberalism had close ties to humanism and Enlightenment rationalism. The other main stream of liberalism, by contrast, was much more bound up with Romanticism – so much so that it can be referred to as Romantic liberalism. Equally, however, it may be called mystical or spiritualist liberalism, for it also drew on the spiritualist trajectory of Christianity.

Within academic theology, by far the most powerful and influential exponent of Romantic liberalism was the German theologian Friedrich Schleiermacher (1768–1834). In *The Christian Faith* (1821–2), Schleiermacher made clear his deep dissatisfaction with orthodox confessional theology. The latter, he claimed, had betrayed the faith by reducing it to a sterile set of propositions and a system that had little or no real contact with the lives of individuals. It was this external, dogmatic theology that had become identified in many people's minds with Christianity itself, and it was this more than anything else that had led to disillusionment with Christianity. Though attacks on this particular manifestation of Christianity might be valid, they left the true Christian religion untouched. This Schleiermacher identified not with propositional belief but with what he referred to as *schlechthinniges Abhängigkeitsgefühl*, which can be translated as 'a feeling of absolute dependence' or 'a sense of being absolutely dependent'. The latter translation more accurately conveys Schleiermacher's meaning, since what he had in mind was not a fleeting sensation, but an individual's deep-seated and permanent sense of dependence upon something greater that himself or herself. (Schleiermacher maintained women's equal, if not greater, religious sensitivity.) Such a sense of dependence was, Schleiermacher claimed, the true basis of faith – something inward and personal rather than something outer and external.

Yet Schleiermacher did not, as his conservative critics have maintained, reduce faith to a subjective experience. He believed that the subjective experience had an objective correlate in God, even though the latter named a transcendence that it was impossible for the finite human mind to grasp. It was the conservatives' confidence that they could control and comprehend God to which Schleiermacher objected. 'Any possibility of God being in any way *given*', he commented, 'is entirely excluded, because anything that is outwardly given must be an object.'[5] Nor did Schleiermacher reduce the status of Jesus. He was entirely orthodox in his affirmation that 'there is only one source from which all doctrine is derived, namely the self-proclamation of Christ'.[6] The affirmation rested on Schleiermacher's belief that it was only in Christ that the perfect consciousness of God was found in so pure a form that it was appropriate to speak of God existing in him, and to endorse the Chalcedonian statement that he was both God and man. Schleiermacher's theology did not, therefore, rest upon subjective experience but upon God's existence in Jesus Christ, to which Christ bore witness in his teachings, life, death and resurrection.

Schleiermacher's balancing of the subjective and objective elements of faith, and his thoroughgoing Christocentrism, mean that the normal categorisation of him as a theological liberal is problematic. He was in fact one of a handful of modern theologians who cannot be easily slotted into the liberal–conservative scheme. The same can be said of the Danish theologian Søren Kierkegaard (1813–55) who, like Schleiermacher, resisted both orthodox and liberal Lutheran attempts to contain and control God, and identified the gospel with the simple proclamation that God became man and with the existential reception of this ultimate mystery by the individual. For Kierkegaard, this truth negated all merely human attempts to contain the uncontainable mystery of the God-man, before whom the individual must submit body, mind and soul in a humility as great as that seen in God himself.

The difference between Schleiermacher and a more radical form of Romantic liberalism can be appreciated by comparing his teaching with that of the American transcendentalists, of whom Ralph Waldo Emerson (1803–82) was the most influential spokesman. Transcendentalism represented a radicalised form of Unitarianism, much of whose dynamism came from its uncompromising rejection of dogmatic Christianity. To Emerson, who resigned his Unitarian ministry in 1832, even the rational faith of New England Unitarianism appeared 'corpse-cold'. He and his supporters were against everything that confessional Christianity was for: external rituals and dogmas, emphasis upon human sinfulness, rejection of the body and sensuality, other-worldliness. Emerson believed that God should not be thought of as outside the world, or as confined to certain places or certain people (not even Christ), but must be sought in the heart and mind of each individual and in the majesty of nature. In terms of ethics, transcendentalism's watchword was 'self-reliance' as opposed to submission to higher authority. As Emerson put it in an eponymous essay, 'What have I to do with the sacredness of traditions if I live wholly within? . . . Whoso would be a man must be a nonconformist.'

Natural theology

As well as the moral-rational and experiential-romantic strategies that many theologians employed to deal with the empiricist challenge, there was a third approach that remained live during the nineteenth century: 'natural theology'. Natural theology had grown out of early Christian confidence in the scientific enterprise, a confidence based on the belief that the book of nature and the book of God could not contradict each other. In the eighteenth century, theologians such as William Paley (1743–1805) still turned confidently to nature to find evidence of God. Paley's *Natural Theology* (1802) contained numerous examples of wonderful contrivances in nature, which, he argued, could be explained only in terms of the existence of a benevolent creator. For Paley, however, the world was still essentially static. The later nineteenth-century heirs of natural theology worked with an alternative, evolutionary picture.

The theological challenge facing the evolutionary theologians was to reconcile the evolution of the world and the species that inhabited it with the existence of the Christian God. While they claimed to embrace Darwin, they in fact paid little attention to his theory of natural selection by random mutation. Their eyes were fixed, rather, on the spectacle of an unfolding world, moving inexorably from simple, lower forms of life to higher, more complex ones. Their this-worldly millenarianism maintained that God was working his purposes out through this unfolding, and that, far from being a threat to Christian belief, evolutionary theory could be its ally. In reality, however, the outlook of evolutionary theology was probably influenced less by Darwin than by contemporary north Atlantic optimism, grounded on a confidence in the supremacy of 'western civilisation' that was based on its economic and political success. Intellectually, it was fed by the Idealist philosophy, which found its most powerful expression in the work of G. W. F. Hegel (1770–1831), but which had spawned a plethora of academic and popular forms by the late nineteenth century. Such philosophy is called 'Idealist' because it posits the ultimate reality of *Geist* (Spirit, Mind, Idea), of which matter is merely an expression. In nineteenth-century Idealism, as in evolutionary theology, Spirit was thought to unfold in a succession of historical stages, leading towards a final epiphany.

After reaching a peak of popularity around the turn of the century, both Idealism and evolutionary natural theology suffered a spectacular fall from grace. The more cautious had long realised that the yoking together of theology and science would bring trouble. One danger was that the falsification of a scientific theory would bring down the theological system that depended on it. In the end, however, it was not changing scientific paradigms that undermined evolutionary theology so much as a changing cultural mood closely bound up with historical events. Some nineteenth-century Christians, such as the popular British poet Alfred, Lord Tennyson (1809–83), had already understood that Darwinism actually gave more support to a view of nature as amoral, wasteful and 'red in tooth and claw' than to any form of natural theology. As the twentieth century unfolded, more came to share his view.

The appalling loss of life in the First World War may have contributed to this development, but it was not the only factor. Easy confidence in the supremacy of western or Christian civilisation was beginning to be shaken on all sides. The failure of Christian missions to convert the world (discussed below) had an effect. In Europe, a gradual loss of power to the USA, setbacks for colonial empires, economic difficulties and mounting social divisions also played a part. 'Modernist' and avant-garde movements in art, literature and philosophy expressed a new iconoclasm and dissatisfaction with what had gone before. In philosophy, the Logical positivists struck out at Idealism and Christianity, and, in literature and art, 'formalistic', 'contrived' and 'bourgeois' modes of representation gave way to new experimental forms of expression, often consciously designed to shock and unsettle what had gone before.

Generally speaking, the more Christianity and theology had validated the existing status quo – cultural, national, social, gendered and party-political – the more it suffered from this reaction. And the greater the loss of confidence in what had previously passed for western or Christian civilisation, the greater the suffering. Those forms of theology that had been most identified with an optimistic liberal mood were now the most likely to come under attack. Not only evolutionary theology but liberal theology more generally was put on the defensive. Its enemies were not so much the secular avant-garde, who tended to abandon Christianity altogether, but fellow Christian theologians of a conservative hue.

THEOLOGICAL RESPONSES IN THE TWENTIETH AND TWENTY-FIRST CENTURIES: THE CONSERVATIVE TURN

Faced by the empiricist challenge that intensified through the eighteenth and nineteenth centuries, Protestant forms of confessional theology had crumbled. Theology gradually split into a number of sub-disciplines, most of them created in the course of contact with the emerging disciplines of the modern university. Philosophical theology engaged with philosophical critiques of Christianity; biblical studies applied the new historical critical methods to the Bible, and church history made accommodations to the new historical method. Theology 'proper' continued as systematic or dogmatic theology, sometimes in distinction from 'Christian ethics' or 'pastoral theology', sometimes as part of a single enterprise. Only in Roman Catholicism did confessional theology continue to flourish, protected as it was by the walls of its intellectual and institutional fortress. When these walls came down in the 1960s, it disappeared almost overnight.

If creative theological endeavour in the eighteenth and nineteenth centuries had taken a liberal turn in its attempts to cope with the challenge of knowledge from below, in the twentieth century – particularly its second half – this direction was reversed. Now it was liberal theology that found itself on the defensive, and conservatism that was in the ascendant. The change of direction accompanied the crisis of the churches after the 1960s, and reflected their largely defensive stand against the massive subjective turn of the general culture.

Neo-orthodoxy

The most influential spokesman for the conservative turn was the neo-Calvinist theologian, Karl Barth (1886–1968). Barth's achievement was to revivify and reinvent confessional theology in a mode that took full account of the challenges posed by both liberal theology and secular knowledge from below, but that refused to submit to them. A Swiss Reformed pastor and theologian, Barth was well aware of the confessional tradition that had been discarded by the liberal theologians who had taught him as a student. Barth's campaign against the latter and against the entire liberal turn in theology was thoroughgoing and single-minded. It had two elements: the construction of an alternative 'neo-orthodox' theological system, and the reinterpretation of theological history in a way that privileged the conservative cause. After Barth, all modern theology would come to be categorised as either liberal or conservative, with the former being understood as revelation accommodated to modern culture and the latter as revelation true to itself.

Though this loaded interpretation of modern theology is now widely accepted, it is in fact a highly controversial way of dividing up the field, for at least three reasons. First, Protestant theology of the eighteenth and nineteenth centuries was actually much less internally divided than the dichotomy suggests. Second, the categorisation assumed that modern culture and Christian revelation were single, homogeneous entities that stood over against each other, not two internally diverse traditions with a complex history of interactions and interrelations. Third, it collapsed the humanistic and spiritualist trajectories in theology into the single category of liberalism, and overlooked the fact that both had ancient roots in the Christian tradition. Nevertheless, Barth succeeded in presenting liberal theology as a by-product of modernisation rather than as a tradition integral to the Christian repertoire, and in positioning conservative theology as the only authentic form of Christian thought.

While few liberals would deny that they were attempting to restate theology in a way that took account of the challenges posed by modernity, most believed that they were doing so not by accommodating the Christian tradition to modern culture, but by drawing on – and drawing out – central elements of the Christian tradition that had been distorted or neglected by confessionalism. Barth begged to differ. He accused the liberals of beginning with man, not God, and with experience, not revelation. The unfortunate results, he argued, were evident in the weak dilutions of Christian truth with which liberals ended up, and in liberal theology's manifest failure to witness to its age. Barth's attack was personal as well as theological. Not only were liberals wrong; they were also immoral – or, more accurately, their theology was an inadequate defence against sin. Barth attempted to discredit the liberal tradition by drawing attention to his teachers' support for the Kaiser and the First World War, though in fact nearly all the German churches had supported the war.

Barth's black and white view was most powerfully expressed in his early 'dialectical' theology whose manifesto was provided by his *Commentary on Romans* (1918). This theology was called 'dialectical' because it set God against humanity, and conservatism against liberalism, in the most uncompromising way possible. 'Let God be God' was Barth's slogan, and the implication was that God was nothing like man. The early Barth went further than even Calvin in denying any point of contact between God and man – in fact, the theologian to whom he was closest in his early writings was probably Kierkegaard. Like the latter, Barth was reacting against the confidence of contemporary liberal culture with the message that God, as God, was utterly beyond the furthest limits of human comprehension. The only appropriate stance before transcendent power was absolute submission. The most important task of the theologian was therefore to deny and negate all human understandings of God, in order to clear away 'religion' to make way for the living God, who infinitely exceeds all human attempts to grasp hold of him.

But if God has absolutely no connection with human beings, why should he be of any concern to them, and on what basis can the theologian write or the preacher preach? It was in tackling this question that Barth moved into the second, confessional, phase in his theology, expressed over forty-one years in his multi-volume *Church Dogmatics*. Barth's answer was that we can know something of God solely because God is a God who reveals himself in the Word. This Word is made flesh in Christ, in the Bible and in orthodox preaching and teaching. (For Barth, the Holy Spirit was not a separate agent of revelation, but the Spirit of Christ, who enables comprehension of the Word.) Because it is revealed that God reveals himself in Christ, Barth believed that there is nothing of God that is not Christ-like. The theology of the *Church Dogmatics* is Christocentric through and through. Indeed, it is more thoroughly Christocentric than even the Reformed theology to which Barth owed so much. Barth does not begin by investigating the grounds of knowledge of God in terms of the capabilities of the human mind, or the preliminary evidences of God in the world. Or rather, he does begin with this task, but in his hands it becomes an exposition of the Trinity, since epistemology for Barth has to do with God's revelation rather than with human capacity.

Barth's achievement was to accomplish what nineteenth-century liberal theology had also attempted, but to do so by conservative means. Like Kant and Schleiermacher, he sought to place Christian thought on foundations secure enough to make it invulnerable to the challenges of knowledge from below. But he rejected what he regarded as the liberal foundation of inner subjectivity in favour of what he saw as its opposite – objective revelation. Since Barth made such revelation the criterion of truth and the starting point of knowledge, he also made it unfalsifiable and invulnerable. For Barth, both the church and theology were somehow located above both culture and society. The position was famously expressed in the Barmen Declaration of 1934, which was, in effect, a statement of the church's distance from all worldly affairs. Though he rejected the fundamentalists' claim that every word of the Bible was literally true, Barth maintained that its inner truths were inerrant. Like his confessional predecessors, he could therefore begin with revealed dogma, and work down to the world. Like their dogmatic theology, the effect was to enhance not only the power of God but that of the approved interpreters of his Word, most notably 'orthodox' Protestant theologians and clergy. Not surprisingly, it is among these groups that Barth's theology was and is best received. Having been marginalised among the modern disciplines, theology and theologians were given a new injection of confidence by the Barthian programme, which presented theology as the master discipline in relation to which all other disciplines must understand themselves.

The transcendent power that Barth ascribed to Christianity meant, in practice, that the most common stance taken by Barthian theology in relation to modern culture and society was one of lofty critique. In its cruder forms, Barthianism dismissed all so-called liberal theology and all modern culture and society as infected by the hubris of the merely human. 'Liberalism' was said to be the cause of war, fascism, communism, capitalism and all the other evils one might like to select. In the USA Reinhold Niebuhr (1892–1971) offered a more sociologically discriminating statement of the neo-orthodox position. Like Barth, Niebuhr was acutely aware of the inadequacy of theology's often complacent baptism of the social status quo in the Gilded Age. His proposal was for a form of theological 'realism'. It was to be realistic not only in its estimation of human sinfulness – a great theme of the Barthian tradition – but in its analysis of the socio-cultural situation in which it found itself, and in its prescription of Christian 'solutions'. In relation to social affairs the watchword of theological realists such as Niebuhr was no longer love but justice. Christians were to give their energy to opposing evil and injustice rather than to building the kingdom of God on earth – a clear indication of chastened hopes. In the immediate aftermath of the Second World War, such realism bore rich fruits in terms of actual policy. For a short time, Christians of both liberal and realist persuasions found themselves able to enter the mainstream of political and economic debate once more, and theologians and churchmen such as Niebuhr and John Bennett played some part in influencing the New Deal in America, just as Archbishop William Temple had some influence on the creation of the welfare state in Britain.

Despite the increasing confidence with which the distinction was being handled, Niebuhr was another of the theologians of the modern period who is actually very hard to pigeonhole as either liberal or conservative. The very title of his major two-volume work, *The Nature and Destiny of Man* (1941–3), might sound liberal to Barthian ears, and its concentration on the theme of man's self-transcendence was a long-standing liberal theme. Yet its emphasis on the reality of human sinfulness struck a more neo-orthodox note. Niebuhr's contemporary, Paul

Tillich (1886–1965), a German exile in North America, also rehearsed themes of human sinfulness and self-transcendence, yet took them in a more obviously liberal direction. Tillich's self-imposed task was to restate the great themes or 'myths' of Christianity and the Bible in terms that could make sense to the modern world. In his interpretation, sin became a sense of estrangement from self, others, the world. God became the 'ground of being'. Salvation became the 'authenticity' one could secure by getting in touch with this ground of being. Though it spoke directly to a generation, Tillich's theological project confirmed many Barthians in their view of liberalism as an accommodation to modernity. (Tillich preferred to speak of 'correlation'.) A serious weakness was that it did not explain why the Christian 'myths' were worth restating in the first place. If they were only picturesque ways of articulating deep existential truths, then why not simply replace them with new, more effective 'myths'? This is indeed what seems to have happened in the late twentieth century, as a generation that had no longer been brought up in a Christian framework found that other sources, such as eastern religions, might prove to be aids just as fruitful to spiritual and personal self-development as stories about fall, virgin birth and resurrection.

Yet the popularity of Tillich in his own day, and the attention given to the popularisation of his ideas in John Robinson's *Honest to God* (1963), made it seem, briefly, as if a liberal revival was under way. Even the Catholic church was said to be liberalising. Much to most people's surprise, Pope John XXIII (1881–1963) brought the era of fortress Catholicism to an end by calling the Second Vatican Council (Vatican II) in 1962. It closed in 1965 under a new pontiff, Paul VI (1897–1978). Charged with the task of *aggiornamento*, with modernising the church in an appropriate fashion, it took some very significant steps in a human-istic direction, albeit within a firmly Catholic framework.

As one of the key statements of Vatican II, the Pastoral Constitution on the Church in the Modern World (*Gaudium et Spes*) declared that 'this sacred synod, proclaiming the noble destiny of man and championing the Godlike seed which has been sown in him, offers to mankind the honest assistance of the Church in fostering that brotherhood of all men which corresponds to this destiny of theirs'.[7] This new more positive estimation of human dignity was echoed in the council's acceptance of the principle of freedom in religious belief, its championship of human rights, and its more positive and open attitude towards other religions and their followers. It was extended into the church's own self-understanding by identifying church not with clergy but with 'the whole people of God'. The new understanding was translated into practice by way of liturgical reforms. The mass was to be understood as a communal feast of the whole church rather than as a priestly action passively witnessed by a congregation; it was to be said in the vernacular rather than in Latin; there was to be greater congregational participation in worship; private oral confession was to make way for a general confession of sins; the laity were to take a more active role in worship and the life of the church in general. By way of all these measures and more, the formality of Catholic worship was diminished, and with it the distance between God and humankind and between the priest and the laity. Less emphasis was given to the objective efficacy of the sacraments and to an understanding of the moral life in which the inexorable build-up of individual sin must be counteracted by regular reception of the sacraments of the eucharist and penance. Instead, greater emphasis was placed on the dignity of human beings, the importance of their inner dispositions, the strength of their natural desire for communion with God, and the fulfilment such relationship would bring.

Vatican II also stimulated the application of a modern historical approach to ecclesiastical, theological and biblical texts, and legitimated the work of a new generation of Catholic theologians including Karl Rahner (1904–84), Yves Congar (1904–95) and John Courtney Murray (1904–67). All played a major role in drafting some of the key conciliar documents, and all, in different ways, were responsible for a recovery of the Catholic humanist tradition and for developing it in a voluntaristic direction. Their view was that the Christian tradition had always attributed to the human being a dignity and a freedom that placed humanity at the centre of the creation, but that this dignity had been obscured by the defensive dogmatic and propositional approach of the theology of the manuals. In his transcendental anthropology, for example, Rahner argued that God is the true depth of the deepest human experiences, while, in his defence of religious freedom, Murray argued – in effect – that it was American rather than European Catholicism that had remained truest to the church's most fundamental insights.

But though Vatican II might seem liberal in comparison with the confessional theology of the fortress Catholicism that had preceded it, by comparison with the temper of its times (the 'swinging sixties') or even the liberalism of a Tillich, it remained cautiously conservative. While it gave liberals within the Catholic church hope that their cause might at last win out, it opened the door to that possibility without stepping through it. And in 1968, in the immediate aftermath of the council, Pope Paul VI (1897 – 1978) issued an encyclical, *Humanae vitae*, which seemed to many to slam that door shut. Disregarding powerful lay and theological opinion and advice in favour of a relaxation of the church's ban on contraception, *Humanae vitae* reinstated that ban with new force. Later popes, most notably John Paul II (1920–2005), continued the conservative retrenchment in relation to theology and ethics (particularly sexual ethics), while developing a more liberal-humanistic position in relation to political affairs. Together with his Prefect of the Congregation for the Doctrine of the Faith, Cardinal Joseph Ratzinger, Pope John Paul II withdrew the church's licence from a number of theologians whose views were considered too liberal, including Hans Küng and Charles Curran. Even liberation theology was criticised for drawing too close to the ideas of secular Marxism (see below).

By the 1980s the conservative turn of western theology, both academic and ecclesiastical, was becoming more entrenched. Since the churches now articulated their official theological positions within the context of cultures and societies that were drifting ever further from belief in higher, dominating power to commitment to the empowerment and self-development of every unique individual subject, the appearance of conservatism was heightened. A stance such as that against contraception, which, a century before, had been part of a wide cultural consensus, now appeared reactionary. Of course, many of the mainline liberal churches supported a more moderate theological stance, yet even in their official documents, and in a number of attempts to reach 'agreed' ecumenical statements, the initiative appeared to have shifted to the more conservative in their ranks. In broad churches such as the Anglican, liberal churchmen became increasingly afraid of offending conservative opinion, and liberals seemed to find it hard to answer conservatives' claims to represent 'true' Christianity. The claim that theological liberalism had been discredited, or had simply run out of steam, was made with a new sense of certainty. Such certainty was bolstered by the decline of the liberal-mainline churches. What is more, the conservative trend became self-reinforcing. Having failed to win the baby-boom generation by developing more tolerant, democratic, 'subjectivised' forms of Christianity, the churches became a refuge for those who were out of sympathy with such values.

Conservative postmodern theology

Academic theology of both a conservative and a more liberal tendency gained a new injection of intellectual vitality after the 1970s from an unlikely direction: secular postmodernism. The latter was an intellectual movement, generated from within a number of university disciplines, that expressed dissatisfaction with the entire 'Enlightenment project'. 'Modernity' was presented as the attempt on the part of reigning elites (white, male, western, bourgeois) to impose their 'rationality' upon unsuspecting 'others' (colonial, female, homosexual). All 'totalising' 'metanarratives' were rejected as destructive of a 'difference' that should be celebrated, not universalised and 'essentialised' out of existence.

This radical attack on power from on high might seem like the natural enemy of conservative theology, particularly since it took a dim view of all forms of 'foundational' knowledge and the grand narratives that supported them. What it offered, however, was a sweeping critique of secular modernity that was immediately congenial to the conservative mind. A 'right wing' of academic theology influenced by postmodernism not only developed this critique, but began to suggest the importance of moving to a 'post-secular' epoch. Postmodernism supplied conservative theology with a powerful new tool kit with which to deconstruct the modern world, and allowed it to enter into dialogue with secular postmodernists on equal, if not superior, terms. A new method developed whereby theologians would use the tools of a Foucault, a Derrida or a Baudrillard to critique modern culture, and then move on to argue that only the churches and 'the Christian tradition' or 'the Christian narrative' could provide the cure for the contemporary malady.

Yet postmodernism did not merely supply theologians with a new form of critique. It also offered a new anti-foundational foundation for theological truth, one that avoided the dangers of both the Barthian appeal to a supra-cultural revelation and the liberal appeal to individual experience. Postmodernism claimed that all universal truth claims were totalising and oppressive, and that the way forward was to embrace epistemological diversity with self-conscious conviction. Truth was relative to the particular narratives in which it was embedded, and to the particular communities that sustained them. But who had a better claim to a foundational community ('the Christian church') and tradition ('the Christian tradition') than Christians? Some philosophers, such as Alasdair MacIntyre, did the theologians a favour by saying as much, and MacIntyre's work was seized on with alacrity.

A revival of the Eastern Orthodox theological tradition also proved influential. Influenced in part by the Russian émigré theologians of the first part of the century (see previous chapter), this revival took place after the 1960s and involved a confident restatement of selected Orthodox themes. Such themes were used to critique the 'western tradition' in theology and philosophy. Particularly important was a recovery of the theme of relationality, which was said to be exemplified by the internal relations of God the Holy Trinity. The *perichoresis*, or mutual moving towards and indwelling in one another of the divine persons, was presented as the model of authentic life – divine, ecclesiastical and human – and set against the atomistic individualism of the western philosophical tradition and the monarchial emphasis of much western theology. Such ideas were presented in English by Nikos Nissiotis (died 1986), Christos Yannaras and, most influentially, by John Zizioulas in *Being as Communion: Studies in Personhood and the Church* (1985). The broadly conservative implications of the position are clear in Zizioulas's work, in which the church, its sacraments and its bishop become the indispensable focus of a unity-in-diversity that anticipates God's ultimate will for creation.

An important effect of the conservative postmodern turn in theology has been a new appreciation of the importance of concrete Christian communities, traditions, rituals and liturgies. It is in these that many theologians now began to locate truth, rather than in a supra-historical revelation or an invisible church. In the theological ethics of Stanley Hauerwas, for example, it is the Christian community and its 'story' that has a foundational status in the moral life. This is not merely some abstract community, but the concrete bodies of men and women who meet regularly on Sundays to pray, worship and associate with one another. Only in their midst, argues Hauerwas, can the 'peaceable kingdom' be incarnated.[8]

Liberal postmodern theology

In the sort of grounded postmodern theological turn taken by Hauerwas, we find once more the interesting spectacle of a theologian who cannot easily be categorised as liberal or conservative. (The same might be said of the contemporary German communitarian theologian Jürgen Moltmann). While he sees himself as an unsparing critic of liberalism, both secular and theological, in practice Hauerwas has nevertheless attempted some sort of rapprochement between knowledge from below (the stories of actual Christians in actual communities) and knowledge from above (the Christian story told in the Bible). This attempt to take both approaches seriously in a way that dissolves the long-standing modern opposition between liberal and conservative and its theological recapitulations is also evident in two earlier developments in theology: liberation theology and feminist theology. Both date from the late 1960s, though the roots of feminist theology go back to the late nineteenth century.

· Since both liberation theology and feminist theology were founded on the attempt to do theology on the basis of knowledge from below, both have tended to be categorised together and dismissed by conservatives as 'liberal'. What this analysis obscures is the fact that the 'experience' that both forms of theology regard as foundational is not necessarily identical with the inner subjectivity to which some earlier forms of theological liberalism tended to appeal. In different ways, much liberation theology and feminist theology attempted something new, less individualistic and more sociologically acute.

Liberation theology, which grew out of the situation of the poor and oppressed under the totalitarian regimes of Latin America in the 1960s and 1970s, tried to take seriously the contextual nature of all knowledge. Rather than relying on some apparently unsituated individual consciousness that was actually the production of an ideology of bourgeois individualism, liberation theologians argued that a theology that took seriously Jesus' ministry to the poor could be practised only by and among the poor. 'Base communities' of Catholics were established to engage in the theological task, which must be regarded as inseparable from the general cause of 'liberation'. The scriptures were read within this context, and interpretation that emphasised not personal salvation, but social and economic liberation, resulted. Though the demise of liberation theology since the 1980s has been cheerfully announced by its conservative critics, the base communities have in fact proved flexible enough to adapt to changed conditions, and have been creative in their theological embrace of new initiatives including feminist and ecological issues.

Feminist theology has also undergone some significant changes since it first made its appearance on the theological scene in the 1970s. Pioneering feminist theologians such as Mary Daly and Rosemary Radford Ruether did indeed begin from the liberal presupposition that all knowledge is based on individual experience.[9] Following the lead of secular feminism, their challenge to academic theology has been to point out that all that had hitherto been written about God and humanity had been based on partial, male experience. Their contribution would be to do academic theology on the basis of women's experience – for the first time. What Daly and Ruether did not fully appreciate, however, and what the secular feminist Luce Irigaray pointed out, was that in an important sense women do not yet have experience.[10] For experience is not a pure inner consciousness, untouched by social and cultural contexts and straightforwardly available to introspection as a new foundation for feminised knowledge. Only if women were to achieve positions of greater power and influence in the world and in the shaping of knowledge would a genuinely female experience and knowledge develop.

Like much conservative theology, therefore, feminist theology was also revitalised after the 1980s by the influence of postmodernism (to which feminism and gender studies had made a vital contribution). The result was a liberal rather than a conservative theological postmodernism that was particularly influenced by postmodern secular feminism. Like the latter, it gives a new importance to empirical attempts to uncover women's experience, rather than simply to pronounce upon its essence. The result, in the work of the theologian Mary McClintock Fulkerson (for example), is a new and experimental rapprochement between theology and social scientific method.[11] Again, knowledge from on high and knowledge from below appear to be coming together in fruitful ways that may begin to break through the old liberal–conservative stalemate. Yet feminist theology and liberation theology still tend to be marginalised within ecclesiastical and academic theology, and women and non-whites continue to be under-represented in both spheres. The preponderance of men within academic departments of theology, and the contrast this now presents with a trend the other way in

Table 7.1 *Affiliation to Christianity on six continents (millions), 1995*[12]

Europe	557
Latin America	445
Africa	318
Asia	282
North America	251
Oceania	24

the humanities and social sciences more generally, is a telling indication of the continuing conservative agenda of theology as it enters the new millennium.

Post-colonial Christianity

The same period that witnessed the decline of the churches and the challenge to theology in the northern hemisphere also witnessed the upsurge of Christianity in parts of the southern hemisphere, most notably in the post-colonial societies of Latin America, Africa and parts of Asia. Though the decades after 1960 were characterised by secularisation in the west, they were characterised by sacralisation in the south. Nearly all forms of Christianity have experienced growth outside the west – the colonial 'mother' churches, the independent churches that first developed under colonial rule and, most dramatically of all, the new charismatic churches. Growth is related not only to conversion but also to a high rate of population growth (during the same period that the west experienced a declining birth rate). As tables 7.1 and 7.2 indicate, if these trends continue at their present rate, the number of Christians in the southern hemisphere will soon greatly exceed the number of Christians in the west – an unprecedented situation.

Christianity in the southern hemisphere finds itself in a significantly different context from the churches in the west. Both belong to an increasingly globalised capitalist system, but the southern nations participate as weaker members, experiencing fewer of its benefits and more of its costs. While the standard of living has risen for some sectors of the population, and while an affluent middle class has established itself in nearly all countries that have at least a basic level of political stability,

Table 7.2 *Projected affiliation to Christianity on six continents (millions), 2025*[13]

Latin America	641
Africa	634
Europe	555
Asia	465
North America	290
Oceania	32

a significant proportion of the population still struggles to secure minimal material comfort. The provision of healthcare and education is far more patchy and precarious than in the west, and the task of 'bettering' oneself socially and materially and entering into the ranks of the middle classes much harder. Upward social mobility is possible chiefly by seeking employment in the rapidly expanding cities. Vast numbers leave the relative security of established rural communities to settle in the rapidly expanding towns, where extremes of fortune, both good and bad, await them.

All these conditions appear to favour religion in general and, in those places where it has a foothold, Christianity in particular. They ensure that there is a strong demand for the services that Christianity, particularly in its charismatic guise, seems well equipped to supply. Such demand stems from the nature of people's needs and desires, and from the fact that these are generally much harder to satisfy than in the west. At the most basic level, many still struggle just to maintain 'raw life' – to secure food and healthcare for themselves and their families. In the absence of developed welfare systems, even those in paid employment may suddenly find themselves thrown into a situation of desperate material need by illness or unemployment. At a higher level of needs, many people see the rewards that successful employment in the capitalist system may bring, and strive to attain them. To do so requires a great deal of the individual: health, mobility, education and personal 'virtues' of reliability, hard work, self-reliance and so on. Useful connections to people in positions of influence are also important. At this level what is desired is not just raw life, but a secure and prosperous life – like that enjoyed by most people in the west.

While the churches cannot supply all these needs or satisfy all these desires, they can assist in extremely important, even indispensable, ways. They can provide strong communities whose members serve as 'family' to one another, providing practical and emotional support. They can provide welfare by redistributing money from wealthier members and from donations from Christians in the west to those who are in need. They can provide moral order and guidance for people struggling with the confusions and temptations of the city. They can help inculcate the dispositions and virtues that allow people to succeed within global capitalism, and can provide essential training: by learning how to read the Bible people gain literacy skills; by learning how to preach they learn how to speak in public; and by helping to administer a club or church group they develop skills of organisation and leadership. For men in particular, the ministry or the priesthood may also provide a valuable outlet for talents and skills and an effective point of entry into the middle classes. For women, the gifts of the Spirit can offer empowerment, while the conversion of their menfolk from machismo to gentler domestic virtues can be an additional benefit.

In all these ways, then, the churches in the southern hemisphere have real and important roles to play, which those in the north have largely lost. While the churches in the south help people maintain or attain a basic quality of life, in the north generations born after the Second World War experience a much higher quality of life almost automatically. As noted above, many westerners now enjoy the luxury of a 'post-materialist' condition in which basic needs are met, and the enrichment of inner, subjective life can take priority over the pursuit of material necessity. In the west, as we have seen, recent generations are therefore likely to turn to religion or spirituality – whether Christian or alternative – if they find there resources that can help them cultivate their unique spiritual lives; but they are likely to turn away from it if it cannot.

But even though these differences can go some way to explain the contrasting fortunes of Christianity in north and south, it is important not to overdraw the comparison. For both regions have experienced a subjective turn, and both have been affected in related ways. Thus in both places Christianity has become voluntaristic and focused upon individual well-being rather than on social or political well-being, and in both it offers individual empowerment. Indeed, in some ways Christianity in the southern hemisphere can now be said to sustain and reinforce the upsurge of power from below to a greater extent than the churches in the west. For one thing, the upsurge of Christianity in post-colonial societies represents a political reversal whereby a religion that was once brought from outside and associated with colonial power has been appropriated by those who were once colonial subjects. For another, charismatic Christianity in particular arises from the grassroots and does away with official, centralised hierarchies of ecclesiastical power. It has little or no direct involvement with political and economic systems, and little desire to influence or control them (which is not to deny that it may have important political and economic effects). Its focus is not on improving society, but on improving and empowering the individual, and it does so first and foremost by spiritual means – by offering direct empowerment through the gifts of the Holy Spirit. Yet it does all this while retaining a basically conservative moral framework, particularly with regard to biblical authority and personal, family-based morality. Like charismatic-evangelical Christianity in the west, it seems to succeed by having the best of both worlds.

MODERN MISSION, GLOBAL CHRISTIANITY

Though the globalisation of Christianity has forced itself on western consciousness only very recently, its antecedents lie much further back in the colonial activity of western nations and the missionary activity of the western churches. The impact of such activity has been significant not only for the peoples and cultures at which it was directed, but for its agents as well.

While the first phase of Christian mission abroad (in the sixteenth and seventeenth centuries) went hand in hand with colonial conquest and was led by the regular and secular clergy under the ultimate control of secular rulers (see previous chapter), the second phase of mission (in the nineteenth and twentieth centuries) differed in a number of ways. Its pioneers were Pietists and Baptists acting largely independently of colonial powers. Their goal was 'confessional': to spread the gospel, to save souls and to win members for their own churches. Very quickly Catholics also entered the field, and competition between different types of Christian confession became another major feature of this phase of mission. Connection with colonial power, though important, remained less direct than in the earlier phase of mission. The role of the 'missionary' developed as a semi-professional one distinct from existing offices of the church.

Despite the important initiatives of individuals at the start of modern mission, centralised church bureaucracies quickly attempted to take control. Their aim was to send ordained clergy and ministers into the mission field to convert 'the heathen' and make them good Christian citizens and loyal church members. Many favoured the establishment of mission compounds overseas, in which the clergy maintained paternalistic control over model 'villages' of native converts (a reversion to an idealised picture of medieval life and of ecclesiastical domination of society). This strategy was frustrated by a lack of funds, a lack of volunteers and a lack of success on the ground. The solution, resisted by church officials until its momentum became unstoppable, was to laicise mission: to send lay people into the mission field and to allow lay-run missionary associations to fund them. An unanticipated result was that women became central in modern mission – both at home, where they were active in the work of the mission societies (see ch. 5), and abroad, where they became increasingly involved in missionary activity, first as wives and later in their own right (though always under at least nominal male control). Women also became prominent in Catholic mission, both as fundraisers and as members of the growing number of religious orders devoted to missionary work.

A gradual change in mission strategy also took place. Ideas of mission from above slowly gave way to a greater openness to mission from below. By the end of the nineteenth century the theories of Henry Venn (1796–1873) were beginning to be taken seriously. Largely because of the shortage of priests, Venn had popularised a 'three-self formula' for the creation of indigenous churches – they should be self-supporting, self-governing and self-propagating. Such ideas were revived by mission strategists such as John Nevius, who devised a policy of itinerate mission work, indigenous leadership and financial self-support for Korea. While it did not abandon its commitment to clerical leadership, the Roman Catholic church began to ordain native priests. In *Maximum Illud* (1919), Benedict XV (1854–1922) laid down three principles to guide the spread of Catholicism outside the west: the recruitment of native clergy, the renunciation of nationalistic concerns, and the recognition of the dignity and worth of the people and cultures who were evangelised. Pope Pius XI (1857–1939) continued these policies, and was responsible for consecrating indigenous Chinese, Japanese and Indian bishops. (At his accession there had not been a single one.) By 1939 the Catholic church had forty non-western bishops and over 7,000 non-western priests.

The relationship between mission, politics and colonialism remained complex. Most modern missions were independently organised by their various churches and were independent of the state. In some cases colonial agents actively obstructed mission; it was only evangelical lobbying in Britain, for example, that eventually resulted in missionaries being allowed to enter the Indian sub-continent. For the British empire in particular, which operated by way of co-operative collaboration between a tiny British elite and native rulers, missionary activity constantly threatened to disrupt delicate balances of local power. The status of the missionary himself or herself remained anomalous; he or she belonged neither to colonial nor to native society, but was often more closely identified with the latter. Yet missionaries travelled in the wake of colonial settlement, and depended greatly upon the infrastructure and resources of empire to do their work, to guarantee their safety and to claim their status. Examples of missionaries who opposed the colonial enterprise are so rare as to be virtually non-existent. In certain instances mission and colonialism might exist in even closer relationship, as in the Belgian Congo, where political and religious conquest went hand in hand, sometimes in a brutal fashion.

For good or ill, then, the credibility and power of the modern missionary were closely bound up with his or her relationship to western culture and colonial power – however much he or she might have wished it to be otherwise. In the main the missionary ended up strengthening rather than undermining the colonial enterprise, not least by becoming responsible for basic health, welfare and educational provision in colonial countries (which in turn helped give a moral rationale for colonialism). Care for the bodies and minds as well as for the souls of native peoples became an increasing priority of mission in the late nineteenth and twentieth centuries, and helped establish the churches as centres of material as well as spiritual provision. The strategy was successful in bringing large numbers into contact with the church, though the extent to which it won souls for the gospel is more debatable.

It might be fair to summarise the effects of modern mission by saying that native peoples drew selectively on what was offered them. They

Plate 27   *The Secret of England's Greatness,* by Thomas J. Barker (1815–82)
The British often legitimated their global empire as a means by which Christian 'civilisation' could be spread more widely, and the churches concurred. Thomas Barker's painting
gives visual expression to this idea by depicting the queen and empress, Victoria, handing
the Bible to a grateful subject.

took advantage of educational and medical provision, and some gave
their allegiance to the colonial churches. But, on the whole, modern
mission failed to win the large-scale conversion to Christianity – or,
more specifically, to the western churches – that had been hoped for. The
short-lived optimism that reigned at the start of the twentieth century
and was encapsulated in the mission slogan 'The evangelisation of the
world in this generation' quickly dissipated as the expected harvest of
souls failed to materialise. Though the foundations had been laid, it was
only once the colonial powers had departed that Christian growth really
took off.

But the impact of modern mission is to be looked for 'at home' as well
as 'overseas', for the churches that helped organise such mission were
not unaffected by it. The most important effect was in the gradual and
still incomplete reshaping of many 'western' churches to become 'global'

churches. The indigenisation of mission was crucial in this development, not least through the creation of a native clergy. Even more important was the elevation of such clergy to positions of real power in the church. In some respects the Roman Catholic church led the way. By the time of Vatican II, over half the 2,800 bishops came from outside Europe, and Pope Paul VI went further by including a large number of Third World bishops in the College of Cardinals. Vatican II also helped pave the way for 'indigenisation' within post-colonial Catholic churches by articulating a new, more open and receptive attitude towards other faiths and cultures, and by allowing for the creation of more inculturated liturgies and church practices. For Protestants and Orthodox the World Council of Churches played an important role. Founded in 1948 (though conceived in 1937), it grew out of a post-confessional ecumenical sense that was born in the mission field and that aimed to encourage co-operation rather than competition between denominations. It currently works as an agent of mutual influence between the churches of north and south.

Ironically, however, such steps towards global churches and global Christianity arise from the west rather than from 'the rest'. The attempt to indigenise, in other words, is not always an indigenous one. It is often badly received outside the west, and is criticised for reflecting a foreign agenda of a liberal variety. By the beginning of the third millennium, it was clear that there were two very different strategies for global Christianity at play in the world: the 'official', liberal one, and a more conservative one. The latter, best exemplified by charismatic Christianity, globalises not by way of a self-conscious policy of synthesis between the best in northern and southern cultures, but by jumping over existing ethnic and cultural frontiers to create trans-cultural communities of individuals without these prior commitments. The latter process gains momentum from the way in which conservative Christians in the west are increasingly forming alliances with their counterparts in the southern hemisphere to present a united front against the 'liberal' developments they dislike in their own churches, particularly those that encourage a relaxation of family-based sexual norms. And the irony is that their sympathy with a tolerant, multi-cultural ethos makes it hard for liberal globalisers to ignore or override 'indigenous' voices, even when they support conservative policies.

CHARISMATIC UPSURGE
Pentecostal origins

Though charismatic Christianity is not the only successful form of Christianity in the southern hemisphere, it is the fastest-growing. In the last quarter of the twentieth century it is estimated to have won up to a quarter of a billion converts in Latin America, Africa and parts of Asia. Not only has it won adherents from other churches, both Catholic and Protestant; it is also having an increasing influence on the style of these churches.

The charismatic movement developed out of the Pentecostal upsurge of the early twentieth century. The origins of the latter were in a periphery of the USA (Los Angeles) and a periphery of Great Britain (Wales). As well as growing on the margins, Pentecostalism attracted those marginal to social power, particularly the working classes, blacks and women. It was primarily an urban movement, appealing to those who had swapped the established order of rural life, or semi-slavery, for the uncertainties of the city. Its supporters tended to be those who stood on the margins of capitalism, aware of the riches on offer, providing the labour on which the wealth and well-being of the middle classes depended, yet unable to enter into their kingdom. Unlike the fundamentalists, they knew of no golden age to which they longed to return, and their hopes tended to be focused on the heavenly Jerusalem rather than on old-time America.

The main thing that fundamentalism and Pentecostalism had in common, besides their contemporaneous origins, was a love of the written word of scripture, often the King James version of the Bible. In this sacred book both fundamentalists and Pentecostals found their map of the world, the heavens, the future and their own lives. It served as a blueprint of reality, more solid and reliable than the deliverances of science, the judgements of the law, and the shifting sands of modern culture. What is more, the Bible required no mediating authority. With their ultimate origins in Reformation biblicism, fundamentalists and Pentecostals were united in their belief that they needed no pope, priest or theologian to interpret God's Word.

In other respects, fundamentalism and Pentecostalism differed completely. Though Pentecostalism tended to form itself into centrally organised denominations, it had a much greater orientation towards power from below, expressed in a much higher doctrine of the Holy Spirit and a more flexible authority structure. Such flexibility was enhanced in the 'charismatic revival' that took place worldwide after the 1970s. For this reason, Pentecostal-charismatic Christianity has affinities with both the biblicist and spiritualist strands of Christianity, for the authority of the Word is always qualified by that of the Spirit, and vice versa. Thus it is not only the man (and occasionally the woman) learned in scripture who is authorised to preach in charismatic churches, but the one who is inspired by the Holy Spirit. Likewise, the Holy Spirit descends on people without regard for their earthly condition, bestowing on them the 'charismata' (gifts of the Spirit) of prophecy, healing, speaking in tongues, miracle-working, exorcism, and acts of love and service. Charismatic worship is immediately recognisable by its 'enthusiasm'. Religion becomes a matter of the deepest experience, as God's Spirit moves the believer, encouraging him or her to sing, dance, cry out and be 'slain in the Spirit'.

Thus charismatic Christians do not merely listen; they speak. In every sense, they find their voice. Under the inspiration of the Holy Spirit, prophecies may be given, responses to the sermon may be shouted out, healing may take place, demons may be cast out, and powerful displays of emotion will occur. Such partially unregulated access to divine power opens up possibilities of individual empowerment and advancement both within and outside the church that traditional forms of Christianity find it hard to rival. In many of the rapidly expanding cities of the southern hemisphere a small army of preachers have established their own churches, based around personal inspiration and sited in any available space – whether a shop, shack, tent or the open air. Here, where the doctrine of the priesthood of all believers combines with the opportunities of the religious free market, power from below finds support in divine power from above.

Charismatic upsurge in Latin America, Africa and Asia

Though the charismatic revival had an impact in the west as well as the south, it is in Latin America, Africa and Asia that its effects have been most profound.

In Latin America the alliance of colonial church (Roman Catholic) and colonial power (Spain and Portugal) was overthrown by the rise of secular regimes from the start of the nineteenth century. Due to a lack of power and social control, however, such regimes were often obliged to tolerate Christianity and even to enlist the support of the church. In some cases this led to Catholic alliance with the political right; in

Plate 28   Charismatic 'churches' in a suburb of Santiago, Chile

These photographs convey something of the ease and the speed with which charismatic Christianity can spread in the southern hemisphere. Rather than depending on official legitimation from an authoritative ecclesiastical body, individuals who believe they have received the call of God can 'set up shop' whenever and wherever the opportunity arises.

others – particularly after the 1960s – with the left. In Brazil, for example, the Roman Catholic church eventually became a qualified supporter of democratisation and even of social revolution, manifest eventually in sporadic support for base communities and liberation theology. Even so, the traits of non-voluntary Catholicism persisted in Latin American Catholicism, not only in the retention of clerical power but in the churches' continuing desire for control over society and in their repeated gravitation toward alliance with military and political power.

Though the Roman Catholic church in Latin America gradually became more of a church 'for' the people, it did not necessarily become a church 'of' the people. A new desire to take control over one's own life, and a disillusionment with existing forms of power, both religious and political, led many in the later part of the twentieth century to a conversion from Catholicism to the more subjectivised options of either charismatic Christianity or neo-nativist systems of individual spiritual empowerment such as Umbanda. So sizeable has been the walkout from Catholicism that the official Roman Catholic church has become increasingly alarmed at the development, and has encouraged various measures designed to win back its lost sheep (including introducing a charismatic element to its own worship).

Yet the 'conversion' to Pentecostalism or Umbanda is not always as decisive as that term might imply. Recent research reveals that increasing numbers of Christians in Latin America (the majority of them female) now move freely from one such form of religion or spirituality to another, depending on changing personal needs and commitments. Commitments that might be thought incompatible, such as to Catholicism and Pentecostalism, can be held simultaneously. The latter, for example, is evident in the way that a significant number of women and men in Brazil belong both to a base community in the Catholic church and to a charismatic renewal group. It is no longer the church that prescribes the course of their life, but the course of their life that prescribes their commitments.

In Africa charismatic upsurge is linked to a much more recent colonial past. In most African countries independence was achieved in the decades immediately after the Second World War. One of the earliest and most visible results of missionary activity in post-independence Africa was the creation of a new African elite, educated by the missionaries, who took power after independence and tried to steer their newly created nation states down western paths of 'development', often of a secular nature. It was partly disillusionment with the results of such secular 'solutions' to Africa's problems that highlighted a different result of missionary activity, namely the creation of conditions that have made possible the extensive growth of Christianity since the 1960s, particularly in the sub-Saharan regions, where Islam does not provide as much competition to the churches as in the north. By the end of the twentieth century around 360 million Africans identified themselves as Christian.

Nearly all the churches in Africa have benefited: the colonial churches (the largest being Anglican and Roman Catholic), the independent churches that developed in the colonial era (such as the Kimbanguist church) and post-colonial churches, of which the most important are the ever more numerous charismatic churches. Even the colonial churches have attempted to distance themselves from power from on high, particularly of a colonial form, and have indigenised by replacing western clergy with native clergy and allowing a degree of inculturation in worship and even in lifestyle (hence the ongoing debate about the permissibility of polygamy in the African context).

But it is the charismatic churches that have grown the fastest. Some belong to wider charismatic federations of churches, some with an international reach. Others are tiny, independent congregations founded by a single pastor and belonging to no broader grouping. In Africa to an even greater extent than in Latin America, charismatic Christianity focuses upon the most basic needs of the individual, and the twin themes of healing and prosperity are central. It has also been extremely successful in harnessing the energies of indigenous African religions and turning them in a Christian direction. For example, the pervasive sense of the presence and efficacy of spiritual forces, both good and bad, is echoed directly in the supernaturalism of charismatic Christianity. Healings, exorcisms and miracle-working are important elements of African charismatic life. In all these respects, and in its lack of historical connection with colonialism, charismatic Christianity can claim to be more truly indigenous than its competitors.

In Asia, Christianity has made far less headway. The chief reason has been the strength and cultural entrenchment of competing world religions – Hinduism, Buddhism and Islam. The battle between Islam and Christianity continues as bitterly into the present day as before, with militant forms of Islam breaking down ancient forms of Christianity in such places as the Lebanon, Palestine and Pakistan. Generally speaking,

Christian mission made headway in Asia only when it managed to win converts among groups peripheral to major socio-religious formations – such as some outcaste Christian groups and tribal peoples in India, ethnic peripheries in Nepal, Thailand, Burma and Indonesia, and, more recently, evangelical middle-class transnational groups in Singapore and some other small 'tiger economies' in Asia. Apart from the Philippines, where Christianity was established by the Spanish after the sixteenth century, the only Asian country in which Christianity has made real headway has been South Korea, where over 30 per cent of the population now identify as Christian. Here, by contrast with the rest of Asia, Christianity was brought from China by native Koreans, and its later spread under the direction of western missionaries was by means of the method of indigenous growth mentioned above. What is more, Christianity in South Korea managed to make a positive association with internal modernisation, progressivism and the cause of national autonomy by providing a rallying point for South Korean identity over against Confucian conservatism and Japanese colonialism. Since the 1970s, charismatic upsurge has also fuelled evangelical growth in South Korea.

The case of China is rather different, not least because it was here that Christians had long held the greatest hopes of winning souls for Christ, and here that their failure was therefore the most profound. In China, Christians had no 'world religion' to contend with, but the inner-worldly socio-cultural system of Confucianism and indigenous forms of religion and spirituality. Though Christian preachers and missionaries often entered on the coat tails of western penetration, they did not come as part of a conquering force, as in Latin America and Africa, and it was always clear that their victory would have to be won through the sheer force of the gospel. As we saw in the previous chapter, it was in India that de Nobili and other Jesuits pioneered a form of indigenous mission by attempting to come among the elite and to appeal to them on their own terms. The experiment was cut short by Roman intervention and by growing Chinese hostility, which led to the first of several expulsions of Christians from the country. When China became a prime target of mission once more in the second phase of missionary activity in the post-Reformation period, it again became the site of pioneering forms of missionary strategy. The most notable were those of Hudson Taylor's China Inland Mission, which pioneered not only an interdenominational form of mission, but lay ministry, the ministry of women, and a semi-covert form of operation by which Christians entered the country to offer education, medical service and welfare. Interestingly, it is this covert form of mission that has been revived after the latest round of missionary expulsion under communist rule.

Though mission historians often appeal to the forceful expulsions of Christians from China in order to explain the failure to Christianise China, what really requires explanation is why the Chinese felt the need to expel the Christians. Sometimes the Chinese authorities were motivated by fear that the Christians were a Trojan horse for western expansionism. Fears that Christianity would undermine the existing socio-political order were also a significant factor, and intensified when the Taiping Rebellion against the Manchu dynasty (1851–64) was identified as Christian, however erroneously. Yet the vast resources pumped into Chinese mission by the western churches during the long periods of toleration (by 1925 there were over 8,000 foreign Protestant missionaries in China) still failed to produce the expected harvest of souls. By the early twentieth century it was clear that a major part of the explanation was simply that Christianity had proved unable to provide the Chinese with viable solutions to the vast problems they faced in the modern period. Communism proved more attractive, and the churches' opposition to communism and their support of the Guomindang during and after the civil war of 1946–9 led to the final expulsion of missionaries. It is only in so far as the secular communist pathway to modernisation has in turn failed to provide lasting solutions that covert Christian penetration, combined with underground support, has made some headway in recent times by identifying itself with the cause of democracy and progress, or, in the case of a large Pentecostal underground whose numbers are hard to estimate, by offering support for individuals in a period of rapid social change.

Right across the world, then, in the south as much as in the north, the Christianity of the late twentieth and early twenty-first centuries seems to succeed best where it is able to offer sacred empowerment to the struggling individual. The nature of the struggle influences the nature of the empowerment. Yet even the massive growth in Christianity in the southern hemisphere – from 94 million affiliates in 1900 to one billion in 2000 – has not been sufficient to compensate for the massive loss in the west during the same period. In 1900, those affiliated to Christianity were estimated to make up 34.5 per cent of the world's population. By 1990, Christian affiliates made up 33.2 per cent of the world's population, and by the year 2000, 33 per cent (two billion).[14]

Despite this loss, however, Christianity entered the third millennium as the world's largest religion. It had achieved that position largely through alliance with power from on high (including colonialism), but it retained it in the latter part of the twentieth century through successful accommodations with power from below. In both north and south such accommodations tended to be partial and piecemeal. There was little departure from the model of deity as a male God of dominating power from on high, and no serious revival of the more subjectivised trajectories within Christianity. Defence of the family and of 'traditional' gender roles continued to be an important part of the modern Christian manifesto. Yet the more extreme doctrines of human sinfulness that had prevailed in confessional Christianity were quietly put on one side, as were doctrines of predestination and election. Likewise, images of God as a mighty and distant king and judge were eclipsed by the image of a loving father and a personal companion, guardian, helper and protector. Christian legitimations of social inequality as God-given slipped into the background, and even legitimations of patriarchy tended to hide behind more positive talk of 'the family' and 'equal but different' gender roles. The message that each individual is loved, cared for and empowered through right relationship with God became more central within all varieties of Christianity. In both north and south, then, Christians distanced themselves from the wider subjective turn of modern culture, while making the necessary adjustments to compete within it.

Further reading
THE CHURCHES IN THE TWENTIETH CENTURY

The majority of studies in this area are empirical and/or sociological, since on the whole Christian history has not yet caught up with the twentieth century. See, however, Hugh McLeod's *Religion and the People of Western Europe 1789–1990* (Oxford and New York: Oxford University Press, 1997), and the many books by the historian of modern American religion, Martin Marty, including his three-volume *Modern American Religion* (Chicago, IL: University of Chicago Press, 1986–96).

Useful sociological studies of the liberal/mainline churches include Wade Clark Roof and William McKinney's *American Mainline Religion: Its Changing Shape and Future* (New Brunswick and London: Rutgers University

Press, 1987), and Nancy Ammerman's more recent empirical study of a variety of American congregations, *Congregation and Community* (New Brunswick, NJ: Rutgers University Press, 1997). On the fortunes of the churches in Britain and Europe see Grace Davie, *Religion in Britain since 1945: Believing without Belonging* (Oxford and Malden, MA: Blackwell, 1994); Steve Bruce, *Religion in Modern Britain* (Oxford and New York: Oxford University Press, 1995); and Grace Davie, *Religion in Modern Europe: A Memory Mutates* (New York: Oxford University Press, 2000).

On evangelical Christianity in the west, from a historical point of view, see George Marsden's *Understanding Fundamentalism and Evangelicalism* (Grand Rapids, MI: Eerdmans, 1991), which offers a sympathetic introductory account. There are a number of illuminating empirical studies of late twentieth-century American evangelicalism, including James Davison Hunter's *Evangelicalism: The Coming Generation* (Chicago, IL: University of Chicago Press, 1987) and Nancy Ammerman's *Bible Believers* (New Brunswick, NJ, and London: Rutgers University Press, 1987). On the subjective turn in American evangelicalism, see Donald Miller's *Reinventing American Protestantism* (Berkeley and Los Angeles, CA, and London: University of California Press, 1997), and Joseph B. Tamney's *The Resilience of Conservative Religion* (Cambridge and New York: Cambridge University Press, 2002).

The idea that conservative Christian churches are growing while liberal ones are declining was made famous by Dean Kelley in *Why Conservative Churches Are Growing* (San Francisco, CA: Harper and Row 1986). Though it is a demanding book, one of the most illuminating accounts of secularisation is still David Martin's *General Theory of Secularisation* (Oxford: Blackwell, 1977). On the churches' 'privatisation' (exclusion from politics) and recent 'deprivatisation' (renewed public and political activity), see José Casanova, *Public Religions in the Modern World* (Chicago, IL, and London: University of Chicago Press, 1994).

MODERN THEOLOGY

David Ford's edited collection, *The Modern Theologians: An Introduction to Christian Theology in the Twentieth Century* (Oxford and Malden, MA: Blackwell, 1997), has become a standard reference work. It contains essays on all the major theologians and theological movements of the twentieth century. Another useful reference work is Alister McGrath (ed.), *The Blackwell Encyclopedia of Modern Christian Thought* (Oxford and Malden, MA: Blackwell, 1995). Both books contain suggestions for further reading.

CHARISMATIC UPSURGE

The origins and growth of Pentecostalism in the west are documented in Walter J. Hollenweger's study, *Pentecostalism: Origins and Development Worldwide* (Peabody, MA: Hendrickson, 1997), whilst Vinson Synan's *The Twentieth-Century Pentecostal Explosion* (second edition, Altamonte Springs, FL: Creation House, 1997) surveys the holiness movement, Pentecostalism and recent charismatic renewal.

On the worldwide charismatic upsurge see David Martin, *Pentecostalism: The World Their Parish* (Oxford and Malden, MA: Blackwell, 2001), which covers Latin America, Africa and Asia; and Simon Coleman, *The Globalisation of Charismatic Christianity* (Cambridge and New York: Cambridge University Press, 2000).

GLOBAL CHRISTIANITY

On mission history and cross-cultural encounter, see Andrew Walls, *The Missionary Movement in Christian History: Studies in the Transmission of Faith* (New York: Orbis; Edinburgh: T. and T. Clark, 1996), and *The Cross-Cultural Process in Christian History: Studies in the Transmission and Appropriation of Faith* (Maryknoll, NY: Orbis; Edinburgh: T. and T. Clark, 2002).

On Christianity in contemporary Latin America, there is a helpful and wide-ranging collection of essays edited by Christian Smith and Joshua Prokopy, *Latin American Religion in Motion* (New York and London: Routledge, 1999). See also John Burdick's engaging empirical study, *Looking for God in Brazil* (Berkeley, CA: University of California Press, 1996). On Africa, see Paul Gifford, *African Christianity: Its Public Role* (London: Hurst, 1998).

The collection edited by Thomas M. Gannon, *World Catholicism in Transition* (New York: Macmillan; London: Collier Macmillan, 1988), offers a useful overview of the state of Catholicism in every part of the world in the 1980s and contains a helpful introductory survey by David Martin.

The figures in this chapter are taken from David B. Barrett, George T. Kurian and Todd M. Johnson, *World Christian Encyclopedia* (second edition, Oxford and New York: Oxford University Press, 2001).

Conclusion

Those who have followed this book from start to finish will notice that the story has come full circle. It began with a religion that was marginal to social power, and it ends with a religion that has become marginal to social power once more. The fact that Christianity lost influence over the spheres of political, economic, military and even ideological power does not, of course, mean that it necessarily loses influence over individual lives. It does, however, mean that such influence is likely to take particular forms. It will be felt at the personal rather than at the public level, and Christian ethics will be concerned with the regulation of personal, intimate and domestic life. In so far as Christianity continues to have an impact on political and economic life, it will do so by shaping behaviour and commitment at the individual level. Some churches may continue to make pronouncements about war, politics and economics, but they will do so from the margins rather than from the centre, and without any guaranteed influence. Grand theological systems are likely to be eclipsed by teachings that have an immediate relevance to the individual in the living of his or her life. Rather than having an established status in society, Christianity has, once again, to fight for that place with a wide range of competitors. In the sphere of the sacred it faces serious competition from a range of alternatives, both old and new, which promise more effective forms of personal or social empowerment.

All these characteristics of a religion of limited social power apply to Christianity in the southern hemisphere as well as the northern. The main difference is that secular power in the latter is more intensive and extensive, and functional differentiation is greater. In the north, there-fore, there is now limited opportunity for the churches to continue as providers of welfare and education, whereas in the south they still have vital roles to play. Imbalances in global development currently tend to favour the churches in the southern hemisphere, where they empower individuals to negotiate the difficult but potentially rewarding demands of capitalist modernity in the way the churches in the west did more than a century ago. Here the sacred succeeds where it supports the construc-tion of selfhood within a framework of clear moral order and strong congregational support.

In the west, where both social and personal secularisation has accel-erated since the 1960s, two main roles remain open to the churches. They can maintain small-scale community and moral order for their members, or they can resource individuals in discovering and develop-ing their own unique spiritual paths. On the whole, they have taken the former option. They have become the carriers of communitarian and relational values in a society that they criticise as unhealthily 'individ-ualistic' and 'materialistic'. Their task, as they see it, is to counteract the 'bowling alone' syndrome by offering warm, supportive community and clear moral values based around church, family and – in the case of parish churches – local society. One reason for favouring this role is that here the churches have few serious competitors. With the breakdown of kin-based and work-based forms of community, and the collapse of externally authoritative moral orders, many churches feel they are now in a unique position to offer social and moral capital. Recently, some western governments have begun to take seriously their claim to be a central support of a healthy civil society, and are considering channelling charitable and social welfare initiatives through the churches. In a few instances, the churches have also been able to retain or even to strengthen their role in educational provision.

A further reason so many western churches are marketing themselves as providers of community is that this role is compatible with the broadly conservative stance that has been their dominant mode since at least the fourth century. This book has traced the nature and changing shape of this conservatism and its connections with Christianity's ascent to social power in the Middle Ages. In the broadest terms, such conservatism is evident in the support of hierarchical structures of power in religion, society, politics and gender relations, and it has been only selectively and partially dismantled in the modern period. Contrary to the common assumption that the whole of Christianity has softened and liberalised in modern times, this volume has shown how Christianity after the seventeenth century entered into a confessional phase that actually saw an intensification of support for power from on high. This was evident not only in a tendency on the part of most churches to align with the right rather than with the left in politics and to oppose any attempts at revolutionary social change, but in a new emphasis upon the almighty transcendence of God and the utter sinfulness of humankind. Some churches, most notably the Roman Catholic, opposed liberalism, democracy, religious freedom and human rights up to the mid-twentieth century. Even those that showed greater support for power from below were generally unwilling to countenance more democratic arrangements in ecclesiastical or domestic life. In the USA, for example, where Christianity became tied to the cause of liberty rather than of reaction after the eighteenth century, it tended to become the guardian of 'traditional values' in private and domestic life. And when the Roman Catholic church reversed its sociopolitical conservatism by embracing democracy and human rights from the 1960s, it retained its conservatism in relation to the family and women's roles. Together with many contemporary Protestant churches, Rome has reacted to the increasing subjectivisation of society since the 1960s not by abandoning support for an 'objective' and 'absolute' Christian morality based around disciplined sexuality, but by intensifying it.

Yet this volume has also suggested that this was never the whole story, since Christianity has never been one thing. As well as sponsoring, supporting and legitimating various modes of power from on high, the Christian repertoire has always contained possibilities of support for power from below. This has been evident in two main trajectories. First, it is evident in the Christian humanist tradition that came to prominence in the Middle Ages (in scholasticism as well as in renaissance thought), influenced some forms of radical reformation, and was revived in the early modern period in both secular and Christian forms, often under the label of 'liberalism'. Second, it is evident in the voluntarist spiritualist tradition that was present from the beginning, flowered in the mysticism of the late Middle Ages, and flowed through various channels, both Protestant and Catholic, thereafter. In its support for the inherent dignity of human beings and their ability to make free and responsible decisions, the liberal-humanist tradition proved congruent with broader currents of political and social liberalism in modern culture. Its main point of distinction lay in its grounding of human dignity in a Christian metaphysic. Such distinctiveness has not always been sufficient to prevent liberal Christianity being subsumed into secular liberalism, and today both liberal churches and liberal theology find themselves in defensive mode. By contrast, mystical Christianity has tended to support power from below, not by dignifying the inherent goodness of the human, but by commending the path by which individual human beings may be transfigured through contact with the divine. Whereas liberalism 'humanises' transcendence by uniting the human and the divine, mysticism 'subjectivises' it by bringing it into transforming relation with each unique individual life. Where liberalism focuses on the value of unity and community, the mystical tradition within Christianity therefore tends towards individualism-in-relationship and diversity.

In relation to modern politics, it has been the liberal strand of Christianity that has been most easily activated, since it makes a natural contribution to debates on liberalism, human rights, distributive justice and so on. In relation to personal life, however, it is the spiritualist strand that now has easy resonance in the wider culture, particularly since the socio-cultural upheavals of the 1960s. The collapse of support for external authority and the flight from deference have dealt a serious blow to churches in which deference to authority, both human and divine, has long been at the heart of things. In religion, as in society more generally, subjectivised selves no longer wish to be told what to think or how to behave by overarching authority, but desire to live their own lives in their own way. Increasing numbers speak of being 'spiritual, not religious', and propel books on spirituality to the top of the 'best-seller' lists. Thus an almighty God of transcendent power becomes less appealing in a democratic age than a 'Spirit' that empowers each individual to live her or his own life in the most fulfilling and authentic way possible. But whereas the mainline liberal churches might have seemed the most likely to interact creatively with the subjective turn after the 1960s, most have in fact remained wedded to residual forms of deference. In so far as they have softened, they have tended to humanise rather than to subjectivise. Individuals who seek more subjectivised forms of spirituality have tended to defect to more spiritualised churches such as the Quakers, or – in far greater numbers – to the rapidly expanding and easily accessible 'alternative' forms of spirituality that now market their wares in shops, spas and health centres.

In practice it has been evangelical Christianity and the voluntarist biblicist tradition in general that have proved more willing to subjectivise than liberal Christianity. The move is not unprecedented, given evangelicalism's long-standing commitment to the importance of individual experience and personal choice, but it has been given new impetus and intensity by the charismatic movement. The subjective turn of the evangelical-charismatic churches has helped them avoid much of the decline that has affected many other churches since the 1960s. This has been evident in the USA, where the ability of many churches to combine a fairly 'hard' moral teaching with a 'soft' stress on experience and personal empowerment has contributed to the success of Christianity in that country. It has been even more spectacularly evident in the southern hemisphere, where the growth of charismatic Christianity has almost managed to keep pace with the equally rapid decline of Christianity in the west. In both places the churches that are doing best are those that offer a combination of strong community, clear moral order and subjective empowerment. God as Holy Spirit enters into the inner life and experience of the individual, strengthening, empowering and calling by name. But God as Word also offers a clear framework of acceptable belief and behaviour within which such empowerment takes place. Thus the charismatic and charismatic-evangelical churches offer subjectivisation within limits. Individuals are empowered to be themselves; but the model of what counts as authentic Christian manhood or womanhood is externally prescribed.

The churches of both north and south have become conservative in relation to ecclesiastical and family life (where they often support an ideology of separate roles for men and women) and somewhat more liberal in relation to political life (where they are now most likely to support human rights and democratic values). In relation to economic life they generally have little to say, for capitalism tends to fall outside the range of contemporary Christian social teaching. This mixture of strictness and laxity in different areas of moral teaching makes perfect sense in relation to a religion that has lost social power but retains the desire to exercise control within society. Thus churches are most directive in relation to the realms over which they retain authority (the family and the church) and most open or disengaged in relation to those where their authority has been eclipsed (politics and the market). It is surely telling that there has been little attempt, even in academic theology, to rethink the nature of divine power, which continues to be conceptualised in terms of dominating, paternalist power from on high – albeit tempered by a new stress on the relational and caring nature of God. An antagonism to 'liberal' tendencies in church and society is currently evident in the extreme tension surrounding issues such as abortion, contraception, homosexuality and the ordination of women bishops. Such controversy is currently drawing in southern as well as northern churches, and may prove to be the place where a truly global Christianity of a conservative hue comes into being in opposition to 'liberalism', both religious and secular.

So the end is not wholly like the beginning. Christianity returns to a marginal position in relation to social power, but does so with a heavy weight of baggage in tow. Above all, it brings with it a history of alliance with higher power that sits uncomfortably with an age that exalts power from below. For those in north and south who are unwilling or unable fully to embrace the subjective turn, this history proves an advantage, as the counter-cultural, counter-modernised, counter-westernised stance of the churches becomes part of their appeal. They become havens of moral support and conservative values in a time of rapid change and dislocation. Even then they have to make some accommodations to the subjective turn in order to survive. But for those who are more accepting of the 'turn to the self', grateful for the enlarged opportunities open to recent generations, and suspicious of external authority, Christianity's heavy freight becomes a stumbling block. The ability of the churches to retain or to win the allegiance of such people will depend upon their ability to move in a more liberal and subjectivised direction. Though we have noted many important historical examples of their ability to do just that, we have also noted the tentativeness of these instances, and the suspicion with which they have been greeted by the official churches. Christianity's potential for a thoroughgoing and convincing embrace of power from below remains unproven. Meanwhile the main action in the unfolding drama of subjectivisation – both spiritual and secular – continues to take place outside the churches rather than within them.

Chronology

Date	Events	Key figures
27 BCE	Octavian named Caesar 'Augustus', emperor of Rome (died 14 CE)	Philo (c. 20 BCE–c. 50 CE)
c. 33 CE	Death and resurrection of Jesus	
c. 37	Conversion of Paul: Paul's letters written c. 40–c. 60	Josephus (c. 37–c. 95)
c. 60–c. 120	Writing of gospels	
64	Nero's persecution	
66–70	First Jewish revolt; destruction of Jerusalem	Ignatius (c. 35–c. 107)
c. 67	Paul executed in Rome	
c. 112	Persecution of Bithynia; Pliny's letter to Trajan	Clement of Rome (c. 67–c. 132)
c. 120	Gnosticism flourishes	Justin Martyr (c. 79–c. 163)
132–5	Second Jewish revolt	
144	Marcion establishes his own church	Marcion (died c. 160)
c. 157	Beginnings of Montanism	
179	Conversion of Abgar, king of Edessa	Origen (c. 184–254)
226	Beginning of the Sasanid dynasty in Persia	Mani (216–76)
270	Antony in the desert; the beginnings of monasticism	

Date	Events	Key figures
280	Conversion of Tiridates, king of Armenia	
284	Diocletian emperor; beginning of the later empire	Arius (c. 250–c. 336)
305	Abdication of Diocletian; new tetrarchy	Eusebius (c. 260–c. 399)
306	Constantine emperor in Gaul; anarchy and civil war	
311	Donatist schism begins in north Africa	
312	Constantine's victory at the Milvian Bridge; adopts Christian symbol for his standards	Athanasius (c. 300–73)
313	Edict of Milan (official toleration of Christianity)	
314	Council of Arles (Donatist affair)	
323	Eusebius' *Ecclesiastical History* (final edition)	
325	Council of Nicea	
330	Foundation of Constantinople (formerly Byzantium)	Basil of Caesarea (c. 330–c. 374) Gregory of Nazianzus (c. 330–c. 389)
361–3	Julian, last non-Christian emperor	Gregory of Nyssa (c. 330–c. 395)
379–95	Theodosius emperor	
381	First Council of Constantinople	Ambrose (c. 340–97) Cyril of Alexandria (365–407) Jerome (c. 340–20)
396	Augustine bishop of Hippo	Augustine (354–430)
398	John Chrysostom bishop of Constantinople	
400	Augustine's *Confessions*	
401–7	Pope Innocent I asserts primacy of Rome	
410	Rome attacked by Alaric and the Goths	Nestorius (c. 386–c. 451)
427	Augustine finishes *The City of God*	

(*cont.*)

Chronology

Date	Events	Key figures
431	Council of Ephesus condemns Nestorianism	
432	Beginning of St Patrick's ministry	
451	Council of Chalcedon	Leo I (died 461)
455	The Vandals take Rome	
476	End of Roman empire in the west	Boethius (c. 480–524)
486	Persian church opts for Nestorianism	Caesarius of Arles (486–529)
496	Clovis king of the Franks converted to Christianity	Gregory of Tours (491–544)
491	Armenian church opts for monophysitism	Benedict of Nursia (c. 480–c. 550) Cassiodorus (died 583)
527–65	Justinian emperor	Pope Gregory I (540–604)
537	Dedication of St Sophia in Constantinople	
c. 540	Benedict's *Rule*	
553	Second Council of Constantinople	Isidore of Seville (c. 560–636)
c. 563	Columba leaves Ireland and makes Iona his centre (died 597)	Maximus the Confessor (c. 580–662)
590–604	Gregory I ('the Great') pope	
597	Augustine, sent by Gregory, arrives in Kent	
622	The hegirah, year 0 of the Muslim calendar (birth of Islam)	
638–56	Arabs conquer Palestine, Iraq, Syria and Egypt; first recension of the Koran	John of Damascus (c. 655–c. 750)
681	Third Council of Constantinople re-emphasises Chalcedonian Christology	Bede (c. 673–735)
711–16	Iberian peninsula (Spain) conquered by Arabs	
716	Boniface's first missionary journey to Frisia	Boniface (c. 680–754)
726	Outbreak of Iconoclast controversy	
732	Charles Martel halts Arabs at Poitiers	

Date	Events	Key figures
751	Pippin anointed Frankish king	
756	Rise of the Papal States	
787	Second Council of Nicea upholds veneration of icons (Seventh Ecumenical Council)	
800	Charlemagne crowned emperor of the west by Pope Leo III; the *Book of Kells* (Ireland)	
848	Evangelisation of Sweden and Denmark	
910	Foundation of abbey of Cluny, a centre of monastic reform	
963	Monastic foundation of Mount Athos	
988	'The conversion of Russia'; baptism of Vladimir, prince of Kiev	
993–1002	Emperor Otto III works together with Pope Sylvester II	Simeon the New Theologian (949–1022)
1049–54	Leo IX pope: beginnings of papal reform	
1054	Fracture of relations between Greek and Roman churches (mutual excommunications)	Anselm (1033–1109)
1073–85	Pope Gregory VII (Hildebrand)	
1095	Urban II preaches to the First Crusade at Council of Clermont	Abelard (1079–1142)
1098	Foundation of abbey of Cîteaux (Cistercian order)	
1099	First Crusade takes Jerusalem	Gratian (died c. 1160)
1122	Concordat of Worms (end of investiture dispute)	
1123	First Lateran Council	Bernard of Clairvaux (1090–1153)
1139	Second Lateran Council	
1146	Bernard of Clairvaux preaches to the Second Crusade	Joachim of Fiore (c. 1135–1202)
?1150	Gratian's *Decretum*	
c. 1157	Peter Lombard's *Sentences*	

(*cont.*)

Date	Events	Key figures
1174	Peter Valdes preaches poverty in Lyons; beginning of 'Waldensians'	Peter Valdes (died c. 1218)
1187	Loss of Jerusalem by the crusaders	
1189	Beginning of the Third Crusade	Dominic (1170–1221)
1198–1216	Pope Innocent III	Francis of Assisi (c. 1181–1226)
1204–61	The Latins take Constantinople (Fourth Crusade)	
1209	Beginning of the Franciscans	
1209–29	Crusade against the Albigensians (Cathars)	
1215	Fourth Lateran Council (annual confession made obligatory)	
1216	Approval of Friars Preachers (Dominicans)	
1232	Papal Inquisition established by Gregory IX	Bonaventure (1221–74)
1244	Jerusalem finally lost to Muslims	Thomas Aquinas (c. 1225–74)
1245	First Council of Lyons	
1273	Aquinas' *Summa Theologiae* completed	Meister Eckhart (1260–1328)
1281	Ottoman empire founded (lasts until 1924)	Marguerite Porete (died 1310)
1291	Loss of Acre and the Holy Land	Duns Scotus (c. 1265–1308)
1295	Conversion of Mongol dynasty to Islam	
1302	Boniface VIII issues *Unam Sanctam*	Marsilius of Padua (c. 1275–c. 1342)
1309–77	Avignonese captivity: popes at Avignon	William of Ockham (c. 1285–1347)
1323	Franciscan doctrine of absolute poverty declared heretical	
1337	Hesychast controversy in the east	
1348–9	Black Death	Gregory of Palamas (died 1359)

Date	Events	Key figures
1378–1414	The Great Schism; two popes, Urban VI and Clement VII	Catherine of Siena (1347–80) John Wyclif (c. 1330–84)
1414	Beginning of Council of Constance (conciliar principle affirmed)	
1415	Jan Hus burned at Constance	Jan Hus (c. 1372–1415)
1431–49	Council of Basle	
1439	Council of Florence	Julian of Norwich (c. 1342–after 1416)
1448	Russian church becomes autocephalous	Nicholas of Cusa (1401–64)
1453	Constantinople taken by Ottoman Turks	Nil Sorsky (1433–1508)
1455	The Bible printed by Gutenberg at Mainz	
1472	Grand Prince Ivan III of Moscow proclaims himself tsar	
1479	The establishment of the Spanish Inquisition	
1491	The baptism of the king of the Congo by the Portuguese	Erasmus (c. 1469–1536) Michelangelo (1475–1564)
1492	Muslims expelled from Spain; discovery of America by Christopher Columbus	Thomas More (1478–1535)
1493	Pope Alexander VI divides newly discovered lands between Spain and Portugal	
1498	The Portuguese reach the Indies (Vasco da Gama)	Martin Luther (1483–1546) Ulrich Zwingli (1484–1531)
1500	Discovery of Brazil by the Portuguese	
1503	Conflict in Russia between 'Non-Possessors' and 'Possessors'	

(*cont.*)

Date	Events	Key figures
1506	Julius II begins rebuilding St Peter's, Rome	Thomas Müntzer (c. 1489–1525)
1511	Erasmus' *In Praise of Folly*	
1516	Erasmus' *New Testament*; Thomas More's *Utopia*	Thomas Cranmer (1489–1556)
1517	Luther posts the ninety-five theses at Wittenberg	Kaspar Schwenkfeld (1489–1561)
1519	Capture of Mexico by Cortes; Magellan's circumnavigation of the world	Ignatius Loyola (1491–1556)
1520	Luther's great Reformation writings	
1521	Excommunication of Luther; the Diet of Worms	
1523	Zwingli leads reform movement in Zurich	Menno Simons (1496–1561)
1524	The Peasants' War in Germany; Franciscans arrive in Mexico	Philipp Melanchthon (1497–1560)
1525	Müntzer's execution after defeat of the peasants; William Tyndale's translation of New Testament published	
c. 1525–c. 1590	Second scholasticism in Spain	Francisco de Vitoria (1483–1546)
1527	Reformation in Sweden and Denmark	
1530	The Augsburg Confession, drafted by Melanchthon	Francis Xavier (1506–52)
1534	Henry VIII recognised as Supreme Head of the Church of England; the anabaptist commonwealth of Münster; Ignatius Loyola founds Jesuits	
1536	Calvin's *Institutes*	John Calvin (1509–64)
1537	Pope Paul III approves Loyola's foundation of the Jesuits	
1541	Calvin finally in Geneva	
1542	The Holy Office in Rome; Francis Xavier in India	

Date	Events	Key figures
1545	The beginning of the Council of Trent	John Knox (c. 1513–72)
1549	Francis Xavier in Japan	
1551	Second period of the Council of Trent	Teresa of Avila (1515–82)
1553	Servetus burnt for heresy in Geneva	
1555	The religious peace of Augsburg: *cuius regio eius religio*	Filippo Neri (1515–95)
1557	The first *Index* of prohibited works published by Catholic church	
1559	The Elizabethan religious settlement in England	St John of the Cross (1542–91)
1560	Scotland adopts Calvinist confession	
1562	The Heidelberg Catechism; beginning of the Wars of Religion in France	
1563	End of the Council of Trent	
1566	*The Roman Catechism*	Robert Bellarmine (1542–1621)
1570	*The Roman Missal*	
1571	Defeat of the Ottomans at Lepanto	
1582	The Jesuit Matteo Ricci in China	
1595	Philip II of Spain's Escorial consecrated	
1598	The Edict of Nantes guarantees freedom to French Calvinists (Huguenots)	
1600	Giordano Bruno burnt in Rome	
1607	The colony of Virginia established in North America	
1608	Francis de Sales's *Introduction to the Devout Life*; founding of Quebec	Francis de Sales (1567–1622)
1610	The first 'reductions' of Paraguay	
1611	Bérulle founds French Oratory; Authorised King James I version of the Bible	Vincent de Paul (1581–1660)
1616	First trial of Galileo	
1618	Beginning of the Thirty Years War; Synod of Dort condemns Arminianism	Hugo Grotius (1583–1654)
1620	The *Mayflower* sails to America	
1622	Gregory XV establishes the Congregation of the 'Propaganda'	Cornelius Jansen (1585–1638)
1623	Second trial of Galileo	

(*cont.*)

Date	Events	Key figures
1629	Vincent de Paul founds the Sisters of Charity	
1638–1715	Reign of Louis IX of France	
1640	Jansen's *Augustinus*	Blaise Pascal (1623–62)
1642	Outbreak of civil war in England	
1647	George Fox begins to preach and organises Quakers	George Fox (1624–91)
1648	Peace of Westphalia	
1659	Creation of vicars apostolic	John Bunyan (1628–88)
1660	Restoration of Charles II and Anglican church in England	
1666	Schism in Russian church, Patriarch Nikon v. Old Believers	John Locke (1632–1704)
1675	Spener's *Pia Desideria*; beginnings of Pietism	Philipp Jakob Spener (1635–1705)
1678	Simon's *Critical History of the Old Testament*; Bunyan's *Pilgrim's Progress* (second part 1684)	William Penn (1644–1718)
1682	William Penn founds Pennsylvania on principle of tolerance	
1685	Revocation of the Edict of Nantes	
1692	Salem witch trials	
1701	Society for the Propagation of the Gospel founded in London	Fénelon (1651–1715)
1713	The bull *Unigenitus* condemns Jansenism	Leibniz (1646–1716)
1721	Peter the Great abolishes the Russian patriarchate	
1722	Count Zinzendorf founds Pietist Herrnhut community in Saxony (The Moravian Brethren reconstituted by Zinzendorf, 1727)	Jonathan Edwards (1703–58)
1726	Beginning of the 'Great Awakening' in America	Voltaire (1694–1778)
1738	The conversion of John Wesley	John Wesley (1703–91)
1740	George Whitefield preaching in America	George Whitefield (1714–70)

Date	Events	Key figures
1751	Beginning of the publication of Diderot's *Encyclopédie*	Alphonsus Liguori (1696–1787)
1759	The Jesuits expelled from Portugal and subsequently (1762) France	Nicholas Zinzendorf (1700–60)
1762	Rousseau's *Social Contract*	Jean-Jacques Rousseau (1712–78)
		Immanuel Kant (1724–1804)
1773	Suppression of the Society of Jesus (Jesuits) by the pope	
1776	Independence of the United States of America; Tom Paine's *Common Sense*	
1782	Publication of *Philokalia* (compilation of Greek Orthodox devotional writing)	
1787	Constitution of United States separates church and state	
1789	Beginning of the French Revolution	
1795	Separation of church and state in France	
1801	Concordat between France and the pope	
1804	Napoleon crowned by Pius VII in Paris	
1807	Slave trade made illegal in Britain; first Protestant missionary arrives in China	
1808–9	Occupation of Rome by the French; arrest of Pius VII	
1813	East India Company allows entrance of missionaries to India	
1814	Abdication of Napoleon; reinstatement of Pius VII; Jesuits reconstituted	Félicité de Lamennais (1782–1854)
1815	Unitarianism organised in America	
1821	Greek revolt against Ottoman rule	
1822	Schleiermacher's *The Christian Faith*; Brazil obtains independence from Portugal	Friedrich Schleiermacher (1768–1834)
1830	Revolution in France; Lamennais's *L'Avenir*	Søren Kierkegaard (1813–55)
1832	Encyclical *Mirari vos* of Gregory XVII	
1835	D. F. Strauss's *Life of Jesus*	Charles Finney (1792–1875)

(*cont.*)

Date	Events	Key figures
1840	David Livingstone begins missionary work in Africa	
1842	Beginning of Nangking Treaties in China	Ralph Waldo Emerson (1803–82)
1846–78	Pope Pius IX	
1848	Revolutions in Europe; Marx and Engels publish *Communist Manifesto*	
1854	Pius IX establishes dogma of the Immaculate Conception	
1858	Appearances at Lourdes	
1859	Darwin's *Origin of Species*	
1860	Amputation of the Papal States and unification of Italy	Dwight L. Moody (1837–99)
1863	Renan's *Life of Jesus*	
1864	Pope Pius IX's encyclical *Quanta Cura* with attached *Syllabus of Errors*	
1865	James Hudson Taylor founds China Inland Mission	
1866	Austro-Prussian War	
1867	Karl Marx's *Das Kapital*	
1868	White Fathers mission founded by Lavigerie	Alfred Loisy (1857–1940)
1869	Opening of the First Vatican Council	
1870	Definition of papal infallibility; close of Vatican I; Franco-Prussian War; end of Papal States	Billy Sunday (1863–1935)
1891	Leo XIII's encyclical *Rerum Novarum*	Walter Rauschenbusch (1861–1918)
1900	Boxer Revolt in Peking	Sergei Bulgakov (1871–1944)
1905–7	Separation of church and state in France	Albert Schweitzer (1857–1965)
1907	Papal encyclicals *Lamentabili*, *Pascendi*; condemnation of modernism	
1910	Anti-modernist oath; Edinburgh Missionary Conference	

Date	Events	Key figures
1912	Ernst Troeltsch's *The Social Teaching of the Christian Churches*	
1914	Beginning of the First World War; Assemblies of God founded (Pentecostal)	
1917–18	Russian Revolution; reinstatement of Russian patriarchate	
1919	Karl Barth's *Commentary on Romans*; Encyclical *Maximum Illud*; World Christian Fundamentals Association	
1921	Church of Simon Kimbangu (of Jesus Christ) founded in Congo	Simon Kimbangu (c. 1889–1951)
1933	Hitler gains power: Concordat with Germany	
1937	Papal encyclicals *Mit brennender Sorge*; *Divini Redemptoris*	Rudolf Bultmann (1884–1976)
1939	Beginning of the Second World War	Karl Barth (1886–1968)
1943	Stalin allows re-establishment of Russian patriarchate	Paul Tillich (1886–1965)
1945	Hiroshima; end of the war	Reinhold Niebuhr (1862–1971) Dietrich Bonhoeffer (1906–45)
1948	World Council of Churches founded; Iron Curtain; missionaries in China expelled	
1949	Billy Graham commences evangelistic work	Billy Graham (1918–)
1950	Pope Pius XII proclaims the Assumption of Mary as an article of Catholic faith	Martin Luther King (1929–68)
1952	Norman Vincent Peale's *The Power of Positive Thinking*	
1958–64	Khrushchev's renewed persecution of Orthodox church; Orthodox churches join World Council of Churches (1961)	
1962–5	Second Vatican Council	

(*cont.*)

Date	Events	Key figures
1966	Beginnings of charismatic renewal worldwide	
1968	Papal encyclical *Humanae Vitae*; Medellín conference (liberation theology); assassination of Martin Luther King	
1978	The year of the three popes: Paul VI, John Paul I, John Paul II	
1978	New Christian Right emerges on political scene in USA	
1979	Liberation theology criticised by the pope	
1988	Election of first woman bishop in the USA (Barbara Harris, Episcopal Church); millennium of Russian Christianity and improvement in state–church relations	
1989–90	Collapse of communist regimes and liberation of churches in communist lands	

Notes

1 How Christianity came to power

1 Eusebius of Caesarea, *Oration in Praise of Constantine, Delivered at the Thirtieth Anniversary of his Reign*, 2, 1–2.
2 Eusebius, *Oration*, 3, 6.
3 Eusebius, *Ecclesiastical History*, 1, 1, 2.
4 In Eusebius, *Ecclesiastical History*, 3, 39, 4.
5 Hippolytus, *Refutation of All Heresies*, 8, 8.
6 Tertullian, *The Prescription Against Heretics*, 41, 1–8.
7 Tertullian, *Five Books Against Marcion*, 1, 23.
8 Tertullian, *Five Books Against Marcion*, 5, 17.
9 Irenaeus, *Against Heresies*, 3, 2, 2.
10 Irenaeus, *Against Heresies*, 3, 3, 2.
11 Mat.16:18.
12 Eusebius, *Life of Constantine*, 1, 28.
13 Eusebius, *Ecclesiastical History*, 1, 2, 5.
14 Optatus, *De Schismate Donatistarum*, 3, 3, in *Creeds, Councils and Controversies. Documents Illustrating the History of the Church AD 337–461* ed. J. Stevenson (London: SPCK, 1993), p. 23.
15 *The Code of Theodosius* 16, 1, 2.
16 *The Code of Theodosius* 16, 10, 19.
17 Rodney Stark, *The Rise of Christianity* (San Francisco: Harper San Francisco, 1997), pp. 6–7.
18 Libanus, *Pro Templis*, 8, 9, in *Creeds, Councils and Controversies* ed. Stevenson, p. 175.
19 *The Desert Fathers: Translations from the Latin* ed. Helen Waddell (New York: Vintage Books, 1998), p. 102.

20 Athanasius, *Seasonal Letter to Virgins*, 31. Quoted in David Brakke, *Athanasius and the Politics of Asceticism* (Oxford: Clarendon Press, 1995), p. 77.

2 Churches of east and west in the early Middle Ages

1 Mani, *Kephalaia*, 154. Quoted in Garth Fowden, *Empire to Commonwealth. Consequences of Monotheism in Antiquity* (Princeton: Princeton University Press, 1993), p. 72.
2 Simeon the New Theologian, *Ethical Orations*, 1, 6. Quoted in Jaroslav Pelikan, *The Christian Tradition: The Spirit of Eastern Christendom 600–1700* (Chicago: Chicago University Press, 1974), vol. 2, p. 257.
3 Simeon the New Theologian, *Hymns*, 15, 141–44. Quoted in Pelikan, *The Christian Tradition*, vol. 2, p. 257.
4 Simeon the New Theologian, *Ethical Orations*, 5. Quoted in Pelikan, *The Christian Tradition*, vol. 2, p. 260.
5 Augustine, Confessions, 10, 29, 40.
6 Augustine, *Letter 93 (to Vincentius)*, 2, 5. Augustine is quoting Luke 14:23.
7 Augustine, *Sermon 24*, 6. Quoted in Ramsey MacMullen, *Christianizing the Roman Empire A.D. 100–400* (New Haven and London: Yale University Press, 1984), p. 95.
8 Augustine, *On the Morals of the Catholic Church*, 30, 63.
9 Gregory, *Pastoral Rule*, 2, 6.
10 Quoted in Richard Fletcher, *The Conversion of Europe: From Paganism to Christianity 371–1386 A.D.* (London: HarperCollins, 1997), p. 242.
11 Quoted in Fletcher, *The Conversion of Europe*, p. 243.
12 Bede, *Ecclesiastical History of the English People*, 3, 6.
13 *The Rule of St Benedict*, chapter 4.

3 Christendom: the western church in power

1 *The Donation of Constantine*, in *Documents of the Christian Church*, 2nd edition, ed. Henry Bettenson (Oxford and New York: Oxford University Press, 1989), pp. 98–101.
2 *The Dictates of the Pope*, in *Select Historical Documents of the Middle Ages* ed. Ernest F. Henderson (London: George Bell and Sons, 1910), pp. 366–7.
3 Gregory VII's *Letter to the Bishop of Metz* 1081, in *Documents of the Christian Church* ed. Bettenson, p. 110.
4 Quoted in Jacques LeGoff, *Medieval Civilization 400–1500* (Oxford and New York: Basil Blackwell, 1989), p. 145.
5 In C. G. Coulton (ed.), *Life in the Middle Ages*, 2nd edition (Cambridge: Cambridge University Press, 1967), vol. 1, pp. 1–7.
6 *The Canons of the Fourth Lateran Council*, Canon 21, in *Disciplinary Decrees of the General Councils: Text, Translation and Commentary*, ed. H. J. Schroeder (St. Louis: B. Herder, 1937) pp. 236–96.

7 Aquinas, *Summa Theologiae*, 2–2, 9, 3.

8 Aquinas' *Letter to Margaret of Flanders ('On the Government of Jews')*, in *Aquinas: Selected Political Writings* ed. A. P. d'Entrèves (Oxford: Blackwell, 1948), pp. 84–95.

9 Marsilius of Padua, *Defensor Pacis*, 1, 12, 5.

10 Marsilius, *Defensor Pacis*, 1, 13, 3.

11 Marsilius, *Defensor Pacis*, 2, 4, 4.

12 Marsilius, *Defensor Pacis*, 2, 4, 1.

13 Geoffrey Chaucer, *The Canterbury Tales, Prologue to The Wife of Bath's Tale*, lines 699–703.

14 Matthew Paris, *Long Chronicle*, 4, 278. Quoted in R. W. Southern, *Western Society and the Church in the Middle Ages* (Harmondsworth: Penguin, 1970), p. 319.

15 Mechthild of Magdeburg, *The Flowing Light of the Godhead*, 1, 44.

16 Julian of Norwich, *Revelations of Divine Love*, 58.

4 The Reformation in context

1 Martin Luther, *The Freedom of a Christian*, 1520, in *Martin Luther's Basic Theological Writings* ed. Timothy F. Lull (Minneapolis: Augsburg Fortress, 1989), p. 596.

2 Bernard McGinn, *Apocalyptic Spirituality* (London: SPCK, 1980), p. 127.

3 Martin Luther, *Letter* 99, paragraph 13. See also 'Letter to Jerome Weller 1530', in *Martin Luther* ed. E. G. Rupp and Benjamin Drewery (London: Edward Arnold, 1970), pp. 150–1.

4 Luther, Preface to the 1522 German New Testament, in *Martin Luther's Basic Theological Writings* ed. Lull, p. 117.

5 Abraham Friesen, *Erasmus, the Anabaptists, and the Great Commission* (Grand Rapids: Wm B. Eerdmans, 1998), p. 102.

6 *D. Martin Luther's sämmtiliche Werke* (Erlangen and Frankfurt, 1826–57), 20, 84. Quoted in Merry Weisner, 'Luther and Women: The Death of the Two Marys', in *Feminist Theology: A Reader* ed. Ann Loades (London: SPCK, 1990), p. 123.

7 *D. Martin Luther's sämmtiliche Werke* 51, 428. Quoted in Merry Weisner, 'Luther and Women', pp. 126–7.

8 *Martin Luther's Werke* (Tischreden, Weimar, 1912–21), 1, 1046. Quoted in Merry Weisner, 'Luther and Women', pp. 128–9.

9 Ernst Troeltsch, *The Social Teaching of the Christian Churches* (London: Allen and Unwin; New York: MacMillan, 1931), vol. 2, pp. 540–4.

10 John Calvin, *The Institutes of the Christian Religion*, 1, 16, 3.

11 In Carter Lindberg, *The European Reformations* (Oxford, UK and Malden, USA: Blackwell, 1996), p. 249.

12 Calvin, *The Ecclesiastical Ordinances of 1541*, in *The European Reformations Sourcebook* ed. Carter Lindberg (Oxford, UK and Malden, USA: Blackwell, 2000), p. 171.

13 Erasmus, *The Education of a Christian Prince*, ed. Lester K. Born (New York: Columbia University Press, 1968), p. 153.

14 In Jill Raitt (ed.) in collaboration with Bernard McGinn and John Meyendorff, *Christian Spirituality II: High Middle Ages and Reformation* (London: SCM, 1988), p. 148.

15 In Ernst Troeltsch, *The Social Teaching of the Christian Churches*, vol. 1, p. 968.

5 Protestant pathways into the modern world

1 John Bunyan, *The Pilgrim's Progress* (Harmondsworth: Penguin, 1987), pp. 81–82.

2 William Perkins, *A Golden Chain*, 1616 edition, 11. Quoted in F. Ernest Stoeffler, *The Rise of Evangelical Pietism* (Leiden: E.J. Brill, 1971), p. 53.

3 From the Journal of John Wesley for 24 May 1738, in *John and Charles Wesley: Selected Prayers, Hymns, Journal Notes, Sermons, Letters and Treatises*, Classics of Western Spirituality series, ed. Frank Whaling (New York: Paulist Press, 1981), p. 107.

4 Quoted in John Kent, *Wesley and the Wesleyans. Religion in Eighteenth-Century Britain* (Cambridge: Cambridge University Press, 2002), p. 32.

5 Quoted in Kent, *Wesley and the Wesleyans*, p. 33.

6 'Fox's Commission', in *The Works of George Fox*, Vol. 1 (1831), p. 111.

7 Margaret Fell, *Letter to the King on Persecution*, 1660.

8 Quoted in Patricia Crawford, *Women and Religion in England 1500–1720* (London: Routledge, 1996), p. 176.

9 Quoted in Marilyn Westerkamp, *Women and Religion in Early America 1600–1850. The Puritan and Evangelical Traditions* (London and New York: Routledge, 1999), pp. 5–6.

10 In Marvin A. Breslow (ed.), *The Political Writings of John Knox* (Washington: Folger; London and Toronto: Associated University Press, 1985), pp. 42–3.

11 Merry E. Weisner-Hanks, *Christianity and Sexuality in the Early Modern World. Regulating Desire, Reforming Practice* (London and New York: Routledge, 2000), p. 90; Brian P. Levack, 'The Great Witch-Hunt', in *Handbook of European History 1400–1600*, ed. Thomas A. Brady, Jr., Heiko A. Oberman and James D. Tracey, vol. 2 (Grand Rapids: Wm B. Eerdmans, 1995), p. 616.

12 Levack, 'The Great Witch-Hunt', p. 620.

13 Quoted in J. William T. Youngs, 'The Social Impact of Puritanism', in *The Christian World: A Social and Cultural History* ed. Geoffrey Barraclough, (New York: Harry N. Abrams; London: Thames and Hudson, 1981), p. 208.

14 Quoted in Kent, *Wesley and the Wesleyans*, p. 133.

15 Quoted in Edmunt S. Morgan, *The Puritan Family*, revised edition (New York: Harper, 1966), p. 18.

16 Quoted in Jon Butler, *Awash in a Sea of Faith: Christianizing the American People* (Cambridge, Mass. and London: Harvard University Press, 1990), pp. 135–6.

17 Albert J. Raboteau, *Slave Religion: The 'Invisible Institution' in the Antebellum South* (Oxford and New York: Oxford University Press, 1980), p. 92.

18 Quoted in Butler, *Awash in a Sea of Faith*, p. 205.

19 Quoted in Butler, *Awash in a Sea of Faith*, p. 204.

20 Abraham Lincoln, Second Inaugural Address, March 4, 1865.

21 Abraham Lincoln, Gettysburg Address, November 19, 1863.

22 Quoted in Michael Hill, *A Sociology of Religion* (New York: Basic Books), p. 201.

23 Caroll Smith-Rosenberg, *Disorderly Conduct. Visions of Gender in Victorian America* (New York: Oxford University Press, 1985), pp. 125–6.

24 In John Atherton (ed.), *Social Christianity: A Reader* (London: SPCK, 1994).

25 In William R. Hutchison (ed.), *American Protestant Thought: The Liberal Era* (New York and Evanston: Harper and Row, 1968), p. 110.

26 In George Hochfield (ed.), *Selected Writings of the American Transcendentalists* (New York: New American Library, 1966), p. 277.

6 Catholic and Orthodox negotiations with modernity

1 Pope Pius IX, 1864, in *Documents of the Christian Church* ed. Bettenson, pp. 272–3.

2 Council of Trent, Sixth Session, 13 January 1547. In *How to Read Church History*, Vol. 2, ed. Jean Comby with Diarmaid MacCulloch (London: SCM, 1989), p. 27.

3 Quoted in Jean Delumeau, *Catholicism between Luther and Voltaire: A New View of the Counter-Reformation* (London: Burns and Oates, 1977), p. 49.

4 Quoted in Felipe Fernández-Armesto and Derek Wilson, *Reformation. Christianity and the World 1500–2000* (London: Bantam Press, 1996), p. 178.

5 Quoted in Fernández-Armesto and Wilson, *Reformation*, p. 171.

6 Quoted in Delumeau, *Catholicism*, p. 193.

7 Quoted in Jo Ann Kay McNamara, *Sisters in Arms: Catholic Nuns through Two Millennia* (Cambridge, Mass. and London, UK: Harvard University Press, 1996) p. 463.

8 Constitution 6, 1, in *Documents of the Christian Church* ed. Bettenson (Oxford and New York: Oxford University Press, 1989), p. 261.

9 *The Spiritual Exercises of St Ignatius,* Rules 13 and 18.

10 Quoted in Fernández-Armesto and Wilson, *Reformation,* p. 70; Adrian Tinniswood, *Visions of Power: Ambition and Architecture from Ancient Times to the Present* (New York: Stewart, Tabori and Chang, 1998), p. 79.

11 Francisco Suárez, *Laws and God the Lawgiver,* 3, 2, in *From Ireneus to Grotius: A Sourcebook in Christian Political Thought* ed. Oliver O'Donovan and Joan Lockwood O'Donovan (Grand Rapids: Wm B. Eerdmans, 1999), pp. 734–6.

12 Quoted in Colleen McDannell, 'Catholic Domesticity, 1860 to 1960', in *American Catholic Women: A Historical Exploration* ed. Karen Kennelly (New York: MacMillan; London: Collier MacMillan, 1989), p. 59.

13 Quoted in McDannell, 'Catholic Domesticity', p. 61.

14 Quoted in McDannell, 'Catholic Domesticity', p. 74.

7 Twentieth-century fortunes

1 Eric Hobsbawm, *Age of Extremes: The Short Twentieth Century* (London: Abacus, 1996), pp. 8–9.

2 Paul Heelas and Linda Woodhead, *The Spiritual Revolution: Why Religion is Giving Way to Spirituality* (Oxford, UK and Malden, USA: Blackwell, 2005), pp. 129; 139.

3 Heelas and Woodhead, *Spiritual Revolution,* pp. 55–7.

4 Immanuel Kant, *Groundwork of the Metaphysic of Morals* (New York: Harper and Row, 1964), 2, 29, p. 76.

5 Friedrich Schleiermacher, *The Christian Faith* (Edinburgh: T. & T. Clark, 1928), p. 18.

6 Schleiermacher, *The Christian Faith,* section 19. Quoted in John Kent, 'Christian Theology in the Eighteenth to Twentieth Centuries', in *A History of Christian Doctrine* ed. Hubert Cunliffe-Jones with Benjamin Drewery (Edinburgh, T. & T. Clark, 1978), p. 504.

7 *Gaudium et Spes,* Preface, 3, in *The Documents of Vatican II,* ed. Walter M. Abbott (London: Geoffrey Chapman, 1972), p. 201.

8 Stanley Hauerwas, *The Peaceable Kingdom: A Primer in Christian Ethics* (Notre Dame: University of Notre Dame Press, 1983).

9 Mary Daly, *Beyond God the Father: Toward a Philosophy of Women's Liberation* (Boston: Beacon Press, 1973); Rosemary Radford Ruether, *Sexism and God-talk: Toward a Feminist Theology* (Boston: Beacon Press, 1973).

10 Luce Irigaray, 'Equal to Whom?', in *The Essential Difference,* ed. Naomi Schor and Elizbeth Weed (Bloomington: Indiana University Press, 1991), pp. 63–81.

11 Mary McClintock Fulkerson, *Changing the Subject: Women's Discourses and Feminist Theology* (Minneapolis: Fortress Press, 1994).

12 David B. Barrett, George T. Kurian and Todd M. Johnson, *World Christian Encyclopedia*, 2nd edition (Oxford and New York: Oxford University Press, 2001), vol. 1, table 1–4, pp. 13–15.

13 David B. Barrett et al., *World Christian Encyclopedia*, vol. 1, table 1–4, pp. 13–15.

14 David B. Barrett et al., *World Christian Encyclopedia*, vol. 1, table 1–1, p. 4.

Index

Index